WITHDRAWN
HARVARD LIBRARY
WITHDRAWN

World Religions and Multiculturalism

A Dialectic Relation

Edited by

Eliezer Ben-Rafael and Yitzhak Sternberg

BRILL

LEIDEN · BOSTON
2010

On the cover: "Paradise" by Lilach Bar-Ami (2010).

This book is printed on acid-free paper.

Library of Congress Cataloging-in-Publication Data

World religions and multiculturalism : a dialectic relation / edited by
Eliezer Ben-Rafael, Yitzhak Sternberg.
    p. cm. — (International comparative social studies ; v. 23)
    Includes bibliographical references (p.   ) and index.
    ISBN 978-90-04-18892-1 (hardback : alk. paper) 1. Religious pluralism.
2. Multiculturalism—Religious aspects. I. Ben-Rafael, Eliezer. II. Sternberg, Yitzak.
III. Title. IV. Series.

BL85.W73 2010
306.6—dc22

2010027848

BL
85
.W73
2010

ISSN 1568-4474
ISBN 978 90 04 18892 1

Copyright 2010 by Koninklijke Brill NV, Leiden, The Netherlands.
Koninklijke Brill NV incorporates the imprints Brill, Hotei Publishing,
IDC Publishers, Martinus Nijhoff Publishers and VSP.

All rights reserved. No part of this publication may be reproduced, translated,
stored in a retrieval system, or transmitted in any form or by any means, electronic,
mechanical, photocopying, recording or otherwise, without prior written permission
from the publisher.

Authorization to photocopy items for internal or personal use is granted by
Koninklijke Brill NV provided that the appropriate fees are paid directly to
The Copyright Clearance Center, 222 Rosewood Drive, Suite 910,
Danvers, MA 01923, USA.
Fees are subject to change.

PRINTED BY DRUKKERIJ WILCO B.V. - AMERSFOORT, THE NETHERLANDS

In Memory of
Shmuel Noah Eisenstadt

CONTENTS

Preface	xi
List of Contributors	xiii
Tables and Figure	xv
Introduction A Dialectic Relation *Eliezer Ben-Rafael*	1

PART ONE
NEW PERSPECTIVES

Chaper One   The New Religious Constellations in the Frameworks of Contemporary Globalization and Civilizational Transformation 21
Shmuel N. Eisenstadt

Chapter Two   Religious America, Secular Europe: Framing the Debate 41
Grace Davie

Chapter Three   Globalization, Nationalism and Religion: A Multiple Modernities Perspective on Imperial and Peripheral Nations in Post-Communist Europe 63
Willfried Spohn

PART TWO
CHRISTIAN FAITHS

Chapter Four   Dynamics of Ultramodern Religiosity and New Forms of Religious Spatiality 85
Danièle Hervieu-Léger

Chapter Five   Pentecostalism: A Christian Revival Sweeping the Developing World 93
David Martin

Chapter Six Trans-national Pentecostalism and Secular
    Modernity 119
    Bernice Martin

PART THREE
ISLAM

Chapter Seven Transnational Islam in a Post-Westphalian
    World: Connectedness vs. Sovereignty 145
    Armando Salvatore

Chapter Eight Autoritarian Persistence and Barriers to
    Democracy in the Muslim Middle East: Beyond Cultural
    Essentialism 159
    Mehdi P. Amineh

Chapter Nine From Medina to the *Ummah*: Muslim
    Globalization in Historical and Contemporary
    Perspective 193
    Peter Mandaville

PART FOUR
ASIAN RELIGIONS

Chapter Ten Establishment of Buddhist Sacred Space in
    Contemporary India: The Ambedkarite Buddhism, Dalit
    Civil Religion and the Struggle Against Social Exclusion 219
    Knut A. Jacobsen

Chapter Eleven Hindu Traditions in Diaspora: Shifting
    Spaces and Places 237
    Martin Baumann

Chapter Twelve Religions in India and China Today 257
    Peter van der Veer

PART FIVE

JUDAISM

Chapter Thirteen   One People? Contemporary Jewish
   Identities 279
   Eliezer Ben-Rafael

Chapter Fourteen   Judaism and Global Religious Trends:
   Some Contemporary Developments 315
   Shlomo Fischer

PART SIX

THE COMPARATIVE DIMENSION

Chapter Fifteen   Religion, Territory and Multiculturalism 353
   Yitzhak Sternberg

Bibliography 367

Index 393

PREFACE

A resurgence of religion and religiosity is taking place in the contemporary world. It is manifest in the rise of new religious movements—especially fundamentalist and communal-national ones—and new forms of action in existing churches. These developments are also reflected in the crystallization of new diasporas and their frequent self-assertion in terms of religious identities. Religion and religiosity thus gain renewed imprint on contemporary scenes, gainsaying the assumption which asserts the weakening, if not disappearance, of religion in modernity.

It is in this context that a large number of new transnational networks develop and transform in communities and their participation in public spheres. In the relations between different dimensions of religion—the cosmological-transcendental and the institutional-organizational—authority and individual orientations are reformulated. Among other expressions, new formulations of the relations of religions with the political arena lead to new societal configurations, confrontations between communities and tensions opposing religious interests and secular institutions. These developments are related to growing contestations by religious organizations and leaders of prevailing interpretations of the modern world and its loci of authority. The weight of religious entities and identities in globalization processes brings about the cristallization of new concepts of secularism and alterations of the social order.

It is in this context that this book explores different developments that pertain to this world's major religions and focuses on their dialectic relation with the forms of multiculturalism which they themselves contribute, more than any other agent, to engender.

It is in this perspective that the contributions to this volume discuss general questions pertaining to the realm of the sociology of religion, and propose a variety of analyses of societal and social issues relating to the present-day evolution of world religions and religious communities. They focus on the range of convergent and divergent courses of development while paying special attention to fundamentalism and sectarian milieus.

Our perspective is basically comparative and we attach ourselves to the major patterns cristallizing within the twofold context of national-regional circumstances and trends of globalization. Following these analyses, we ask about the emergence and assertion of basic changes in religious approaches and modes of action that impact on the development of contemporary societies.

* * *

This volume stems from a series of discussions in the frame of the IIS World Congress in Budapest (June 2008), a Jerusalem workshop at the Israel Academy of Sciences and Humanities (December 2008) and individual interactions with leading scholars in the field. The editors of the book benefited from the support of the Israel Academy of Sciences and Humanities, the Embassy of France in Israel and the Weinberg Chair of Political Sociology of the Tel-Aviv University. We want to express our gratitude to Bob Lapidot, the Director of the International Division and Secretary for the Humanities, at the Academy, who was most instrumental in this endeavor. We want also to thank Diana Rubanenko for her language editing of the manuscript and, last but not least Lilach Bar-Ami for the picture of her beautiful painting for the cover of this book. We are also indebted to Rosanna Woensdregt and Julian Deahl at Brill, and above all to Mehdi P. Amineh, the editor of the ICSS series who has been of the greatest support.

LIST OF CONTRIBUTORS

Mehdi P. Amineh is Senior Lecturer, International School for Humanities and Social Sciences, University of Amsterdam, the Netherlands. His main research interests: international relations; political Islam; political economy.

Martin Baumann is Professor of Religious Studies, University of Luzern, Switzerland. His main research interests: religion; Hindu and Buddhist religions and communities.

Eliezer Ben-Rafael is Professor Emeritus, Department of Sociology and Anthropology, Tel Aviv University, Israel and Co-Director of the Klal Yisrael Project. His main research interests: Israeli society; ethnicity; globalization; sociology of language.

Grace Davie is Professor, Department of Sociology and Philosophy, University of Exeter, UK. Her main research interests: sociology of religion; modernity.

Shmuel N. Eisenstadt is Professor Emeritus, Department of Sociology and Anthropology, The Hebrew University of Jerusalem, Israel. His main research interests: theory, comparative sociology; civilizational analysis; social change.

Shlomo Fischer teaches sociology at Tel Aviv University and the Hebrew University of Jerusalem, Israel. His main research interests: Judaism; religion, politics and class in Israel.

Danièle Hervieu-Léger is Professor (Directeur d'études) and Past President, Ecole des Hautes Etudes en Sciences Sociales (EHESS), Paris, France. Her main research interests: sociology of religion; modernity.

Knut A. Jacobsen is Professor of History of Religions, University of Bergen, Norway. His main research interests: religions in South Asia—Hinduism, Buddhism, Sikhizm and Jainism.

Peter Mandaville is Associate Professor of Government and Islamic Studies, George Mason University, USA. His main research interests are: global studies; political Islam.

Bernice Martin is Emeritus Reader in Sociology, University of London, UK. Her main research interests: sociology of culture and religion.

David Martin is Professor Emeritus, Department of Sociology, London School of Economics and Political Science, UK. His main research interests: sociology of religion; secularization.

Armando Salvatore is Professor of Sociology, School of Arab-Islamic and Mediterranean Studies, L'orientale University at Naples, Italy. His main research interests are: sociology of religion; Islam; modernity.

Willfried Spohn is Professor, Free University of Berlin, Germany. His main research interests: post-communist societies in Europe; modernity; nationalism.

Yitzhak Sternberg teaches sociology at Beit Berl Academic College and the Open University, Israel. His main research interests: theory; Israeli society; nativism.

Peter van der Veer is Professor of Anthropology, University of Utrecht, the Netherlands. His main research interests: comparative religion; religion in Asia.

TABLES AND FIGURE

Tables

Table 2.1	Presidential Vote by Religious Affiliation and Race	44
Table 2.2	Presidential Vote by Worship Attendance	44
Table 11.1	Sympathy for a temple among Hindu Tamils in Germany	249
Table 11.2	Attendance of a temple among Hindu Tamils in Germany	250

Figure

Figure 13.1	The space of Jewish identities by "family resemblance"	314

INTRODUCTION

A DIALECTIC RELATION

Eliezer Ben-Rafael

This book is about new forms of religiosity and religious activity emerging in the context of their dialectic relations with contemporary multicultural realities to whose development those religions are themselves contributing more than anything else. By dialectic relations, we understand, following Rawlins (1988, 1992), a chain of movement, activity, and change involving different but intertwined phenomena. This notion, we contend, applies to world religions and multiculturalism.

Religion, according to Durkheim (2008), is a system of beliefs and practices which unite its membership in one moral community. As underlined by Robertson (1970), these beliefs and practices refer, as a rule, to transcendental non-empirical spheres and follow from a priori assumptions. For many years, it was scholars' conviction that modernity grounded in secularism and rationality would push religion to the margins of society and confine it to the private sphere. Concomitantly, and as stressed by Beckford (1989, 2003), the sociology of religion was 'insulated' and 'isolated' from mainstream sociology. Berger (1999a, b) explains that, on behalf of the expansion of rationality as a principle of action, scholars were convinced that the world is undergoing demystification and religion's delegitimization. They disregarded the fact that, in one form or another, religion has always been present in the building of modern societies, even in the elaboration of national ideologies. This was illustrated centuries ago by historical examples like the creation of The Netherlands and, later on, the formulations of national identities by England or Sweden. The contemporary resurgence is often described as an unveiling of powers that were always at work but which were hidden from the surface as long as modernity aroused the enthusiasm of the many and seemed to make individuals sovereign over their destiny. Those forces revealed themselves together with unavoidable disillusion about the new civilization and the reality of its promises.

However, it is no less undeniable that religion today is not what it was in the past: like society, it has undergone multi-step transformations. As assessed by Hervieu-Léger (1993), far from being antithetical to modernity, religions undergo renewal through changing codes. Under their present formulations, she says, these codes emphasize the private and individualistic character of beliefs and the fluidity of organizational-institutional forms.

The entrance into modernity has brought religions to confront cultures which resist their influences, and ever since they have been subject to chronic crises of authority. Arguments with secular, individualistic, and democratic values challenge many of their old truths, and set off the questioning of dogmas, the desire to keep a distance from cults, and velleities to re-formulate credos. As Riesebrodt (1998) proposes, it is a conflictual endemic condition, that has become the plight of religions in modern times, despite their no less undeniable continuing and pervading influence.

This conflictual condition assumes a diversity of forms in diverse circumstances. Modernity itself is defined in multiple ways, and globalization sets these diverse definitions in direct relation with each other. In this era of globalization, one of the forces that hyphenate these diverse conjunctures consists of the flows of people across the world, who disseminate religions and denominations (Eisenstadt 2003). Increased and increasing global interconnectedness indeed makes migration a major source of religious diversification within individual societies and, concomitantly, global communication that ensures unbroken relationships between people separated by thousands of miles imprints itself in the dynamic of new-type transnational religious communities.

Carriers of given religious convictions, rites and ways of life do not, however, 'remain the same' once they insert themselves in new societies; they cannot but alter their ways of thinking of themselves and of the world. This transformation, moreover, adopts diverse patterns according to place, social context, and cultural encounters. Hence religions, as global entities, can hardly retain a monolithic or even coherent image of themselves. While scattered religious congregations may exploit the new technologies of communication and networking to maintain some unity, these entities inevitably become multicultural wholes of their own. Wherever they constitute a minority, they contribute a factor of sociocultural diversity and multiculturalization, so to speak, and themselves come to illustrate the same principle of socio-cultural heterogeneity as a transnational diaspora. In brief, religions today greatly contribute to a world disorder (Ben-Rafael and Sternberg, eds. 2009) that is multicultural both when viewed as a whole, and from within most societies that compose it. It is a development that contrasts both with Fukuyama's (2006) assumption that globalization implies one-way homogenization and convergence to Western modernity, and Huntington's (1996) expectation that globalization would be bound to polarize homogeneous Western and non-Western civilizations.

These disparate tendencies within and between religions favour the formation of new movements and communities of increasing presence on public scenes. At the same time, however, religions' messages tend to lose their conceptual sharpness while the social boundaries of religious communities become less clear and trenchant. Glock and Stark (1965) who describe how religiosity engenders communities of believers, underline at the same time that such communities are more often in search of truths, rather than effectively armed with well-defined spiritual ambitions; a phenomenon that Wuthnow (1998) describes as 'seekership'. Religions, he contends, gain in presence at the same time as their cohesion and unity weakens. In all religions one finds numerous believers who are uncertain of the universal validity of their convictions, and who ask themselves how to understand, and relate to, other churches and movements around them.

In this very context, and possibly in response to the dilemmas that it imposes on religious faiths, the profusion of types of religiosity often witnesses, if not provokes, the emergence of totalistic and assertive forms of religiosity associated with fundamentalism. As Emerson and Hartman (2006) show, fundamentalism describes groups that aspire to impose religious practices and values in all areas of social life. According to Armstrong (2002), fundamentalism is piety made militant in an uncompromising conflict with evil. The strong interest aroused by this notion—especially when it is linked to violence and terrorism—is not always proportionate with the scope of the phenomenon in reality, but the intensity of its disruptive effect on the daily life of many when it occurs, explains the discrepancy.

Many analysts view fundamentalism as adversative to modern rationality and thus see it as a category that is alien to the general discussion of religion in modern life. In contrast, Bruce (1996) sees in fundamentalism a rational response of peoples who suffer from the assumed downgrading of the prestige and role of their faith in the contemporary world. As a religious reaction to this reality, fundamentalism combats secularism relentlessly. In brief, and as assessed by Marty and Appleby (eds., 1991), fundamentalism is a reaction by religious people to modernity from within modernity—i.e. using modern organizational schemes and rational strategies.

Optimists like Bruce expect that fundamentalism would disappear in a genuinely democratic and secular society. Nevertheless, fundamentalist groups are now more violent than in the past and have actually increased over the decades. Riesebrodt (1993) proposes a new assessment—that modernization and secularization are the very soil for religious resurgence and the development of fundamentalism.

Today, this discussion leads to Islamism which, in recent decades, has become the most salient phenomenon pertaining to fundamentalism as well as by far the most impactful. It derives, according to Ramadan (1999), from the aspiration of masses to empowerment in the face of global capitalism. This kind of interpretation is appealing to many contemporary scholars who speak of a revolt against the West, highlighting the tension between Western values and non-Western values in the global society.

From an altogether different perspective, Lewis (2002) sees in the rapprochement with fundamentalism by many Muslim intellectuals a manner of directing the blame on the West for the perceived failures of Muslim societies and states to manage the public domain in this era of independence. In a similar vein, Dorraj (1992) defines the problématique of contemporary Islam as the painful discrepancy emerging between Islam's rich cultural past and its present-day cultural impoverishment. Which, however, by no means signifies, as Tiesler (2009) asserts, that secularism is dead among Arab and Muslim intellectuals as a whole.

The actual phenomenon of fundamentalism, we are reminded by Segady (2006), appeared decades ago in America where it illustrated a conjunction of literal interpretation of Scriptures and political involvement. True, it has taken on many different forms since then but what still constitutes the common denominator of all past and present cases is the combat against secularism, liberalism and democracy—in addition to their struggling with each other. Hence, fundamentalism does give to the development of our world a flavour of civilizational clash that recalls Huntington's prognosis.

Fundamentalism however draws out but one category of phenomena pertaining to the broad and ever-widening field of contemporary religiosity—whose growing centrality in our social world justifies the increasing interest that social scientists take in it. Spickard and Cragg (2001) believe that scholars' interest in it is particularly attracted by the new importance of religion in many individuals' lives; its part in the awakening of contemporary conflicts often revolving around issues linked to collective identities; and its new organizational schemes in frameworks that transcend societal and national borders.

These aspects lead to the general questioning of further developments of world religions which, by the very essence of their dogmas and the truths they preserve in their respective Holy Scriptures, aspire to offer coherent pictures of the universe. Arguably more than ever before, these aspirations of world religions to coherence are today challenged by the increasingly multicultural, incoherent, even tumultuous, social, societal and global realities which, together with other actors, they themselves have contributed to shape. They have done so by fighting for influence in individual societies as well as at the global level as a whole, both by implanting themselves as a local development and by presenting themselves as transnational forces. Multiculturalism—the at least partial fruit of religious pluralism—cannot but challenge the coherence of the images of the world that the same world-religions carry. Above all, it indicates the endemic problematic dimensions of their co-presence in this era of interconnectedness. Which, however, does not deny that while multiculturalism is the very context where inter-faith contacts easily lead to confrontations, it also represents a window of opportunities for different intra- and inter-religion approaches to embark on elaborating forms of cohabitation.

In other words, multiculturalism—the *Golem* so to speak—has turned on its creators—world religions. It now requests these 'creators' to transform themselves in the very same manner with which they have transformed social reality. This volume aspires to enlarge on this discrepancy by focusing on how the major faiths of today's world respond to the challenge: how do they evolve at a time when 'everything is permanently changing', at least partially, under their own influence?

Under the title 'New Perspectives', Shmuel N. Eisenstadt, Grace Davie and Willfried Spohn set diverse angles from which to observe the changing relations of society and religion in our times and also to assess the diversity of those relations, according to both social contexts and basic codes of the religions themselves. For Shmuel N. Eisenstadt, the new developments in religious arenas herald no less than a new civilizational constellation. The changes we witness include, among others, a multiplying of religious orientations within the religious systems, the privatization of religious experiences, a general weakening of the institutionalization of religions, and the emergence of new types of organizations. Religious identity has become transposed into national, transnational and international arenas—often connected with ethnic components. At their opposed extremes, these changes include the growth of fundamentalist movements at one end, and the increasing popularity of 'New Age' manifestations. Transnational religious networks characterized by decentralized authority develop as ethnic communities conveying diasporan translocal identities. These networks fuel civilizational visions that draw their tenets from sources external to the homogenizing cultural premises of the nation-state. A reconfiguration of the relation between the primordial as against the civil components of collective identities brings about the crystallizing of 'alternative' modernities. A 'New World Disorder' emerges in a context where new forms of international capitalism take shape, and increasing discrepancies and inequalities open up between central and peripheral sectors within and between societies. These circumstances nourish the new diasporas' challenging of today's prevailing modernities in terms of their own civilizational premises. An analysis of religious arenas indicates that they constitute not just changes in religious practices, but are also a part of the transformation of civilizational frameworks and premises.

Grace Davie attacks the same theme, the confrontation of religion and today's social reality, by analyzing the role of religion in American politics and comparing it to Europe in the same respect. This chapter shows the role that religion played in Obama's election and asks why social scientists in Europe encounter difficulties in understanding it. Western European elites generally assume that elections in 'modern' societies are decided on economic issues, rather than religious or moral ones. But in the USA, it is not only elections that are influenced by religious orientations, but also major points on the national agenda, such as who should be responsible for welfare—the State or churches. Liberal social scientists fail to appreciate the continuing role that religious expression plays in communities across this country. America definitely provides proof that there is no incompatibility between being religious and being modern. European scholars are slow learners in this respect because of the different nature of their own religious situation, and their tendency to assume that their model is the global prototype. In fact, the American model is closer to the reality prevailing in the rest of the world. America's 'free market of religious goods' encourages religious initiatives and it shows that secularization is by no means inevitable nor essentially one-directional. The active religiosity of the United States, the massive shift to the south of global Christianity, and the emergence of Islam as a major factor in the modern world-order, are some of the signs of the contemporary importance of religion in social life. A growing body of data indicates that religion is present, pervasive, and increasingly influential in the twenty-first century, and that this influence varies widely according to cultural contexts.

It is not, however, the 'sole' influence: models of religiosity vary from one social context to another, and also, it should be emphasized, from one faith to another. Actually, this influence is not only a current major factor in the multiculturalization of societies but also, in given areas, in the strengthening of uniformizing national cultures. Willfried Spohn shows indeed how post-Soviet Central and Eastern European states follow historical examples of the past, and illustrate the conjunctive revival of nationalism and religion. The break-down of communism has triggered a search not only for democracy and market capitalism, but also a quest for national sovereignty against communist imperial rule, fuelling a return to traditional religious symbols. Nationalism is here given shape by organic ethno-national rather than by democratic-pluralist identities, and combines with a revitalization of religion against the previous imposed secularism and repression of religion. In many instances, moreover, the emerging organic forms of ethno-nationalism are not only shaped by traditional forms of religiosity but also by new forms of religious fundamentalism. These developments comprise varying phases: pre-communist and communist state formation, nation-building and nationalism, as well as religious development and secularization patterns in the context of an increasing exposure to inter-civilizational constellations and global forces. Globalization enhances ethnic and religious fragmentation, exclusion and conflicts in contemporary societies but also entails tendencies towards more inclusive ethnic pluralism and religious-cultural citizenship. Spohn shows that a historical-comparative, multiple modernities approach is better prepared than over-generalized theories of modernization, transformation or globalization to understand and explain the complex, contradictory and varying trends in post-communist Central and Eastern Europe.

Those three chapters lead to a similar conclusion, that religions and religiosity are by no means dwindling phenomena in the social realities of today's world. They are an integral part of both the development of new unifying ideologies and, above all, the diversification of cultural communities. The fact that universal religions aim to offer a coherent view and understanding of the world does not preclude them from constituting a major factor in multiculturalization of the social reality. What is profoundly new in the present-day situation, in this respect, is that it pertains to an era of globalization composed of diversity, where segments and components are part of one whole where each one—or nearly each one—is aware of the others and finds itself in contact with them. It is in this respect that the new era questions the responses of the major religious faiths which aspire to offer a coherent understanding of this world.

Hence, the following essays of this volume ask about the responses of major world faiths to the challenge of multiculturalism. The next three chapters discuss developments among Christian denominations. Danièle Hervieu-Léger elaborates on the contemporary global evolution of Western Christianism that has always presented itself as a world institution. The process of individualization of beliefs and the process of globalization of religion are two cornerstones of the contemporary religious scene. As a result, local religious communities are coming to an end, especially in Western Europe where the decline of the "parish civilization" is now widely recognized. The recording of the fall in (or even the collapse of) church attendance and the diminishing number of priests and ministers attest for a disaggregation. This process can be described as a de-communalization of Christianity in Europe. The Catholic example is particularly acute while the contemporary deterritorialization and reterritorialization of religion reveal not only the tension between the subjectivization of beliefs and the new appeals to affinity communities, but also demonstrate the internal contradictions of religious authority in a world of individuals: a question which goes far beyond the Catholic (and even Christian) case.

David Martin turns to another development unknown until recently—Pentecostalism. This religious trend focuses on the Holy Spirit and sees itself as return to the Primitive Church. Drawing its truths from Luther, Methodism, and Pietism, it constitutes a kind of perspective on modernity, the global reality, and the multicultural tumult. Its first steps were in the USA but it has spread throughout the world, carried by migrants. It attracts marginal peoples and people. Its fusing of technological modernity with a sense of the inspirited world and the daemonic, enables it to cut across cultural barriers. It represents a decentralised and voluntary organisation, separated from territory and state. It is a global movement, often equipped with a portable identity able to adapt to all contexts, based on personal transformation and choice, and may be understood as a narrative of modernity. Pentecostalism emphasizes the inner religious experience at the expense of sacraments, and preaches adherence by choice and conversion; it also shows pacific or even pacifist tendencies. Moreover, it is strongly mission-minded and its perspective contains the idea of a Promised Land. A basic principle is the priesthood of all believers, a ministry open to people of inspiration and charisma. Amongst the 'little people' it fosters discipline and ambitions. In an uneven way, according to contexts and the variance of influences, the Pentecostal model includes competition between rival churches, entrepreneurship, and charismatic and bureaucratic authority. Ultimately, Pentecostalism is a plausible version of modernity.

Bernice Martin pursues the discussion of Pentecostals, emphasizing that they are the younger offspring of the Christian family. Originally a mixture of poor white and poor black religiosity, it has become indigenised in many parts of the globe. It attracts people from many groups and thereby escapes the mono-ethnic condition. Pentecostals build transnational networks and new churches which, as a rule, are scenes of ecstatic worship. It individualises identity, speaks of salvation, and treats all converts as fully equal. The theology is bound to the weakening of traditional ties and identifications. The Pentecostal world is also peopled by demons that can be defeated only by divine power, which reincorporates indigenous religions in the Christian faith. Pentecostals are confident and seek to influence their life and environment. Recent neo-Pentecostalism has emphasized this aspect by a strong world-accepting approach which eases the way for members to live as modern subjects in a geo-politically, economically, and culturally interdependent world.

These chapters about Christian denominations show how far change has become their attribute and has resulted in far-reaching innovations at the heart of their credos. Catholicism in the twenty-first century is 'different', and Pentecostalism is itself a brand new phenomenon that represents an unprecedented Christian experience. It seems that society does imprint itself in the development of the major religious denominations, to no lesser extent than vice versa. At least at first glance, this seems even more true of Islam which is perceived today as a most activist trend of religiosity. The three following chapters consider this question from different angles.

Armando Salvatore discusses this issue by first reminding us that the world system was set down by the Westphalian treaties which instituted the nation-state form of incorporation and the principle of one-state one-religion. This system affected Islamic movements and groups which until now sought to benefit from a positive trade-off of nationalism and transnationalism without assimilating standards that do not warrant cohesion for their communities and polities. Today, however, globalization relativizes the centrality of nation-states. It resonates with a historic Islamic approach privileging ties between locales, groups, and cities more than stressing the sovereignty of national communities. This affinity is bound to the erosion of the legitimacy of post-independence states within Muslim majority societies. While it is still uncertain whether transnational Islam presents a decisive challenge to postcolonial Muslim states, 'integrationist' tendencies seem to prevail today over 'isolationist' temptations. Thus the idea of an integration of Muslim interests and lifestyles into the wider dynamics of the world system is widely viewed among Muslims as subordinated to the possibility of preserving the autonomy of key Islamic notions of a good life. Nor can one dismiss postcolonial resentments and a sui generis 'will to power.'

Mehdi P. Amineh assesses, at this stage, that the lack of democracy and the persistence of authoritarian regimes in the Middle East region relate to socio-economic not geo-cultural, reasons. In the non-European world, traditional cultures are confronted with modernization pressures of colonial and imperial expansion and modernization processes from inside. In these circumstances, they face a structural and consequently mental transformation that makes them vulnerable to internal contradictions. Islam as political ideology emerges in this context through the development of fundamentalist movements. In response to the failure of modernization, this stream of political Islam calls for the creation of a radically non-secular Islamic state. On the other hand, many Muslims relate to "Liberal Islam," an interpretation of Islam that acknowledges democracy, pluralism, and human rights. These ideas gradually increase in popularity, criticizing Islamist radicalism. Hence, whereas some interpretations of Islam impede democratization, others spur democratization. The key to understanding the confrontation between these opposed forces lies in state/society relations rather than in society's norms, values and religions. They widely depend on the changing powers of the actors involved, and especially, on the strength of an independent middle class and civil society organizations.

Peter Mandaville emphasizes his conviction that the discourses of European Muslims have contributed significantly to a critical Islam. Muslims encounter a diverse range of schools of thought in Europe today, and divide themselves accordingly. As a result, a space is created where no particular conception of Islam is *negated*. There are always forces working to narrow the boundaries of the Islamic political community and which seek to control the discourse of political legitimacy. At the end of the continuum, one finds radical tendencies of political activism—some of them requesting that Muslims work towards establishing Islamic states in Europe and refusing to tolerate pluralistic conceptions of Islam. In those cases, the West is viewed as an enemy figure which must be subverted. On the other hand, some Muslim thinkers in Europe problematize the extremists' position by pointing out that it simply serves to reproduce Western hegemony. They oppose pressures for greater 'unity' which, in their eyes, are often nothing more than demands for greater uniformity. Some of those thinkers emphasize that safety in individuality is more important than safety in numbers. Many Muslims are in fact reconciling themselves to Islam heterogeneity and hold a dialogue with other traditions. They see in this posture an intrinsic aspect of their religion. Under this light, the European experience of Muslim intellectuals should contribute to the development of critical thinking in Islam—a critique not only of the West, but also—and more importantly—of Islam itself.

Hence, Islam has now become a major factor of multiculturalism in the non-Muslim world but it itself faces difficulties in meeting the challenge of experiencing this kind of condition which, possibly more than any other actor, it helped to create—but where it finds itself as a minority among others. What we see from these texts is that conflict and tension animated by fundamentalist outlook do result, but, at the same time, some forms of pluralism have penetrated the Muslim population itself. Some of the speakers tend to find, at least partially, a common ground of understanding with 'others' and the culture prevailing in society. Which is not to deny that this friction revolving around the kind of influence Islam may have on the social order, does constitute a major factor of dispute on the contemporary public scene.

An additional question which then arises is whether the very fact of changes in religion and religious communities within the context of societal change—as we have seen with respect to both Christianity and Islam—also affect Asian religions' relations to society. Three more chapters attempt to provide answers to this question.

Knut A. Jacobsen focuses on India and the role of Buddhism in this country where that faith first emerged. He emphasizes that the main symbols of the nation of India are strongly associated with Buddhism. Most central symbols indeed reflect India's past as a Buddhist civilization. In contemporary India, one speaks of a modern Buddhism that has been especially defined and diffused by Ambedkar, the speaker for the Untouchables and father of India's constitution. Ambedkar presents himself as a rational and secular philosopher primarily interested in teaching ethics. The Buddhism he teaches is often considered more as a political identity than a religious practice. It rejects many rituals and magical elements of Buddhism, and sees Buddha as a social reformer oriented toward building a just and happy society. The supreme goal is how to banish poverty, the caste structure, and the injustice done to the marginalized. Here, the Buddhist notion of rebirth means transformation and it incorporates a sharp critique of the Indian caste society. Ambedkar understood Buddhism to be in permanent moral conflict with Brahminical Hinduism. Religion is to be understood in the sense of civic religion aimed at the political mobilization of people. In the same vein, the declared aim of the Buddhist Bahujan Samaj Party (BSP) is to move the lower strata away from the margins of Indian society to the centre. While Buddhism is a relatively very small religious minority in India, it has been in power several times in Uttar Pradesh, a state of 200 million people. Hence, it is a minority that is able to reach major positions of power, even though it is but one component of India's multiculturalism. In the process, however, Buddhism becomes 'modern Buddhism' and switches orientations toward the welfare not only of individuals but also, and mainly, society itself. It becomes a kind of political ideology.

What, however, happens in this context to the majority trend in India and beyond India, the Indian widespread diaspora, i.e. the Hindu tradition?

Martin Baumann firstly shows how Hinduism also has now become a global phenomenon in modern times, through the multiplication of Indian communities throughout the world. Like any world religion today, the primary challenge is to adapt to a huge diversity of contexts with the wish of preserving—through adaptation—basic religious codes, practices, organisational forms, architecture and much more: in a word, re-constructing and re-establishing religion. In this vast space of related phenomena, this chapter analyses one specific aspect of religious change and continuity, i.e. that of the growing importance of temple attendance. This phenomenon focuses on the importance of the temple among Hindu people, even when they emigrate far from their homeland. Especially in the diaspora, the temple has become the main site for rites and the transmission of traditions, at the detriment of the home, a basic change that has also been accompanied by a shift in authority from the family to priests. As attendance at the temple becomes a new routine, it strengthens social relationships and cultural ties, endowing new meanings to the temple. The temple becomes a cultural and religious space on foreign land, a home away from home and, to some extent, a re-established regulator of status. The basic distinction between domestic rites and solemn, public rites, nevertheless remains. Over time, this shift turns standardised Hinduism from a practised and experienced tradition into a considered and systematized religion.

While Jacobsen studies Buddhism as a minority religion in India and Baumann focuses especially on Hinduism as a minority in diasporic settings, Peter van der Veer takes us to the very foci where these religions prevail—China and India, respectively. His comparative analysis shows that each of these systems of belief experiences major transformations in this contemporary area when confronting political systems that define themselves as secular and constitutional. A close-up look relativizes those ambitions, however, and at the same time shows the different directions taken on by each religion under study. In either case, the nation-state continues to be of primary importance for the development of religion formations in Asia today. In China, the Communist Party, though atheist in orientation, is recently developing a more accommodative relation with Chinese religions—Buddhism and Confucianism in particular. Especially at the level of the 'moral state' it tries to align itself with a particular form of Confucian morality as an essential part of national identity—as long as it does not threaten the political status quo. In India the normative secularism of the state has slowly given way to assertions of Hindu majoritarianism. In particular, the state's failure to provide adequate secular education leaves room for communal socialization. This has led to a very volatile situation in which both international (Pakistan) and regional (Kashmir) political developments contribute to the radicalization of religious identity politics. The current phase of globalization does in fact enhance the importance of transnational connections for all world religions, as well as for forms of spirituality unrelated to religious institutions.

Hence, Asian religions are also undergoing changes at the same pace that they bring about changes in societies. This is equally the case when they have the status of a minority and a majority. Buddhism and Hinduism are both undergoing a process of change while the locus in society is changing when facing states that are essentially defined as secular. In China, religion is now cited as a background and acknowledged as a formative element in Chinese civilization; in India, the Hindu religion is being awarded more central roles than in the past. At the same time, both religions are undergoing changes asserting ever more clearly the political messages they convey. As such, they are definitely a factor in the pluralization of their societies, if not of multiculturalism. Concomitantly, diasporan Buddhist and Hindu communities are also attached to the transformation of their faiths in the direction of better adjustment to their actual environments, though at the same time each one may be divided regarding which traditions to retain, and which to neglect. In any event, they pursue paths that make them components of their respective environments' multiculturalism.

Judaism is another world religion, in spite of the fact that it numbers but a tiny cohort of members in the world. As the mother of the world's great monotheisms, with its widespread presence in major foci of civilization, its study merits appearance in this volume about major world religions. This religion as well, it should be stressed, is going through far-reaching transformations in today's multicultural world to whose emergence it is also contributing, together with others.

In the face of today's multiple formulations of Jewish identity and in an attempt to offer a systematic view of this diversity, Eliezer Ben-Rafael proposes a conceptual framework based on the notion of 'space of identity'. This notion encompasses all the varieties of Jewish identities, tries to group them into subgroups according to their relative closeness to each other, and then to explore the deep structures that account for the convergence/divergence of the various subgroups towards and away from each other. In a similar manner, it is discernible that all formulations and groups of formulations may be related, differently but systematically, to the same traditional Judaism that, for centuries, implied a primordial sense of belonging to 'the Jewish People'; the perception of the 'God and Torah of Israel' as Jews' collective singularity; the place or status of the collective vis-à-vis 'others' defined as 'exiles' everywhere outside 'the Land of Israel'. These unequivocal assertions have been questioned ever since the dawn of modernity, and answered in many different ways according to moral attitudes, life experiences, and historical circumstances. Jewish identity has definitely lost its uniformity with the emergence of three flows of identity formulations—the ultra-Orthodox, ethnocultural, and national—themselves subdividing into numerous varieties. The perceptions of these three facets of identity as well as the facet to which each formulation grants greater emphasis, now distinguish the different formulations, and beyond them, the different flows of Jewish identity. It is a diversity marked both by clashes over influence and leadership, as well as by a basic family resemblance. In other words, we again witness here a confrontation of a religion with multiculturalism whose creation itself contributed to, and which in the final analysis penetrates it as well.

Shlomo Fischer completes this analysis of contemporary Judaism by emphasizing the dual factors of geography and sectorial segmentation. This chapter shows that the dynamism of the Jewish world scene is marked by the diverse accentuation of the various salient components of social and religious action. Some trends accentuate the importance of individual or personal meaning, experience and self-realization, with or without reference to collective membership, while others focus upon that collective membership, downplaying individual religious observance or belief. The other major aspect is that all these new trends that appear as Jewish manifestations are also present in other religions, or are global trends in religion. Thus the focus upon personal religious experience and self-realization is present both in contemporary American Evangelism and European Islam. 'Belonging without believing' characterizes the historical European Christian religions, as well as moderately committed American Jews and Israeli *Mizrahim-Masoratiim*. And the abstraction or de-coupling of religion from culture and life distinguishes both Islamic and Jewish fundamentalism. Thus while Judaism certainly has its own history and structural features, in the contemporary world it cannot be understood apart from general trends in religious life and belonging.

In the discussion about the major impacts of the globalization process on recent and contemporary religious life, prominent place is given to global flows of goods and people—often described as deterritorialization, delocalization and transnationalization. However, as researchers also indicate, this does not gainsay that local and territorial aspects lose their general importance. Regarding religions, more especially, one knows their longstanding connection with 'sacred spaces' or 'sacred lands'.

In the final chapter, Yitzhak Sternberg compares a few examples of such relations of world religions and territories and places where it appears that these are understood in most diverse manners according to circumstances and basic codes. It is in this respect that the significance of multiculturalism stands out. Multiculturalism assumes the coexistence of different neighbouring faith communities commanding a degree of intra-religious and inter-religious tolerance. This, however, does not concur with their inherent intolerant conviction, dictated by their very nature as religions, of representing the 'only valid truth' about the world. The comparative analysis shows that one cannot speak of uniformity or symmetry in this regard. Institutionalization of churches and mission-orientation of the faith community are but two of the variables that may explain the diversity of patterns of coexistence and conflict that world religions articulate vis-à-vis each other in the social reality of this era, namely—multiculturalism.

It is at this point that we conclude this volume which aspires to evince the dialectic relation of world religions with multiculturalism. Globalization and migration have, in a way, been the implementation of the very calling of world religions by disseminating them to all corners of the world: Buddhism, Hinduism and Shinto have reached Western Europe and North America; Episcopalism and Pentecostalism have spread throughout Africa and Asia; Catholicism has increased its presence in the USA; Islam is now a major European religion; the Jewish diaspora is today more scattered than ever—despite the large concentrations of Jews in Israel and the USA.

The multiculturalism that has emerged—with unique contours in each place—is widely the expression of these dispersions of world religions that was not only the effect of the inner drives of religions to conquer new disciples in new places, but mainly of general sociological and political developments where modernity, in highly diverse forms, has penetrated all civilizations of this world. Though, 'on the ground', we observe that the multiculturalism which has been engendered or amplified by world flows of migrants towards—more or less—democratic and—more or less—developed societies, is strongly marked by the co-presence of faith communities. In other words, world religions are effectively a major agent of the multiculturalization of contemporary societies.

The growing salience of multiculturalism in many societies, does not mean that people are more and more enclosed in their own enclaves and more and more close to others. We know that multiculturalism also means increased contacts between individuals of different backgrounds, cultural hybridization, fluidity of social boundaries, and individualization of the spiritual and religious life. This reality, we have seen, does impact on the transformation of the world religions which, as a rule witness the weakening of their institutional frameworks while forms of cult and religious experiences tend to look for new ways of expression. Hence, one may speak in general terms of multiculturalism as a category of phenomena engendered, at least partly, by world religions but which in turn brought them to adjust to new circumstances and experience transformation. What we also know now, is that in this multicultural reality—or more accurately, in these multicultural realities—inter-religion and intra-religion conflict may also develop not only for the souls of potential adherents but also over the control of territories, allegiance to which may be variously defined through the different prisms of those religious systems. Hence, multiculturalism, which is somehow the offspring of world religions, pushes them not only toward change and reforms, but also toward new conflicts between and within them.

This process should remind us of the Jewish legend of the Golem—an animated being created by man which finally challenges the latter's control over it—a dialectic relation, indeed.

PART ONE

NEW PERSPECTIVES

CHAPTER ONE

THE NEW RELIGIOUS CONSTELLATIONS IN THE FRAMEWORKS OF CONTEMPORARY GLOBALIZATION AND CIVILIZATIONAL TRANSFORMATION

Shmuel N. Eisenstadt

Introduction

Many new developments in the religious arenas are taking place in the contemporary scene—developments which entail changes, transformations of the place of religion on the world scene, and which herald a new civilizational constellation.

These developments go far beyond being the usual picture of 'religion' and constitute a very strong challenge to the widely accepted assumptions in the hitherto predominant academic and public discourse in which the extension of modernity, the modernization of societies, seemingly as it were naturally entails the secularization of the world; the weakening of religion in its predominance in the hegemonic worldview and of its central place in public spheres—especially in the major modern revolutionary and nation-states—the institutional epitome of the modern programs—and the concomitant removal, as it were, of religion to the private spheres.

In the first stages of the crystallization of the post-Second World War social and political scene, it seemed as if the major developments in the religious arenas in most modern societies indeed provided, as it were, proof of major assumptions about the continual tendency to secularization as epitomizing modernization. Among the most important of these developments were, first, the growing crystallization of the religious sphere in the modern world as just one—among many others—institutional spheres; second, the weakening or loss, as compared to other periods, of the predominant place of religion in the constitution of hegemonic world views; third, the weakening of religious authorities and of religious practices, and concomitantly the seemingly growing de-ritualization or apparent desacralization, both of central public arenas, as well as of private life.

This situation epitomizing the apogee of the classical age or models of modernity has started to change—first slowly, then much more intensively—from about the last two or three decades of the twentieth century—changes closely connected with the development first in the West and then throughout the world of several processes which crystallized across the world in different constellations, and which also entailed far-reaching changes in the religious arenas.

The Crystallization of New Patterns of Religiosity and Religious Constellations

In all—especially but not only in the 'Great'—religions, albeit of course, in different concrete formations—a new religious constellation has developed on the contemporary scene, characterized on the one hand by the multiplication and privatization of religious orientations, sensibilities and practices; the decline of institutionalized religion; the development of multiplicity of new 'informal' types of religious orientations, activities, movements and organizations, of the hitherto major official religious institutions and organizations and of their membership—combined, on the other hand, with the move and transposition of different religious activities and orientations into various frameworks of political activity in the constitution of collective identities. Religious identity and practices, which in the classical model of the nation-state were delegated or confined in theory, although far less so in practice, to private or secondary semi-public spheres, have become transposed into national, trans-national and international, in some cases central, public arenas. Indeed, one of the most important developments in the constitution of the political arenas and collective identities on the contemporary scene has been the 'resurgence' of religious—often connected with national-ethnic—components, their move as it were into the centres of national and international political activity and in the constitution of collective identities. At the same time they have greatly changed the relations between 'local' and 'global' settings, as well as those between overall, grand-narratives and more localized social and cultural visions. Such transposition did not however entail a simple return of some traditional forms of religious organizations, authority or practices but rather a far-reaching reconstitution of the religious components in the overall cultural and institutional formations.

Closely related were the changes in the structure of religious authority—manifest in the weakening of the major ecclesiastical institutions and in growing contestations between different religious organizations, movements and leadership about the loci of religious authority and their legitimation; about the proper interpretation of the basic premises of their respective religions and of their relation to the modern world. Such multiple challenges developed above all by means of a great variety of new popular religious leaders, promulgating—as against the older, above all the 'traditional' religious authorities—especially through the new electronic media, new religious conceptions and interpretations of the basic premises of their respective religions, as well as a multiplicity of new practices, creating new national and international religious public spheres not regulated by the hitherto predominant religious or by new political authorities.

In tandem, there developed in all religions, albeit of course in different degrees, changes in the relations between, on the one hand, religious beliefs, and practices, and, on the other hand, 'official' authoritative religious codes. Thus there developed far-reaching changes in the relations between different cosmological and doctrinal dimensions or components: in individual religious sensibilities and practices; the institutional-organizational ones; the structure of religious authority, as well as in their relations to the major political and institutional formations; and to the constitution of collectivities and collective identities, as well as in the relations between major religions.

All these developments did not necessarily denote the disappearance of strong transcendental and religious orientations from the cultural and political panorama of contemporary societies. Rather, they entailed the development of multiplicity of orientations to the transcendental realm, often giving rise to new religious sensibilities, practices and commitments. Nor did these developments necessarily give rise to the disappearance of religion from the public arenas of their respective societies and in the constitution of collective identities. In fact they were closely connected with the very forcible, as it were, re-entry of religion into the centres of these areas—but indeed in new ways, signalling far-reaching new civilizational formations.

Closely connected—and one of the most interesting characteristics of the contemporary world religious scene—is the world-wide growth of many new types of religious movements, communities, organizations, and various informal relations. One such type were the fundamentalist movements which burgeoned especially in the monotheistic civilizations; and the communal-national or ethnic ones which developed above all in the other-worldly, especially Buddhist and Hindu communities—both of which aimed, even if in different ways, at reconstituting the basic contours of the political regimes and national collectivities, and of new types of religious arenas.

Second, there developed throughout the world sectarian and semi-sectarian groups and activities, probably the most visible of them being Presbyterian sectarian groups and movements which expanded throughout the world, in South America, Korea, and other Asian countries. Many such sectarian groups, movements or informal formations—be it different Sufi orders or Buddhist groups, also developed, even if being less visible on the international scene, in many other, religions—especially the Great Religions—burgeoning together with many cults throughout the world. Concomitantly there developed what may be called new overall religious or 'spiritual' orientations or tendencies such as 'the New Age' ones. While these movements, groups and tendencies were not organized in any overall national or international frameworks, yet there developed between them multiple 'trans-national' networks which constituted a new element on the overall global scene.

Third, one of the most important developments in the contemporary global scene has been the development of virtual transnational religious, as well as ethnic associations and communities, including new Diasporic ones. Truly enough, 'diasporic' communities such as 'overseas' Chinese or Indian ones have existed for long periods of history—as did similarly, transnational or trans-imperial religions such as the Catholic, the 'Orthodox'-Christian, as well as Buddhist ones and of course, the Jewish ones. However, under the impact of extensive movements of migration attendant on processes of globalization, and the closely related development of new electronic media, not only did a large number of such Diasporic networks, and organizations develop—many of them new. Far-reaching transformations also took place in their constitution and new modes of participation in them, as well as their participation in national and international public spheres and in the constitution of collective identities. The result was far-reaching changes in the very constitution of trans-national religious organizations, in their relations with the state and civil society and in inter-religious relations.

In most of these communities, orientations to some 'home' base developed, but basically they all went beyond them. Within most of these communities, strong tendencies developed for the denial of various local traditions, the promulgation of new universalistic translocal identities, carried above all by numerous translocal networks which connected directly—without the mediation of the 'home' centres—indeed of any single territorial centre or regulated by them—between similar 'ideological' religions and communities or networks. Concomitantly, many new trans-state religious organizations and encounters took shape, as well as a far-reaching shift in the relations between the major religions.

All these communities and networks, including indeed the fundamentalist, communal national ones, as well as different sectarian ones and different cults, were characterized by new, basically decentralized patterns of religious authority and accountability thereof, and of participation in the religious frameworks. These developments were closely connected with growing contestations within each religion between different religious organizations, movements and leadership about the proper interpretation of their basic premises and of the relation to the modern world and about the loci of authority within them.

All these new trans-world communities, networks and organizations constituted not only a new organizational or structural element on the contemporary scene, but also important foci of the reconstitution of collective identities, and of new civilizational visions and contours.

These networks, movements, or communities, including indeed the fundamentalist ones, also promulgated far-reaching claims with respect to the redefinition of citizenship and the rights and entitlements deriving from it. They do not see themselves as bound by the strong homogenizing cultural premises of the classical model of nation-state, especially by the places allotted to them in the public spheres. It is not that these movements or communities do not want to be 'domiciled' in their respective societies. Part of their struggle is to become domiciled in their respective countries—more than according to classical models of assimilation—but on new, more pluralistic, multifaceted and multinational terms. They want to be recognized in the public spheres, in the constitution of the civil society, in relation to the state as culturally distinct groups promulgating their collective identities, and not to be confined solely to the private sphere. They do indeed make claims—as illustrated for instance in the new debate over *laïcité* in France—for the reconstitution of the symbols of collective identity promulgated in respective states.

The Crystallization of New Civilizational Constellations

These new religious constellations developed throughout the world, with far-reaching 'local' differences between them. Their distinct features were shaped by their specific traditions, historical experiences and the concrete contemporary context of their respective societies. Indeed, many of the new religious networks, virtual communities and movements, strongly emphasized their distinct authenticity—in fact, their continually reconstructed traditions. Indeed the constitution and the promulgation of such traditions constituted a very important component of the activities of many such groups.

All this great variability in the new religious constellations entailed not only parallel developments in different parts of the world, but also constituted components of new civilizational frameworks of new civilizational constellations.

Notwithstanding such multiple 'local' differences, the major constellations of this new religious scene are to be identified throughout most of the world—especially but not only—among the classical 'Great Religions'. All these new—especially but not only—trans-world communities and networks constituted not only multiple new organizational or structural elements on the contemporary scene, far exceeding the multiplicity that could be found among Axial religions, for instance. They are also important foci of the reconstitution of new civilizational visions which constitute a response to major changes in the overall frameworks of modernity; of the civilization of modernity as it is being crystallized in the contemporary scene—indeed, beyond the classical contours thereof, and heralding a new civilizational constellation.

Furthermore, the global civilizational constellation entailed a combination of changes in the structure of social relations; of far-reaching cultural changes; as well as in the constitution of major political boundaries, of international arenas and processes of globalization.

These changes first developed in the West, spreading throughout the world and crystallizing in various constellations in different parts of the world. They were rooted in the original civilization of modernity but went far beyond it, and indeed generating new civilizational constellations.

Patterns of Social Relations and Institutional Formations

Several phenomena formed the common core of processes that transformed the hitherto prevalent hegemonic patterns of social relations and institutional frameworks. First was the growing dissociation of the main—social, economic, political, family and gender—roles, organizations and relations from broader macro formations, especially from the hegemonic formations of the nation and revolutionary states and from the 'classical' class crystallization characteristics of the formative and mature stages of development of industrial capitalism. Second—far-reaching changes and shifts in the crystallization of overall social formations, of class and status relations; third, dissociations between political centres and the major social and cultural collectivities; and fourth, the development of multiple networks and clusters which cut across many organizations and 'societies.' Under the impact of intensive globalization processes, far-reaching changes concomitantly developed in the constitution of many social boundaries—weakening and diversifying hitherto hegemonic collectivities and social arenas; and the crystallization of new cultural and social identities that transcend existing political and cultural boundaries; the closely related reconstitution of the place of territoriality in the structuring of social roles and of collective identities and the decoupling of the hitherto predominant relations between local and global frameworks. In tandem there developed continual processes of decomposition of the relatively compact image of the styles of life, of the constitution of life worlds of different social sectors and classes, of the conceptions of 'civilized man' as embodied in the classical nation-state. Closely related was the crystallization of a multiplicity, pluralization, and diversification of semantic-ideological and institutional connections between major arenas of life—between public and private arenas, between work and culture, occupation and residence, as well as between primordial and/or sacred and civil components in the constitution of collective identities. Concomitantly there developed multiple, continually changing combinations of many cultural themes and tropes brought together from different cultures around the world, as well as new patterns of syncretization between different cultural traditions, so aptly analyzed by Ulf Hannerz (1996, 1999) among others. Often these developments culminated in the crystallization of shifting 'alternative' modernities which challenged the existing hegemonic ones, and entailed new modes of exclusion and inclusion.

Cultural Transformations

The crystallization of the patterns of social relations and of institutional patterns were closely connected with new cultural developments which started in the West and then expanded throughout the world. These new cultural trends entailed a far-reaching critique of the cultural program of the Enlightenment and also, to a very great extent, of the Romantic criticisms thereof as it was promulgated and institutionalized as the hegemonic discourse of the classical period of modernity. A weakening began of the definition of ontological reality as promulgated during the Enlightenment and which was hegemonic in the classical period of modernity, especially the emphasis on the exploration of continuously expanding human and natural environments and destiny and the belief that they could be mastered by conscious effort of man and society. Cognitive rationality—particularly as epitomized in extreme forms of scientism—which was often conceived as the epitome of the Enlightenment, has been dethroned from its relatively hegemonic position, as has been the idea of the 'conquest' or 'mastery' of the environment, whether of society or nature. The validity of the presumed predominance of the scientific worldview, as well as of any future common to the whole of humanity, based on the ideas of progress, of any common criteria—of liberty, freedom, or progress—according to which different societies, can be compared or evaluated, were questioned or denied.

Closely related was the weakening of the hitherto predominant grand narratives of modernity, with their very strong emphasis on the historical process of progress, which in many versions of the Enlightenment and revolutionary visions entailed the transformation, in 'secular' terms, of the eschatological visions of numerous sectarian movements. This gave rise to more pluralistic 'multicultural' and postmodern orientations with a strong relativistic bent.

Thus, throughout the world a continually growing tendency developed to the distinction or even dissociation between *Zweckrationalität* and *Wertrationalität*; and to the recognition of a great multiplicity of different *Wertrationalitäten*—and to a growing emphasis on the possible plurality of cosmological visions and different ways of combining a 'bracketed out' *Zweckrationalität* with different modes of *Wertrationalität*—be they aesthetic, social or moral.

Transformations of National and International Political Arenas

These changes in the structure of hegemonic patterns of social and institutional relations, as well as in cultural premises, that have taken place throughout the world—first in the West and then spreading beyond it—were closely connected with the transformations of the premises and institutional arrangements of nation-states, and indeed of entire political constellations and the transformation of the boundaries of political and 'national' communities (Saskia Sassen 2006).

While the political centres of the nation and revolutionary states continued to constitute the major agencies of resource distribution, as well as very strong and important actors in the major international arenas, the control of the nation state as the hegemonic centre—over its own economic and political affairs—despite the continual strengthening of the 'technocratic' 'rational' secular policies in various arenas, be it in education or family planning—was reduced. Many global, above all financial, actors became very powerful. The nation and revolutionary states lost also some of their—never total—monopoly of internal and international violence to many local and international groups of separatists or terrorists. Neither nation-states nor the concerted activities of nation states were capable of controlling continually recurring occurrences of such violence. They also lost their centrality and semi-monopoly over the constitution of the international playgrounds and of the rules regulating them. Above all, the ideological and symbolic centrality of the nation and revolutionary states, their perception as the major bearers of the cultural program of modernity, the basic frameworks of collective identity, and as the principal regulator of the various secondary identities, became weakened and they are certainly no longer closely connected with a distinct cultural and civilizing program.

Among the most important repercussions of these developments was the emergence of very strong tendencies to politics of identity, to the redefinition of boundaries of collectivities, and of new ways of combining 'local' and global, transnational or trans-state components in the processes of constituting these collectivities. They heralded far-reaching transformations of cultural and political frameworks, and of public spheres and civil society.

Most hitherto 'subdued' identities—ethnic, local, regional, and religious—have indeed acquired a new prominence, in some cases possibly a central role on the contemporary national and international public scenes. They moved, as it were, naturally in a highly reconstructed way, into the centres of their respective societies and international arenas, claiming their own autonomous places in the central symbolic and institutional spaces, whether in educational programs or public communications and media, and posed far-reaching claims to the redefinition of citizenship and the rights and entitlements connected with it.

These developments entailed the expansion of new types of collective identity grounded, on the one hand, in smaller continually reconstituted 'local' settings; and on the other in trans-state and trans-national frameworks; the concomitant development of new political transnational or trans-state frameworks and organizations—the most far-reaching being the European Union—as well as the reconfiguration of the relations between the primordial and/or sacred (religious), and as against civil components in the constitution of collective identities entailing new modes of exclusion and inclusion.

These new collective identities which have been indeed promulgated above all by various 'new' social movements, frequently in new social settings, especially indeed in Diasporic ones, contested the hegemony of the older homogenizing programs of the nation and revolutionary states. In many such settings, the local and the transnational orientations, often couched in universalistic trans-state themes, such as new European ones; or those rooted in the great religions—Islam, Buddhism, in different branches of Christianity—reconstructed in modern ways, were often brought together in new ways.

Closely related was the development within different social sectors of new, less ideologically homogeneous, interpretations of national identity and modernity, in terms different from those of the Enlightenment, that redefined modernity; for instance urban or regional settings, in terms of their own distinct Greek or Turkish, Islamic, Indian, or Chinese models.

International Formations

A fourth component in the crystallization of the new civilizational formations that occurred at that period was the shifts in hegemonies in the international order; the development of new power relations between different states; as well as the emergence of new actors, institutions and new regulatory rules in the international arena. All of them attested to the disintegration of the 'Westphalian' international order, and contributed to the development of a 'New World Disorder' (Jowitt 1993). The development of disorder intensified with the demise of the Soviet Union, the disappearance of the bipolar relative stability of the 'Cold War', and of the salient ideological confrontation between communism and the West. With one remaining superpower, the USA, greater autonomy was gained by regional and trans-state frameworks and emerged new combinations of geopolitical, cultural and ideological conflicts.

Concomitantly, the international financial agencies created after World War II, the World Bank and the International Monetary Fund, became more prominent. Often pursuing American interests and ideologies, they also developed as relatively independent actors and regulators of the international economic trends which ultimately would challenge those interests. In addition, new international NGOs acted beyond the scope of any single nation-state and even beyond the more formal international agencies.

Prominent in the international scene were first of all the major international agencies—the UN, and regional agencies, above all those of the European Union. Second, a plethora of new legal institutions were created, such as the International Court and the European Constitutional Court, as well as multiple new international professional, legal, and economic regulatory institutional networks.

At the same time, new principles of legitimation took shape which undermined the premises of state sovereignty that had prevailed since the 1815 Congress of Vienna. Most important of these were the principles of human rights transcending existing state boundaries and calling state agencies to accountability. Coalitions of different trans-state, as well as nation-state political actors with new social movements around these principles influenced the political dynamics of states, including the authoritarian ones. Some actors have presented these developments as constituting arenas of a new international civil society which transcends existing political boundaries.

All these developments entailed far-reaching changes in the distribution of power in the national and above all international arenas. On the one hand, they entailed a far-reaching transfer of power from the hitherto hegemonic nation-state to new centres of hegemony, to various global political institutions and organizations. This gave rise to multiple new and more dispersed centres of power which were often connected with the new actors on the international scene, all of which constituted continual challenges to the existing international order and hegemonic institutions. When combined with changes in the internal institutional arrangements of different states, all these developments on the international arena greatly increased the international system's instability and the new world disorder. The latter have been further intensified by the inability of different international actors and agencies to cope with many of the problems attendant on the process of globalization which developed in this period—be it environmental, epidemiological, or nuclear—as well as social problems generated by the globalization process.

This increase in dispersed centres of power, often connected with the new actors in the international scene, challenged the existing international order and hegemonic institutions, and constituted a central component of the new civilizational framework—rooted indeed in the classic civilization of modernity, but going far beyond it.

New Patterns of Globalization

These numerous changes were indeed all very closely related to the new patterns of globalization that developed in the contemporary scene, and which constituted a central component of the new civilizational frameworks. The most distinctive characteristic of the contemporary globalization processes in comparison with 'earlier' ones, were not just the extent of the global flow of different resources, especially economic ones, and the concomitant development of new forms of global capital and economic formations, to which we have already referred above, important, of course, as they have been. Global flows of economic resources that developed in this period were not necessarily greater in comparison to some during the late nineteenth- and early twentieth-century. Rather, the specific characteristics of contemporary globalization have been first the predominance of new forms of international capitalism—extinguishing other 'older' ones based to a large extent on 'Fordist' assumptions; the transition from industrial to service, financial or administrative arenas; the reduction of different segments of the workforce, especially those connected with the high-tech and financial activities; the growing autonomy and relative predominance of 'denationalized', 'deterritorialized' 'global' capitalist financial forces. Second, the tendencies to the global economic neo-liberal hegemony promulgated among others by the major international agencies—

the World Bank, the IMF, and the World Trade Organization, fully embodied in Washington's consensus. Third were international processes of migration, which brought in their wake the dispossession of many social sectors from economic and cultural niches that were previously relatively stable, even if not highly developed; the concomitant continual movements of hitherto non-hegemonic, secondary, or peripheral societies and social sectors into the centres of the respective national and international systems—often bypassing both the existing national as well as trans-state institutions.

Fourth, was the continual growth of discrepancies and inequalities between various central and peripheral sectors within and between societies. Of special importance in this context were first the combination of discrepancies between social sectors which were incorporated into the hegemonic financial and 'high-tech' economic frameworks, and those which were left out; the closely connected far-reaching dislocation of many of the latter sectors, suffering decline in their standard of living and generating acute feelings of dislocation and dispossession among them. Most visible among such dislocated or dispossessed groups were not necessarily—and certainly not only—those from the lowest economic echelons—poor peasants, or urban *lumpenproletariat*, important as they were in those situations. In fact, most prominent among such dislocated sectors were first, groups from the middle or lower echelons of more traditional sectors, hitherto embedded in relatively stable, even if not very affluent, social and economic frameworks or niches and cultural frameworks, and which were transferred into mostly lower echelons of new urban centres; and second, various highly mobile, 'modern' educated groups—professionals, graduates of modern universities and the like who were denied autonomous access to the new political centres or participation in them—very much against the premises thereof; and third, large social sectors which were dismissed from the work-force.

A crucial aspect of these developments was the fact that many of the inequalities and dislocations that developed in the wake of these processes of globalization both within different states and between them, coalesced with religious, ethnic or cultural divisions. At the same time, continually growing mutual impingement began throughout the world of different societies, civilizations and of social sectors of 'peripheral' societies and sectors on different centres of globalization. These constellations of processes of dislocation and the concomitant movement of 'peripheral' sectors or societies into different hegemonic centres have become especially visible in the diasporas of religious, ethnic, and national virtual communities which became a highly important new component of the international scene. To use Arjun Appadurai's (2006) felicitous expression, they attested to 'the power of small numbers,' constituting an important element of the new social movements, especially of various anti-globalization ones.

These changes were related to, and in fact closely intertwined with, the crystallization of the major religious constellations analyzed above; especially with the 're-entry' of religion into both the national and international public spheres, which in a way epitomized those changes. One of the most important manifestations of such close interweaving between these new religious constellations and the emerging civilizational frameworks was the world-wide development of new types of protest movements: the anti-globalization movements that developed in this period constituted an important component. The movements were closely related to and interwoven with, a far-reaching transformation of movements and ideologies of protest which developed throughout the world from the last decades of the nineteenth century.

Intercivilizational Settings—Transformation of Movements and Ideologies of Protest

One of the most important manifestations of the new civilizational framework that developed together with all the processes analyzed above has been the close interweaving between the numerous new religious constellations and the new types of orientations and movements of protest that first developed in the late 1960s.

Protest movements with potentially revolutionary visions indeed continued to constitute important components of the social and political scenes—but their structure, as well as their goals and visions, have been continually reinforced and radically transformed by the globalization process. Movements and symbols of protest continued to play a very important central role in the political and cultural arenas—as they did in the constitution and development of modern states. The most important of them were the new student and anti-(Vietnam) movements of the late 1960s—the famous 'movements of 1968,' which persisted in a highly transformed way in the great range of movements that have since developed. These movements and orientations went beyond the 'classical' model of the nation state, and the 'classical' or liberal, national and socialist movements, and developed in two major seemingly opposite but in fact often overlapping or cross-cutting directions. On the one hand, various 'post-modern' and 'post-materialist' movements took shape, such as the women's, ecological, and anti-globalization movements. On the other hand, many movements flourished that promoted highly ideological, often assertive and aggressive, particularistic, local, regional, ethnic cultural autonomous movements, as well as various religious-fundamentalist and religious-communal ones. They promulgated different conceptions—of identity above all, though not exclusively—among different sectors dispossessed by globalization processes and gained great prominence.

The themes promulgated by these movements, which were often presented or perceived as harbingers of the far-reaching changes in the contemporary cultural and institutional scenes—and possibly also the exhaustion of the entire program of modernity—entailed far-reaching transformations, both in internal state and in the international arenas, of the orientations and themes of protest and of the revolutionary *imaginaire* that were constitutive of the development of the modern social order, and above all of the modern and revolutionary states (Mann, 1997).

The common core of the distinctive characteristics of these new movements, attesting to their difference from the 'classical' ones, was first the shift of the central focus of protest orientations away from the centres of the nation and revolutionary states, and from the constitution of 'national' and revolutionary collectivities as the charismatic bearers of the vision of modernity. They made the transition into various diversified arenas of which the, by now transformed nation states was only one. Second, the 'classical' revolutionary *imaginaire* as a major component of protest grew weaker at the same time; third, new institutional frameworks developed in which these options were exercised; and fourth, new visions of inter-civilizational relations were generated.

Contrary to the basic orientations of the earlier, 'classical' movements, which focused primarily on the constitution and possible transformations of the socio-political centres, of the centres of the nation or state, or of the boundaries of major macro-collectivities, the new protest movements were oriented to what one scholar has defined as the extension of the systemic range of social life and participation, manifest in demands for growing participation in work, in different communal frameworks, citizen movements, and the like. Perhaps the initial simplest manifestation of change in these orientations has been the shift from the emphasis on increasing the standard of living which was so characteristic of the 1950s as the epitome of continuous technological-economic progress, to that of 'quality of life'—designated in the 1970s as a transition from materialist to post-materialist values. In Habermas' (1981: 33) words, these movements moved from a focus on problems of distribution to the emphasis on 'grammar of life'. A central aspect was the growing emphasis, especially in movements which flourished in sectors dispossessed by globalization processes, on the politics of identity; on the constitution of new religious, ethnic and local collectivities promulgating narrow, particularist themes often in terms of exclusivist cultural identity—often formulated in highly aggressive terms.

Closely related to these processes has been the transformation of the utopian, especially transcendental orientations—whether of the totalistic 'Jacobin' ones that were characteristic of many revolutionary movements, or the more static utopian visions which promulgated a flight from various constraints and tensions of modern society. The focus of transcendental utopian orientations shifted from the centres of the nation-state and overall political-national collectivities to more heterogeneous or dispersed arenas, to different 'authentic' forms of life-worlds, often in various 'multicultural' and 'postmodern' directions.

In the discourse attendant on these developments—above all in the West, but spreading rapidly beyond it—a strong emphasis evolved on multiculturalism as a possible supplement or substitute for that of the hegemony of the homogeneous modern nation-state model, and possibly displacing it altogether.

The various themes of protest and utopian orientations became connected with multiple demands made by many single-issue groups which proliferated in this period, as well as with many national, regional and trans-state movements promulgating patterns of identity, often cutting across state boundaries, and above all with the numerous anti-globalization movements which gathered great momentum in the final two or three decades of the twentieth century.

All these distinct new orientations of protest indeed became closely interwoven with the new religious constellations analyzed above, most particularly with the various anti-globalization ideological movements.

While intercivilizational 'anti-globalization' or anti-hegemonic tendencies combined with an ambivalent attitude to the cosmopolitan centres of globalization developed in most historical cases of globalization—be it in the Hellenistic, Roman, the Chinese Confucian or Hindu, in 'classical' Islamic, as well as early modern ones—on the contemporary scene they become intensified and transformed. First, they were disseminated by the media throughout the world. Second, they became highly politicized, interwoven with fierce contestations formulated in highly political ideologies and terms. Third, they entailed a continual reconstitution in a new global context, of collective identities and contestations between them. And fourth, the reinterpretations and appropriations of modernity, giving rise to new inter-civilizational orientations and relations were attempts by these actors to radically decouple modernity from Westernization, to take away the monopoly of modernity from the 'West', from the original Western 'Enlightenment' and even Romantic programs; to appropriate modernity and define it in their own terms, often in highly transformed civilizational terms. A central component of this discourse was a highly ambivalent attitude to the West, most particularly to the USA, its predominance and hegemony; it was most powerfully manifest in the spread of strong worldwide anti-American movements that burgeoned in this period, in several European countries too.

These movements were on the one hand closely related to changes in the major religions referred to above, especially to the 're-entry' of religion into both the national and international public spheres, which in a way epitomized those changes. On the other hand, they were closely related to, indeed interwoven with, a far-reaching transformation of movements and ideologies of protest which had developed throughout the world since the final decades of the nineteenth century.

All these developments were perhaps most clearly visible in the various new diasporas and virtual communities and networks: at the same time, those new developments became closely interwoven with the multiple new social movements which burgeoned throughout the more 'established' societies. Indeed, it was within these virtual communities and networks that extensive and highly transformed intensified 'reactions' to the processes of globalization flourished, especially to hegemonic claims by different, often competing, centres of globalization, attesting, to quote Arjun Appadurai (2006) again, to 'the power of small numbers,' and constituting one of the most volatile and inflammatory components on the global scene; as well as an important factor in the transformation of inter-civilizational relations in the contemporary arena, often promulgating visions of clashes of civilizations.

Crucial differences are discernible with respect to their attitude to the premises of the cultural and political program of modernity and to the West, from the perspective of civilizational orientations between—on the one hand the major 'classical' national and religious, especially reformist movements—and on the other, the new contemporary communal, religious movements, above all the fundamentalist movements. All of them were closely connected to the constitution of the new virtual communities.

These developments signalled far-reaching changes from the earlier reformist and religious movements that developed throughout non-Western societies from the nineteenth century on. The confrontation with the West within these contemporary anti-global movements, does not take the form of searching to become incorporated into the modern hegemonic civilization on its terms, but rather to appropriate the new international global scene and modernity for themselves, on the terms of their own traditions.

Their aim is to take over, as it were, the modern program in terms of their own civilizational premises, which are rooted, according to them, in basic, and highly reformulated images and symbols of civilizational and religious identity—very often formulated by them as the universalistic premises of their respective religions or civilizations—and aimed at transforming the global scene in such terms.

They constitute part of a set of much wider developments which have been taking place throughout the world, in Muslim, Indian and Buddhist societies, seemingly continuing, though in a markedly transformed way, the contestations between other earlier reformist and traditional religious movements that developed throughout non-Western societies. These movements do indeed promulgate a markedly confrontational attitude to the West, to what is conceived as Western, and attempts to appropriate modernity and the global system on their own non-Western, often anti-Western, terms. This highly confrontational attitude to the West, and what is conceived as Western, is closely related in the movements either to attempts to radically decouple modernity from Westernization and to take away from the West the monopoly of modernity, and to appropriate the contemporary scene—contemporary modernity—in terms of visions grounded on their own traditions.

At the same time, however the vistas grounded in these traditions have been continually reconstituted under the impact of 'modern' programs and couched paradoxically—indeed reinforced—in terms of the discourse of modernity in the contemporary scene. In many ways, these discourses and the discussions around them resemble the discourse of modernity as it developed from its earliest beginnings in the very centres of modernities in Europe, including far-reaching criticisms of the predominant Enlightenment program of modernity and its tensions and antinomies. Thus for instance, many criticisms of the Enlightenment project made by Sayyid Qutub, possibly the most eminent fundamentalist theologian, are in many ways very similar and often also related to the major religious and 'secular' critics of the Enlightenment from its origins. They start with de Maistre, the romantics, also many of the populist (Slavophiles and the like) in Central and Eastern Europe above all but not only in Russia, and in general those who, in Charles Taylor's (2007) words, emphasized the dimension of human experience, and then of course moving through Nietzsche up to Heidegger. Or, in other words, these different anti-global and anti-Western movements and ideologies reinforce in their own terms the basic tensions and antinomies of modernity, attesting—perhaps paradoxically—that they constitute components of a new common global civilizational framework rooted in the program of modernity, but also going beyond it.

Another very important component of the contemporary religious scene attesting to the fact that different religions are now acting in a common civilizational setting is the changing relation between the different—especially the 'major'—religions. Competition and struggles between religions often became vicious—yet at the same time strong tendencies could be discerned to the growth of common, encouraging interfaith meetings and encounters focused on their relations to some of the premises of the new civilizational framework. They are rooted in the original program of modernity and on the possibility of cooperation between them—but in fact transcend it.

Such attempts at the reformulation of civilizational premises have occurred not only in these movements, but also—though perhaps in less dramatic forms—in new institutional formations such as the EU, in different local and regional frameworks, as well as in the various attempts by the different 'peripheries'—such as the discourse on Asian values—to contest the Western, especially American, hegemony, as well as to forge their own constitutive modernities. These reformulations of rules and premises have been also taken up by many developments in the 'popular' cultural arenas challenging the seeming predominance of the American vision thereof, seen as being promulgated by the media, above all allegedly dominated by the USA—but also giving rise to distinct new trans-state Indian and East Asian media with very far-reaching realms.

The debates and confrontations in which these movements or actors engage and confront each other may often be phrased in 'civilizational' terms, but these very terms—indeed the very concept 'civilization' as constructed in such a discourse—are already couched in the language of modernity, in totalistic, very often essentialistic, and absolutizing terms derived from the basic premises of the discourse of modernity, its tensions and antinomies, even though drawing on older religious traditions. When such clashes or contestations are combined with political, military or economic struggles and conflicts, they can become very violent.

Indeed, at the same time, the combination of far-reaching changes in the international arena and globalization processes, the combination of distinct characteristics of the contemporary processes of globalization with changes in the structure of the international arena has also generated dramatic results. Among them are the multiplication and intensification of aggressive movements and inter-civilizational contestations and encounters, and the development of the new international disorder. The multiple responses to them provide the basic frameworks for the development of asymmetrical warfare as analyzed by Herfried Münkler (2003), as the major type of contemporary warfare, to a very large extent carried by such multiple movements.

The analysis of developments in the religious arenas presented above indicates that they constitute not just important changes in different aspects or dimensions of religious behaviour, practices, beliefs and organizations, but also a highly important component of the far-reaching transformation of civilizational frameworks and premises, and of religion's place within these frameworks, far beyond the dynamics that developed in the classical Axial and early modern periods, when the very constitution of basic hegemonic institutional and ideological formations was deeply rooted in religious premises and institutional frameworks. In the contemporary scene, different components of 'religion' compete with other ones, for their place in the new framework.

CHAPTER TWO

RELIGIOUS AMERICA, SECULAR EUROPE:
FRAMING THE DEBATE

Grace Davie

This chapter[1] takes the election of Barack Obama as the forty-fourth president of the United States as its starting point, but uses this to ask deeper questions. In the first section it examines the role which religion played in the electoral process itself and—more importantly—the reactions of Europeans to this. The answer is interesting and reflects both the realities themselves and the capacities of European commentators to grasp what was happening. These issues, however, provoke a second set of questions which penetrate more deeply: they ask to what extent the tools of social science, which have largely emerged from the European case (i.e. from the philosophical principles elaborated in the European enlightenment), are appropriate if we are to understand fully the religious situation not only in the United States, but in the rest of the world.

Three clarifications are necessary before going further. The first concerns the trigger for the chapter itself. This came from a seminar in a British university a few days before the 2008 Presidential election—a moment of considerable excitement. At the end of the afternoon, a question was asked from the floor concerning the role of religion in the campaign so far and its likely importance in the forthcoming election. I was struck by the inability of any of the participants—all of them well-informed specialists on America and electoral politics—to deal adequately with this question or even to grasp its implications. What follows is very largely an attempt to understand why this was so. I am fully aware, however, that to extrapolate from the speakers at this seminar to "European commentators" more generally is a large step.

---

[1] An earlier version of this chapter is to be published in Ferrari, S. and Cristofori, R. (eds) (forthcoming). I am grateful to the editors for permission to reuse part of this text. What follows also draws extensively on Berger, P., Davie, G. and Fokas, E. (2008).

In this respect, the claims of this chapter must remain speculative, though I believe them to be true.

The second clarification follows from this. In using the term "Europe", it is important to grasp the diversity within the continent as well as the contrast with the United States. If the countries of North West Europe (the Nordic countries, the Netherlands, Belgium, Germany, France and the United Kingdom) are markedly secular and are probably becoming more so, the rest of Europe looks rather different. It is true that Spain is, in many respects, catching up with France, but Italy is not, and Orthodox Europe looks different again. The presence of communism over two generations has also left its mark—countries that suffered the imposition of atheism at first hand are rather more wary than their Western neighbours about abandoning their religious traditions. Finally, recent immigration into many countries within Europe has altered their religious profiles. One result of this has been the increasing—and not always welcome—presence of religion in public as well as private debate even in the more secular countries listed above.

The third point is related. It is often the case that the political commentators of Western Europe (the primary focus of this chapter) assume that they are speaking for more people than they really are. The political class, even in the broadest sense of the term, is by no means typical of the population as a whole. The same is true of the United States. The US is one country, not several, but there is a world of difference between the dominant and moderately secular elites of the coastal cities and the inhabitants of the bible belt, both in their practice of religion and in their views about this. It is important not to jump to conclusions, however; America, just like Europe, is changing—and not always in ways in which the "traditionally" trained social scientist might expect. Precisely this question is addressed in the final section of this chapter.

Did Religion Make a Difference in the 2008 Presidential Election?

At one level the answer to this question is straightforward: of course religion made a difference. It always has in a nation in which well over 90% of the population declare themselves to be believers, and over 40% report that they attended a place of worship in the previous week (a figure that rises to 60% if the period in question is extended to a month)?[2] If a would-be president does not take these figures into account, he or she is unlikely to be elected—something that the Democrats learnt to their cost in both 2000 and 2004. At the same time, however, it is clear that the 2008 election was won, ultimately, on the capacity of the Democrat Barack Obama, rather than the Republican John McCain, to deal with the global economic crisis that became ever more dominant as the election approached. How then can we reconcile these points of view?

The answer lies in the detail rather than in general statements. The following paragraphs set out the bare bones of this analysis drawing on data taken from exit polls on 4 November 2008 and found on the website of the Pew Forum on Religion and Public Life.[3] An excellent overview can also be found in Green (2009).[4]

The argument can be summarized as follows. It is broadly speaking the case that in the recent history of the United States, it is the Republican Party which has both attracted and represented the religious voter. That was certainly true in 2000 and 2004, and up to a point remained so in 2008—but not entirely. Broadly speaking, there are two reasons for this change. The first is widely agreed and reflects Obama's capacity to mobilize sections of the population who "normally" do not vote: that is the substantial ethnic vote, which includes both black Protestants and (mostly) Catholic Latinos. The black Protestant vote is particularly striking—well over 90% of this constituency supported Obama.[5] The second reason is rather different and is less frequently reported. It lies in the fact that sufficient, if not large, numbers of religious individuals turned themselves into floating voters, notably in the swing states of the Midwest. This propensity was fully

---

[2] This is not the place for an extended discussion on the accuracy of these figures. Suffice it to say that these figures are relatively stable over a long period and have as much to do with the desire of Americans to demonstrate that they are a churchgoing nation as they do with actual behaviour. Good up to date statistics regarding the religious situation in the United States can be found on the website of the Pew Forum for Religion and Public Life. See "US religion landscape survey", http://www.pewtrusts.org/our_work_detail.aspx?id=568.

[3] See "How the faithful voted", http://pewforum.org/docs/?DocID=367.

[4] The very recent *Oxford Handbook of Religion in American Politics* puts these findings in a broader perspective. See Smidt, Kellstedt, and Guth (2009).

[5] See "A look at religious voters in the 2008 election", http://pewresearch.org/pubs/1112/religion-vote-2008-election.

understood by Obama and his team, who worked hard to encourage this trend, targeting to considerable effect the religious populations of the states that he needed to win. Indeed it is hardly an exaggeration to say that the success of this policy constituted a key to the 2008 result (see below).

Table 2.1: Presidential Vote by Religious Affiliation and Race (%)

	2000		2004		2008		Dem change 04–08
	Gore	Bush	Kerry	Bush	Obama	McCain	
Total	48	48	48	51	53	46	+5
Protestant/other Christian	42	56	40	59	45	54	+5
– White Prot/ other Christan	35	63	32	67	34	65	+2
– Evangelical/ Born-again	n/a	n/a	21	79	26	73	+5
– Non-evangelical	n/a	n/a	44	56	44	55	0
– Catholic	50	47	47	52	54	45	+7
– White Catholic	45	52	43	56	47	52	+4
Jewish	79	19	74	25	78	21	+4
Other faiths	62	28	74	23	73	22	–1
Unaffiliated	61	30	67	31	75	23	+8

Notes:
Throughout the report, 'Protestant' refers to people who describe themselves as 'Protestant', 'Mormon', or 'Other Christian' in exit polls.
Throughout the report, figures may not add to 100 and nested figures may not add to the subtotal indicated, due to rounding.
Source: 2008, 2004 and 2000 national exit polls. 2008 data from MSNBC.com.

Table 2.2: Presidential Vote by Worship Attendance

	2000		2004		2008		Dem change 04–08
	Gore	Bush	Kerry	Bush	Obama	MacCain	
Total Attend worship…	48	48	48	51	53	46	+5
– weekly or more	39	59	39	61	43	55	+4

Table 2.2 (*cont.*)

	2000		2004		2008		Dem change 04–08
	Gore	Bush	Kerry	Bush	Obama	MacCain	
– more than weekly	36	63	35	64	43	55	+8
– once a week	40	57	41	58	43	55	+4
– Monthly or more	53	43	53	47	57	42	+4
– few times a month	51	46	49	50	53	46	+4
– few times a year	54	42	54	45	59	39	+5
Never	61	32	62	36	67	30	+5

Source: 2008, 2004 and 2000 national exit polls. 2008 data from MSNBC.com.

Taking each of these points in turn, there are two ways of looking at the figures. The first is to compare the success of the 2008 presidential candidates in attracting the religious vote. In this respect, John McCain is the clear winner—a fact that becomes increasingly striking when the frequency of churchgoing is taken into account. The second way of working is to look at the same constituency and compare this with the position of the respective Republican and Democrat candidates from the 2000 and 2004 elections. It is at this point that the relative success of Obama begins to become apparent. Both points are illustrated in the following tables. The Democratic gain amongst religious voters between 2004 and 2008 is not huge, but it is consistent and was sufficient to make a difference. Equally interesting, however, is the marked gain for the Democrats among the religiously non-affiliated—the picture should not be oversimplified.

Even more important, however, is the fact that the position varies considerably between states. In order to demonstrate this point with maximum clarity, it is worth concentrating initially on the evangelical vote—in itself a substantial section (circa one quarter) of the electorate. Using the data from the Evangelical Electoral Map compiled by Christianity Today,[6] it becomes abundantly clear that evangelicals

---

[6] See http://blog.christianitytoday.com/ctpolitics/2008/11/the_evangelical.html and http://www.spiritual-politics.org/2008/11/results_evangelicals.html.

behaved differently in the swing states of the Midwest compared with their coreligionists in the South. Specifically, in the Midwest, evangelicals tended to vote 3–1 for George Bush over John Kerry in 2004; in 2008, in contrast, they voted only 2–1 for John McCain over Barack Obama. Conversely in the South, evangelicals voted 3–1 or better for Bush over Kerry in 2004, and—in many states—by an even greater margin for McCain over Obama in 2008.

Particularly sharp is the contrast between Indiana and Oklahoma: in the former, for example, evangelicals favoured Bush by 77–22 in 2004 but McCain by only 66–41 in 2008; in the latter, they voted 77–23 for Bush and 77–22 for McCain. Indeed in Indiana, at least half of the 21 point shift to the Democrats came from the shifting position of evangelicals. More generally with regard to this constituency, compared to Kerry in 2004 Obama gained 11 points in Ohio, 13 in Michigan, 11 in Iowa, 11 in South Dakota, and 19 in Nebraska, but lost one point in Alabama, five in Mississippi, three in Kentucky, five in Tennessee, eight in Louisiana, and five in Arkansas. In other words the overall swing of evangelicals to Barack Obama should not be exaggerated. It was however a decisive factor in some places, notably the swing states.

American Catholics are equally interesting. They too moved towards the Democrats in 2008. Overall, Catholics supported Obama over McCain by a nine-point margin, reversing the position four years ago when Catholics favoured Bush over Kerry by five percentage points. It is important to note however that much of this shift can be accounted for by Latino rather than white Catholics, remembering that Obama was markedly successful in mobilizing this constituency. That said, appreciable numbers of all Catholics shifted their vote from 2004— responding, perhaps, to the cultural Catholicism of Vice-Presidential candidate Joe Biden. In this sense Biden's firsthand experience of the economic difficulties of the rust belt may have counted for more than the "values" questions, which in recent years have drawn Catholics, like most evangelicals, towards the Republican Party. The overwhelming importance of economic issues at the time of the election is clearly a factor in this respect.

Steve Waldman in the Wall Street Journal[7] asks how Obama achieved his goal of "closing the God gap". His answer is two-fold. Firstly

---

[7] See "Analysis: How Obama lured millions of religion voters", http://pewforum.org/news/display.php?NewsID=16835.

Obama emphasized his personal faith (see below) and in so doing reclaimed the right to make connections between personal belief and public issues. Secondly he exploited the rise of what has been termed a "religious left"—i.e. seriously religious individuals and groups who are looking for a space other than the Republican Party to express their political views. The two dimensions came together in June 2006 when Barack Obama spoke to Jim Wallis's "Call to Renewal" conference.[8] He argued that Democrats should indeed support the separation of church and state, but they should also be more welcoming both to individual believers and to those who affirm a proper role for faith in the public square. There is a critique here, not only of the Republican right, but of the secular left, who—it is clear—had alienated a significant body of voters. It was almost certainly this that cost the Democrats the 2000 and 2004 elections.

An interesting article in Prospect Magazine (Crabtree 2008), published shortly before the election itself, notices these shifts and puts them into a broader context. It recognizes not only that the evangelical constituency in the United States is growing in importance, but that it is changing in nature. Younger, more progressive evangelicals are questioning some inherited assumptions, are gaining confidence in the public square, and are ready to do business with a Democratic candidate who recognizes their needs.[9] Rick Warren, author of the hugely successful The Purpose Drive Life (Warren 2002), and pastor of a mega-church (Saddleback) in Southern California exemplifies this trend perfectly. It was Warren moreover who staged the first public encounter between Barack Obama and John McCain—it took place at the Saddleback Civil Forum in August 2008.

To what extent did Europeans grasp what was happening?

Prospect is published in London, but many Europeans (notably those that dominate the media in the advanced economies of West Europe) began, it appears, from a rather different position—they were concerned not so much with the detail as with the big picture. They noted that most religious voters supported McCain and drew the obvious

---

[8] See "Obama's historic 'Call to Renewal' speech", http://blog.beliefnet.com/stevenwaldman/2008/11/obamas-historic-call-to-renewa.html.
[9] The broader sociological literature on American evangelicals echoes this point. See, for example Smith (1998) and Lindsay (2008).

conclusion—that "progressive" Americans had other priorities. Such Europeans, rather like their American equivalents,[10] were also attracted by what might be termed the more newsworthy aspects of the election. Regarding religion, there were several of the latter: among them the notion that Barack Obama was a Muslim; the controversy engendered by the public statements of his former pastor in Chicago, Jeremiah Wright; and, most of all, the nomination of Sarah Palin as the running mate of John McCain.

The first of these was not taken seriously by the European press, except to note with incredulity that between 10 and 12% of the American population remained convinced that the aspiring president was a Muslim, despite repeated statements to the contrary. That said, it is clear that significant members of Barack Obama's African family are indeed Muslim, a fact that he notes with pride (Obama 2008a: 441–2). The second—the strained, and eventually severed relationship between Barack Obama and Jeremiah Wright—was potentially more serious, but it rapidly became clear to the European commentators, as indeed to all supporters of Obama, that to pursue this issue to its logical conclusion was simply going to damage their preferred candidate at a time when the Democratic nomination was still uncertain. It was more important to affirm the politically astute way in which Obama extricated himself from a difficult situation, whilst at the same time recognizing the damage done by Jeremiah Wright's inflammatory sermons.

The third question, however, ran and ran, for entirely understandable reasons—here was a stick to beat not only Sarah Palin herself, but McCain as well, who was, it became increasingly clear, guilty of a bad error of judgement. In the short term, however, the nomination of Palin as McCain's running mate did what it was supposed to do: it enthused the evangelical constituency who had not previously been enamoured of McCain as the Republican candidate. Following the declaration of her candidature, poll-ratings increased, fund-raising improved and James Dobson, the influential head of "Focus on the Family",[11] declared his support for McCain—reversing an earlier decision. But in the long term, Palin became a liability—so much so that

---

[10] See "How the news media covered religion in the general election", http://pewforum.org/docs/?DocID=372.

[11] Focus on the Family's mission statement reads as follows. 'To cooperate with the Holy Spirit in sharing the Gospel of Jesus Christ with as many people as possible by

she was turned increasingly into a scapegoat, someone to blame for the disaster.

In terms of democratic politics, a more general and to my mind very encouraging point is worth noting before going further. Palin's nomination is in many ways symptomatic of one of the most interesting aspects of the 2008 election as a whole. At no stage in the entire process, from the selection of the candidates onwards, was it possible to predict the final outcome. Very few commentators, for example, would have put their money on Barack Obama as the Democratic candidate or John McCain as his Republican opponent. Equally unpredictable were the choices of running mates—the announcement of Sarah Palin's nomination astonished the world. The "logic" of Palin's appointment in the summer of 2008, however, is clear enough: McCain's intention was to reduce the gap between himself and the new Christian Right—a section of the electorate who were manifestly delighted at his choice.

Europeans, conversely, were appalled—as indeed were many Americans. Why was this so? Was it Palin's all too evident lack of experience which revealed itself in not one, but several misguided statements and a worrying lack of competence? Or was it her association with the New Christian Right, more specifically with (among others) a Pentecostal church in Alaska? And were these factors ever considered separately? In many cases, it was simply assumed that anyone with religious affiliations of this nature was bound to be incompetent—he or she would, necessarily, be an unsuitable candidate for the vice-presidential role.

Two provocative extracts from a prominent European commentator (Bates 2008a), himself the author of a book on religion in the United States (Bates 2008b), capture this confusion perfectly. The opening paragraphs convey the distaste of most Europeans (Bates uses this term) both for Sarah Palin herself and for the religious right; they also evoke the attitude of Palin's supporters for their European detractors:

> *Every word Europeans (and many Americans) hear about Sarah Palin chills their blood—none more so than her <u>religious beliefs</u>, or at least those of her pastors at the Wasilla Assembly of God church, or the Juneau Christian Centre. But even as it does so, the social conservatives of the American religious right flock ever more enthusiastically to her support. She's saying all the right things for them, and what does it matter what effete, Islamo-friendly, panty-waisted, God-denying,*

---

nurturing and defending the God-ordained institution of the family and promoting biblical truths worldwide.' See http://www.focusonthefamily.com/about_us.aspx.

> *anti-Christian, sopping wet liberal European surrender monkeys think? They don't have a vote, so there.*

It is important to underline that these are stereotypes, not facts, but the mutual contempt is palpable and centres on the religious convictions of one group and the lack of them in the other. But as Bates explains, what Europeans consider to be extreme to the point of being ridiculous, is commonplace in the United States—more so in some places than others, and among some sections of the population rather than others—but, overall, an essential ingredient in the complex mix that makes up religion in modern America.

The final sentences of Bates's piece, however, are even more provoking in that they link Palin's nomination to the exponential growth of Pentecostalism in the modern world—exposing the possibility that it is Europeans, rather than Americans, who might be out of step in global terms:

> *...there are plenty of Pentecostalists in the US and across the third world— Pentecostalism being arguably the fastest-growing religious movement in the world and now the second-largest Christian denomination with 500m followers—who would find her beliefs perfectly unexceptionable. In that sense, the raucous religious right in the US is correct to jeer that it is Europe that is out of step in deriding fundamentalism, rather than the likes of Sarah Palin.*

We can only speculate what might have happened in the 2008 US election had the global economic crisis not taken over as the dominant issue for most Americans—a fact that not only gave Barack Obama an increasingly clear advantage as the election approached but allowed European pundits to declare, in an otherwise rigorous seminar, that religion was simply not an issue.

Why then were these analysts so keen to "change the subject"? The most obvious reason for ignoring the question of religion is that you do not expect it to be there as a significant electoral factor in a modern Western democracy. That, however, simply leads to the second point: why do European commentators have such expectations, or rather the lack of them? And what does this tell us about Europeans, quite apart from the American election itself?

Rightly or wrongly, and displaying significantly short memories regarding their own past, West European elites assume for the most part that elections in "modern" societies are decided on economic rather than religious or moral issues, bearing in mind that there are different interpretations of the word "moral". Rejecting the values questions that are dear to many Republicans (among which abortion remains paramount), European experts are primarily concerned with the economy as such, and with topics such as healthcare, welfare, inclusion and exclusion (in which race, ethnicity and immigration are central), interest groups, the environment and so on. Many of these are of course "moral" questions in a broader sense, but we can leave that possibility on one side for the time being.

No serious commentator would deny the importance of these issues to what was happening in America in November 2008, and indeed since. It goes without saying that the election of the first black president of the United States in November 2008 was a truly momentous event for the entire world order, not only the United States itself. It is also worth pausing for a moment to consider the question of welfare—given its close association with religion in the United States, the absence of such a relationship in Europe, the very different views of Americans and Europeans regarding the underlying philosophies of welfare provision, and the significance of all these questions for Barack Obama himself.

There is a certain amount of truth in the statement that the welfare state (including the health service) in Europe has replaced religion, but it is not the whole truth. A good deal of care in Europe, notably its more informal aspects, is still delivered by the churches.[12] It is also the case that the welfare states of almost all European societies are rather less confident than they used to be about delivering a comprehensive service from the cradle to the grave—a situation compounded by the demographic changes taking place in all developed societies. Ageing populations absorb ever larger welfare budgets, meaning that a wider range of groups—including the churches—are likely to become increasingly involved in the delivery of services alongside the state. All these things are made more difficult in times of economic uncertainty.

The situation in Europe, however, is qualitatively different from that in America, in that significant sections of the American population

---

[12] See for example the work on religion and welfare in Europe carried out by the Centre for the Study of Religion and Society at Uppsala University. Information about these projects and the publications emerging from them can be found on http://www.crs.uu.se/en/node99 and http://www.crs.uu.se/en/node185.

regard even the principle of state-funded welfare negatively. For these people, a comprehensive system of care delivered by the state impedes the economy rather than underpinning it. That said, debates regarding welfare reform are heated in the United States and include as a central, if controversial component faith-based initiatives (FBIs)—that is the delivery of welfare by means of the myriad religious organizations that exist in every corner of the nation. The policy is contentious. Supporters of FBIs argue that formalizing these groups as the providers of welfare simply legitimates what they do all the time, often very effectively. Those who are opposed to this view are convinced that the state, or non-religious community organizations are much better suited to the job.[13] The real sticking point, however, is not so much the existence of FBIs themselves, as the fact that their hiring policies might be restricted to certain religious groups and/or that they might use public funds to proselytize—indirectly, if not directly. Both these things would seriously compromise the establishment clause of the First Amendment in that FBIs would be using money raised through taxes to fund religious activities.

Obama's own position is revealing in this respect. Drawing very directly on his experience in the Developing Communities Project on the south side of Chicago, he has chosen to continue what was originally a Bush initiative. He has renamed the White House Office of Faith-Based and Community Initiatives, the White House Office of Faith-Based and Neighborhood Partnerships, and has kept this as part of the Executive Office of the President. Obama's familiarity with the situation in Chicago was clearly an important factor in this decision. His engagement with some of the most deprived communities of the city instilled in him an understanding of what can be achieved by faith-based organizations in neighbourhoods where living conditions are precarious, to put it mildly. It is these initiatives that he wishes to encourage.

Quite apart from the organizational aspects of this work, Obama's personal views on religion developed at this time, a story which he describes in detail in Chapter 6 of The Audacity of Hope (Obama

---

[13] See the data collected by the Pew Forum on Religion and Public Life, "Religion and social welfare", http://pewforum.org/social-welfare/. See also Cnaan (2002) and Cnaan, R., Boddie, S., McGrew, C. and Kang, K. (2006).

2008b). The moment of decision is captured in the following frequently quoted passage:

> *It was because of these newfound understandings—that religious commitment did not require me to suspend critical thinking, disengage from the battle for economic and social justice, or otherwise retreat from the world that I knew and loved—that I was finally able to walk down the aisle of <u>Trinity United Church of Christ</u> one day and be baptized. It came about as a choice and not an epiphany; the questions I had did not magically disappear. But kneeling beneath that cross on the South Side of Chicago, I felt God's spirit beckoning me. I submitted myself to His will, and dedicated myself to discovering His truth. (2008b: 208)*

More importantly for this chapter, what follows is a well-worked out philosophy—or perhaps theology—of life which openly acknowledges the inspiration that Obama finds in his own faith and his conviction that religion is a positive ingredient in the search for a common good. Clearly he had no difficulty expressing these ideas in the course of his campaign—demonstrating, in fact, a considerably greater facility in this respect than John McCain. Interestingly this reverses once again the positions of the respective predecessors of each of these candidates: in 2004 John Kerry was much less at ease with religious language than George W. Bush, who emphatically made such language a hallmark of his campaigns and presidency.

George Bush's convictions in this respect became, of course, the butt of a great deal of European criticism. Such views were seen as an inappropriate inspiration for the leader of a modern democratic state. Such distaste found a new focus in the contempt expressed for Sarah Palin. Much more perplexing therefore for many Europeans is Barack Obama's own position. It is probably fair to say that his religion is tolerated rather than embraced, a point of view shared in fact by the less religious constituencies in the United States—those, paradoxically, who normally vote Democrat. Interestingly Madeleine Bunting (a British journalist) makes exactly this point in a piece entitled "Religions have the power to bring a passion for social justice". She concludes thus:

> *So those liberal secularists who thought that they had seen the end of praying in the White House will have to think again. They might want to overlook Obama's faith, but he won't make it easy for them. Like it or lump it, he unequivocally believes that <u>religion</u> can be a force for progressive ends. A liberal secular elite on both sides of the Atlantic is going to have to deal with a much more challenging form of religious belief than*

> *those they have been wont to ridicule among George Bush and his cronies.*
> *(Bunting 2009)*

Bunting's argument affirms the ideas presented in this chapter in several respects: it challenges the liberal secularist view (on both sides of the Atlantic); it recognizes—with Obama—that religion can be a force for good (the collective good); and, more specifically, it endorses the role of religion in the delivery of welfare, particularly in the more deprived areas of our cities. Equally interesting is the fact that it provoked 347 online responses, the majority of which were negative.

Grasping the Implications for Social Science

In the early part of Chapter 6 in The Audacity of Hope, Obama writes more generally about the religious situation in the United States. This is an interesting read for any sociologist of religion who has had to come to terms with the failure of the sub-discipline to predict accurately the place of religion in the United States, and more generally in the modern world order. Expectations (of decline) that were commonplace in the 1960s, in the United States as much as in Europe, have not come to pass. Equally acute are Obama's own observations about the reasons for this mistake. They rest, among other things, on the point already mentioned: the inflated influence of the liberal elite who "failed to appreciate the continuing role that all manner of religious expression played in communities across the country" (Obama 2008b: 200). Precisely this failure, moreover, encouraged what Obama calls a "religious entrepreneurship", particularly amongst evangelicals, whose highly successful initiatives are not only independent of the dominant cultural institutions (they had to be), but are unparalleled elsewhere in the industrialized world. America, in this sense, emerges as an exceptional case. But is it? My answer is yes in terms of the modern West, but what is happening in America needs to be seen in a wider context.

Before embarking on the big picture, however, it is important to grasp the political implications of this displacement from the centre of American life. As Obama rightly says, it was Jimmy Carter (a Democrat) who first had the courage to introduce evangelical language into the political discourse of post-war America. It was, however, the Republican Party—no doubt for a complex mixture of motives—who saw the potential in the mass of evangelical voters who felt aggrieved and excluded from the system, a point which returns us to the analysis set out in the first section of the chapter. As we have seen, this is a story in which the Democrats in 2008 were playing catch-up. Catch-up, that is, from the presidential campaigns of 2000 and 2004 in which the Party constructed itself as self-consciously secular and—as a result—lost a significant proportion of the religious vote. Identifiable groups within this constituency (some Catholics and the more reflective evangelicals) returned in sufficient numbers to the Democrats and ensured Obama's election.

In short, both in personal and electoral terms Barack Obama has recognized what every social scientist needs to know: that there is no incompatibility between being seriously religious and fully modern. The problem, if such it is, lies in the eyes of the beholder, not in the religious individuals or constituencies themselves.

European scholars are particularly slow learners in this respect, a reluctance that can be explained first by the very different nature of their own religious situation, but also by the tendency to assume that their own—the European—model is the global prototype. In other words, what Europe does today in terms of its dealings with religion is what the rest of the world will do tomorrow. It is for this reason that European commentators display a mixture of bewilderment and contempt when it comes to the place of religion in the 2008 American election. Rather than engaging the detailed analyses that are required to grasp what was going on the minds of many Americans who were traditional (more often than not evangelical) Republican voters, but who wanted a change, they focus on personalities such as Sarah Palin, using her as a focus for derision rather than scrutiny.

Underneath these attitudes lies something more serious: the persistent difficulty that many Europeans have in grasping the continuing significance of religion in the modern world order. The following paragraphs look in more detail at these questions, using as a pivot a recent—somewhat provocative—publication by two senior journalists from The Economist (Micklethwait and Wooldridge 2009). The fact that both of them work for the most influential public affairs journal that currently exists is worth noting in itself. Equally striking is the uncompromising title of their new book: God is Back: How the Global Rise of Faith is Changing the World. Their core argument is easily summarized. Not only is the religious situation in the United States markedly different from that in Europe, it is the American model that is likely to export itself to the rest of the world rather than the European one. The reasoning is simple: the freer the market in religious goods, the more space there is for successful entrepreneurship—precisely the point made by Obama himself. Conversely, the relatively restricted religious market in Europe, dominated by Europe's state churches, depresses rather than encourages initiative. Herein lie the reasons for the relatively secularity of Europe.

This look, however, needs to be placed in a broader perspective. Is it the case that God is back? Or is it simply that the perceptions of two senior journalists (among others) have caught up with reality? Could it be that religion, in most parts of the modern world, including America, has never gone away? It has simply been ignored by most economic, political and social commentators. To be fair, Micklethwait and Wooldridge are aware that the renewed interest in religion in the modern world lies only partly in the empirical data themselves. Equally important are the ways in which such data are perceived. And they too see the descendants of the European Enlightenment as some of the most culpable in terms of their inability to recognize this fact—an observation that reveals, in turn, two very different approaches to modernity. On the one hand, following Micklethwait and Wooldridge, are the Europeans, who—with varying degrees of success—marginalized religion from the public sphere from the time of the Enlightenment onwards and who remain perplexed by its recent manifestations. Americans, conversely, embraced religion as an integral part of their growing nation, and (like Obama) see no incompatibility in the notion of being fully modern and fully religious. The central chapters of God is Back work through this contrast, concentrating initially on the difference between Europe and America but then widening the perspective to embrace the rest of the world (or most of it). It is, moreover, American forms of religion rather than European ones that are thriving, given that pluralization (unlike secularization) is a necessary feature of modernity. It follows that only those forms of religion that can hold their own in a growing and truly global market are likely to succeed in the current century.

Is this simply a free-market solution from a free-market journal—in other words something that we might expect? The cynic might say yes. The more discerning reader would also be correct in questioning the assumption that America is simply "exporting" a particular version of religion to other parts of the world. The reality is much more complex than that. Indeed at this point, it is important to link this chapter to others in this book (notably those that deal with Pentecostalism) and to appreciate that some very notable scholars have been asking these questions for several decades and have been providing answers that are rather more nuanced than those that are currently in the public eye.

David Martin is a key player in this respect, for two reasons. His work underlines both the importance of the data per se and the difficulties that Martin himself encountered in persuading the majority of his colleagues that Pentecostalism was a topic of key importance not only to its adherents but to scholars of religion—one, moreover, with largely positive outcomes. As he explains in a semi-autobiographical essay (Martin 2000), it was not easy to convince the social scientific establishment that they should take Pentecostalism seriously—the more so given the nature of this particular phenomenon (its emotional, seemingly irrational, dimensions flew in the face of "scientific" explanation). So much so that "[I]t was incorrect even to report what theory forbade" (2000: 27). Martin's correct insistence that Pentecostalism was an indigenous movement of some power for certain kinds of communities in (initially) Latin America, rather than an imposition of American imperialists, was equally problematic. This was not what most people wanted to hear in the sense that it removed the most acceptable explanation for something that—according to the received wisdom of the day—should not have occurred in the first place.

For Martin himself however, the logic is clear. Right from the start he has been less convinced than others about the inevitability of secularization. As early as the 1960s, for example, he expressed serious misgivings about the concept itself. These were voiced in a much quoted article, published in the Penguin Survey of the Social Sciences, under a provocative title "Towards eliminating the concept of secularisation" (Martin 1965). Such were the confusions surrounding the concept that it might be better to abandon it altogether. It is, however, Martin's classic text, A General Theory of Secularization (Martin 1978) that offers the key to his thinking in this area. The initial chapter, itself a reprint of an earlier piece, takes the form of a five finger exercise in which Martin sets out the different trajectories that the secularization process takes in different parts of the world and the key reasons for these contrasts. Not only does he underline the marked difference between Europe and America, he also points out the different patterns in different parts of Europe. The analyses that follow, many of which have become classics in the literature, work through the detail of the different cases.

Just over a decade later, Martin published a further article, with an equally significant title. The initial pages of "The secularization issue: prospect and retrospect" recall Martin's earlier analysis—i.e. that theories of secularization were essentially one-directional in so far as they embodied "covert philosophical assumptions, selective epiphenomenalism, conceptual incoherence, and indifference to historical complexity" (Martin 1991, abstract). The second section articulates an increasingly recognized theme: the connections between stronger versions of the secularization thesis and the European context from which they emerged. In other words, there are particular circumstances or conditions in West Europe that account for the relatively strong indicators of secularization that can be discerned in this part of the world (though more in some places than in others). But outside Europe—and even in the parts of Europe that experienced communism at first hand—very different outcomes have occurred. The active religiosity of the United States, the massive shift to the south of global Christianity, and the emergence of Islam as a major factor in the modern world order are some of these—the understanding of which is ill-served by theories that emerge from a specific, but atypical context. The question moreover is urgent: it becomes abundantly clear that we need new and different concepts if we are to understand properly the nature of religion in the modern world.

Martin himself has worked in two areas in particular: on the post-communist situation in Central and East Europe and—as we have seen—on the exponential rise of Pentecostalism in the Southern hemisphere. It is these empirically driven cases that have led him to articulate even more forcefully than before his initial misgivings about the secularization thesis. The penultimate paragraph of the 1991 article contains a final sting in the tail. The very factors that across Europe accounted for the erosion in the historical forms of religion (the negative associations with power and the rationalist alternative associated above all with the French Republic) are themselves in decline, liberating spaces hitherto occupied by opponents of certain forms of religion. At precisely the same time, new forms of religion (both Christian and non-Christian) are flooding into Europe, not least a significant Muslim population. One effect of these shifts is the return of religion to the public square in Europe.

Martin is not the only scholar to question the wisdom of generalizing from the European case. Among others, we should note Peter Berger's change of mind regarding the relationship between secularization and modernization—a link considered self-evident in the 1960s and 1970s, but no longer supported by the data. In his more recent writing, therefore, Berger affirms not secularization, but pluralization as the essential concomitant of modernization, noting that pluralization is as likely to stimulate faith as to undermine this (Berger 1999). Jose Casanova (1994) echoes these sentiments, both refining the concept of secularization as such and insisting that religion is—and always has been—present in the public square; it is not simply a private matter. Interestingly in his more recent writing, Casanova is also sharply critical of the self-fulfilling nature of European secularism, arguing that the secularization of Western Europe has more to do with the triumph of intellectual knowledge regimes, than with structural processes of socio-economic development—a clear echo of the argument stated in this chapter (Casanova 2006a: 84). My own contribution to this debate can be found in the increasing recognition of Europe as the exceptional case in global terms, meaning that it is the secularity of Europe that requires an explanation, not the continuing religiousness of the rest of the world (Davie 2002). Philip Jenkins (2002), finally, has stressed the extraordinarily rapid growth of Christianity in the global South, calling attention to the demographic revolution that is taking place in all the Christian churches with important consequences for almost every aspect of their existence. No longer can the more "liberal" North dominate the agenda, a fact with serious implications for theology as well as social science.

Such approaches are, of course, entirely consonant with Shmuel Eisenstadt's notion of multiple modernities. If, as Eisenstadt suggests, the best way to understand the modern world (in other words to grasp the history and nature of modernity) is to see this as "a story of continual constitution and reconstitution of a multiplicity of cultural programs" (2000: 2), it is easier to accommodate the religious factor. The argument is rigorously sociological. These on-going reconstitutions of modernity do not drop from the sky; they emerge as the result of endless encounters on the part of both individuals and groups, all of whom engage in such activities but within different economic and cultural contexts. Among these very varied actors are religious movements of all kinds, including those whose dominant philosophies are vehemently opposed to some aspects of modern living. Indeed one of the fundamental paradoxes of Eisenstadt's writing is the following: that to engage with the Western understanding of modernity, or even to resist it, is as indisputably modern as to embrace it. Hence his approach to fundamentalism. It is true that fundamentalist groups are opposed to the West and to the ideologies embodied therein. Fundamentalist movements are, however, quintessentially modern in the manner in which they set their goals and in the means that they adopt to achieve them: their outlooks are truly global and their technologies highly developed. And just like their secular counterparts, they are constantly redefining and reconstituting the concept of modernity, but in their own terms (Eisenstadt 1999).

God is Back should be seen in this light. In this respect, it is not the argument as such which is new (many scholars of religion were already aware of what is happening in different parts of the world), but the fact that two senior journalists from a secular and highly influential public affairs journal are now paying attention to such matters. It is regrettable that the authors do not always take sufficient note of the existing literature and the nuanced nature of the arguments to be found therein—there are conspicuous gaps in their references. The publication of God in Back is, however, of considerable significance in the sense that it will bring these important debates to a much wider circle of readers than is usually the case—an entirely positive feature. Equally significant is Micklethwait's and Wooldridge's assertion that the presence of religion as a powerful factor in modern as well as modernizing societies is set to continue for the foreseeable future. If this is indeed the case, some radical rethinking will need to take place in the economic and social sciences, given that their approaches are underpinned by a markedly secular philosophy. Such views are stubbornly persistent, despite the growing body of data that indicates that religion is present, pervasive and increasingly influential in the twenty-first century.

The implications of these statements are immense if they are taken seriously. Religion continues to influence almost every aspect in human society—economic, political, social and cultural. No longer is it possible to relegate religion to the past or to the edge of our analyses; it must return to the core as an independent as well a dependent variable. Hence the challenge: scholars in many different disciplines must acknowledge the place of religion both in the empirical realities of the modern world, and in the paradigms that are deployed to understand them. In short, social science itself, just as much as its subject matter, must respond to the exigencies of an increasingly religious global order. If we fail in this endeavor, our disciplines will no longer be fit for purpose.

In conclusion, exactly the same point can be made even more sharply by considering three events in the late twentieth and early twenty-first century which changed the world. These are the Iranian revolution of 1979, the fall of the Berlin wall in 1989 and the attack on the Twin Towers in 2001. The striking thing about all of these episodes is that Western social science failed completely to see what was coming. Why was this so? It would be naïve in the extreme to say that each of these events was simply, or even primarily, a religious event. All of them were both motivated by and depended on a wide variety of economic, political, social and cultural factors. It would be equally foolish, however, to exclude religion from the analysis—indeed it was the visible presence of religion and religious motivation in all three episodes that shocked the world, not least the Western pundits.

Why was it, for example, that a pro-Western, relatively secularized Shah was obliged to flee before an Iranian Ayatollah clearly motivated by conservative readings of Islam? Such a scenario had not been anticipated. And why was it that an aggressively secular ideology, not a religious one, collapsed so comprehensively throughout the Soviet bloc—a part of the world that has seen subsequently a marked, if uneven, renaissance of both Christianity and Islam? And why, finally, did the terrifying events of 9/11 come as such a bolt from the blue? Quite simply the unimaginable had happened, requiring—amongst many other things—a radical rethink of the paradigms that are supposed to explain, and indeed to predict the events of the modern world. Hence an inevitable, if somewhat disturbing, question: could it be that a more careful grasp of the continuing place of religion in the late modern world—i.e. of its capacities to resist Western influence in the Muslim world, to withstand harassment and persecution in the Soviet bloc, and to motivate terrorism across the globe—might have led to more accurate predictions of these events? It is time, surely, to take these questions seriously beginning with the 2008 American election.

CHAPTER THREE

GLOBALIZATION, NATIONALISM AND RELIGION: A MULTIPLE MODERNITIES PERSPECTIVE ON IMPERIAL AND PERIPHERAL NATIONS IN POST-COMMUNIST EUROPE

Willfried Spohn

A conspicuous characteristic of post-communist transformations in Central and Eastern Europe since 1989 has been the parallel—though considerably varying—revival of nationalism and religion (Spohn 1998, 2002a, 2008). There have been several general reasons for this. The break-down of communism was not only triggered by a search for democracy and market capitalism but also the quest for national sovereignty against communist imperial rule. The related nationalism was often shaped by organic ethno-national rather than democratic-pluralist identities. This organic ethno-nationalism often combined with a revitalization of religion as a counter-move against the previous state-imposed secularism and repression of religion.

In the framework of modernist and neo-modernist approaches that informed post-communist transitology and transformation research, this parallel revival of nationalism and religion was not foreseen (Bönker, Müller and Pickel 2002, Dawisha and Parrot 1999, Linz and Stepan 1996, Outhwaite and Ray 2005). Rather, it was expected that along with political transitions to democratic regimes and socio-economic transformations to market capitalism and continuing communist secularization also secular-civic forms of nationalism, even if gradually, would emerge. Even if the rise of ethno-nationalism was analyzed, the religious sources and components were seldom addressed. However, in many instances, the emerging organic forms of ethno-nationalism were shaped by revitalizing traditional forms of religiosity as well as new forms of religious fundamentalism and thus represented a key factor in the wide-spread ethno-religious mobilization, conflict and war.

In order to solve this theoretical dilemma between an evolutionist modernization-*cum*-secularization framework and actual post-communist transformation processes, globalization approaches have become attractive, criticizing the methodological nationalism of modernization theory and explaining the revival of nationalism, religion and fundamentalism as a defensive reaction to intensifying global forces in the contemporary era (Beyer 2004, 2006, Juergensmeyer 2003). From that perspective, the impact of global capitalism on post-communist societies leads to sharp social disparities and inequalities and thus creates favourable conditions for ethnic and religious defensive reactions. However, the reasons for the considerable variations in the ethnic and democratic as well as religious and secular components in the post-communist Central and Eastern Europe revival of nationalism remain unclear.

From my own multiple modernities perspective both paradigms share a common bias in one-sidedly reifying or over-generalizing either internal modernization processes or external globalization processes. Instead, I propose to consider varying long-term aspects: communist and pre-communist trajectories of state formation, nation-building and nationalism as well as religious development and secularization patterns in the context of inter-civilizational constellations and global forces. Such a comparative historical-sociological orientation allows also for explaining the considerable variations in the contemporary relations between nationalism and religion in post-communist Central and Eastern Europe. In particular, it provides an explanation for the differences between the two main types of imperial and peripheral forms of nationalism and their relationship with religion and secularization—the core aim of this comparative study.

In the following, I will firstly outline my multiple modernities perspective; secondly, consider the main types of empire-contracting nation-state formation and their relation to nationalism, religion and secularization in Central and Eastern Europe; thirdly compare them to various cases of peripheral nation-state formation and their relations to nationalism and religion in East Central and South Eastern Europe; and fourthly consider the differing impacts of inter-civilizational interconnections and global forces in these empire-contracting and peripheral cases of nationalism, religion and secularization.

Nationalism, Religion and Secularism—A Multiple Modernities Perspective

Let me begin with some introductory remarks to my multiple modernities approach to nationalism, national identity, religion and secularization. Following but also modifying Shmuel Eisenstadt's comparative civilizational perspective (Eisenstadt 2002b, 2003), I assume that modern nationalism and national identity in the context of state formation and nation-building are shaped by three basic—primordial-ethnic, cultural-religious and political-legal—codes (Eisenstadt and Giesen 1995). Whereas most sociological approaches to nationalism and national identity presuppose only two basic dimensions: the ethnic and political ones, the multiple modernities perspective includes also the cultural-religious dimension as crucial. The core premise, here, is that processes of modernization, nation-state formation and democratization evolve within the frameworks of different civilizations—axial-age civilizations as well as non-axial-age civilizations—that are constituted by different types of religion and shape different kinds of modernization and modernity. Accordingly, the compositions of these three codes in collective identities vary according to their different civilizational contexts of modernity and modernization, nation-state formation and democratization as well as religious development and secularization. Modern nationalism and national identity thus comprise, in varying compositions, ethnic and civic as well as secular and religious components.

This multiple modernities perspective on collective movements and identities revises wide-spread modernization approaches that presuppose a world-wide evolutionary trend in the context of global modernization and secularization processes to a secular or civil-religious form of collective identity (e.g. Martinelli 2005, Schmidt 2007, Schwinn 2006). These still prevailing modernization approaches reflect particularly the European experience and assume in a nutshell that the long-term processes of social differentiation and individualization, industrialization and urbanization as well as state-formation, nation-building and democratization are accompanied also by secularization—in the sense of increasing differentiation between organized religion and secular institutions as well as the decline and privatization of religion (Casanova 1994). As a corollary, the construction of collective identities is primarily conceived of as the formation of secular identities spreading with expanding Westernization over the globe. By contrast, the multiple modernities perspective presupposes the varying religious-cultural dimensions—despite undeniable secularization processes—as constitutive for the formation of multiple modernities in the many different civilizations of the world. As foundational sources the religious-cultural dimensions shape not only the type of secularization but also the structural-institutional socio-economic, political and cultural dimensions and thus the multiple forms of modernity and modernization.

On this background, the multiple modernities perspective contrasts also the predominant globalization approaches (Held and McGrew 2002, 2007, Lechner and Boli 2002). Here, the forces of globalization are primarily identified with economic, political, and secular-cultural globalization as consequences of Western modernity. They lead to a converging global modernization by generalizing the European nation-state model of modernity and increasingly transcending it by an overarching Western form of global economy and global governance. As a corollary, they are accompanied by a global expansion of Western forms of secular culture and communication as an emerging world culture. These globalization forces impact also on the various forms of world and local religions by transforming them into a Western-Christian form of differentiated and privatized religion (Beyer 2006). Against this globalist trend in globalization theories, the multiple modernities perspective assumes the continuing relevance of different civilizational religions in the context of axial civilizations, their internal pluralist and fundamentalist tendencies as well as their ecumenical and conflictive potentials in a globalizing compressing world (Eisenstadt 2003). From that perspective, globalization is seen as an intensifying interaction of different and diverging civilizations and nation-states as the complex basis of an emerging world society and globality.

This critical multiple modernities perspective within the social theoretical field of modernization and globalization goes hand in hand with parallel developments in two related fields of research: the sociology of religion and the sociology of nationalism. In the sociology of religion, on the one hand, the received secularization thesis as an evolutionary decline of religion has been replaced by distinguishing several dimensions of secularization such as differentiation between state and religion, public and private religion, decline and revitalization of religion as well as political and secular religion (Beyer and Beaman 2007, Casanova 1994, Joas and Wiegandt 2007, Martin 1978, 2005). These distinctions allow combining modernization and globalization not only with the decline but also rise of religion; to specify varying institutional configurations of differentiation between religion, politics and society; to consider the privatization as well as the de-privatization of religion; and to conceptualize also secularized forms of movements, identities and world-views as alternative forms of religion. In this context, the multiple modernities perspective emphasizes particularly the continuing relevance of axiality in most world civilizations, the axial foundations of world revolutions and the contradictions and antinomies of modernity between pluralizing and totalizing forces (Eisenstadt 2003). At the same time, the multiple modernities approach should include more the conceptual distinctions and comparative analysis in the revised sociology of religion in order to explain the varying configurations of religious and secular components in the pluralizing and totalizing forces in the modern world.

In the sociology of nationalism, on the other hand, the wide-spread evolutionary thesis towards a modern secular, political and civic nationalism has been contested by cultural and ethno-symbolic approaches to nationalism (Armstrong 1982, Brubaker 1996, Hastings 1997, Smith 2001, 2005, van der Veer and Lehmann 1996). They claim that modern nationalism is not only based on an orientation to and identification with the modern nation-state and democracy and thus political-civic values but contains also linguistic, cultural, ethnic and religious components. These components have their origins in pre-modern formations of ethno-genesis, cultural-linguistic homogenization and ethno-religious community that precede and remain an integral part of modern nationalism and national identity. In this context, the multiple modernities perspective emphasizes the continuing relevance of sacred—be it in religious or secular-religious, pluralist or totalizing forms—layers in modern collective identities pertaining to religious communities, social movements, ethno-national groups or transnational civilizations (Eisenstadt 1999). At the same time, the multiple modernities perspective should include more the insights in the sociology of religion on differing secularization dimensions and patterns in order to grasp the varying combinations of religious and secular components in the construction and re-construction of collective identities in the course of modern state formation, nation-building and democratization in the context of processes of modernization and globalization.

The following comparative analysis of empire-contracting and peripheral nationalism in Central and Eastern Europe as two basic opposite types of the relationship between religious and secular components in collective identities attempts to develop the multiple modernities perspective in such a historical-sociological direction. This analysis starts from four theoretical-methodological premises: Firstly, instead of presupposing an ideal-typical opposition between West European political-civic and East European ethnic-cultural nationalism, it is more adequate to distinguish within the structural and cultural pluralism of the European civilization (Eisenstadt 1987) different configurations of primordial-ethnic, cultural-religious and political components in the formation of nationalism and national identity. Secondly, in the context of the European civilization a crucial difference pertains to the distinction between empires and peripheries and related forms of empire-contracting and related forms of peripheral nationalism. Thirdly, regarding the configurations of religious and secular components, empire-contracting nationalisms, due to sovereign imperial statehood, are influenced by stronger religious-pluralist and secular components, whereas peripheral nationalisms are shaped by stronger religious and homogenizing tendencies. And fourthly, to explain the different kinds of revitalization of nationalism and religion in post-communist Central and Eastern Europe, it is necessary to consider not only the communist legacies but also the pre-communist foundations of nationalism and collective identities in the main political and religious European regions.

Empire-contracting Nationalism, Religion and Secularization

As well-known, there have been several attempts to map the different kinds of European state formation, nation-building and nationalism as constitutive parts of the structural and cultural pluralism of the European civilization. In comparative research, focussing on the guiding ideas in nationalist movements, the influential key distinction of Hans Kohn between the Western political-civic and the Eastern ethnic-cultural nationalisms has been questioned and reformulated as varying dimensions in Western and Eastern European nationalism (Delanty and Kumar 2004). Among others, Eugen Kamenka (1960) differentiated between West European political-civic, Central European cultural and Eastern European ethnic nationalism, or Theodor Schieder (1992) distinguished between the Western European state-led nationalism, Central European unifying nationalism and East-Central European separating nationalism.

These different kinds of nationalism have been connected to different time zones of state formation and nation-building. For instance, Ernest Gellner (1983, cf. Szűcs 1990) distinguished four main timezones of state formation and nation-building: the Western early state formation zone, the Central European late formation of nation-states in the context of an over-arching imperial high culture, the East-

Central peripheral zone and the Eastern European imperial zone. Or in an even more complex manner, Stein Rokkan in his European analytical map differentiated all in all eight European regions (Flora 1999). A key element of Rokkan's European typological comparison has been his systematic attempt to take into account not only as usual the big states but also the many peripheral states in the various European regions (cf. also Krejci and Velimsky 1981). However, in all these typologies of European state formation, nation-building and nationalism, there is also an underlying modernist assumption that these processes of political modernization combine with the formation of a secular nationalism and thus the role of religion in European nation-building and nationalism remains unclear.

In order to include systematically the religious developments and related secularization patterns for explaining the varying religious/secular compositions of European nationalism, it is best to turn above all to the general theory of secularization as developed by David Martin (1978, 2005). In a nutshell, Martin proposed an inverse relationship between the degree of institutional religious pluralism or monopolization and the degree of cultural secularization: the more plural the religious landscape, the lower the cultural tendency towards secularization; and the more monopolistic the form of organized religion, the stronger the cultural secularization tendency. Accordingly, considering the main types of religion in Europe, the pluralizing Protestant cultures in Europe are characterized by weak secularization—though with considerable differences between Calvinism and Lutheranism. Monopolistic Catholic cultures lead to a sharp opposition, strong secularization and a Catholic organic reaction. A similarly strong religious-secularist cleavage is characteristic for Orthodox Christianity with its close connection between state and church as well as Islam with its interconnection of law and religion—though with characteristic differences due to their particularities in religious institutions and cultures.

It is however needed to connect Martin´s general model to the actual variety of secularization patterns in European religion. To explain the varying religious/secular composition of European nationalism, one has to consider the center-periphery relations in European state formation and nation-building as contexts of religious developments and secularization patterns. The Martin ideal-typically formulated relations between the institutional and cultural dimensions of religious development and secularization are primarily valid for independent sovereign nation-states, whereas in dependent or peripheral nations without sovereign state and legal institutions the secularization patterns are considerably modified. As a general rule, religious integration remains stronger and the tendency towards secularization is weaker in peripheral nations in contrast to core nation-states. Hence, also peripheral nationalism has a stronger religious component, whereas core nationalism combines with a stronger secular component. However, this general rule has to be specified in relation to the predominating type of religion in the different zones of European state formation, nation-building and related nationalism.

Turning first to the big nation-states in Europe, the German world historian Jürgen Osterhammel (2008) has emphasized that the European big states were not simply nation-states but imperial nation-states with not only a considerable multi-ethnic but also pluri-religious composition. As a consequence, the processes of state formation and nation-building in the 19th and 20th centuries consist of varying empire-transforming and empire-contracting trajectories. At the same time, they combined with civilizing missions—not only as part of European colonialism and imperialism but also as part of the cultural construction and homogenization of the European big nation-states themselves (Barth and Osterhammel 2005). A key component, here, was the predominant type of religion: in Great Britain Anglican and Methodist Protestantism, in France Catholicism and laicized republicanism, in Germany predominant Lutheran Protestantism, in Habsburg Counter-Reformation Catholicism, in Russia Orthodox Christianity and in the Ottoman Empire Sunni Islam.

In Central Europe, both Germany and Austria were imperial nation-states with extending political spheres and civilizing missions to East Central Europe until World War II and only thereafter developed through catastrophic empire-contraction into modern democratic federal nation-states. In the German case, the trajectory of state formation and nation-building was essentially shaped until 1945 by the Old German-Roman Empire, the Protestant Reformation and German high culture. Although dissolved under the impact of the Napoleonic wars, the imperial foundations remained a frame of reference for unified Germany from the Second Empire to the Third Reich and became dissolved only with post-WW II German division and re-unification in 1990 (e.g. Breuilly 1994, Dann 1990, Giesen 1998, Minkenberg 2005). A crucial cultural background was the Protestant Reformation that split the developing German nation into a Protestant and a Catholic part and formed the basis of the predominance of Lutheran Protestantism and German enlightenment in German cultural nationalism. At the same time, the predominant place of Protestantism against sub-dominant Catholicism in German nation-building generated an asymmetric pattern of secularization: strong in Protestant and weak in Catholic regions. Against this historical background, contemporary German national identity is characterized in its Western Protestant-Catholic mixed part by a combination of secular and Protestant-Catholic components and in its Eastern largely Protestant part by a—as a legacy of the communist period—strong secularist component (Spohn 2002b).

Also in the Austrian case, the imperial and religious backgrounds are of crucial importance. As an integral part of the Old Empire and its German high culture, Austria had become also the centre of the Habsburg Empire and thus torn between two projects of an either pan-German or Austrian empire-contracting nationalism (Kann 1974). At the same time, Habsburg Austria was the centre of Counter-Reformation Catholic Europe and thus in the German-speaking lands a counter-project to Protestant German nationalism as well as a Catholic variety of a German cultural mission to the East. Also here, only the catastrophe of World War II destroyed the imperial framework of Austrian nation-building and turned Austria into a small Central European democratic-federal nation-state. It combined with an Austrification of German-Austrian culture and cultural nationalism with a strong Catholic component—despite increasing, though in comparison to Germany weaker, secularization (Bruckmüller 1996, Spohn 2005).

Turning to the Eastern empires in and beyond Europe, both the Tsarist Empire and the Ottoman Empire underwent processes of empire-contraction on their paths to post-Soviet Russia and modern Turkey (Barkey and v. Hagen 1997). The Tsarist Empire, rapidly expanding to Central and East Asia through colonial conquest since the 16th century, formed an enormously complex multiethnic empire under the domination of the Russian ethno-national group and the Orthodox-Christian Church. The Bolshevik revolution transformed it into the Soviet Empire that expanded its imperial scope even further but Soviet nationality policies and the intensification of Russian nationalism prepared also the ground for the contemporary post-Soviet contraction to a Russian dominated Eurasian empire (Eisenstadt 1994, Khazanov 1995, Motyl 1994). Through the Soviet intermezzo the originally close caesaro-papist connection became substituted by a secularist ideocracy that persecuted but also accommodated, since World War II, with Orthodox Christianity. On this basis, the contemporary post-Soviet Russian nationalism as one pillar of the break-up of the Soviet Union—in addition to the separating nationalism of the East-Central European and Central Asian spheres—combines with a strong revival of Christian Orthodoxy in state and society. This is indicated particularly in the enormous growth of Orthodox religiosity, the reconstituted role of the Orthodox Church in state and politics and its strong influence on Russian nationalism and national identity in a mixture with communist-secularist elements (Sakwa 1996).

Also the Ottoman Empire as a multi-ethnic and pluri-religious empire under the domination of the Ottoman state centre and Sunni Islam became transformed through the Kemalist revolution into a modern-secularist Turkish nation-state (Barkey 2008). This state secularism, however, is not identical with Western European secularization processes in terms of differentiation between state and religion. Instead of privatization of religion, it rather imposed an authoritarian-secularist state control on Islam and other religions by simultaneously prioritizing Sunni Islam as an integral part of Turkish cultural nationalism. In the context of increasing pressures towards democratization and pluralisation, contemporary Turkish secularist nationalism and national identity is confronted with a growing mobilization of ethno-national and religious minorities and as a reaction with growing Sunni-Islamic currents. As a consequence, Turkish secularist nationalism is torn between secularism, Sunni-Islam and religious pluralism (Bazdogan and Kasaba 1997, Yavuz 2003, Zürcher 2004). Thus, both the Russian and Turkish trajectories of empire-contracting nationalism are not simply characterized by the evolution of a secular national identity but rather by oscillations between religious and secularist canopies that differentiate in more pluralistic but also conflictive configurations.

Peripheral Nationalism, Religion and Secularization

All four empires: the German, Habsburg-Austrian, the Tsarist and Ottoman empires ruled or dominated until World War I most of the peripheral regions with their national and ethnic groups in East-Central, South-East and Eastern Europe. Through the retreat and final collapse of these empires, a diverse mosaic of independent nation-states in the in-between peripheral regions on the basis of separating nationalisms emerged after World War I. However, the reversal to imperial conquest through World War II renewed imperial domination in East

Central, South Eastern and Eastern Europe until the break-down of the Soviet Empire in the late 1980s and early 1990s. This long-term historical imperial domination created specific frame conditions for the formation of peripheral nation-states, nationalism and religion. Generally speaking, the absence of an independent sovereign statehood along with autonomous political, social and religious institutions weakened the dimensions of a political-civic nationhood, limited secularization and strengthened an ethnic-cum-religious nationalism. Peripheral nationalism is characterized by strong religious and weak secular components. Its particular form thereby depends on the external imperial legacies and the internal ethnic and religious composition of the peripheral nations. Let me exemplify this thesis with reference to five regional clusters of peripheral nationalism in East-Central, North-East, South-East and Eastern Europe as well as the Caucasus.

In East Central Europe Poland is a typical case. In the transition era to modern Europe in the late 18th century, the Polish-Lithuanian Commonwealth had been partitioned between the three surrounding German, Habsburg and Russian empires, regained its national independence only after World War I, but soon became again the victim of imperial onslaughts from the West and the East and regained its renewed national sovereignty only with the transformation to post-communist Poland (Davies 1981, Zernack 1994). In this context, Polish nation-building, for a long time, was not embedded in autonomous state and church institutions, but rather opposed to the political institutions imposed from outside. As a consequence, the Catholic clergy played an important role in Polish nation-building and nationalism throughout the 19th and 20th centuries (Kriedte 1997, Luks 1997). This constellation got even strengthened in the communist period and this explains the high level of Catholic religiosity and the strong Catholic component in post-communist Poland—though now slightly weakening in the present post-communist constellation (Pollack et al. 1998).

Three other cases are characteristic for East Central Europe, though as former parts of the multi-national Habsburg Empire with important differences. On the historical foundations of Bohemia and Moravia as two core regions of the Habsburg Empire, modern Czechoslovakia gained its national independence after World War I, lost it again with Nazi Germany's annexation and its inclusion into the Soviet hemisphere after World War II (Krejci 1990). The renewed national independence with post-communist transformation was soon accompanied by the separation of the Czech Republic and Slovakia. An important reason for this national separation played the diverging role of Catholicism in both cases. Interwar modern anti-Habsburg Czechoslovakian nationalism contained a crucial cleavage between the predominant liberal-Hussite Czech and the more ethnic-Catholic Slovakian part (Schulze Wessel 2002). On this basis, the communist period continued the uneven secularization pattern. This resulted in the post-communist period in a strongly secularized Czech national identity which contrasts with the more Catholic Slovakian national identity. Also in the case of Hungary the historical status of a co-centre in the Habsburg Empire that it had gained after its liberation from Ottoman rule during the 19th century played a constitutive role. Though predominantly anti-Habsburg Catholic, Hungarian nationalism contained considerable liberal, Protestant and multi-religious components and shaped its composition after Hungarian post-WW I independence (Brandt 2002, Spannenberger 2002). Also here, the communist period was accompanied by further secularization—but less than in the Czech case—and the post-communist present by a revitalized Catholicism and Catholic component of Hungarian nationalism—though on a much lower level than in Poland (Pollack et al. 1998)

In North-Eastern Central Europe the religious-secular composition of peripheral nationalism contrasts to the East-Central European cases on the basis of its predominant Protestantism and the legacy of the Tsarist and Soviet Empire. Originally Christianized under the influence of Latin Christianity, most of this Northern periphery—Finland and the Baltic states except Lithuania—turned under the influence of Sweden and Prussia to Lutheran Protestantism (Hope 1995). Protestantism also contributed to stronger contours of ethno-genesis, however, since the 17th century under imperial dominance and conflict between Sweden, Prussia and Tsarist Russia. Since the early 18th century, Estonia, Latvia and Lithuania (following the Polish partitions) came under Russian rule, followed by Finland during the 19th century. For the Baltic states, national independence after the Bolshevik revolution was short-lived and only regained with the break-down of the Soviet Union, but also Finland remained until then in a sort of semi-dependent status. Lutheran Protestantism and particularly its pietist-popular variety continued to be at the heart of the developing ethno-nationalism, but its inward-directedness and state orientation contributed also to strong privatization and secularization. This tendency has particularly played out in Finland with high secularization of pre-dominant Protestantism but accompanied by a high proportion of new religions (Kaplan 2000). In post-communist Estonia and Latvia, secularization and related secular elements in national identity as a consequence of Soviet impact is also rather strong but countered by a certain Lutheran revival in addition to that of Orthodox Christianity in the numerous Russian minority (Kaplan 2000). By contrast, in post-communist Catholic Lithuania, secularization is much weaker and the Orthodox element less weighty while the Catholic component in national identity considerably stronger (Meissner 1990).

South-Eastern Europe has been over long stretches of time a contested zone between Western Christianity, Eastern Christianity and Islam and in modern times related to the Habsburg, Tsarist and Ottoman empires. The related regional and religious fragmentation is particularly pronounced in the case of Romanian dependent state formation and peripheral nation-building. Due to the geo-political constellations after WW I, an independent Great Romania came into being torn by internal regional and ethno-religious fragmentation. The Romanian Orthodox Church with more than 2/3 of the Romanian population competed with substantial Greek-Catholic, Roman Catholic and Protestant minorities and was unable to materialize its claim to be the true core of Romanian national identity (Maner 2002). In the post-WW II communist period, the secularization pressures by the communist state were primarily directed against the ethnic-religious minorities, whereas Orthodox Christianity accommodated to national communism (Scharr and Gräf 2008). In post-communist Romania, therefore, the enforced secularization process left its marks, but was countered by a revival particularly of the minority religions and Pentecostalism (Martin 2006), less so by Orthodox Christianity, and accordingly the predominant secular-Orthodox core of Romanian national identity became contested by minority religious elements (cf. Brubaker et al. 2006).

A similarly fragmented, but more conflictive and unsuccessful form of a common state formation and nation-building is represented by (ex)Yugoslavia. Against the historical background as contested territory between Western and Eastern Christianity and later Islam as well as some late-medieval ethno-political kingdoms, the collapse of the Habsburg and Ottoman empires enabled after WW I a common South-Slavic monarchical state based on similar languages, a regional Illyrian identity but also Serbian hegemony (Banac 1981). Through WW II and an anti-Nazi partisan movement, it turned into a centralized communist-secularist state which continued Serbian hegemony and an asymmetric ethno-federalism. As a countermove, there remerged Slovenian, Croatian, Bosnian and Serbian ethno-nationalisms in close entwinement with a resurgence of Catholic, Orthodox and Islamic religions and triggered with the communist break-down the internecine war and state dissolution of Yugoslavia (Roudometof 2001). As a result, there is now in the Balkans a multitude of small states—all with a relatively high level of religiosity and ethno-national homogenization as well as strong currents of religious nationalism (Todorova 1997).

Strong sacralized ethno-nationalism with rather low secularization and high multi-ethnic conflict potential have been also characteristic for other cases of peripheral state formation and nation-building in South Eastern Europe at the edges of the contracting Ottoman Empire. In this region, with the collapse of the Byzantine Empire through the expansion of the Ottoman Empire to South Eastern Europe, Orthodox Christianity became included as millets into the Ottoman-Islamic imperial edifice (Barkey 2008). Against this historical background, Greek nationalism succeeded with the help of the European imperial powers to separate from the Ottoman Empire in the early 19th century and embark on the trajectory of modern state formation and nation-building. But Greek nation-building included a catastrophic population exchange after the foundation of modern Turkey and the lost dream of a Greater Greece after World War I and democratic nation-building set in only after World War II (Kokosolakis and Psimmenos 2005, Legg and Roberts 1997). In this context, Greek nationalism was closely intertwined with Greek Orthodoxy. Secularizing processes remained limited and Greek national identity characterized by strong religious components (Fokas 2006, Roudometof 2001). Similarly, though with a time-lag, Bulgaria succeeded shortly before and during WWI in founding a separate nation-state. Also, here, the tendency to construct national identity on the basis of majority Orthodoxy was predominant but at the same time connected with an incorporation of the Muslim and Jewish ethno-religious minorities. In the communist period, the secularist regime accommodated more with Orthodoxy than the minority religions and this resulted in the post-communist transformation period in a revival of a predominantly Orthodox Bulgarian nationalism in tension particularly with the Muslim-Pomiak minority (Karagiannis 2005).

Moving on, finally, to the Eastern European Southern tier of the former Soviet Union, Ukraine and the Caucasus may serve as opposite examples. Also in this region, competing surrounding empires had a crucial impact on the forms of national state formation during the Tsarist and Soviet periods and now in the post-Soviet phase. In the case of Ukraine, the imperial division originally between the Polish-Lithuanian Commonwealth in the West and the Tsarist Empire in the East, then the Habsburg Empire and the Tsarist Empire in the 19th century and between Poland and the Soviet Union in the inter-war period in the early 20th century formed also contours of Ukrainian nation-building and religion. First in the Western Ukraine, later also in the Eastern Ukraine, there emerged a common sense of a separate Ukrainian nation based on a common language, Western Greek Orthodoxy and Eastern attempts towards an autonomous Ukrainian Orthodoxy against imperial Russian Orthodoxy (Vulpius 2005). Strongly discriminated against during Tsarist times and severely suppressed during Soviet times, Ukrainian nationalism re-emerged in the late Soviet Union and constituted the basis for the formation of an independent Ukrainian nation-state with the breakdown of the Soviet Union (Hosking 1991, Szporluk 2000). However, though the Soviet period was accompanied by a considerable secularization process, contemporary Ukraine is haunted by the continuing strong religious-national divisions between Western and Eastern Ukraine as well as autonomous national and pro-Russian currents (cf. Casanova 1998).

By contrast, the Caucasus with its many small ethno-national groups resembles in many respects the fate of the Balkans. Geographically, it is a similarly mountainous terrain and, historically, it was shaped as a conflictive imperial influence zone originally between the Roman/Byzantine and Persian empires, later the Ottoman, Persian and Tsarist empires and finally the Soviet Union, modern Turkey and Iran. Based on ancient civilizations, multiple languages, different religions, small kingdoms and related forms of ethno-genesis, an over-arching pan-Caucasian state has not been a historical viable option. Rather, the Caucasian people became a plaything and victim of imperial conquest and domination. As a corollary, ethno-genesis and nation-building were strongly entwined with overlapping ethno-national groups and multiple religions—varieties of Orthodox Christianity and Islam (Stölting 1990, Suny 1983). With empire-contraction and empire-contracting nationalism—modern Turkey since WW I and Russia with the break-down of Soviet communism—the geopolitical situation of the Caucasian ethno-national groups became extremely precarious (Mann 2004). On the one hand, the contracting empires perceived them as potential foes of their national homogenization, on the other, the ethno-national groups became opposed to each other in ethno-national rivalry underpinned by strong religious identities. This is characteristic also for the current ethno-national conflicts in the post-Soviet Caucasus (Herzig 1999).

Globalization, Nationalism and Religion

As Shmuel Eisenstadt argues, the contemporary globalization processes are leading to far-reaching changes in the constitution of nation-states, collective identities and inter-civilizational relations (Eisenstadt 2003: 925–935). Indeed, there is the growing weight of transnational and global, socio-economic, political-military and cultural-religious forces that considerably change the external and internal conditions of state sovereignty, national autonomy and democratic participation. In this context, also the international and inter-civilizational power relations between nation-states and civilizations are transformed. As a consequence, also collective identities in their internal composition and boundary constructions are reconstructed. At the same time, it would be misleading to view these changes through globalization simply in the direction of the decline of nation-states. Rather, as Michael Mann (1997) argued, nation-states are multiplying and diversifying; or as Mitchell Young and others (2007) stated, nations are persisting. At the same time, it is true that many existing states have been threatened by the external and internal impact of global forces, enhanced ethno-nationalist conflicts on the basis of increasing ethno-national diversity and growing forces of disintegration into smaller ethno-national units (Sassen 2007).

However, globalization has multi-dimensional effects on nation-states, nation-building and democratization. As I argued regarding Central and Eastern Europe, there are crucial differences between long established old states and newly emerging nation-states, particularly between empire-contracting big states and separating peripheral small states. Empire-contracting big states on the historical basis of multi-ethnic empires have gone through considerable conflicts and crises but in the end are characterized by a rather stable institutional stateness that allows for political, cultural and ethnic differentiation and thus more pluralistic forms of political and civic inclusion. By contrast, peripheral nations in a conflict zone between these contracting empires have been characterized by weak stateness, a multi-ethnic composition of the population, cultural heterogeneity, ethno-national hierarchies, a low level of national integration and organic forms of ethnic and cultural nationalism. Under those circumstances, transnational and global forces that increase social inequalities and ethnic diversity and decrease state sovereignty and power control have indeed threatening and conflictive effects.

In this context, the revitalization of religion in the contemporary global era cannot be seen in a one-directional way as a defensive reaction to globalization alone. Rather, it is a complex phenomenon that combines a sense of global human threats (Robertson 1992) with a continuing expansion of world religions (Berger 1999) and varying secularization trends (Beyer 2006)—closely entwined with the proliferation of nation-states and mobilisation of ethno-national conflicts. Regarding post-communist Central and Eastern Europe, the revitalization of religion is first and foremost a counter-reaction to the former communist-secular regimes that has re-opened spaces of religious freedom, where traditional and new forms of religiosity revitalize and compete with secularism and religious pluralism. These renewed religious spaces go hand in hand with an intensification of trans-national forms of missionary activities, particularly by evangelical Protestantism, social Catholicism and political Islam (Martin 2006, Byrnes 2001, Eickelman and Piscatori 1996). A special role is also played by the increasing volume of international migration as an important element of pluralizing the religious landscape. The resulting complex revival of religion is closely intertwined with claims to collective and individual autonomy and thus with contradictory processes of ethnic and national mobilisation as well as individualization and pluralism. The impacts of global forces on each post-communist society therefore depend on the specific national configurations of the religious/secular and monopolistic/pluralistic components in the construction and reconstruction of collective identities.

Regarding the four empire-contracting cases in Central and Eastern Europe, the imperial legacies such as strong stateness, high national integration of the dominant ethnic group and multi-ethnic and pluri-religious experiences support, under the contemporary conditions of globalization and immigration pressures, also the tendencies to more pluralistic forms of citizenship, religion and collective identity. How these tendencies play out, however, depends amongst other factors, on the dominant religion and the form of secularization. In Germany the recent shift of citizenship to more civic elements, the increasing efforts to integrate immigrants and the attempts to include Islam have been crafted under the impact of coming to terms with the past and particularly the Jewish question. In post-Habsburg Austria, even if now a small nation particularly fearful of foreigners and the opening of the East, there is also the legacy of a multi-religious citizenship (Permoser and Rosenberg 2009). In post-Soviet Russia, despite the re-establishment of Orthodoxy and mobilization of nationalist and xenophobic sentiments, there is also, even if hierarchical, the legacy of a multi-national citizenship and religious pluralism (Sakwa 1996). And similarly in post-Ottoman Turkey, in spite of growing mobilization of Sunni-Islam and its impact on Turkish nationalism, the Ottoman legacy serves also as a framework for secular/religious and multi-ethnic pluralism.

Regarding the many peripheral cases in the four major European peripheral zones analyzed, by contrast, they combine weak stateness, an ambiguous national identity, revitalized religiosity and re-emerging currents of religious nationalism though on varying secularization levels—and all these factors contribute to strong tensions and high conflict potentials between the national majority and ethnic minorities as well as the dominant religion and minority religions in the context of continuing ethno-national rivalries and growing immigration movements. In predominantly Protestant North-East Europe, particularly in post-communist Estonia and Latvia, despite continuing conflicts with the large Russian and Orthodox minority, the tendencies to civic and religious pluralism are relatively strong. In predominantly Catholic East Central Europe, civic and religious pluralism in the context of Catholic and secularist legacies is more limited, despite strong variations in religious composition and secularization levels. In South East Europe shaped by long-term incorporation in the Ottoman Empire and protracted separating nation-building, the tendencies to civic and religious pluralism are even more restricted and ethno-national rivalries underpinned by competing religious identities more pronounced. In the southern tier of post-Soviet, predominantly Orthodox-Christian Eastern Europe, there are similar tendencies of ethno-national fragmentation and religious diversity. These tendencies play out in very different ways in multi-religious Ukraine and the ethno-nationally fragmented new Caucasus.

In all these empire-contracting as well as peripheral cases of nation-building and nationalism in post-communist Central and Eastern Europe, economic, political, cultural and religious forces of globalization represent different pressures, challenges and opportunities. Here, empire-contracting big states are better prepared and more powerful than peripheral small states. This relates also to the new forms of regional integration and transnational governance that develop in the context of historical civilizational complexes as countermoves to the destructive forces of globalization and are primarily driven by the empire-contracting big states and their former imperial spheres. A particular role here is played by the European Union that, on the one hand, facilitates economic, political and cultural globalization but, on the other, through the Eastern and South Eastern expansion of European integration and European partnership association, also contributes to state formation, democratization, economic development, protection of ethnic and religious minorities as well as the implementation of human and civil rights in the peripheral zones in post-communist Central and Eastern Europe (Byrnes and Katzenstein 2006). Turkey—either as a future member or only as a privileged partner of the European Union—could play a similar role in the newly emerging Mediterranean Union and the Near/Middle East. Post-Soviet Russia still tends to follow a course of imperial re-construction instead of promoting a course of regional integration in cooperation with the newly independent, but peripheral nation-states and the European Union eastern partnership association (Spohn 2008).

Globalization thus enhances ethnic and religious fragmentation, exclusion and conflicts in contemporary societies but also entails tendencies towards more inclusive ethnic pluralism and religious-cultural citizenship. In order to explain these tendencies it is needed to compare the varying trajectories of state formation, nation-building, religious development and secularization as well as their transformation in the changing global, inter-civilizational and transnational constellations in the present. Such a historical-comparative multiple modernities approach, as I tried to outline, is better prepared than over-generalized theories of modernization, transformation or globalization to understand and explain the complex, contradictory and varying trends in post-communist Central and Eastern Europe.

PART TWO

CHRISTIAN FAITHS

CHAPTER FOUR

DYNAMICS OF ULTRAMODERN RELIGIOSITY AND NEW FORMS OF RELIGIOUS SPATIALITY

Danièle Hervieu-Léger

The process of individualization and subjectivization of beliefs which allows the spiritual mobility of individuals on the one hand, the process of globalization of religion which encourages the circulation of ideas and symbols on a worldwide scale, on the other, are currently two cornerstones of the sociological description of the contemporary religious scene. The combination of these two series of observations leads us to suggest that a world of religious communities, organizing regular practices on a local basis and carrying out the transmission of religious identities from one generation to another could possibly be coming to an end. This proposal sounds particularly relevant to the case of Christian churches in Western Europe where the decline of the so called "parish civilization" has been recognized and measured for more than 60 years (Lambert 1985).

Made directly visible through the fascinating proliferation of steeples and church towers all over the European landscape, the parish civilization was the materialization of a regime of religious communalization combining a spatial organization (in fact: a territorial meshing), a system of religious authority (embodied in the figure of the parish priest or pastor) and a comprehensive administration of social times (through the cycles of practices and feasts, and daily, through the ringing of bells).

The recording of the fall in (or even the collapse of) church attendance and the diminishing number of priests and ministers everywhere have attested for a long time to a disaggregation which is the direct counterpart of the increasing inability by the Church to provide the symbolic frameworks of collective reference. Of course, we know that the rate and historical process of this decline vary, according to the different national contexts in Western Europe. But the conclusion remains very clear: the new directions of religiosity in these societies irremediably dissolve the local fabric of religious sociability.

Does it mean the inevitable virtualization of socio-religious links? Is Western Europe entering into a time of "above ground religion" (as one speaks of "above ground agriculture"!)? I would like to question this hypothesis of a possible de-communalization of Christianity in Europe, in two steps: first, I examine the paradoxical tension between the process of individualization of beliefs, and the recurrent calls for intensive forms of communalization that are developing at the same time; secondly, I would consider the no less paradoxical contradiction between a general movement of deterritorialization of religion—that is supposed to be linked to the collapse of natural communities in all ultramodern European societies—and the unexpected ways by which contemporary religiosity inserts itself into new forms of religious spatiality.

I suggest that it is possible, by crossing these two sets of observations, to go beyond the superficial equivalence posited between the processes of individualization, de-communalization and deterritorialization of religion in Western Europe.

For more than 20 or 30 years, sociologists of religion have admitted that the institutional deregulation of religion (which is the very core of the process of secularization in Europe) perfectly cohabits with a proliferation of beliefs, made more active by the increasingly fast rate of technological and cultural change, and the multiple uncertainties of the present social and economic situation.

What is new indeed is not that proliferation in itself. It is the fact that the great "codes of meaning" run by historical religious institutions are less and less able to frame the individual sets of belief. Individuals claim to make by themselves small systems of meaning that are able to put in order their own subjective experience. In religious matters, as in all matters that are supposed to request a full involvement of personal subjectivity, the demands for personal authenticity take precedence over external obligations of any sort.

However, this process of subjectivization must not be misunderstood as a complete individualistic dissemination of small narratives produced by freely floating believers. Individuals freely assemble their personal belief solution, but they do so using symbol resources whose availability remains confined within certain limits, according to the cultural environment and to the access that each person has to these resources. The contemporary *bricolage* of beliefs operates through a limited number of cultural patterns, in a way which is not so far from the *bricolage* of myths so magnificently analyzed by Claude Levi-

Strauss (1958). I let this point aside. There is no doubt, however, that the pool of symbol resources upon which individuals are likely to draw, in order to make their own personal narrative, is undergoing a considerable expansion. The general increase of cultural opening, linked to the development of communication and professional and geographical mobility, brings individuals into contact with a diversified range of cultural worlds during the course of their lives. The weakening of the family structures and processes of religious transmission also generate and contribute to the diversification of personal trajectories of identification, and gives room to the subjectivization of these trajectories.

It occurs at the very moment when the ready availability, with no special access code, of multifarious symbol stock on offer to individuals has expanded quite phenomenally. The profusion of religious sites on the web offers a perfect illustration of this open market of spirituality, in which individuals move around and choose what they want. But this is the visible part of the iceberg: alongside the explosion of virtual religion, the proliferation of published matter on religious topics, television, films and the mainstream press all contribute to placing at everyone's disposal information which—however partial or superficial it may be—broadens the "well known religious landscape" of individuals.

In Western Europe, much is made of the dangers, perhaps even the impending "cultural catastrophe", entailed by such a chaotic spreading around of references to tradition known only fragmentarily and indirectly. The fact remains that it is here, from this kaleidoscope of disparate data, almost invariably dislocated from the symbolic syntax which made them readable within the great narratives of Tradition, that individuals build their own capacity for spiritual and religious home-compositions.

But contrary to all expectations, this process of subjectivization, far from implying the atomistic dispersion of small narratives, reveals a paradoxical tendency towards their standardization, that makes possible—in a context of cultural globalization—their arrangement into networks on a world-wide scale. In the spiritual domain, as in all areas of mass production (including artistic and cultural production), standardization appears to be the direct consequence of the process of liberalization, here made possible by the abolition of the institutional monopoly of truth.

This paradoxical homogenization is well documented—especially in the European charismatic field (Protestant and Catholic)—by the expansion of a "theological minimalism"—frequently associated with an emotional religious style which promotes the value of personally experiencing the presence of the Spirit, and tends to put the intellectual mind on the back-burner. This religiosity reduced to effects, allows its efficient adaptation for self-fulfilment and personal realization. It encourages the migration of believers, who define and modulate spiritual courses that pay less and less heed to denominational boundaries. But it also paradoxically feeds a need for places where the specificity of an irreducible distinctiveness of personal quest can find recognition.

These dialectics, between the standardization of theological and spiritual contents on one hand, and the extreme valorization of personal expression of experience, on the other, is one of the major traits of the Christian charismatic currents and so-called "new communities" unfurling inside and outside the main Churches in Europe: the very fluidity of individual spiritual journeys encourages the play of mutual authentication, which occurs within small affinity groups, where individuals seek for and find the confirmation of their own subjective productions of meaning. The most striking paradox is this: the more beliefs circulate, the less they determine tangible social affiliations, and the more they further a desire for community which is likely to evolve into intensive forms of religious communalization.

How to Make Sense of this Tension?

In the European Christian sphere, an obvious paradox of religious high modernity lies in the fact that the fluidity of belief, which bears witness to the (at least relative) emancipation of the individuals from the tutelage of the Church, rarely provides them the minima of certainty which they need in order to create their personal identity, as believers called upon to assume their own personal autonomy in all areas of their life. They claim to direct their spiritual courses by themselves, and give precedence to the authenticity of their personal quest over any form of compulsory conformity to official truths. But, at the same time, they aspire to dialogue with others as the only way to testify to their experiences. By means of mutual validation, they seek an intersubjective sharing of certainties which can compensate for the collapse of the institutional regime of truth, which had organized for centuries the collective regulation of beliefs.

This tendency, empirically documented, in particular, in the so-called Catholic "new communities", which organize, on an affinity basis, the sharing of community certainties, does not challenge the general movement towards individualization of belief. Quite the contrary, it can be considered as the exact counterpart of this movement. The approaches to the contemporary European Christian scene which deal exclusively with the individualistic *bricolage* of beliefs and the metaphor of the symbolic supermarket regularly miss that point: the need for subjectivization—which is indeed the very dynamics of religious high modernity—cannot really be met just through personalized consumption of increasingly standardized symbolic goods. Because it has the more fundamental aim of making meaning out of individual experience, the construction of a personal spiritual narrative implies the confrontation with an otherness outside which no language—and hence no personal recognition—is possible.

More than that, it is the process of mutual recognition—through face-to-face interactions and dialogue—that makes possible the grounding and stabilization of individually produced meaning systems within a symbolic genealogy—a chain of memory—which constitutes the structural axis of any religious identity. In other words, there is no possible rendering of spiritual experience as a religious narrative unless the individual, at some point, meets other individuals able to confirm it for him: "what makes sense for you, also makes sense for us".

To take on this process, individuals must have sufficient access to symbolic resources, cultural references and circles of dialogue. If these relational means are missing, for different reasons, efforts to obtain authentication of belief may move towards other ways, far more structured, of joining religious groups in which a substantial sense of security may be found in the sharing of a community orthodoxy.

A call to recreate a community of shared truth thus arises, paradoxically, at the very breaking point of tangible socio-religious links. At this extreme limit, a need to define a "base-platform of certainty" stands out, within closed spaces, made as impermeable as possible to communication with the outside world, where an intense sharing of a common objective truth is exclusively vouched for by the magic of language of a charismatic leader.

In that sense, the "fundamentalist threat" which is an obsession—as a sort of exogenous cultural trend—to European democratic societies, is not something that comes from outside. It is also a paradoxical (and even contradictory) tribute to pay for the advent of individual religious autonomy. This threat does not receive the same political treatment in the different European countries, according, in particular, to the way they used to manage religious plurality within their specific political culture. But, from a sociological perspective, the process is the same everywhere: individualization which dissolves inherited cultural identities, also leads, as the other side of the coin, to the reconstitution, activation and even invention of small community identities, that can drive—at the extreme limit—towards compact, substantial and compensatory forms.

Individualization and New Calls

Can this paradoxical tension between religious individualization and new calls for more or less intensive forms of communalization find a concrete spatial expression? My suggestion here is that this tension is also materializing itself concretely within the double process of deterritorialization and reterritorialization (Hervieu-Léger 2002) which is currently characterizing the spatial configuration of Christian European ultra-modernity.

A great number of empirical studies have documented the fact that the collapse of the parish civilization, which had (ideally) involved for centuries the utopia of the Christian integration of all human communities on a territorial basis, dismantled the traditional bonds between believing and belonging. They confirm, at the same time, the dynamics of deterritorialization that characterize the most contemporary forms of religious sociability (a deterritorialization which finds its more complete demonstration with the virtual spiritual communities that are currently mushrooming on the net).

But, in the same way that the subjectivization of beliefs does not mean the pure and simple atomistic dissemination of believers, deterritorialization does not imply the total delocalization of religion. One notices, when observing the European Christian field, the appearing of new spatial configurations that parallel the new forms of religious sociability and embody the tension between individualistic dissemination on one hand, and the need for communities where the process of mutual recognition is able to work, on the other.

The exploration of these configurations does not constitute an absolutely original theme for sociologists of religion. At the beginning of the century, Ernst Troeltsch (1960) marked out the way in that direction by introducing, alongside the classic types of "Church" and "Sect", another form of Christian communalization, characteristic, in his view, of the modern culture of the individual. The "mystic type" of Christian community (Spiritualismus), which connects individuals through mobile, precarious and fluid networks, embodies—according to Troeltsch—the features of religious modernity that directly imply the delocalization of socio-religious bonds: the individualization and subjectivization of religious life, the primacy given to personal and intimate experience; the privilege of interpersonal relationship over any forms of collective validation of beliefs or institutional mediation; the insistence placed upon the importance of emotional spiritual exchanges etc. Following the same direction, present-day scholars studying contemporary Christian movements in the West are particularly interested in the relational forms of religious communalization working as a network, that are presently imposing themselves as one of the chief modalities of a deterritorialized form of religious communities, including virtual communities, completely detached from any sort of local expression.

This process of deterritorialization of religion is congruent, from an ideal typical point of view, with the process of individualization of beliefs. However, it finds its limits when it meets the claims for recreating concrete communities of shared truths, which imply personal and direct interactions that cannot remain entirely virtual. Varied studies concerning the expansion of Pentecostal churches on a world scale bring telling elements that throw light on the dialectic of deterritorialization and reterritorialization of religion, through the different scales of sociability and participation offered to the faithful, combining a distended network sociability (using all modern means of communication, such as TV or Internet) and an intensive participation within proximity groups.

In new European Christian movements—both in Catholic and Protestant fields—one can follow the same dynamics operating through a specific tempo of religious life which alternates between loose relationships within affinity networks on one hand, and on the other, occasional large emotional gatherings where individuals have the opportunity of expressing collectively the convergence of their personal experiences. The meetings of the *Taizé* Community, which attracts young people from everywhere in Europe during the summer, the Youth World Days, made famous among young Catholics by John Paul II, the fascinating contemporary renovation of the European historical pilgrimage roads (Hervieu-Léger 2001), or the successful renewal of monastic hospitality, are telling examples of this "sociability of high places and peak moments", which is currently creating a new Christian geography in Europe: more exactly, a "neo-traditional" geography which offers believers a chance to summon up their imaginary spiritual roots, while extending their freedom to come and go, and to choose places where they "feel at home".

However, this logics of "relocalization of affinities" has by no means been fully reconciled with the logics of territories, which remains the organizing principle of ecclesiastical control, specifically in Roman Catholicism. The problem is all the more complicated in the most secularized European Catholic countries, where the local parishes show less and less traces of the concrete presence of a dominant religion claiming to permeate the whole culture and society: becoming the refuge of a minority of believers, they tend themselves to operate on a voluntary basis.

In this new context, Catholic authorities are driven to acculturate themselves to a networked sociability, even encouraging the formation of spiritual interest groups currently assuming transnational dimensions. But this strategy clearly induces boomerang effects and often confronts them with centrifugal tendencies and lobbying practices, which they are poorly equipped to deal with. The only way for them to thwart the potentially destructive consequences of these tendencies is the constant reaffirmation of the centrality of a parish model which remains the imaginary emblem of an authentic Catholic sociability, but which has less and less to do with the aspirations and experiences of "delocalized" and freely circulating believers.

The Catholic example documents, in a particularly acute way, to what extent the contemporary process of deterritorialization and reterritorialization of religion reveals not only the tension between the process of subjectivization of beliefs and the new appeals to affinity communities. But it also demonstrates the internal contradictions of religious authority in a world of individuals: a question which goes far beyond the Catholic (and even Christian) case.

CHAPTER FIVE

PENTECOSTALISM: A CHRISTIAN REVIVAL SWEEPING THE DEVELOPING WORLD

David Martin

What is Pentecostalism?

Pentecostalism mostly sees itself as a unique return to the Primitive Church, though its more knowledgeable representatives have been well aware of similar attempts to recover the pristine rapture presumed to inspire the first Christians. Perhaps the most important of such attempts is the Lutheran appeal ad fontes, from which, as I shall suggest, many of the emphases of Pentecostalism ultimately derive. Above all Pentecostalism looks back to the outpouring of the Spirit 'on all flesh' dramatised in the second chapter of the Acts of the Apostles. In the later liturgy of mainstream Christianity, and still today, Pentecost is celebrated as the third most important feast in the calendar and regarded as the manifestation of the Holy Spirit that gave birth to the Church. However, insofar as this implies a major discontinuity in the action of the Spirit it is problematic, even in Christian terms, because a wider understanding locates many earlier manifestations of the Spirit, not only at the birth and baptism of Jesus, but as ruah or the power of the wind of the Spirit present throughout salvation history, above all in the creation of the world and in the coming of the Law on Sinai.

Within salvation history as recounted in the Hebrew Scriptures/the Old Testament, a Christian hermeneutic understands the story in the Acts by referring back to the story of the confounding of a common language following the attempt to build the Tower of Babel, as well as to the outpouring of the Spirit promised both to men and to women by the prophet Joel. Pentecostals in particular stress the coming of 'the latter rain' (Joel chapter 2, v.23, and elsewhere) seen as a premonition of the divine goal of history. The promised outpouring of the Spirit realised at Pentecost looks forward to that final goal, and finds it anticipated by the reversal of the linguistic confusion of Babel. Humankind once more enjoys a shared understanding conferred through the gift of tongues, which for Pentecostals is linked to a new personal and life-changing baptism in the Spirit manifest, for example, by dancing in the Spirit. Of course, the Christian Pentecost, placed fifty days after the Paschal season, also refers back to the Jewish Pentecost or Shavuot, celebrated fifty days after Passover to mark the ingathering of the harvest. This spiritualisation of material goods, such as the harvest, is just one of many other spiritualised metaphors of universality, such as the temple and the city 'which is above and the mother of us all'. Pentecostalism expects a universal heavenly harvest marked by miracles, deliverance from daemonic possession, spirit baptism and the gift of tongues.

One can understand the first century Pentecost as a response to the universal oekumene created among the peoples of the Roman Empire. Similarly, the twentieth century Pentecost can be seen as a response to modern global communications and accelerated transnational movement, above all in the multicultural and multicoloured tumult of the United States. From the moment of its inception, in the USA and in places as far apart as Wales and India, Pentecostalism spread like a star-burst along global trails laid down by Evangelical mission, much of it Anglo-American, such as the Holy Ghost Empowerment movement founded in England at Keswick in 1875 and the China Inland Mission. Thereafter Pentecostalism was increasingly carried by people on the move around the world, and appropriated by the imagined communities created by modern media (Meyer 2005).

As in mainstream missions the primary carriers were indigenous, though that could mean a partial reversion from the transnational to nation making under Christian auspices, especially where marginal peoples as well as marginal people were attracted (Peel 2000).

Pentecostalism was pre-adapted, therefore, to multicultural and migrant situations. It was also pre-adapted to non-Western contexts, especially Africa, through its fusion of black and white revivalism. It fused technological modernity with a lively sense of the inspirited world and the daemonic, and this carried it across cultural barriers hitherto blocking the advance of mainstream Christianity, in India, China and Latin America as well as Africa. The main resistances come from secular Europe and Islam, the former because it represents a territorial and clerical Christianity under severe strain, and the latter because it represents a revived sense of a common religious universe organically related to politics, power and territory. Pentecostalism, by contrast, promotes a decentralised and fissile form of lay voluntary organisation, separated, at least in its initial governing ethos from territory and state, and operating on an open competitive market. An endless capacity for fission helps it adapt to any number of indigenous contexts.

How did Pentecostalism Originate?

In looking for Pentecostal origins one has to remember that origins are inherently contested, partly because they were fought over at the time between rival innovators, and partly because stories about how it all began include claims concerning the true line of descent. I have already referred to the clash between understandings based on continuity and those based on discontinuity, whether we think of Pentecostalism in relation to Christianity or Christianity in relation to Judaism. Plainly it matters whether Pentecostalism is seen as a recrudescence of an ancient theme in Christianity, amongst (say) Montanists in the Early Church or 'Catholic Apostolics' in mid-nineteenth century Britain, or is promoted as an entirely new beginning. It also matters a great deal whether Pentecostalism had black or white (even racist) origins. It matters whether it was multi-centred or centred mainly in the USA. It matters whether the global carriers of its messages were cultural colonisers or emerged 'spontaneously' among indigenous peoples. It matters whether Pentecostalism made crucial and lasting breakthroughs to racial and gender equality or in more important ways reverted to both forms of discrimination as it semi-stabilised and entered new social contexts, for example South Africa. Were Pentecostals poor and disregarded or were they ignorant and intolerant? Were they participatory and mutually supportive, a kind of trade union of the dispossessed, including women and a buried intelligentsia, or patriarchal authoritarians exploiting their charisma, sexually and financially? Did they exhibit agency or inhibit it? Like its Methodist forebear Pentecostalism has always been potently ambiguous. Ambiguity is more potent for change than outright challenge, especially perhaps when it comes to mutations in gender relations: for example Pentecostalism can undermine gender hierarchies, but it does so by requiring mutual respect not by directly demoting the male.

In *The Fire Spreads* Randall J. Stephens has given an account of the genesis of Pentecostalism that treads delicately through the ambiguities (Stephens 2008). The main source was the holiness tradition in Methodism, which arrived in the American South from the North in the 1860s. There it received a frosty welcome from the dominant Southern Methodists and Southern Baptists, still smarting in the aftermath of the Civil War, and it was not until the 1880s that local holiness leaders started to emerge. Once Southerners started to embrace holiness they adapted it to their plain-folk, largely rural needs, and identified with the poor, even though many of the key figures, black as well as white, held positions of authority in church and society. This was a time when the tastes of Methodists in the urban middle classes of the wealthy New South often ran to Victorian Gothic and pew rentals, as well as theatre-going, smoking and drinking. Rural southern holiness advocates battled against what they saw as over-sophistication and moral decay, and flaunted markers of difference and dissent. They disapproved, for example, of coffee, pork and neckties. Yet although these attitudes were rooted in rural southern values, holiness people reached beyond the South. They fostered a nationwide commitment, and their views on gender, race and class put them at odds with Southern hierarchical traditions. They looked back, for example, to Phoebe Palmer, the original mother of the holiness movement, who believed that all the sanctified were endowed with both purity and power. African-American stalwarts likewise fostered nationwide contacts. Naturally, they execrated the 'peculiar' institution of slavery, and some white holiness leaders agreed with them. The very lively and fractious holiness press and holiness gatherings provided liminal spaces where blacks and whites could interact, even though local hostility was powerful enough to inhibit moves to integration.

Holiness preachers grew frustrated with denominational authorities that saw them as dangerous religious tramps, and they challenged a culture they saw as going to hell in a handcart. Increasingly they drew on English as well as American sources, including the Keswick Convention and the dispensationalist and pre-millennial views of the Plymouth Brethren. Just as holiness had originated in the North before moving South, so did millennialism, and far from fostering passivity it unleashed furious energy, in religion if not in politics. Several fledgling denominations emerged, each seeking to restore the one, true, sanctified Church of God. End-time expectation also generated a search for those gifts of the Spirit, such as divine healing and the fire-baptism promised in St. John's Gospel, believed to presage the Second Coming. The stage was set for Pentecostalism, for the tongues of fire, and for the premonitory patter of the 'latter rain' before the final harvest.

One outbreak of the Pentecostal tongues of fire occurred in Kansas in 1901, and was associated with Charles Parham, a white Methodist preacher, later to acquire an interest in Anglo-Israel and a Jewish homeland. Another outbreak was associated with William Seymour, a black holiness preacher, in 1906. Seymour sparked off wildly enthusiastic, and to some extent multiethnic and interracial, manifestations, including speaking with tongues, at Azusa St., Los Angeles. The West coast enthusiasm rapidly spread back to the South, fanned by a furore in the press. Southern holiness people either provided a conduit for Pentecostalism or disdained its unfettered worship style, for example fast-paced spirituals quite unlike the old Evangelical hymns. Just as the original Methodists in England and Pietists in Germany had disrupted their established Churches, and the holiness offshoots of Methodism had criticised staid denominational authorities for losing their original fire, so Pentecostals outflanked the holiness movement. The rest of Randall Stephen's book is given over to the way many white stalwarts of Pentecost transformed themselves after the Second World War from social and religious pariahs into middle class Republicans.

Analytic Overview: Is it Sectarian? Is it Fundamentalist?

The growth of Pentecostalism since the middle of the twentieth century represents the largest shift in the contemporary religious landscape, running deep into nine figures. It suggests a religious future characterised by voluntary transnational associations of largely lay inspiration. It is a global movement of people, often migrants to the mega-city, equipped with a portable identity, and in its operations decentralised and fissiparous. Pentecostalism is based on personal transformation and choice, and likely to appear anywhere from Haiti to Burkina Faso, Kiev to Kyrgyzstan, Singapore or Jakarta to Manila or Seoul. You can liken it to a bush fire of the spirit, picking up modern spirituality at one end and ancient inspired universes at the other.

My approach implies two notes of dissent. One arises as a response to the profoundly insightful analysis of the Christian sectarian roots of Jacobinism by S.N. Eisenstadt (1999). I do not think Pentecostalism belongs in this company. It is true one can trace certain Pentecostal links back to the 'sectarian' or Radical Reformation, but I see Pentecostalism as closer to the American Revolution than the French, and fitting into Gertrude Himmelfarb's (2004) discussion of Methodism in her classic account of three different roads to modernity. The other note of dissent is more substantial, and it relates to analyses that both assimilate Pentecostalism to fundamentalism and treat it as a reaction to modernity rather than as a major narrative of modernity central to what S.N. Eisenstadt (2000) has termed the 'multiple modernities' of our time. This term captures an important truth, and one which I have consistently adhered to in my critique of the ideological elements in the unilateral view of the inevitable course of secularisation and my analysis of its very different and historically inflected trajectories. Moreover, I have tried to set out in what way Pentecostalism constitutes one of the master narratives of modernity, and done so by reference to Halevy on the role of Methodism in England (and therefore by extension in the USA) in preventing the kind of violent revolutionary trajectory that convulsed France. Of course, Weber on the Protestant Ethic always hovers off-stage.[1]

To call Pentecostals fundamentalists is to see them through the prism of America's culture wars, and to treat them as an American cultural export. It is true there have been and are important American connections, and that Pentecostals retain a conservative approach to Scripture. Aimee Semple Macpherson, for example, the flamboyant creator of the Angelus Temple in Los Angeles, not only crossed racial barriers but explicitly linked herself to the fundamentalist cause. But the distinctive note of Pentecostals is a response to the breath of the Spirit by people all over the developing world who seek their own religious route to the global modernity of which the USA is the most conspicuous example.

Back to Luther

The genealogy of Pentecostalism is, of course, mixed, Reformed as well as Lutheran. But given its immediate source lies in the Holiness tradition of Methodism, and given the Methodist debt to German Pietism, I trace the Pentecostal genealogy back to Luther rather than to Calvin.

---

[1] My earliest published critique of secularisation as a universal, unilateral trend to a common modernity dates from 1965 and was included as chapter 1 in my *The Religious and the Secular*, London: Routledge 1969. My first full-scale account of Pentecostalism was *Tongues of Fire*, Blackwell, Oxford, 1990 and I specifically argue for Pentecostalism as a major narrative of modernity in Part III of David Martin '*On Secularization*' Aldershot: Ashgate 2005

There is, of course, a Calvinist and Puritan sense of an inner pilgrimage marked by crisis and conversion, but Pentecostals do not create godly and disciplined territorial cities 'set on a hill'. Moreover, Calvinist devotion focuses on the Father in a rather Judaic manner, and carries a potential for a rationalistic Unitarianism, whereas Pietism and Methodism focus on the all-atoning Son, and Pentecostalism on the consoling, enabling and energising Spirit. A warm stream of sweetness and experiential devotion runs through Pietism, Methodism and Pentecostalism which is paralleled in music all the way from Buxtehude and Bach to the Methodist hymn and Pentecostal chorus. In early Methodism there was an overlap with late eighteenth century ideas of Sentiment, while in modern Methodism there is a distinct deposit of sentimentality also characteristic of modern spirituality in general.

I assume a close relationship between an accent on inner experience at the expense of objective sacrament and ceremonious conformity and the kind of voluntary associational religion to which you adhere by mature choice, emotional crisis and conversion. Total immersion in the Pentecostal liturgy of Baptism does not so much effect a change of status as mark an inner condition. I also assume that breaking away from territory and from any symmetry between social and ecclesiastical power, is associated with increased participation and the emergence of pacific or even pacifist tendencies. Within the state religion of Lutheranism the imperatives of the Kingdom of God, including sanctification and non-violence, were of necessity relegated to the heavenly rather than the earthly realm, whereas in both Methodism and Pentecostalism they could seep out as the division between the two realms became more porous. As the Russian experience makes clear there is always some potential in Evangelicalism for passivity and apolitical pacifism. At the same time, as the American and British experience makes clear, social pressures and/or realities may engender reversals of attitude: Aimee Semple Macpherson became a recruiting sergeant, and some erstwhile pacific Methodists became bellicose under the pressures of the Boer War. Partial reversals are always possible in every sphere, since—as I shall indicate—popular participation requires strong leadership and inner purification needs support from tangible devotional objects.

I organise my analysis of Pentecostalism around the *implications* of the principles dramatised by Martin Luther's stand at Worms in 1521 when he faced the combined powers of Church and State. At Worms in 1521 we see the 'inner man' representing a priesthood of faith, conscientiously interpreting the Bible for himself, abjuring idols, and joining voluntarily with others of like mind and heart. I am drawing out what is implicit in the very act of arguing a case against all constituted hierarchical authorities, and assuming it takes time for the implicit to become explicit.

One such shift occurs with the birth of Pietism. The Pietists formed voluntary groups to seek sanctification inside the territorial Church and weakened the hold of a ceremonial and outward conformity. In company with some strains in the Reformed tradition in Holland and England they were the progenitors of a free, voluntary and mission-minded Church. The developments broached in Holland and England included a competitive pluralism which came to fruition in the open spaces of British North America and the USA. On the one hand there is the role of an institution such as the Methodist class meeting in the expansion of American voluntary associations, and on the other the impact of a theology of choice and of salvation for all.

These are bold claims based on sociological premises. One premise is that Christianity establishes advance bases in the consciousness of a vanguard, for example the followers of Jan Hus in Prague. The vanguard creates forward positions for future occupation, even as it retires or is overwhelmed in the face of reaction from threatened power structures. The Radical Reformation withdrew in traumatised shock from the anarchic potential it let loose, and the furious reaction of constituted authorities, both Catholic and Protestant. In the Magisterial Reformation part of the initial thrust of change came from the interests of landed, national and noble elites, and it was these interests that, after much blood shed for any number of reasons, stalled further change and re-established instead the territorial concept eventually embodied in the Westphalian Settlement of 1648. A period of latency is likely to follow before the pressure of the temporarily suppressed principles creates a fresh opening as opportunity arises. The invention of printing offered just such an opportunity for the principle of private judgement.

The initial seeds sown by radical vanguards are reburied in protective sectarian capsules to emerge later in more favourable circumstances, sometimes in secularised forms that once more unleash anarchic potential, or through educational reforms, for example as proposed by Comenius and his long line of successors, or peace movements, such as those—particularly from 1816 onwards—that trace their genealogies back to George Fox and Menno Simons. Many of the positions taken up by religious vanguards fructify outside the institutional walls of the Church. Thomas Jefferson's principle of beginning all over again in every generation translates the Anabaptist principle of making Christian commitment a matter of mature choice, while William Godwin's proposals for dispensing with all institutions represents a secular millenarianism. The same holds true today. Contemporary spirituality takes Protestant interiority to a self-destructive extreme through its detachment from religious institutions, and the consequent loss of any ability to pass a faith from one generation to another. Individualistic European spirituality, shorn of the communal and familial aspects of religion, is the ghostly complement of the operation of the Spirit through the vigorous institutions of Pentecostalism in the developing world.

Neither the practitioners of contemporary spirituality nor the Spirit-filled preachers of Pentecost recognise the inevitability of suffering and frustration coded in the narrative of the Passion. Both have left behind the territorial principle represented by the parish and the national Church. Together they embody the contemporary shift to pluralism and voluntarism, which is in one sense the wave of the future, though the communal and/or the territorial are resistant and resilient, for example in Catholicism, Judaism, and Islam. The vanguards of the future do not represent all the future there is. Community and place, and community in a place, are always with us. The idea of Promised Land destined for a people has never yet lost its potency, for good and for ill. Christianity began as a voluntary movement spiritualising land, city and temple, but once it became established, land, city and temple returned, initially in Rome, Byzantium and Moscow, and then anywhere from the USA to South Africa and the Congo. Zion makes a partial return even in Pentecostalism, particularly in countries where national consciousness is still in formation, for example South Africa, Nigeria, Zimbabwe and Zambia.

Characteristics and Varieties of Pentecostal Spirituality

How to assess and characterise the varieties of Pentecostal spirituality? A profit and loss account might run as follows. Appealing to the poor and marginalised is likely to generate anti-intellectualism and what David Lehmann (1996) describes as indifference to the sponsorship of intellectual elites—though that may be no bad thing, and certainly helps explain why those elites in the West and Africa are often so hostile. Turbulent participation may generate charismatic authoritarianism. A capacity to cross cultural species barriers and indigenise may lead to the incorporation of local practices, as in the case of African Big Men reappearing as Big Pastors, male or female. On the other hand the pursuit of global modernity may require a rejection of local practices defined by elites as 'authentic' traditional culture. Mutual help fostered in a protective capsule may create a strong rejection of 'the other' standing for the enticements of "the world", and that may extend to withdrawal from political systems where Pentecostals are the least regarded among potential clienteles. A pursuit of respectability in the sense of receiving respect can result in righteousness, while an attempt to share in the goods of prosperity easily overvalues enrichment. The stabilisation of moral and material gains may hold up the changes required for yet further gains. The rough comes with the smooth, as now illustrated by four recent studies of the varieties of contemporary Pentecostalism.

Four Examples: Venezuela, Ghana, Nigeria, South India

My examples are David Smilde's (2007) study of Pentecostal men in the classical Pentecostal tradition in Caracas, Venezuela, Jane Soothill's (2007) study of women in Neo-Pentecostal mega-churches in Accra, Azonzeh Ukah's (2008) study of a mega-church in Nigeria, and Michael Bergunder's (2008) analysis of Pentecostalism in South India.

In his *Reason to Believe* David Smilde (2007) reported on years of interviewing the men of two churches in dangerous parts of Caracas during the period just before Chavez. He showed that Pentecostalism offers visions and revisions of lives changed for the good. Of course, things do not always work out as hoped, and many believers find themselves sorely tried or sucked back into the old ways by boon companions. Getting right with God may turn out easier than getting right with a wife or partner. When the going is rough Pentecostals have recourse to ancient theodicies: that God teaches his children through adversity, that his ways are not as our ways, that treasures on earth corrupt, and that the believer has somehow been displeasing in God's sight. In the course of their pilgrimage here on earth Pentecostals traverse an almost Faustian landscape where the foul fiend contends with God's Son and his Holy Spirit for victory.

Compared with other coping strategies, such as gambling, alcohol, drugs, violence and macho irresponsibility, Pentecostalism saves lives rather than destroying them. It restores the primacy of the family, and creates networks of mutual support through principled living. Usually it is the men who adopt the deleterious strategies and the women who suffer them, through bodily or psychic distress. People experiencing dis-ease of body, mind and spirit find healing and hearts-ease in an awakened sense of wholeness, and in a supportive, disciplined community with a protective boundary against the contemptuous outside world.

Smilde also describes the social and economic crises that hit Venezuela in the last two decades of the twentieth century, after decades of rising prosperity based on oil revenues. The period of decline saw the rise of Pentecostalism, so that the overall Evangelical proportion of a population of twenty million has now reached about 5%. He tells a tale of several cities: the faded remnants of a disorganised colonial society and a fractured Church, the monuments of a once triumphant liberal anti-clericalism, the rapidly fading modern city of the oil boom, the gleaming post-modern city of global capitalism, and the vast informal city of the marginalised and impoverished, where the Pentecostals live. In spite of a secular surface the people of Caracas mostly cherish a sense of the holy attached to the Bible, which offers a slipway for Evangelical conversion through a near-optimum relation between the familiar and the novel. On the one hand there are inspirited orientations shared with the wider society, on the other a rejection of "idols" reminiscent of the Reformation, for example the supplication of the Virgin. The classical Pentecostals in the two churches studied by Smilde, *Emmanuel*, and *Raise Your Voice to the Lord*, voiced vigorous criticisms of the utilitarian attitudes of Neo-Pentecostals, and of the spin a prosperity gospel lends to words like "rich" and "fruitful".

Pentecostals are powerful preachers, often in the open air, and they base their appeal on the chance to leave behind disastrous vices through the grace of the Spirit. That could mean, for example, renouncing the male culture of reciprocal violence, once honour is impugned, to embrace peace with God and with neighbour. Thus a believer finding himself threatened by a robber in a dangerous part of the city responded initially with an act of witness to Christ. When that failed he tried to witness in another way by freely offering all he had to his assailant. So doing he saved his honour as a follower of a new Way, one who has given up the camaraderie of violence for the fellowship of peace.

Jane Soothill's (2007) *Gender, Social Change and Spiritual Power* focuses on women in charismatic mega-churches in Accra, Ghana. In Ghana, life and politics alike are saturated in the world of the spirit, without even the veneer of secularity found in Venezuela, though the historical sequences are strikingly similar. They are the effects of IMF intervention, and the emergence of groups mobilising as part of an incipient civil society. However, Ghana's oil was cocoa. What specially characterises Ghana is a semi-mythical evocation of pre-colonial gender equality, a tendency on the part of the sometime colonial government to work with local male leaders, the political co-option of women's movements after independence, and the re-emergence of "Queen Mothers" as powerful "First Ladies".

Jane Soothill addresses such established features of Pentecostalism as orality and the extraordinary power of media in Pentecostalism as well as the freedom of the Spirit and participation, and the role of networks and aspiration in promoting social and geographical mobility. American influence is linked to rapid indigenization, and individuation to the strong ties of the emergent nuclear family. The names of the churches she studied emphasise victorious living rather than patient suffering. Indeed, *Action Chapel International*, *Alive Chapel International*, and *Solid Rock Chapel International* resemble their American counterparts in promoting self-realization for both sexes instead of the more patriarchal emphases still found in fundamentalist Christianity. Gender is potently ambiguous. Pentecostalism reinforces patriarchy by its emphasis on domesticity but also transforms the patriarchal family by feminizing the man and by teaching that male and female alike should feel good about themselves. All this illustrates the influence of an American optimism fused with an African emphasis on religion as based on the pursuit of "goods" here and now. The African tradition of Big Men reappears in Pentecostal leaders, and these include Big Women leading others in the role of Small Girls.

Pentecostal sermons offer vigorous advice about the replacement of African traditions by more Christian attitudes. Charismatic comments on male misconduct and the proper conduct of love-making might raise eyebrows even in the more liberal churches of Europe and North America. "You had fun for five minutes, and she carried the burden for nine months…O, God! If I had a cane, we would lash all the man on their backs, on the bare behind". Success in spiritual warfare against satanic and demonic influence comes with fulfilled responsibility, and when men fail, as they do, women are their salvation through their appropriation of spiritual power. Ancient and modern here come together, as they so often do in Pentecostalism.

Jane Soothill questions the negative judgements made by African and Western theologians and intellectuals about this kind of Christianity, especially its African authenticity. For charismatic Christians, however, Africa is the problem, not the solution, and yet their own solution is clearly framed by the African religious imagination. Female pastors adopting the role of "Big Women" are "post-colonial hybrids" disjoined and yet connected to Africa's pre-colonial and colonial past. As for authenticity it is in the eye of the beholder, and it is notorious that Pentecostals are indifferent to the sponsorship of intellectual elites. In the mega-churches of West Africa it is not the God of the philosophers that is worshipped but Jesus the Winner Man.

Azonzeh Ukah's (2008) *A New Paradigm of Pentecostal Power* deals with the extraordinarily successful *Redeemed Christian Church of God in Nigeria* and its flamboyant prosperity teaching. The RCCG is one of the most controversial of the new mega-churches, in part because it combines the organisational format of an international corporation with an ethos rooted deep in Yoruba tradition. Ukah brings out its extraordinary ability to fuse deep roots in local African spirituality based on healing, protection against malign powers, prognostication, trance and visionary dreams, with a go-getting organisation promoting itself through modern media and every marketing device. He also traces its origins in a much smaller and very different body, the *God's Glory Church*, founded in 1952 by a semi-literate prophet and healer. This was in turn nurtured in the traditions of the Aladura Church known as the *Eternal Sacred Order of Cherubim and Seraphim (Mount Zion)* in Lagos. The *God's Glory Church* enforced an ascetic regime, made no collections, eschewed politics, forbade jewellery, and excluded people associated with corrupt professions, like the military, the police and purveyors of alcohol. By contrast the RCCG, as re-founded in the 1980s by a university teacher of mathematics, Enoch Adeboye, sought out the rich and powerful, negotiated deals with partners in the socio-economic elite, and made much-criticised forays into the political arena.

This shift was facilitated by the regress of post Civil War Nigeria towards a kleptocratic, and electorally corrupt state, and by the mass unemployment brought about by neo-liberal reforms. The national hopes of a frustrated new middle class shifted from politics to religion, so that the RCCG, and similar bodies like the *Deeper Life Bible Church* and *Winners Chapel*, are ventures in the autonomous creation of social capital. They provide an all-embracing environment with educational and health facilities in return for investment in sacred bonds, divinely guaranteed. In the RCCG the traditional belief whereby one enters into a covenant with the celestial powers-that-be, has fused with the more optimistic elements in the Hebrew Bible, promising the righteous shall not want for bread, to create what might well be called an Afro-Jewish amalgam. The teaching and practice of Jesus are read in a way which stresses prolonged prayer, fasting, and exorcism (or deliverance). Jesus is the Winner Man who became poor for our sakes that we might become, quite literally, rich.

The title of General Overseer used by Adeboye is apt, because the RCCG is a huge conglomerate engaged in mass economic mobilisation and linked to, or operating, media enterprises, an insurance company, and community banks, such as the massive Haggai Community Bank. It also runs a business school to equip those inspired to defy what another Pentecostal leader, Ezekiel Guti in Zimbabwe, calls 'the spirit of poverty'.[2] This kind of venture in social and financial capital, of which there are hundreds all over the developing world, also provides a protective trades-union for women, giving them greater mutuality in a stable monogamous family and help in the travails of barrenness or childbirth far from modern health clinics.

A highly spiritual faith, claiming to be guided solely by the Bible, comes once more to value tangible sacred objects. It has been revealed to Adeboye that he should wear three shirts for a time so that some of his own anointing can be transferred to them. He places one of the shirts in a bath of oil, and members use the bath to anoint themselves on the head, mouth and hand, to bring healing and prosperity. Adeboye is also the chief actor in the choreography of worship during the monthly Holy Ghost Night held in the Redemption Camp, a 10 square kilometre site with an auditorium holding half a million people. The Redemption Camp is a pre-emptive territorial strike establishing a colony of heaven to be expanded to all Nigeria and eventually

---

[2] David Maxwell has provided a major study of Ezekiel Guti and the Zimbabwe Assemblies of God Africa in his '*African Gifts of the Spirit. Pentecostalism and the Rise of a Zimbabwean Transnational Religious Movement*' Oxford: James Currey, 2006

the world. This is explicitly the Mecca of the RCCG, and the personal office of Adeboye is its Vatican. A faith that once transcended locality goes back to the land and to the elect nation, and a church that gloried in what Zechariah called 'the day of small things', rejoices in the arrival of the Big-Time as well as the End-Time. A transnational, decentred, voluntarism may be the wave of the future but it is not all the future there is.

Michael Bergunder's (2008) study of Pentecostalism in South India parallels Randall Stephens' study of its emergence in the American South: both involve the clash between caste-like social arrangements and an egalitarian movement powered by universally available charismatic gifts. In South India Pentecostalism ran into layers of earlier Christianity attuned to caste, notably the high caste Thomas Christians, some of whom had become Plymouth Brethren before converting to Pentecostalism. Most of the other converts were low caste and naturally the sometime Thomas Christians assumed the right to lead.

As Bergunder points out, Pentecostalism becomes what local people make of it. The (then) *Ceylon Pentecostal Mission*, emerging in Kerala in the mid-1920s, came under indigenous leadership, and had several distinctive characteristics: it was centralised, it straightforwardly rejected western medicine, and its full-time workers, Sisters and Brothers alike, sold their property and adopted celibacy. The *Indian Pentecostal Church*, which broke away from it, was also indigenously led, and became the strongest Pentecostal church in Kerala, much stronger that those founded by western missions.

Bergunder traces the growth of Pentecostalism in other regions beside Kerala, including the growth of regional churches and of churches with a powerful local influence, for example in Madras. He also charts the arrival in the 1980s of expansive 'faith' (or health and wealth) churches, worshipping in cinemas and concert halls. In Andra Pradesh some churches were established by expatriate Indians returned from the USA: clearly the flow of influence in the contemporary world runs in every possible direction. Whatever the profusion of independent churches, run by rivalrous captains of religious industry, there was also a grass-roots ecumenism 'in the Spirit' fostered by itinerant evangelists, including women, by pastor's fellowships, and by large rallies. All over the world, from Guatemala and Brazil to Korea and the Philippines, big rallies encourage the faithful and disregarded to believe they (literally) count for something. One woman evangelist, Sarah Navroji, became famous for the composition of Tamil hymns in the style of popular film music, and these soon reached virtually every Christian home. Like their Methodist forebears Pentecostals sang their message in a contemporary idiom, often in prolonged sessions like holy rock concerts. If caste was a barrier, there was much in Indian Christian culture, and in Indian culture generally, that resonated with Pentecostalism, notably healing miracles, 'leadings' in the spirit, invoking the holy name, ecstatic possession, exorcism, and the aura attaching to fasting, prayer and holiness. At the same time Pentecostalism also appealed because its exuberant use of a modern technology came with a western guarantee. Pentecostals were spirit-filled people ready to bestow powerful blessings, to offer healing to the poor lacking access to modern medicine, and to confront head-on malignant and daemonic forces. Bergunder analyses many personal testimonies of spiritual rebirth where addictions are converted into aversions, and where the weight of cumulative malignancy finds release in exuberant joy and in worship marked by murmurous and urgent prayer. It is this urgent prayer and praise, together with a sense that whatever may befall the net of Providential care can never be removed, that make Pentecostalism tick.

Mutations of Lutheran Themes

In a general way I emphasise the democratisation of Protestantism as it "steps westward", meaning the increasingly popular, even populist, character of Protestantism as it appealed to groups further and further down the social scale in an increasingly voluntary mode, in Britain, in the USA, and now throughout the developing world. In a more particular way I trace what happens to themes explicit or implicit in the repertoire of the original Reformation once replayed in different and distant popular milieux. I shall, for example, suggest what happens to the priesthood of all believers when played out in milieux informed by an unstable mixture of popular mobilisation and authoritarian clientelism. I shall indicate what happens when the immediacy of personal experience of the Spirit overwhelms the principle of sola Scriptura. Liberal Protestant theologians may sit loose to Scripture but they are far outstripped by the *Friday Apostolics* studied by Matthew Engelke (2007), who have abandoned Scripture altogether.

Some features of the Lutheran tradition that find answering resonance in Pentecostalism, whether or not traceable along identifiable conduits, are the priesthood of all believers and participation; the specifically Pietist pursuit of sanctification in small cells of the committed; the rejection of external "idols" in favour of inward heart-work and experience in communion with an open Bible; and the idea of mission, originating as it did in Germany and Denmark, before being rapidly taken up in the Anglo-sphere. In what follows I shall also indicate reversals of these features.

The Priesthood of all Believers—and the Uses of Authority

The priesthood of all believers is one of those clarion calls of Protestant rhetoric that either proves impossible to realise in practice or gives rise to unintended and perhaps dubious consequences. These are very like those following from the call for universal participation in politics and society in general: instability, uncertainty about what to expect, time wasted in defending one's space against marauders, a fragmentation of authority countered by reversions to all-commanding authority, confusion, and unseemly jostling for position. In Lutheranism the priesthood of all believers becomes transmuted into a learned ministry and a discipline that is potentially useful to the national state. In Methodism it morphs into a partly learned ministry, a version of the Pietist creation of an ecclesiola in ecclesia found in the 'class meeting', the development of lay preaching, with a residue of anti-intellectualism and sentimentality,—and the rise of a bureaucracy. In Pentecostalism it results in a mixture of elements, such as a ministry open to people of forceful inspiration, training on the job and in Biblical Institutes, a charismatic leadership with some authoritarian potential, and a combination of religious entrepreneurship with bureaucratic management. Amongst the 'little people' it fosters discipline, confidence and aspiration while in the mega-churches it often explicitly fosters business and is organised on business lines. Hence the suggestion that it fits well with the neo-liberal project. In the mega-churches as distinct from the myriad 'small firms' on the religious market Pentecostalism creates cell groups that are the lineal descendants of the Methodist class meeting.

In an uneven way this represents movement towards voluntary organisation, competition between rival churches, entrepreneurship (with multiple fissions as new entrepreneurs challenge older ones), and various combinations of charismatic and bureaucratic authority. The authoritarian potential latent in free-floating charisma goes hand in hand with turbulent popular participation, because only a commanding authority can rein in potential anarchy. The learning of a vested ministry invested with authority, gives way to the business know-how of men in suits able to sway and manage mass audiences. If one wants to follow the course of such changes then the history of Methodism as the body midway between Lutheranism and Pentecostalism is instructive. Methodist history is marked by tussles between the power of a ministry and assertions of lay control, between centralised power and local initiative, between learning and organisational savvy, between seemly worship with organs and choirs and popular and spontaneous revivalist choruses, and between sartorial markers of vested ecclesiastical authority and plain but respectable lay clothing.

In the Methodist case one can observe a reversion to sobriety and a learned ministry trained in colleges, and indeed in Methodist universities like Boston, Emory or Duke. That brought with it ecclesiastical architecture instead of functional meeting places or preaching in the open air, as well as formal liturgy, robed choirs as well as ecumenical enthusiasm. In the earlier history of Methodism the plain functionality of the worship spaces took an aesthetically pleasing classical form, and even some of the later Gothic chapels are now listed buildings much admired by connoisseurs. As the worshipping community has disappeared the preservationists have moved in. That symbolises one possible trajectory for a popular religious movement: a return to forms and formalities as a disciplined life creates social mobility. Once people arrive in the middle classes they review their relationship to the older established churches and sectarian fissions become ecumenical fusions.

The big question hanging over Pentecostalism is whether the empty if attractive chapels left by earlier revivals, say in Wales, presage the future of the thousands of churches of religious bodies "in renewal" all over Latin America. It may be that as the lava cools it is replaced by new fires spreading among new groups arriving at modernity through religious re-formation. Perhaps as Methodism loses its consuming fire and moves to the centre ground of Christianity, Pentecostalism takes up its unfinished task. The cycle then begins again as Pentecostalism generates its own intelligentsia and enters its own phase of cathedral building. The suspicion of theology once felt by Methodist laypeople and still felt by many Pentecostals shows that enthusiastic believers guess where formal training and the social acceptance that goes with it might lead. Indeed. John Wesley was quite explicit about the danger, though he did everything in his power to educate his followers practically and intellectually. What we do not know is whether the secular developments in Europe are the model for the future, so that the cycle of fission and renewal at last comes to an end. A partial exception to the cycle, found even in secular Britain, might be charismatic movements in the new middle classes. These are made up of people in search of spirituality within a Christian framework, who enjoy warm and friendly relationships in close–knit groups, seek family stability, and are also happy with an organisational ethos familiar from the world of business (Heard 2007).

Interiority, Purification, the Rejection of Idols

There are several scenarios of a Pentecostal future. One possibility, observable all over the developing world, combines the achievement of modernity en route to salvation, most clearly manifest in the business model and the virtuoso deployment of media technology, with a return to tangible embodiments of spiritual power, including colourful religious dress and extravagant titles. There is a classic tension between the purification of faith through interiority and sincerity, and tangible, external manifestations of spiritual power. Though the Reformation withdrew power from talismans and idols, following the denunciations of the Hebrew prophets and the Gospel demand for purity of heart, Neo-Pentecostal churches in West Africa and the Brazilian Church known as The Universal Church of the Kingdom of God adopt a more Catholic and a more traditional African approach. Some of the practices of Neo-Pentecostal mega-churches in West and East Africa come close to selling salvation in a way Martin Luther would find familiar.

This tension goes back to the Hebrew prophets and has been set in a modern anthropological framework by Webb Keane (2007) in his study *Christian Moderns*, where he deals with the problems faced by Dutch Calvinist missionaries in Indonesia. Keane shows how the Reformed attempt at purification devalued the ritual bonds of indigenous people as merely utilitarian. He also argues that purification and interiority encounter an inbuilt limit, since one needs external codification of the need to purify, even if the external code is only a verbal formula. Another way of tracing this tension would be to follow through the mutations of ideas about Christ's body and blood. Catherine Bynum

(2007), in her study of the *Wonderful Blood* of Christ as it manifested itself to the laity in pilgrimage sites in late medieval Germany, shows how this extra-mural power challenged the formal channels of clerical power realised in the Eucharist. With the Reformation these extra-mural sites once available to the laity through pilgrimage were relocated in the blood of Christ applied internally in the Christian soul. In an analogous way in some reformed liturgies the body of Christ, once objectified by powerful priestly speech, was fed on by faith within the heart, even where the sacramental forms were retained. Nowadays in some versions of Neo-Pentecostalism known as Faith Teaching, as analysed by the anthropologist Simon Coleman (2000), one finds the body of Christ once again finding external embodiment through building up the muscle-power of the Christian body.

Sin, Frustration,—and Optimistic Anticipation

Another shift is generated by the opportunities opened up in the wide open spaces of the USA, where a moderate Enlightenment became fused with a voluntary associational Christianity in a surge of optimistic anticipation. This newly optimistic environment meant that the tragic drama of the passion central to Lutheranism, and indeed to Methodism, could mutate into a celebration of the power unleashed by the original Pentecost. In Latin America the profound frustration coded by the Passion of Christ is carried, literally, by processions of people bearing a dead Christ or by images of laceration. With their sense of the power of the Spirit, and also with a confidence in the Pauline promise that all things are possible, Pentecostals abandon such images for pictures of flowing streams and cleansing waters. In that sense Harold Bloom (1992) is right to characterise Pentecostalism as an American religion. The hope implicit in the modified Arminianism, announcing that salvation is available to whomsoever wills to be in Christ, is reinforced by the faith that all things are possible, whether it is the expulsion of the demons that assault and hurt the soul or the diseases that attack the body. Clearly this hope is eschatological and relates to the coming Kingdom Pentecostals so vigorously proclaim. Whereas in "Old Europe" anticipations of the world to come on earth are largely confined to liturgy and creed, or given a meliorist inflection through liberal theology, in the preaching of Pentecost they recover a pristine immediacy. The Kingdom is not just hereafter. Pie in the sky becomes available on earth through Pentecost, particularly when a secular eschatology, whether Marxist or liberal, proves to be pie in the sky. Where earlier religion seemed to have failed, generating a move towards politics, now politics seems to have failed, generating a move towards faith.

Mission: from Western Senders to Indigenous Carriers and Reverse Mission

The last element in the Lutheran repertoire transmitted to Pentecostalism is mission. The origins of Protestant mission lie in the German Pietism of the eighteenth century. Pioneers in Germany and Denmark conceived of world-wide mission and the vast enterprise of biblical translation (Iversen and Oommen 2005). Danish missions established themselves in India, and Moravian missions in Central America. It was Moravians who convinced John Wesley of the need for inner conversion and second birth, providing one of the sparks that set off the Evangelical Revival and the Great Awakenings. One puts Awakenings in the plural because, like Reformations, they constantly recur: semper reformanda. Early Methodism was a missionary faith and John Wesley famously declared that the world was his parish. Protestant Christianity shifts from the territorial to the transnational. Methodist missionaries died by the score bringing the Evangelical message to disease-ridden areas of West Africa, sowing seeds that grew later in educational and medical institutions that, with other missions from Britain and Northern Europe, nurtured the elites that led Africa after independence.

The gift of tongues speaks of a message that crosses barriers, though these always reassert themselves, whether of gender or of race. Early Pentecostalism, like early Methodism, generated possibilities for female ministry which were later attenuated, and both movements experienced the re-emergence of colour barriers. Many early Pentecostal missionaries, both men and women, even supposed that the gift of tongues not only empowered them to preach to all nations but enabled them to communicate with anybody anywhere without effort. When canvassing the transnational potential of Pentecostalism it is important always to keep in mind that it was multi-centred in its origins and its dispersion, particularly after white and black revivalism came together in 1906 at Azusa St., Los Angeles. As with the mainstream missions of the nineteenth century the effective missionaries were the indigenous catechists. The carriers of messages today are people moving around the globe, for example Koreans in the Philippines, or Brazilians in Portugal, North America, northern Europe or Southern Africa. One of the most active mission fields lies in the Ukraine, where the market has been deregulated and competition between several traditional churches has created a quasi-pluralism. The most successful Church, with 25,000 members, is the Embassy of God in Kiev, run by a Nigerian (Wanner 2007).

Eschatology, the Bondage of the Will, and Empowerment

What then of the variable presence of eschatology? The millennial expectation present in Methodism, though much less intense than millennial expectation in the English seventeenth century England, was influenced by Bengelius in Germany. In the case of Pentecostalism a distinctively pre-millennial hope came through the various holiness traditions of Methodism, the Brethren and the Keswick movement. Obviously an open Bible is always prone to arouse eschatological hope. Similar considerations apply to the Lutheran concept of the bondage of the will, always likely to emerge from any close scrutiny of the letters of Paul. The natural bondage of the will and the divine possibility of a dramatic release through the conversion experience are central to Methodism. Charles Wesley wrote: "Long my imprisoned spirit lay/ Fast bound in sin and Nature's night,/ Thine eye diffused a quickening ray,/ I woke, the dungeon flamed with light". Such an experience of renewed agency and power appears again and again in the spiritual autobiographies of Pentecostals. The Spirit fills the soul so completely it overcomes the chronic weakness of the will and makes everything possible, including holiness. Pentecostals discern potentials in the most unpromising people and circumstances.

Scripture Alone? Spirit Alone?

Pentecostals are avid readers of the Scriptures and for Protestants Scripture alone is finally authoritative, whatever subsidiary principles of reason, tradition, and experience may be invoked. However there are always selective hermeneutic principles at work, both among liberal Protestants and Pentecostals. Clearly the earliest Christians spoke in tongues, even though the supreme theological virtues were faith, hope and love. It is also clear that the Hebrew prophets and some of the psalms are a major source of the prosperity teaching embraced by Neo-Pentecostals, and that healing and exorcism were practised by Jesus himself. What is selected in part depends on felt needs in particular situations, so that where prophecy is a traditional practice or where penury is ever-present and medical care usually absent, the Pentecostal selection from Scripture makes sense (Jenkins 2006). Of course, such a selection from Scripture accentuates well-known problems of theodicy. When healing fails and the wicked prosper, Pentecostals have recourse to the understandings detailed in Smilde's ethnography in Venezuela (Smilde 2007). Some conclude that their God has failed. When a faith promises too much the potential for disillusion is obvious.

Scripture releases as much as it binds, depending on how you use it. Though St. Paul had qualms about some positions of authority being held by women, what women can do in practice depends on how an activity is classified. That is clear from Jane Soothill's account of the role of Big Women (Soothill 2007). The Prophet Joel, in his prophecies concerning the gifts that fall on women and men alike in the Age to come offers a plenary inspiration to female prophecy that women embrace enthusiastically, especially where there are antecedent traditions of women as prophets and healers. Pentecostal gifts of the Spirit enable young men and women alike to move out from under the power of the elders, a process highlighted by David Maxwell (2006) in his work on Zimbabwe. Some of the releases offered by Scripture can be startlingly radical, for example in the case of the Friday Apostolics studied by Matthew Engelke (2007) in Zimbabwe. According to Scripture, the letter kills while the Spirit gives life, so the Friday Apostolics dispense with Scripture altogether. Prophets unhappy about the fetters imposed by a stable text find that appealing. As ever, Pentecostals combine the pre-modern with the post-modern, and post-modern spirituality could hardly ask for more.

Transnationalism—and the Hope of Earthly Zion?

There is a Zionist element in Pentecostalism. Though this may surprise anyone acquainted with Luther's ferocious strictures on the Jews, it may seem entirely unsurprising when one considers the intermittent symbiosis of Calvinism and Judaism from Amsterdam to modern

America. Pentecostal Zionism, like Christian Zionism generally, has its roots in the pluralistic and voluntary associational trajectory gradually realised in the Anglo-sphere. Of course, insofar as this voluntary and associational model rejects the local and quasi-familial bonds, boundaries, territorial imperatives and ritual continuities of birth-right religion it lies at the other end of the spectrum to Zionism, religious or otherwise. But there is always a potential pull back to the Land, reinforced in Christianity by its retention of the Hebrew Bible. Protestantism is pregnant with two possibilities: the voluntary and potentially pacific group, and the nation seen through the lens of the Hebrew Bible as a New Israel. The question then becomes whether the New Israel replaces the Old Israel or continues to stand in some kind of positive relation to it. Notions like British Israel lean towards replacement, but ideas of a continuing relation are also present, reinforced by readings of the Old Testament assuming the Hebrews are right and the Philistines wrong (Katz and Popkin 1999). Those who set up the (proto-American) republican Commonwealth in mid-seventeenth century England, and in 1655 invited the Jews back, were steeled and steeped in eschatological hope and the Hebrew Bible. Christian Zionist motifs also emerged in the turbulent times of the late eighteenth century. There is therefore a range of possibilities on which Pentecostals and Evangelicals can draw: a generalised identification with God's chosen people; an identification of a particular country, (say) the USA or contemporary Zambia, Korea or Nigeria as a chosen (and Christian) nation; and an expectation that the return of the Jews to Israel initiates the End-Time scenario. Much depends on the salience of the End-Time, which may well be occluded by the arrival of the Big-Time.

The range of possibilities is considerable. There are para-Pentecostal movements that aim to create their own Zion, whether in Africa or in Latin America, for example the temple and the landscape of Jerusalem recreated in Guadalajara by *La Luz del Mundo*, with roots in Mexican nationalism and anti-Catholic sentiments accentuated by the Civil War. Alternatively the Jewish infusion into Pentecostalism may be simply an elective affinity between the more up-beat aspects of the Hebrew Bible concerning God's providential care for the peace and prosperity of the righteous, and an inspirited African religious imagination linking the goods with the gods and the good. However the link is articulated, the image of Jerusalem is ubiquitous. Pentecostalism has supported Israel and the Jewish people.

A few versions of Pentecostalism may even adopt Jewish practices, as Kristina Helgesson (2006) shows in her study of two churches of the Pentecostal Assemblies of God in Durban, South Africa. One, known as Red Hill, is predominantly Indian and coloured, the other, Olive Tree, is mainly white, and it attracts a considerable part of its congregation through its commitment to Israel, which it combines with the extensive social outreach characteristic of the AOG in South Africa. Both congregations are simultaneously transnational and seeking to handle the apartheid past and the future by locating Heimat. For Red Hill their sufferings under apartheid parallel the sufferings of the Jews in Egypt, just as they have done for black Evangelicals in North America. For Olive Tree, however, the identification with Israel goes much further than elsewhere in the AOG. It invokes a mandate to be 'a prophetic voice to the Land and People of Israel' and its leader, Malcolm Hedding, who was an anti-apartheid activist, directs the 'International Christian Embassy Jerusalem'. His understanding of 'Messianic Theology' includes celebrating Passover and Yom Kippur, as well as singing Hebrew songs and dancing Jewish dances. This is not widespread in Pentecostalism or South Africa, especially given the rising presence of Islam, but it is part of the spectrum of possibilities.

For Judaism and Israel there are problems in all this. Israel may invite Pentecostal leaders to Jerusalem but feel less happy about attempts at conversion or local fusions of Judaism with Evangelical or messianic Christianity. David Lehmann in his study with Batia Siebzehner (2006) of Shas has even suggested that Latin American Pentecostalism shares some characteristics with Shas, (as maybe Methodism shared some characteristics with Hassidism). Clearly there is an important difference between a religion of required ritual performances ensuring the continuity and solidarity of a people from generation to generation, and the increasing emphasis on interiority, sincerity and personal experience that runs from Jeremiah to Jesus, and from Augustine to Luther. Adam Seligman discusses this bifurcation in monotheism in his *Modernity's Wager* (1999) and more recently, with co-authors, in *Ritual and its Consequences* (2008). My concern here has been with the massive contemporary appropriation in the developing world of the Pentecostal emphasis on personal and mature experience as manifested in and controlled by the disciplines of a voluntary and supportive community. This close-knit and communal Christianity of the Holy Spirit, manifest in Tongues and Spirit Baptism, both parallels and stands in vivid contrast with the relativistic and privatised spirituality of contemporary Western Europe. Contemporary European spirituality is inimical to the continuities secured by religious institutions, and it characterises societies, particularly in north-west Europe, where ancient religious establishments and national narratives are under severe strain.

A Master Road to Modernity?

Unless modernity by definition excludes religion as a vital force and Europe anticipates the global future, then it is perfectly plausible to regard Pentecostalism as a master narrative of modernity. If Martin Luther, facing the combined powers of Pope and Emperor, dramatised the onset of early modernity, then the voluntary movement of the Spirit in Los Angeles in 1906 could be a parallel dramatisation for a later modernity. In her discussion of different roads to modernity, Gertrude Himmelfarb (2004) traces one major road through Methodism, seeing it as complementing Enlightened Moral Benevolence in Britain, just as Pietism complements as well as running counter to the German Enlightenment. Reformations, Revivals and Awakenings are continuous, and maybe Pentecostalism is also a major road to modernity (Fernandez-Armesto and Wilson 1996).

CHAPTER SIX

TRANS-NATIONAL PENTECOSTALISM AND SECULAR MODERNITY

Bernice Martin

Introduction

Terms such as "modernity", "religion" and "secularity" can no longer be used without mental quotation marks to indicate their ethnocentricity, their status as constructions of a very particular western (and colonial) cultural history (Asad 2003; Fitzgerald 2007). Nevertheless, I shall use these terms, subject to the caveat just indicated, because the problem I want to address is how contemporary Pentecostals achieve a modern identity that differs in significant respects from the modernity of that familiar, and dominant, western cultural construction. Is Pentecostal modernity part of what S.N. Eisenstadt identifies as the Jacobin element of modernity, or a distinct variety in the range of what he has taught us to call "multiple modernities" (Eisenstadt 1999, 2000)? Pentecostals do not pose quite the same kind of problem for western secular modernity as Muslims, for example, because, though they look at first sight like alien cultural matter in the secular West, they are younger offspring of the Christian family and so incorporate a good part of the repertoire that underlies what Charles Taylor calls "the modern moral system" and the "modern identity". In a series of books from *Sources of the Self* (1989) to *A Secular Age* (2007) Taylor has constructed what I interpret as a set of implicitly Weberian ideal types of the core elements of western, or, as he prefers, European and North Atlantic, cultural modernity (Taylor 1989, 2007). Taylor has been attacked for western ethnocentricity (Masuzawa 2008), but he has never suggested that the processes he anatomises are universal, or the end point of an evolutionary procession that relegates non-western traditions to backwardness or faces them with a need to catch up. There is, of course, a sense that this western construct of secular modernity is peculiarly privileged and powerful because the civilisation that produced it has been geo-politically and economically dominant for the last three or so centuries, though the current rise of non-western powers such as China and India suggests that dominance may be waning, in spite of the set-backs they may expect from the current economic crisis. Taylor very explicitly argues that the "modern moral system", the "modern identity" and the purely secular perspective are the historical product of Christian theistic sources secularised in the European Enlightenment and further mutated in Romanticism and varieties of Modernist vision after Darwin. The western paradigm of modernity that emerged from these transmutations was globalised, first through European colonialism, and later through American economic, military and cultural dominance. But what Taylor calls the "occluded" sources of the putatively universal values enshrined in international organisations such as the United Nations and the European Court of Human Rights and the International Criminal Court—individual human rights, the imperative of human happiness and avoidance of suffering—rest on secularised Christian bedrock. The focus of my chapter is therefore limited to the disjunctions between this specific historical construct of secular modernity and the distinctive modernity of Pentecostal moral imperatives and the Pentecostal modern self.

As an offshoot of the holiness movement within Protestantism, Pentecostalism stresses the gifts of the Spirit even above the sanctity of the biblical text (Anderson 2004; cf. Engelke 2007 on an African church that has abandoned the Bible altogether). The distinctive beginning of the movement is usually traced to the 1906 Azusa Street Revival in Los Angeles, though some scholars of Pentecostal history claim it was the simultaneous product of many parts of the Protestant mission field (Bergunder 2008). American Pentecostalism was a mixture of poor white and poor black religiosity from the outset (Corten 1999, Stephens 2008), and it finds a ready response in cultures with a tradition of belief in spirits and spirit possession, particularly among marginalised ethnic and cultural minorities. Hence, the movement was quickly indigenised in every part of the globe as it fanned out not only from Los Angeles but from Wales, Sweden, India and many other places to Latin America, Africa, Asia, China and the Far East (Anderson 2004; Dempster, Klaus and Petersen 1999). The latest wave of Pentecostal growth began in Latin America in the 1960s, with peaks in Africa and Asia following in the 1980s and 1990s, reaching virtually every part of the developing world today (Martin 2006). It has only the most modest foothold in Western Europe despite its established position in the United States, but it had some success in Eastern Europe and Central Asia in the period of Soviet hegemony, and immediately after the fall of communism, increased its penetration despite the reassertion of ethno-religion in much of the region (Hann et al. 2006; Wanner 2007).

The Pentecostal/charismatic movement has been part of the mobilisation of the masses in the trek from the small town and rural areas of the developing world to the megacities, and on to the cities of the developed world. Pentecostals have distributed themselves all over the cities of the West by mass migration from the global South to the North, and from the East to the West, for economic, political or survival reasons, and/or as "reverse mission" to the increasingly secular "old world" of the erstwhile imperial centres, though most migrant churches tend in Western, though not in Eastern, Europe to remain mono-ethnic diaspora enclaves. Pentecostals are enthusiastic users of modern means of communication to build transnational networks that ease migration and facilitate the establishment of churches in each new area of migration (Meyer and Moors 2006; Oosterbaan 2009). Here these actively religious new moderns build their noisy churches and sometimes fill vast stadiums with ecstatic worship and spectacles of healing and exorcism that stand in sharp relief against the religious indifference of most First World populations.

The cruder, unilinear versions of the classic secularisation thesis today look both empirically dubious, in some respects even in relation to Europe (Davie 2002; Berger, Davie and Fokas 2008, Casanova, 2007), and, in view of the dramatic revivals in most of the major religious traditions in recent decades, blinkered and philosophically arrogant (Asad 2003). Although Charles Taylor constructs an ideal type of western secularity he makes clear, especially in *A Secular Age* (Taylor 2007), that there are many secularisation stories, even within Europe, with subtle and not-so-subtle differences in the relative influence of secular and religious forces. He accepts that Eisenstadt's concept of "multiple modernities" makes good sense of the very considerable variety of patterns in the different societies of the developed world (Martin 1978; Casanova 1994).

"Societies" here, of course, mostly means "nation states", and modern nation states were formed on the model of the Westphalian settlement, that is, as territorial units in which one particular religion had a monopoly. Although subsequent history has complicated the pattern, most nation states have had a religious component in the myth of their national identity, even when, as in, say, France, Spain, or Turkey, it is a dual myth of struggle between religious and secular forces. The twentieth century from around 1914 on saw a recurrent drive to re-homogenise, "purify", the population of the nation state in ethno-religious terms through population extrusion, exchange and massacre in the name of nationalism; the latest episode followed the fall of the Soviet Union (Judt 2005). The process is never complete, and national homogeneity remains a fictional construct that seeks to gloss the inevitability of internal differences under a constructed cultural unity. Yet it is a powerful myth that underlies many of the deep-rooted, semi-invisible assumptions of national identity, and it is not always comfortable when confronted with the effects of recent global migrations.

The admixture of new migrant populations, particularly since the 1990s, plants new variants of all the major religious traditions, most of them with "alien" ethnic and sometimes civilisational characteristics, in the heart of all these imperfectly "purified" nation states. Potential tension therefore exists not only between migrant religious and ethnic identities and the religiously inflected myth of the nation state, but with the "secular" paradigm of western modernity, also inflected by particular Christian histories, including the variable way in which the religious tradition absorbed or rejected Enlightenment ideas (Himmelfarb 2004). Multiple modernities are therefore not territorially insulated, but must accommodate the global distribution of multiple religious and ethnic identities, including transnational Pentecostalism, within a polyglot, and often makeshift, pluralism. The situation generates attempts, usually by progressive political elites, to re-calibrate national identities in Europe as multicultural, or as manifestations of precisely those values Charles Taylor calls the "modern moral system", though such initiatives often feel artificial rather than organic. This, nevertheless, is the context that leads some to talk of a "postsecular" turn (MacLennan 2007) and to agonise over the epistemology through which religious and secular citizens might conduct democratic discussion (Habermas 2008).

Charles Taylor: The "Modern Identity", the "Immanent Frame" and Pentecostal Modernity

In *Sources of the Self* Charles Taylor showed how the Christian master narrative mutated over time in conjunction with other master narratives, notably Enlightenment, Romanticism and Modernism, to yield the "modern moral system" and the related "modern identity" (Taylor 1989). The imperatives of this moral system are threefold: the dignity of the individual (derived at several removes from the doctrine of the *imago dei*); the value of preventing human suffering and promoting happiness (derived from the gospel injunction to love your neighbour as yourself); and the value of ordinary life as distinct from the heroism of both the warrior ethic and the ethic of virtuoso religious asceticism (derived in part from the Reformation emphasis on the religious calling exercised in the mundane sphere of work and domesticity). Taylor represents these constructs as having become stabilised and immanent in the "civilised" social order that emerged out of the post-Reformation settlement. The modern self, constructed by these values, evolves out of the doctrine of humans as made in God's image, Christian rationality, the Augustinian turn "inwards", Romantic expressivism, Darwinian recognition of instinctual, animal nature, and Freudian stress on the multi-layered self.

In *A Secular Age* Taylor extends the analysis to the process by which the West invented an exclusively humanist paradigm that dispensed altogether with the transcendent dimension which every other human society had taken for granted (Taylor 2007). He points to a sequence of crucial historical moves. The distinction made in Latin Christendom between sacred and secular time and space gradually gave way to a unitary conception of time and space as the same for everyone. Episodes of ritual release from the moral disciplines of Christianity were progressively banished by movements of "Reform" that sought to impose the Christian moral structure more rigorously and uniformly. This process was associated with what Taylor calls the Disciplinary Society in which sex and violence were restrained and public displays of bodily functions were curbed, making progressive instalments of privacy possible. New social imaginaries emerged stressing horizontal rather than vertical relations, and the conception of an autonomous individual became "thinkable". Together these developments provided the crucial historical turning point, the age of Providential Deism, where transcendent goals (notably, salvation) were progressively eclipsed by this worldly ends that Taylor refers to as "human flourishing".

This turning point is characterised by several new features. The first is the "buffered self" that cannot be invaded by supernatural forces. This is combined with what Taylor calls "disembedding" from the "paeleo-Durkheimian" social order, that is, the capacity of the individual to distance him- or herself heuristically from the social context rather than take it for granted as immutable. This is linked with a "disenchantment" of the world, that is, the investment of all agency in humans rather than in transcendent spirits and supernatural forces. And finally the Enlightenment notion that both the cosmos and humanity are essentially benign replaces the Augustinian doctrine of original sin and the Fall.

This incipiently secular picture of reality quickly splintered in a "nova effect", producing a myriad of "thinkable" pictures, including for the first time in human history an exclusively human paradigm that Taylor calls "the immanent frame". The Darwinian revolution undermined the assumption of cosmic and human benevolence and created a new problem of meaninglessness. In the 1960s the radical "turn to the self" with its ethics of authenticity led to a further "supernova" of pictures of reality, many of them based on "a narrative of self-authorization". Taylor believes that the "secular age" has released new possibilities because, though the "immanent frame" is the default position of most western people, it can accommodate both Open and Closed World Systems, that is, open or closed to a transcendent reference. Today there are innumerable hybrid pictures of reality on offer, frequently as a result of recombinations of elements from the existing repertoire of religious and secular positions.

Despite the title of his book, *A Secular Age*, Taylor's is not just another secularisation thesis, but rather an account of how religion, rather than becoming definitively obsolete, is constantly reconfigured, sometimes in ways that are not immediately apparent (as when religious sources become "occluded"). Moreover, Taylor believes, and the anthropological record largely supports his view (Davie 2006; Stringer 2008), that few people hold a single consistent picture of reality. Rather, they shift between pictures depending on need and context: a picture of reality that suits scientific research may be found inappropriate as the basis for personal relationships, for example. He calls this being "cross-pressured". Some of these pictures of the world allow the return of the transcendent dimension repressed by the strict epistemology of secular naturalism. In that sense, anything is compatible with contemporary life, including Pentecostalism, because the "supernova" precludes nothing that is "thinkable".

How, then, does Pentecostal modernity diverge from the *secular* model presented in Charles Taylor's work, since it is that model which dominates the public sphere? First we must recognise the considerable overlap before focusing on the divergences.

Pentecostalism is a transformative system that individualises personal identity through its distinctive theological and liturgical practices. It has a model of individual salvation that treats all converts as fully equal. This is in sharp contrast with the de facto gendering of the process of salvation in many cultures based on honour and shame, such as the Mediterranean or Latin America, where men and women, or, in other places, elder and younger, have a different relationship to honour and agency, and therefore different routes to salvation, whatever the official soteriology (Cucchiari 1988 and 1991). Pentecostal liturgies centrally involve *individual* conversion, often acted out dramatically in ritual exorcisms, and Pentecostals talk a new, post-conversion self into being in the frequent, ritualised repetition of their individual conversion history (Meyer 1998). "Before" and "after" conversion may be partly mythic constructs, but they serve to stabilise the Pentecostal identity around a moral order that incorporates much of Taylor's "modern moral system". Because Pentecostals are typically mobile, this theological stress on the individual also legitimates and accentuates the weakening of traditional ties of obligation and identification with the extended family, and often the tribe or village community, which anyway has often been geographically left behind, in favour of narrower identification with the nuclear family and the new community of the church.

Pentecostal identity is often referred to as "portable", "made to travel", or "transnational", (Martin 2006; Dempster, Klaus and Petersen 1999; Maxwell 2002, 2006), indicating both the strength and the flexibility of the mobile Pentecostal self and of the networks the movement constructs to support it. Nevertheless, Pentecostal individualisation stops well short of the economistic atomisation of the individual, or the "expressive" hyper-individualism of the 1960s' "turn to the self" and what Taylor calls "narratives of self-authorization". Indeed, many Pentecostalite and neo-Pentecostal megachurches, that typically attract new professionals, have a special mission to re-integrate the casualties of excessive individualism, especially in its hedonistic form (Martin 1998; Wanner 2007). Elisabeth Brusco made the point in her pioneering study that the primary unit for Colombian evangelicals was not the individual but the nuclear family (Brusco 1986). This partial brake on western style individuation will be important when we come to consider gender relations and modern western feminism below.

The other area of overlap with western modernity is Pentecostal enthusiasm for science and technology, particularly the technologies of modern communications which Pentecostals harness for the benefit of missionary outreach and the building of church networks, as well as in putting on spectacular public events and media productions (Meyer and Moors 2006). They mistrust some uses to which modern media are put if they encourage immorality and hedonistic excess, but it is the morality of content not the science of means that matters. The Pentecostals of the global South have much in common with American Evangelicals. Many of them happily combine a "pre-millennial" theological doctrine of imminent apocalypse with taking careful pragmatic thought for the morrow, and the habitual resort to faith healing does not imply rejection of modern medicine, which is in any case barely accessible to most Pentecostals in the developing world (Chesnut 1997). There is distrust of Darwinian evolutionary theory, and, even more, of modern biblical criticism, but not of the hard physical sciences, and particularly not of the applied sciences and technology. So it is only selected parts of the programme of scientific naturalism, and some of the uses to which it is put, that cause problems. It appears that Pentecostals are not unlike some other moderns in this inconsistency and capacity to compartmentalise aspects of scientific and religious pictures of the world.

The disjunctions between Pentecostal modernity and the model of western modernity presented by Charles Taylor at first sight look pretty sharp. Pentecostalism lacks most of the features that characterised the crucial turning point towards secularity in the West. In the first place the Pentecostal world is not "disenchanted" any more than are the societies in the global South from which most Pentecostals come. The Pentecostal world is peopled by demons, supernatural beings that can possess human individuals and cause all the ills flesh and soul are heir to, and that can only be defeated by the divine power of Jesus Christ and the Holy Spirit. The Pentecostal world is a permanent psychomachia where the powers of good and evil battle for each human soul; they live in the same enspirited world as the apostles in the New Testament and the prophets and heroes of the Old Testament whom they often treat as their own familiar friends.

Despite the central significance of conversion, the battle just ended is never the last: the demons are ever watchful to retake the citadel of the soul. For this reason exorcism is not a once-for-all ritual cleansing but a perpetually renewed prophylactic. The demons are often a negative transmutation of the spirits of the indigenous religions that Pentecostalism has superseded, and the practice of repeated exorcism is precisely what perpetuates them as powerful forces within the new Christian dispensation (Anderson 2004). In this way indigenous religion is transmuted and reincorporated into the hybrid form that is modern Pentecostalism (van Dijk 2002). This means that Pentecostals are not "buffered selves" in the same way that post-Lockean Europeans are. Or rather, as Birgit Meyer has recently suggested, the superior power of the Holy Spirit ensures a provisional and renewable "buffering" that facilitates individual human agency and control over the self, but without wholesale "disenchantment" (Meyer 2009). But when the "buffering" fails the backslider has to exercise individual *willpower* in order to seek the help of the Holy Spirit through the church.

The duality in Pentecostalism between ecstatic release in worship and sharp moral control in everyday life likewise suggests that the "buffering" of the self and the associated assertion of individual human agency is incomplete. In worship the Pentecostal becomes a vessel for the gifts of the Spirit—speaking in tongues and prophesying, or healing and casting out devils, or dancing to the Lord—that is, the everyday self is laid open to invasion, quite literally inspiration, by spiritual agents. This is ritually enacted and bounded by liturgical limits. Yet these same abandoned worshippers are dressed modestly according to the code of the church, often segregated by sex, and they are constrained by strict moral rules that usually forbid alcohol, drugs, sex outside marriage, and commercial entertainments such as theatre and concert hall, even football, as sources of temptation to promiscuity, immodesty and excess. In some countries including Brazil and, above all, Ghana, Pentecostals compensate for these restrictions by producing films and television programmes through their own mass media offering all the excitement and colour of secular soap operas and serial plays, by staging healing spectaculars, "miracles", and Pentecostal dramas of conversion, actual and fictional. In Ghana they dominate the airwaves (Meyer 2004; Meyer and Moors 2006).

"Disembedding" from the "paeleo-Durkheimian" social context is also ambiguous so far as Pentecostals are concerned. Pentecostals are, in a literal sense, typically disembedded from their original context both by choosing to reject their inherited religious identity, and, very often, by moving geographically. Here again we see the significance of the "portable" Pentecostal identity that is bounded by the Pentecostal moral order and therefore secure enough not to be at the mercy of every new context it encounters. David Maxwell puts the point strongly in relation to transnational Pentecostals in Zimbabwe: "they are not refugees retreating from frightening new circumstances, but are courageous, confident and able people who actively seek to influence their lives and social environment according to their own ideas and aims, their conduct motivated by hope, optimism and determination rather than despair and defeat" (Maxwell 2002: 223) The self-confident mobility of Pentecostals also suggests that one of the predisposing features of those who become Pentecostals may be a capacity to imagine a life other than the one you were born to. But this is not the heuristic distancing that the Enlightenment devised as part of the recipe for scientific naturalism requiring objectivity in empirical observation. Pentecostal disembedding depends on the transnational network of connections with other Pentecostals that recreates the Pentecostal moral order and support structures in every new setting. It also requires the communications media that convey images of non-traditional life lived by Pentecostals in other societies. Many studies of conversion stress the importance of images of technical modernity and individual dignity and prosperity denied in the traditional setting. Such images of the possible inspire groups and individuals to leap-frog over their traditional "betters" into the superior Pentecostal modernity often associated with city life in the developed world. This sometimes suggests that images of America, the geo-political and economic "winner", feed the Pentecostal sense that it is a progressive, modern option, superior to the indigenous culture which is by comparison "backward" (Meyer 2009; Coleman 2000).

Taylor sees the shift of emphasis from transcendent goals to the goal of "human flourishing" in this world as a prerequisite of the crucial turning point of western modernity, and associates it with the Enlightenment replacement of the doctrine of original sin by a semi-secular theory of original goodness in both the cosmos and humanity. He links this development with the emergence of everyday life as the proper arena of the struggle for salvation rather than the heroic warrior ethic or monastic asceticism. Pentecostalism unequivocally accepts the latter position as part of the Protestant holiness legacy, but its relation to the goal of purely human "flourishing" is not quite so straightforward. Pentecostalism in the global South has been a wildfire success in part because it reincorporates aspects of indigenous pre-Christian religious sensibilities within a Christian frame (Meyer 1999). One common characteristic of this pre-Christian layer is to make little or no distinction between different aspects of human well-being, spiritual, physical and material, and to see the spirits and gods as having the power to grant or thwart such blessings here on this earth, with worship as the means to secure them. The American black religiosity that was part of the original Pentecostal hybrid in Azusa St. already incorporated such residues. It is the root of what some mainstream Christians disdain as the relentless *cheerfulness* of charismatic Pentecostalism—all celebration and no long-drawn-out penitence.

An illustration of the way such perspectives were perpetuated and partially transformed, in this case under the cover of Iberian colonial Catholicism in the New World, comes from a hymn in Nahuatl, the language of the Aztecs which would have been one of the popular interpolations in the (Spanish) mass, probably in late sixteenth-century Mexico (though the hymn was part of a collection found in Lima, Peru). The hymn asks first for "protection of spiritual strength", then for "escape from the sins of the devil" and finally for "fortune":

> *Increase my store of gold and silver*
> *Being well provisioned, it will be stored up.*
> *There will be great food harvests.*
> *Defend me from famine.*
> *Let me rest well here.*

Even a verse about the joys of heaven is very earthy, concluding with the lines:

> *For the life of all sustenance*
> *May there be delight (Skidmore 2007).*

Pentecostalism never carried the weight of asceticism that characterised European Christianity, both monastic and Reformation, nor the emphasis on exemplary suffering so strong in the images of Iberian Catholicism with its anorexic virgins and tortured martyr saints. Pentecostalism does not dwell on the tragedy of Jesus crucified but on the power of the risen Christ and of the Holy Spirit to defeat the powers of evil in this world, the devil and his demons, and to grant health, prosperity and spiritual peace to believers. It is Lutheran rather than Calvinist in its emphasis on the free gift of grace: anything is possible for those who truly have faith. Where the holiness tradition is strongest the moral perfectibility of the believer on earth is emphasised, but the indigenous and black contribution to the hybrid makes it perfectly normal for believers to desire the good life, healing on all fronts, here and now, or, as David Martin puts it, the good and the goods without distinction (Maxwell 1998, 2006; Coleman 2000). This is why mainstream Christian leaders, both Catholic and Protestant, tended to dismiss the upsurge of the newer "autonomous Protestant" (Pentecostal) churches in Brazil in the 1970s and 1980s, what Allan Anderson calls the "third wave", as "First Aid Churches" (*pronto socorro*) only concerned to repair the health and worldly fortunes of their members, and why there was a widespread suspicion that the movement could not be indigenous but must be evidence of the cultural imperialism of capitalist America. In fact the very elements identified as obviously American had been prominent in the semi-autonomous black brotherhoods all over Latin America in the centuries of colonial Catholicism (Meyers and Hopkins 1988).

Pentecostalism does not emphasise the doctrine of the Fall and original sin but rather the ability of every human to access the power of the Holy Spirit to defeat evil. It does not have a Rousseauean view of human goodness because the human is always beset by temptation in the shape of the demons, the manifestations of all imaginable evils. But it does have an optimistic expectation that human wholeness and the good life is attainable in this world by the power of the Spirit. The good things of this world are what *God* desires for us, and it is only when we cross clear moral lines that those good things turn evil, particularly when we become enslaved by the demons of alcohol, drugs or promiscuous sex. So Pentecostals celebrate the healthy body, good food, good sex within marriage, and Christian conviviality. At the same time, because the demons are seen as the real agents of evil, there is a sense that people who are freed of demons cannot be continually held responsible for what the demons led them into. However appalling the sins a Pentecostal recounts in his or her "witnessing", (and there is heroic kudos in having escaped from dramatic evils, particularly for men), these sins are not what defines the converted person in his or her own sight or in the eyes of the congregation of the believers. The convert can start again with a clean slate.[1] Though this

---

[1] In one case David Martin and I encountered in research in Brazil in the 1990s this proved a problem. The congregation of the God is Love church was happy to give the man a fresh start, but his wife, who had seen several other conversions break down, was not. She clearly had a sense that his sins *did* represent a thread of continuity in her husband's personality.

runs counter to the secular modern notion of human agency and the continuing deposit of the past in the personality, it also leaves converts more confident in their new, converted identity than do many secular accounts of personality, and many secular therapies: indeed, Pentecostalism is very often more successful than secular therapies in treating addictions (Wanner 2007). Human autonomy in Pentecostalism is therefore ambiguous and contested in theory and theology, but in many concrete ways Pentecostals appear to exercise a new, more effective control over their lives.

This is not a new paradox in religious history. In the course of his excavation of the genealogy of the concept of "agency", particularly in relation to pain, Talal Asad shows what a variety of meanings it has historically encompassed. He points to the case of the early Methodists who acquired a sense of confident individual agency only by total submission to the will of Jesus, though the notion of their own agency became so naturalised in some of them that they forgot the religious submission in which it had originally been grounded (Asad 2003). Of course, the notion of perfect individual autonomy is a sociological oxymoron which many observers, including Asad, see as one of the problematic cultural legacies of the Enlightenment conception of individualism. Humans are created through dependence on other humans and remain ineradicably interdependent throughout their lives. The notion of perfect autonomy or total individual agency is therefore an ideological fiction if it means any more than the human capacity for a degree of self-reflection. We should not apply to Pentecostals tests of total autonomy and agency that secular Europeans, enmeshed in the networks of interdependence, obligation and coercion that constrain us all, would also fail.

The "Protestant Ethic" and the Pentecostal Economic Ethic

Charles Taylor's account of the evolution of western modernity is remarkably silent on the economic component of the modern identity, apart from his discussion of proto-economists such as Adam Smith, where Taylor is mainly concerned with the Enlightenment's optimistic take on human and cosmic benevolence, particularly through the doctrine of human sympathy and the theory of the "invisible hand" that was supposed to turn individual self-interest into optimal economic benefit for society as a whole. Yet economic activity and motivation is a central component of modern culture.

Max Weber's classic account of the Protestant ethic was designed to explain the role of Protestantism in the rise of capitalism in Europe (Weber 1920). It famously attributed the process of capital accumulation to a combination of Calvinist asceticism, which led to saving rather than spending the wealth amassed by unremitting devotion to work and duty, and the existential anxiety about personal election where salvation or damnation was predestined and unknowable. Weber speculated that this existential anxiety was, irrationally but understandably, assuaged by looking for possible clues to election, in particular the worldly prosperity that might be interpreted as a mark of divine favour. Weber's essential insight was that there was something very unlikely in the practice of capital accumulation, the impulsion to make but not to enjoy riches, among a whole new class of economic actors. He speculated that only a pre-existing cultural force as powerful as religion could make sense of the riddle. He found the answer in the "inner-worldly asceticism" of seventeenth century Protestantism, and his argument in the essay "The Protestant Sects and the Spirit of Capitalism" broadens to take in what had long been a truism, that morally disciplined Protestants tend to be more economically successful than others of their class that lack these characteristics (Gerth and Mills 1948). In his essay "Religious Rejections of the World and their Direction" Weber categorised the main religious traditions in terms of their degree of world acceptance or world rejection (Gerth and Mills 1948). Christianity, like other religions of brotherhood, lay towards the world rejection end of the spectrum and therefore would display some degree of tension with the economic sphere, on Weber's reckoning. The relative economic success of those imbued with the Protestant ethic was therefore paradoxical, exactly as John Wesley himself found it. For Weber, however, all this was only important insofar as it helped to explain the capitalist take-off: thereafter, rationalisation and routinisation would institutionalise the necessities of capitalism without need of religious reinforcement.

Capitalism today is very different from its seventeenth-century prototype, and pioneer entrepreneurship is not the calling of most Pentecostals who anyway, as the great-grandchildren of Luther rather than Calvin, do not tend to have existential problems over predestination and election. David Martin has suggested that Elie Halévy may be a better guide than Weber to the economic culture of Pentecostals, though in fact Halévy was more concerned with the politics than the economics (Martin 1990, 2006). Halévy argued that Methodism in

Britain in the eighteenth century did much to prevent revolution in the French style by bringing about a cultural revolution of morals and manners among the lower orders and, crucially, the new urban artisan class. Histories of Methodism on the disorderly American frontier tell a similar story. Certainly, Pentecostalism is in the direct line of descent from Methodism and shares many of the moral priorities of early Methodism. It seeks to bring moral order into the chaotic lives of people flocking to the megacities, prey to all the consolations and excesses of urban life, and mostly entering the labour market at the lowest rungs, often via the informal economy. Pentecostals even in the most unpropitious economic conditions tend to find that moral discipline has an immediate economic pay-off. It is debatable whether this is the straightforward pay-off of "inner-worldly asceticism". In one sense it is. If you stop drinking, taking drugs, fighting, womanising, you are more likely to find and keep work and to be able to put food on the family table and send the children to school. Yet, there are sometimes economic downsides to Pentecostal conversion, for example when your principled objection to violence or to corruption leads to losing your job in the security service or the bank and throwing you back on your own resources. That can stimulate entrepreneurial effort, or it can land you in penury. It is difficult to see unequivocal evidence as yet of the kind Peter Berger hopes for, that a critical mass of Pentecostals definitively stimulates economic development (Berger, Foreword in Martin 1990). Though Berger and his associates detect a hint of such a trend in recent South African data, Birgit Meyer remains unconvinced (Centre for Development and Enterprise 2008; Meyer 2009). There is little doubt that Pentecostal self-discipline aids the survival of the poor in the most difficult circumstances and often leads to micro-entrepreneurship, but the jury remains out as to the long term economic mobility of the next generations.

When the new wave of Pentecostalism first appeared in Latin America, there was a pervasive suggestion, particularly from the Left which had hoped for revolutionary political achievements from liberation theology, that Pentecostalism was the cultural arm of American capitalism. It encouraged individualism rather than collective action, and passivity in the face of economic and political oppression. The fact that its moral reforms made it possible for a sector of the poor to survive even the debt crisis of the 1980s meant that there would be no mass challenge to capitalism. That, of course, without the normative disapproval, was more or less Halévy's argument about early Methodism.

There is a large body of traditional Pentecostalism where the holiness tradition remains strong, mostly composed of relatively poor people, who display the classical work ethic that would have been familiar to early twentieth-century Methodists and that Weber characterised as Protestant "inner-worldly asceticism". They give good measure on biblical grounds, they feel obliged to work hard and conscientiously, they are honest and trustworthy (which makes Pentecostal women particularly sought after as domestic servants in many places). By the same token, many pastors give their services without pay and get paid work to support themselves and their families. While they trust that the Lord will never see a believer lack bread, they also are wary of riches which can as easily be a moral test or the work of the devil as a blessing from the Lord (Martin 1995).

Since the 1980s a new layer of Pentecostalism and neo-Pentecostalism has emerged which has developed the positive, world-accepting elements of the faith into a gospel of prosperity that clearly builds on the pre-Christian fusion of the spiritual, physical and material dimensions into one seamless vision of "human flourishing" in this world. I have argued elsewhere that where this neo-Pentecostalism appeared among the poor of the Latin American megacities it showed a striking elective affinity with the imperatives of so-called postmodern capitalism (B. Martin 1998). By tithing in your church, giving sacrificially large offerings, and having the faith to "name and claim" particular goods (a car or house or particular household goods) you can be assured of having your prayers answered by a miracle. This expectation of miracles tends to have the effect of bolstering the self-confidence and energising the efforts of believers who are cobbling together a living out of the service economy, often in the informal labour market. Such workers have to display certain entrepreneurial skills and styles of self-presentation that help in inventing work for themselves or marketing their services, for example making and selling goods on the street, collecting and selling waste materials, servicing the twenty-four hour economy of the megacities by, for example running a single battered taxi or running errands and making deliveries. Their faith inspires them to make their own small miracles and then give the glory to the Lord.

But this neo-Pentecostal development has made even more headway among professional and business class populations, and is particularly strong in Africa (Maxwell 1999, 2006). Pastors in particular make a display of their own prosperity in their clothes, their cars and their homes, using their own conspicuous consumption, which depends largely on the offerings of the members of the church or on the profits of Church media and other enterprises, as a demonstration of what faith can deliver. Some pastors with poorer congregations do the same. Though in our research in Chile, Brazil and Mexico, David Martin and I concluded that Pentecostal pastors constitute a "buried intelligentsia" of able and ambitious autodidacts, some neo-Pentecostal pastors also adopt many of the characteristics of the secular media celebrity whom they resemble in style if not wholly in substance. Birgit Meyer has recently suggested that this reflects the latest stage of neo-liberal capitalism in stressing not a *work* ethic but what Colin Campbell calls "the spirit of consumption" (Meyer 2009). This chimes with my own view that this variety of neo-Pentecostal prosperity cult fits with those elements of finance capitalism that make money out of taking risks, essentially by gambling, and where those outside its professional ambit see the wealth it generates not as the result of work and technical knowledge but as akin to an inexplicable miracle (B. Martin 1998). Something similar is true of the wealth that celebrities in the entertainment industry acquire, often for doing only what the young audience believes they could do just as well if the chance arose. Celebrities, too, provide models for many pastors. Again it is prosperity as unearned good fortune. None of this suggests a work ethic, but it does suggest that consumption and the status that goes with it, is desirable. Birgit Meyer has shown how prevalent the stories of riches acquired by witchcraft are in the Ghanaian churches and in the surrounding popular culture, and she and Paul Gifford are both concerned that the African economies are such that very few of the ordinary members of neo-Pentecostal/charismatic churches have a realistic chance of matching the conspicuous consumption of their pastors (Meyer 2009). Elsewhere, for example in the Swedish megachurch studied by Simon Coleman, this theology of being an economic "winner" may be more realistic where the congregation is drawn from securely based knowledge and business elites (Coleman 2000). (One charismatic/Pentecostal Church popular in Africa and favoured by the business class is called Winners Chapel.) Nevertheless, the knowledge and business class in the economies of the global South, even the apparently successful BRIC economies, will be particularly vulnerable to the effects of a global economic crisis, though we should also recall that the neo-Pentecostal prosperity gospel took off precisely during the Third World debt crisis of the 1980s.

The Pentecostal Gender Paradox and Secular Feminism

The new wave of secular feminism of the 1970s, and its analogue in the liberal wing of western Christianity, was based on an extension to women of the principles of individual autonomy and human equality that underlie the post-Enlightenment notions of agency in the West. It was adopted in principle, (though rather seldom consistently in practice), by liberation theology, but the explicitly patriarchal theology of most of the Pentecostal/charismatic movement contradicted it head on. In the 1980s and 1990s the "sexist" position of the movement was widely deplored and its theology of complementary gender roles, with the man as "head" of the woman, was regarded as reactionary and oppressive to women, not least by secular feminists.

However, once research on the new wave of Pentecostalism began to be published in the 1980s it became clear that the movement was attractive to women, who currently constitute over 60% of the membership, in spite of the paucity of female pastors and the insistence on formal patriarchy. Nancy Ammerman's studies of gender relations among conservative evangelicals in America, and even more importantly, Elisabeth Brusco's early research on Colombian evangelical and Pentecostal migrants in the USA, suggested that the social reality was subtly different from the patriarchal legitimation in ways that made sense of women's attraction to such morally conservative movements, especially in third World contexts (Ammermann 1987; Brusco 1986, 1995). Brusco was the first to show how the movement reformed the machismo culture of Latin America by domesticating men, aggressively de-legitimating the traditional double standard of sexual morality (officially disapproved of but in practice connived at by Catholic culture) and stabilising the nuclear family. Her findings were amplified in a range of studies not only in Latin America but in the southern Mediterranean, the Caribbean, Africa and Asia (e.g. Lancaster 1988, 1992; Ireland, 1991; Burdick, 1993; Smilde, 2007; Austin-Broos 1997; Cucchiari, 1988 and1991; Marshall 1993; Maxwell 1999, 2006; Soothill 2007). Diane Austin-Broos detects a powerful liturgical process at work. In purifying themselves from sexual sin, Caribbean women Pentecostals symbolically take on the whole burden of the defilement of slavery, and ritually create a new start for both sexes and the whole black community: through accepting their own abjection and their scapegoat role they free themselves and their men from an imposed taint and are thus able to inaugurate a new moral order (Austin-Broos

1997). David Lehmann has suggested that the transformation of gender relations in Pentecostalism may be more wished-for than actual, but his is a minority voice, though Jane Soothill believes the changes in the Ghanaian churches she studied are something short of "empowering" women (Lehmann 1996; Soothill 2007).

The key element is the stabilisation of the nuclear family (B. Martin 2001). Very many of the contexts in which Pentecostalism has taken off in the global South in the last few decades have been radically disruptive to family systems and gender relations—fast social and economic change, migration, war, civil war, arbitrary exercise of totalitarian state power, intermittent and sometimes prolonged breakdown of law and order, and the prevalence of AIDS and the devastations attendant on an international illicit drug trade. In addition, most parts of the global South have traditions of male domination, and, particularly in postcolonial contexts, a pattern of multiple households in which lower status women are often abandoned to fend for themselves and their children. Even where economic modernisation is occurring, women's involvement in the official labour market tends to be considerably less than in the West and their earning power markedly lower than that of men. It is not surprising that many women in such contexts prefer the stabilisation of the nuclear family to the kind of autonomy valued in the West but barely thinkable, let alone achievable, especially by poor, uneducated women in the global South. The research shows a de facto exchange between Pentecostal men and women by which men are accorded dignity and deference as official heads in the family and the church but are subject to new constraints on their freedom to indulge their appetites at the expense of women and children. Though there are constraints on women, including a dress code, the moral constraints bite far deeper on the men who are expected not only to be as chaste as they require their womenfolk to be, but to give up the drink, drugs and brawling of the life of the street and the bar through which they have customarily demonstrated their masculinity. They are reintegrated into monogamous domestic life, and though they are the official decision makers, they are required to consult those for whom they take responsibility, making marriage more of a partnership and the family a more peaceful and co-operative enterprise. In practice, women acquire more "agency", that is, control over their lives, even while accepting what are officially subordinate positions. The same pattern can be observed in church life where the male pastors have the authority of the Word, especially in preaching and teaching, but women deploy their "gifts" of prayer, prophecy and healing, as well as their role of teaching and preaching to children and other women, to acquire areas of authority and to develop a theologically legitimate alternative gender discourse without directly challenging or threatening men. Of course, many women fail to draw their menfolk with them into the movement, or remain without a male breadwinner, but they find a supportive female network in compensation. It is significant, too, that most Pentecostal churches have policies about marriage and divorce that allow people to begin again after conversion and enter a new partnership. This is easier than it might seem since so many of the marriages of the poor are "informal" without legal or church sanction.

These developments in the Pentecostal movement took place in parallel with the global movement of secular feminism whose imperatives were largely adopted by the mainstream Christian denominations and by international political and legal institutions and NGOs in the last decades of the twentieth century. Pentecostalism was not unaware of this secular development. Rather, it operated as an implicit critique of the secular/liberal movement while in practice both adopting and delivering some of its objectives to Third World women. More recent research suggests there is a degree of self-consciousness, even irony, in the way Pentecostal women relate to secular feminist programmes and sometimes incorporate parts of them. For example, in her study of Pentecostal congregations in Accra, Ghana, Jane Soothill shows how women use their spiritual independence to subvert aspects of "submission" to their husbands and to male pastors (Soothill 2007). They also incorporate western ideals of romance into their discourse of womanhood and marital relationships, subtly altering the nature of the marital bond, much as Cucchiari found among Sicilian Pentecostals in the 1980s (Cucchiari 1988, 1991). The women leaders in the Accra churches studied by Soothill, including influential women pastors, "draw on multiple models of power and authority in which 'modern' and 'traditional' patterns often co-exist and overlap" (Soothill 2007: 229). Some of the most highly educated and westernised of these female leaders operate with an "imperial" or colonial model in which the source of authority is male leadership (they are usually wives of Big Men pastors), while those appealing to models of African "authenticity" claim to follow a distinctively Ghanaian tradition of matriarchy (Soothill 2007). Of course, both of these models of authority are constructed selectively out of patchworks of practices that can be used to justify new patterns by claiming their historic authenticity. The important point, however, is that they are amalgams of the two facets of Pentecostalism, the western and the indigenous. The point has a wider significance for Pentecostal "modernity".

Pentecostal Antinomies and Secular Modernity

I have outlined three particular areas in which Pentecostalism is markedly paradoxical, poised between antinomies in respect of the individualism, agency and autonomy of the Pentecostal self; the Pentecostal economic ethic; and Pentecostal gender relations. These are not the only antinomies, paradoxes or tensions in Pentecostalism. Indeed, it could be argued that the essence of Pentecostalism lies in these contradictions held in mostly creative tension though always in danger of tipping to the one side or the other, with, as we saw in respect of economic behaviour, serious potential consequences. Many of them stem from the constitutive hybridity of the movement, the combination of European Protestantism and indigenous spirit cults which, in Allan Anderson's words results in "a globalized Christianity that has not lost touch with its local context" (Anderson 2004: 286). The tension between a literal (though, in fact, selective) reading of the Bible and the gifts of the spirit has wide ramifications. It institutes, on the one hand, the Word, which inspires literacy and a desire for education and intellectual control, but confronts it, on the other hand, with kinaesthetic bodywork and pneumatic ecstasy that releases emotion and excess. If the Word is the primary, though not exclusive, arena of men, women excel in the gifts of the spirit. If intellectualist Protestant denominations are off-putting to the illiterate poor then pneumatic spirit-filled Pentecostalism can make them feel at home, and lead them gently towards the literacy of the Word.

Pentecostalism's ready adaptation to the local and indigenous is always liable to tip into re-territorialisation through mirroring traditional ways of doing things, especially in the matter of authority structures. So you can have Big Men and Big Women pastors in Ghana and *caudillist* pastors in Chile, charges of political corruption against Pentecostal politicians in Brazil and cases of witchcraft for political advantage in Ghana, but patterns of Pentecostal voting in Central America are a little different from others of the same class. At the same time, the transnational networks of connection act as a constant corrective to definitive capitulation to the local context. And in the matter of authority, while local patterns tend to favour centralising, and sometimes corrupt, unaccountable, or clientelist systems of pastoral and bureaucratic authority, especially in the larger churches, the principle of direct inspiration from God to every believer can act both as a corrective to that authoritarianism and even as a pathway to potentially democratising processes. The very fissionability of Pentecostalism is a brake on authoritarianism in the pastorate. The tendency of Pentecostalism to expand its operations to cover every aspect of the life of its members leads to internal differentiation of roles and responsibilities, especially in the newer megachurches such as those studied by Catherine Wanner in the Ukraine and Simon Coleman in Sweden, which dilute the power of even the most charismatic pastors, who can't do everything and therefore tend to specialise in the media performances that are the church's outreach to the general public (Wanner 2007; Coleman 2000). There are choirs, educational agencies, business schools, publishing enterprises and welfare agencies, even therapy centres, as well as the church's liturgies, Bible classes and children's and youth activities to be organised, each by a team of responsible officers. These are often thoroughly modern structures by any definition of "modern", even while they also remain modes of institutionalising and perpetuating an "enchanted" view of the world.

Insofar as Pentecostalism displays points of tension with the "immanent frame" of secular modernity, very few of them are not also one side of an antinomy internal to the movement itself. It is morally rigorous (but no more morally conservative than the Catholic Church, even over homosexuality) but also world- and body-affirming. There are tensions in the intellectual and educational sphere over Darwinian evolution and biblical criticism but not over the main body of science. Indeed, the imaginative arts pose more problems for Pentecostals than the sciences, but even that is not a uniform avoidance. Music is a central aspect of Pentecostal life, of its liturgies and its evangelism, as is rhetoric: Pentecostal preaching and witnessing is an art form in itself. Pentecostalism's commitment to proselytising can cause tensions and even violence when it is practised on, say the Hindu majority in parts of India or the Muslim majority in Iran, though in most of the West Pentecostal proselytism rouses little more than indifference. Far from initiating any kind of threat or violence, Pentecostalism tends to be pacific, even pacifist. In short, it is hard to see Pentecostalism as a serious thorn in the side of civic society, or as intrinsically difficult to incorporate in democratic structures, in spite of its points of difference from western secular modernity. In fact, the consensus of the research literature is that, for the most part, Pentecostalism eases the way for its members to live in and adapt as modern subjects in a geo-politically, economically and culturally interdependent world.

PART THREE

ISLAM

CHAPTER SEVEN

TRANSNATIONAL ISLAM IN A POST-WESTPHALIAN WORLD: CONNECTEDNESS VS. SOVEREIGNTY

Armando Salvatore

Introduction

This chapter articulates a transnational issue that concerns a classic topic within sociology and social theory: the public sphere. It focuses on the metamorphosis of the public sphere out of the straitjacket represented by the modern nationalist myth of the sovereignty of *demos* that overlaid the early modern image of Leviathan. I examine here the scope of a transnational 'Islamic sphere' from the viewpoint of its long term emergence as a form of civilizational challenge to the international order centred on the European Westphalian state, which crystallized in the 17th century, around the time Thomas Hobbes theorized about Leviathan. After summarizing the historic characteristics of Islamic civilization according to Marshall Hodgson, I will first revisit the issue of the public sphere as situated mid-way between social connectedness and state sovereignty. Understanding the tension between these two normative poles in the theory of the public sphere, to be situated in the context of its emergence and metamorphosis, will finally facilitate a diagnosis of transnational Islam.

The Islamic Civilizational Sphere of Connectedness: Anything Wrong With It?

As suggested by the scholar of Islamic civilization Marshall Hodgson a few decades ago, the potential modernity intrinsic to the civilizational visions of Islam could not have germinated from the chrysalis of a fully sovereign state but rather responded to egalitarian and cosmopolitan (and to some extent populistic) presuppositions (Hodgson 1993). These premises might resemble a kind of super-*shari'a* centred on flexible visions of the 'common good.' This potential strength of a long term trajectory could be interpreted as a sublimation of the more particularistic tendencies of Islamic normativity, and therefore as a magnification of the universal power of ethical prophecy that characterizes the Irano-Semitic civilizational realm.

Therefore in the case of Islamic civilization the issue of transnationalism cannot be simply framed as a response to contemporary developments. According to Hodgson, Islamic civilization (which he called 'Islamdom') was a transstate ecumene that resulted from a hemisphere-wide, and within these limits global, expansion. The impetus supporting this expansion originated from the more narrow Irano-Semitic civilizational premises from which Islam sprung up. The strong impulse to colonize culturally, before than politically, the depths of the Afro-Euro-Asiatic macro-civilizational realm reached its peak in the so-called 'Middle Periods' (10th to 15th centuries), which Orientalists before (but also after) Hodgson have mainly depicted as a phase of decadence and lack of creativity (it is the period that roughly goes from the decline of the Abbasid caliphate to the rise of the early modern 'gunpowder empires': the Ottoman, the Safavid and the Mughal). The Middle Periods were an epoch, cut in the middle by the Mongol invasion, during which political domination was weak and fragmented. Exactly for these reasons the cultivation of the relationship between *siyasa* (which is a term of Mongol origin that means sheer 'government') and *shari'a* (meaning 'Islamic normativity' more than simply 'Islamic law') entered a phase of intense elaboration.

During this era, governance and its legitimacy were largely divorced from state power and related to the manifold vistas opened by Islam's steady growth: territorial, social, intellectual. During this era Sufi *turuq* (brotherhoods) played a key role in Islam's global expansion into the Eurasian depths, into the Subcontinent and Far South-East Asia, and into Sub-Saharan Africa. Their flexible and semi-formal model of organization and connectedness, of balancing competition, cooperation, and hierarchy quite well suited the political characteristics of the epoch. Sufism also provided new sources for a fresh wave of reflection on the integration of various dimensions of Islam: juridical like philosophical, exoteric like esoteric. The expansion of Islam enhanced the global interconnectedness of civilizational realms within the hemisphere but also contributed to a process of re-entrenchment of subregions: i.e. the perception of a 'Muslim peril' incarnate in the expansive universalism of Islam was to aid the formation of a Western-European and of an Indian identity. In this sense, the egalitarian potential of Irano-Semitic civilization reached its zenith during a period that saw the eclipse of the legitimacy of state sovereignty in Islamic terms, which Persianate court culture had long cultivated and instilled in different types of regimes. This was also the high time of the social power of the ulama, of their autonomous culture providing cohesion to intricate yet well-ordered social arrangements, kept together by an articulate yet shared Islamic idiom. As synthetically put by Hodgson, at the end of this era, at the threshold of the modern era, 'Islam promised itself, not without reason, that it would soon be absorbing the whole world' (Hodgson 1993: 24).

The spread of Islam as a transcivilizational ecumene solidified the predictability of transactions and patterns of mutuality and solidarity over long distances without the need of enduring centralized state authorities and therefore without governance, as it came to be formulated in the Leviathan's shadow, where any convergence of interest and cohesive pattern is considered accidental, inherently unstable, and therefore threatening (Bamyeh 2000: 39–40). In this perspective, the famous question asked by Bernard Lewis (2002) with regard to Islam's relation to Western modernity *what went wrong?* should be turned around into: what's wrong with Islam's patterns of premodern connectedness? Hodgson, who was only six years younger than Lewis but passed away prematurely in 1968, famously wrote: 'In the sixteenth century of our era, a visitor from Mars might well have supposed that the human world was on the verge of becoming Muslim' (Hodgson 1993: 97). Following Hodgson, one should first of all ask the question of the extent to which the (then hegemonic) Islamic proto-modernity enshrined in the power and culture of the three great empires that flourished from the 16th century onwards was not an adequate response to the ideal of societal autonomy and long distance interconnectedness that had been deployed in the Middle Periods within the Islamic transcivilizational ecumene—before it turned out to be an inadequate response to the development of a Westphalian type of modern sovereignty in Western Europe.

The main infrastructure of the Islamic sphere and of its sense of publicness was the *waqf* (Eisenstadt 2002a). The *waqf* is an endowment made with pious intentions by anybody who can afford it. It is the source of funding for a variety of services, most of them essentially public. Endowers were mainly the rulers and the political, bureaucratic and economic elites. The centrality of the *waqf* increased instead of declining in the Ottoman empire, which was the clearest case in Islamic history of a political-administrative, territorial, state-like entity entailing an organization and hierarchization of public offices in quasi-Weberian terms. In the Ottoman context, the *waqf* did not change its function because of the stronger centralization and legitimacy of political power, but became more complex and finally ubiquitous, enclosing numerous villages and several revenue-consuming institutions, such as the Friday mosques, *madrasas*, poor kitchens, etc. Even when rulers were vested with a stronger legitimacy inherent in their office, they preferred to provide basic services in the form of personal bestowal rather than through a faceless bureaucracy (Gerber 2002: 75). We see here the operation of a type of public space that has a subnational rooting and a potentially transnational projection even when it is deployed within a territorially sovereign state. Within this space, there was a continuous negotiation and interpretation of a variety of interests that the consensus of the community considered legitimate, and out of which an elaborate discourse on the common good gained ever clearer contours. In this context, Hodgson has spoken of an Islamic moral-contractualist vs. a European formal-corporative view of the social bond (Hodgson 1993: 149–58). This phenomenon foregrounds the role of flexible and often inclusive Islamic understandings of the public in historical perspective, within a variety of instances of public goods and enterprises—schools, fountains, hospitals, burial societies, as well as various configurations of public urban spaces: markets, large mosques, public squares. Most importantly, a sustained juridical as well as sociological justification of the mechanisms of provision and adjudication of public goods was a further distinctive achievement of the 'Middle Periods' (Salvatore 2007).

Based on such historical precedents, the comparative sociologists should not be obsessed with assessing the insufficient differentiation between state and religion within Islamdom, measured on the basis of Westphalian parameters, but should take the chance to analyze what was specific to the institutional crystallization of differentiated roles in the framework of specific, non-Westphalian notions of governance, more than sovereignty. Even at the peak of the power of the three modern empires, the state form remained at best in tension with the formative ideals of the *shari'a*, intended as Islamic normativity. The Persianate ideal of the 'circle of justice' appropriated by the Ottoman sultans mediated between the two levels of solidarity and governance as well as between the two components of the administration, the *ilmiyye* of the ulama and the *kalemiyye* of the scribal class. The tension erupted into an open crisis when Western states started to impinge on the Islamic world on a variety of levels, including via direct colonial domination. While state sovereignty has appeared since then as defective in several Muslim majority societies, the long term trajectory of universal sublimation of the cosmopolitan potential of Islamic formative ideals has not been completely aborted. It might be still detected in latent and less latent forms related to current and future developments of a transnational Islamic sphere.

From Leviathan through Demos to Apocalypse: How to Rehabilitate European Politics?

The world hegemonic model of sovereignty was the outcome of the peace of Westphalia of 1648, which sanctioned the principle *cuius regio eius religio*, before it became the universal standard of statehood in the era of colonialism and imperialism. The principle's goal was the outright taming of religiously motivated conflict by sanctioning the religion of the ruler in each and every state as the only legitimate one. At a deeper level, the Westphalian state reflected a polar relationship between subjects' inwardness and state publicness, which became a visible token of sovereignty. The emerging states not only gained a legal legitimacy in governing the religious field, but also operated as the collectors of the surplus of sacral meaning left uninvested by religious traditions and ungoverned by the forms of authority they used to produce. The unique character of this outcome is unmistakable.

Looking by contrast to the early modern configuration of Muslim power, it is moot to reiterate the motive of a blockage of political and economic development brought about by an all-encompassing doctrine of divine authority that withheld a full legitimization of political power and so prevented a modern state formation based on a radical differentiation from a religious field. The question that is most interesting to raise from a contemporary perspective concerns the aborted yet latent potential of a modern type of religious cosmopolitanism that might find a more congenial social and communicative environment in a post-Westphalian world. Viewed from the perspective of the much more seminal developments of the 'Middle Periods,' the three modern Muslim empires achieved a remarkable centralization of political power and also based their power on specific patterns of differentiation of state and religion. Yet such crystallizations could only partially capitalize on the creative impetus of the Middle Periods, when a cosmopolitan high culture thrived alongside a dense social autonomy balancing horizontal cooperation and solidarity with hierarchy and command: a socio-cultural pattern that facilitated a penetration of the piety-minded and populistic ethos of Islam into the practices and cultures of lower strata and the flexible expansion into new territories (Salvatore 2009).

Keeping this historical background in mind, one can revisit the issue of the public sphere from the viewpoint of its dispersion in a globalizing framework, via a dilution of its adherence to a Westphalian framework linked to the state and more specifically to the nation-state. If contemporary Islamic visions of the common good have in the colonial and post-colonial eras partly fed into imitative-competitive Westphalian, nation-state oriented projects, they have also traced a vector of escape from the Westphalian frame and have nested at subnational and transnational levels, thus bypassing or transcending the Westphalian order. In order to show the potential of this development in terms of a competitive or eccentric modernity (Salvatore 2011), I would like to suggest that this trajectory of escape reflects quite neatly some key presuppositions of Habermas' idea of the type of communicative connectedness that underlies the working of a public sphere. It is true that the public sphere is in many ways the icon of the critical power of Western intellectuals and appears therefore as closest to their Enlightenment bias. The ideal of the public sphere might therefore appear, at a superficial scrutiny, most distant from the formative ideals of Islamic civilization and in particular from those grounded in the centrality of a *shari'a* oriented legitimacy of the socio-political body. Upon a more careful obsevation, however, the public sphere is a much more ambivalent concept, which stresses the primacy of communication and connectedness as a counterweight to the sovereignty of the state and the autonomy of the citizen. For sure, sovereignty and autonomy are also considered essential presuppositions of communication and connectedness and in some Western approaches are hypostatized in the guise of a culturally and linguistically compact *demos*. Yet the re-examination of the theory of the public sphere can contribute to conceptualize present and, even more, potential future developments of what transnational Islam has to offer to an analysis of the exit of the public sphere from the Westphalian straitjacket (Salvatore 2007).

Nancy Fraser has recently argued that the notion of the public sphere developed by Habermas was primarily intended to contribute a normative theory of democratic politics in a Westphalian framework. Accordingly, this notion should be considered wanting in a context of crisis of this framework, of transnationalization of social movements and globalization of communication and politics (Fraser 2007). Yet Habermas' approach was from its inception much more ambivalent towards issues of state sovereignty. It was part of an effort to cope with modern Germany's trajectory of political authoritarianism and totalitarianism. It was the answer to another and indeed more legitimate *what went wrong?*—this time referred to the trajectory of German modernity. The answer implicit in the question, as it was faced not only by Habermas but also by a generation of scholars coming before and after him, pointed out the insufficient work done by a bourgeois intelligentsia to tame the inherently destructive potential of modern state sovereignty. The problem appeared to be a deficit in the degree of immunization of national political cultures from the destructive and self-destructive potential of what we might call the Westphalian political imagery or even mythology. Nazi Germany was the nearly apocalyptic culmination of this syndrome.

Some of the implications of this theoretical concern were put in relief by a work more or less contemporary to Habermas's *Habilitation* thesis. In his book *Critique and Crisis* the historian Reinhart Koselleck (1988 [1959]) showed how the Enlightenment intelligentsia inherited and metamorphosed an absolutist conception of sovereign power incorporated in the Leviathan. Another *Habilitation* thesis, written by a pupil of Habermas, Klaus Eder, originally combined the approaches of Habermas and Koselleck and explicitly addressed the pathogenesis of German modernity (Eder 1991). Yet it is important to understand that from the viewpoint of all these scholars the real question of what went wrong was not just a German issue. Between World-War-I and World-War-II Germany had been at the centre of an earthquake that deeply de-legitimized all myths that had justified the Westphalian framework, from Leviathan to *demos*. Germany was the epicentre of the drama of Europe and more specifically of the frustrated will to power—turned first into impotence vis-à-vis the destructiveness of the political-military machine of the state and then into a guilt complex—of European intellectuals.

Habermas contributed to this issue a type of ex-post immunization by depicting the golden age of a bourgeois public sphere, whose liberal premises are allegedly still present in the genes of the political body of European societies. Yet Habermas was, quite early, well aware of the ambivalence of this historic model and of its subsequent trajectory, as proven by the energies he invested in what is to date his main project: the theory of communicative action (Habermas, 1984 [1981]; 1987 [1981]). There were at the time some people in the closer Habermas circle who were quite worried when he published this work. There was a fear that he would overlay the neat narrative of the rise and structural transformation of the public sphere with an insidious concept and an obscure argumentation which needed a detour through several and quite distant branches of social theory. Yet this might have been, at a deeper level, the fear to erode at its fundaments the last bastion of the self-understanding of the European public intelligentsia linked to state service: the singular combination of autonomy and sovereignty enshrined in the Habermasian public sphere.

Perhaps not by chance the risky theoretical deepening of Habermas' work is not even mentioned by Fraser's critique, although the key point of this conceptual operation revolved precisely on the search for a potential escape from the strictures of the Westphalian trajectory. Especially through the traumas of the 1848 revolution and the Paris commune, the trajectory at stake had been delineated by Habermas as one of erosion of critical publicity. Instead of keeping this free floating critical power, publicity ended up permeating several sectors of society, thus becoming a sphere of spheres, a disciplining force favouring either authoritarian twists or a welfarist degeneration of participative citizenship (Habermas, 1989 [1962]: 140). With his theory of communicative action Habermas attempted to pose remedy to what, from a historical viewpoint, seemed a much too suffered trajectory without a guarantee of final redemption and decided to construct a more transhistorical argument on the virtues of communicative action, intended as a connective type of human action facilitating understandings and cooperation among individuals in a largely power free environment. Through this theoretical leap beyond the tormented history of the hard political kernel of Western Europe, the continual negotiation and reconstruction of the common good via communicative action and the ensuing dynamics of the public might therefore be also relocated outside of a Westphalian framework, where it no longer primarily depends on the patterns of solidarity and governance tied up to the modern state. By its now quite abstract, yet malleable nature, communicative action could be shifted onto a simultaneously sub-Westphalian and trans-Westphalian level.

A Transnational Islamic Public?

The myth of incorporation of the body-politic, represented by the Leviathan, is a European myth that was globalized not only via European colonialism and world hegemony, but also through the intense and tense interaction between Europe and the Ottoman empire. Contemporary globalization is nowadays too often identified with the erosion of the governance and solidarity attached to nation-states. Yet at a more careful attention globalization started with the global affirmation of the state as the hub of territorial governance. The contemporary unfolding of a globally Islamic, post-Westphalian sphere of connectedness builds on the earlier illustrated historical experiences within Islamic civilization, while it also responds to Western norms raising the banner of global governance and to the deep ambivalence of the current processes of globalization, which create new dependences and constraints but also new occasions and spaces for collective action. Although the eyes of Western observers are mainly focused on so-called global jihadism and transnational networks of migration, transnational Islam includes a myriad of forms of local, transborder and virtual interconnectedness, ranging from women networks through the development of new life style patterns to the collective mobilization for political causes identified as genuinely Islamic (from Bosnia through *al-Aqsa* to Kashmir), which capture the attention and support of otherwise non-politicized Muslim subjects and groups. Underlying all these forms is an abstract notion of a global *umma*, which superimposes social relations and political contests that are still mainly framed within nation-state frameworks and their narrow patterns of governance and solidarity.

What is interesting from this perspective is not the quite obvious fact that transnational Islam does not merely include a disciplined deliberation among key public intellectuals and the responses of their audiences—the core of Habermas' 'golden age' model of the public sphere. It also depends on those sensory dispositions and engagements that seem to blur the boundaries between ethical messages and the show business, art and entertainment. In the particular case of Islam in Europe and in the West, Muslim spokespersons nourish a rising feeling of participation in a universal *umma* by also capitalizing on critical events, from the Rushdie affair to 9/11 and the ensuing 'war on terror.' Muslim global solidarity is reconstructed in the face of a threatening Western posture also via the work of actors and thinkers often grown up in the West and who often frame Muslim causes as tied up to wider battles for global justice. Neither is Sufism, which innervated the Islamic globalism of the 'Middle Periods' also by facilitating travelers across wide distances, out of the contemporary scenario. Postcolonial labor migration has been for several decades linked up with the success of some Sufi orders in the West, which often include a grey zone of Western practitioners and sympathizers who are formally no Muslim converts.

The emerging forms of transnational Islam exalt movement and dispersion and shun institutionalization, or at least contribute to lower its threshold. They have the potential to represent a hypermodern return to the ethos of the 'Middle Periods,' where membership was often left underdefined through the myriad organizations like Sufi brotherhoods, youth chivalry bonds, guilds and tribal confederations. Such phenomenon would not represent the feared return to the dark Middle Ages of European history but to the expansive 'Middle Periods' of Islamic history. This type of transnational sphere might not fully satisfy the prerequisites of openness and autonomy entailed by the Habermasian model, but might promote horizontal ties and articulate inclusiveness in more practical ways, i.e. by accommodating and circumventing traditional types of authority without unsettling them. Precisely in this sense, it might represent a shift from the 'public' to the 'virtual.'

The Westphalian framework of the Islamic sphere was shortlived, only gaining momentum during the colonial and post-colonial eras, when political and cultural elites largely failed in incorporating wider masses in their programs of national liberation and social justice. The emerging 'public Islam' appealed largely to state-national arenas, yet relied on networks of transnational solidarity and patterns of local participation. In this sense, public Islam denotes new forms of institutionalization of modes of social governance and normative power of the Islamic traditions, which largely rely on civic associations and new media. In both these nationalist phases competition within the public sphere implied a game of staging virtue in a way that referred back the more general construction of the virtuous citizen, that the nation needed in order to free itself from the colonial oppression, since the public sphere operated (along with schools) as the arena of definition and disciplining of the nation. Yet the definition of the virtuous citizen overlapped to some or a large extent the definition of the good believer, the good Muslim, whom God created equal to any other human being (including the ruler) and empowered to perform the good for the welfare of community or nation. The normative framework associated with public Islam did not fit nation-state-building as a hand in a glove.

Overall, both the 'neo-Westphalian' and the 'non-Westphalian' streams of Islamic engagement have gained part of their strength from subsequent waves of Western-led economic globalization, which enfeebled first of all the developmental states after a brief interlude of autonomy and autarchy and thereby favoured transnational communication and networking. Islamic articulations of a global vision have been particularly well supported by the exponential growth, since the late 1990s, of satellite channels and web sites with an explicitly Islamic orientation: often associated with public intellectuals, opinion leaders and even ulama, like in the case of Yusuf al-Qaradawi (Gräf and Skovgaard-Petersen 2009). In such cases the activist level of globalization faces the fact that global media enterprises need the support of wealthy states (like those of the Gulf) or corporate investors. A hybrid character of transnational Islam, resulting from the push and pull between market constraints and participatory activism, is the emerging figure of the 'new preacher,' who in spite of lacking the formal credentials of ulama, is able to attract large audiences across national borders often via a combined use of satellite TV, internet web sites and even via cooperation with international organizations: this is the case of 'Amr Khalid, who, banned from Egypt in 2003, resettled in England and intensified his presence on a variety of Arab satellite channels, while also cooperating with the World Health Organization. Such phenomena signal a proliferation of the political signifiers legitimizing the various messages, and which the international state system is no longer able to contain within conventional views of participation, citizenship and rights. At a deeper level, the new communicators seem to both reflect and support the more general phenomenon of a growing focus on the centrality of life styles and modes of expression, which, though framed by global genres and styles, reconstruct specific identities (see e.g. the case of 'Muslim hip hop' as a culture of urban youth protest).

Conclusion

The modern Westphalian world system privileged the nation-state form of incorporation, but then favored its erosion; non-state systems of solidarity could always negotiate their alternate insertion into the system, but their chance has improved with the weakening of the iconic legitimation of the nation-state, its being an organic body (Bamyeh 2000: 109). This development deeply affects Islamic movements and groups, who seek to benefit from the positive trade-offs between nationalism and transnationalism without assimilating into standards that do not warrant cohesion for their communities and polities, nor the preservation of inherited notions of good life.

Globalization relativizes the centrality of any rooting of human communities in territorially and corporately defined communities, like the nation-states. It therefore resonates with an historic Islamic approach privileging ties between locales, groups and cities more than stressing the autonomy of cities or the sovereignty of national and corporate communities. This affinity is strengthened by the erosion of the legitimacy and by the institutional ossification of post-independence states within Muslim majority societies, which since the 1970s have been losing their capacities of effecting sociopolitical integration by acting as trustees of public welfare.

It is still uncertain whether the emerging patterns of transnational Islam present a decisive challenge to the postcolonial states in the Muslim majority world. Yet 'integrationist' tendencies seem to prevail over 'isolationist' temptations. It remains that even within the former approach the idea of an integration of Muslim interests and life styles into the wider dynamics of the world system is subordinated to the possibility of preserving the autonomy of key Islamic notions of solidarity and good life vis-à-vis the process of global standardization associated with the dissemination of consumerist models. Therefore, voicing fears of globalization in an Islamic idiom is often the expression of a will to negotiate a fair insertion into the world system in ways that avoid a civilizational sell-out. It also reflects a will to support the sub-institutional impetus of globalization processes without surrendering to rootlessness and homogenization.

Transnational Islam can be particularly interesting for its capacity to articulate an alternative, yet quite Habermasian view of connectedness and 'communicative action.' A comparable type of worldliness can be seen at work at different levels, in spite of the institutional polarizations between the historic, European, state-oriented political arenas and the more fluid transnational processes, and in spite of diverging symbolic repertoires providing ideological cohesion to conflicting articulations of the public sphere. In its present shape and future projection, transnational Islam can either magnify the weakness of the

Habermasian vision (in many ways a reflection of the frustrated will to power of European intellectuals) or remedy some of its shaky presuppositions, by drawing on the latent premises of Islamic egalitarianism and cosmopolitanism—which are far from extinguished and can be easily revitalized by post-colonial resentments and the concomitant formation of a sui generis 'will to power.'

CHAPTER EIGHT

AUTHORITARIAN PERSISTENCE AND BARRIERS TO DEMOCRACY IN THE MUSLIM MIDDLE EAST: BEYOND CULTURAL ESSENTIALISM

Mehdi P. Amineh

Introduction

The Middle East is often regarded as an 'exceptional' region where democracy and democratization struggle to take hold. In the so-called 'third wave' of democratization, new democracies emerged in all the regions of the world, with the exception of the Middle East. Of all the global regions, the Middle East has the least number of democracies (Israel and Turkey only) and shows no signs of a shift away from authoritarianism toward democratization either (see Lust-Okar 2003; Weiffen 2004; Resul 2004; Carothers & Ottaway 2005; Hinnebusch 2006; Perthes 2008).

For this reason, the Middle East has gained a lot of scholarly attention in recent years. The lack of democracy, the persistence of authoritarian regimes and the radicalization of political Islam in the region gives rise to the question, what are the causes and conditions of authoritarian persistence and the lack of democracy in the countries of the Muslim Middle East? In fact, there are extensive debates on and various approaches to the causes and conditions of democratization that provide insight into the factors that facilitate and impede democracy in the Middle East.

Samuel Huntington perceives the phenomenon of Islam as a characteristic of the inevitable "clash of civilizations," according to which conflicts and threats to global peace and security in the twenty-first century will be carried out along "civilizational fault lines." His concept of a "clash of civilizations" originated in Bernard Lewis's work *'The Roots of Muslim Rage'* (1990). Huntington brings Lewis's construct to the global level by arguing that humanity is divided among internally homogeneous civilizations. In his popularly cited article from 1993,[1] Huntington predicts that the fundamental source of conflict in the post-Cold War world will not be primarily ideological or economic, but rather that "the great divisions among humankind and the dominating source of conflict will be cultural." Moreover, whereas international conflicts of the past involved alliances of nations adhering to one political ideology against an alliance of other nations with an opposing ideology, Huntington suggests that future world conflicts will not be carried out between ideological blocks but between "civilizations." He anticipates a twenty-first century in which the revolutionary impact of globalization induces irrational violence along axes of religious values on which the "orientalism" of Lewis is based. Huntington shares Lewis's opinion that religious values are at the heart of human civilizations, and he applies it universally. "The clash of civilizations will be the battle lines of the future," he contends. His approach treats "Confucianism," "Buddhism," "Hinduism," "Islam," and "Western culture" as distinct cultural unities that are often played off against each other.

Cultural-essentialists like Huntington (see also Patai 1983; Kedourie 1992; Weiffen 2004) render the Muslim countries of the Middle East as a culturally exceptional region with strong aversions to development and democracy. In *'The Arab Mind'*,[2] Raphael Patai (Ibid.) depicts Islamic culture as primitive, violent and irrational and the outcome of backward peoples with fanatical psyches. Some scholars correlate the region's political history with Islamic culture, assuming that Oriental despotism is inherent to the political traditions of the Arab world.[3] These culturalist arguments suggest that Islam is not compatible with democracy as it rejects the notion of the nation-state and the separation of state and religion. Lewis (2002) in *'What Went Wrong? The Clash Between Islam and Modernity in the Middle East'*, for example, asserts that the region's emersion in a cultural milieu is antithetical to modernity and its various accompaniments and has crippled the Middle East on its path to democratization. Elie Kedourie (1992) in *'Democracy and Arab Political Culture'* considers Islam, Oriental despotism, clientelism, patriarchalism and patrimonialism part of the Arab culture

---

[1] It was published later as a book: *"The Clash of Civilizations and the Remaking of World Order"* (Huntington 1996)

[2] Raphael Patai's 'The Arab Mind' (1983) bursts with racist stereotypes, prejudices and Western generalizations.

[3] See, for an interesting criticism on cultural essentialist scholars: Kamrava (2007).

and incompatible with democratic values. Brigitte Weiffen (2004), in her article '*The Cultural-Economic Syndrome: Impediments to Democracy in the Middle East*' argues that prerequisites of democracy such as individualism, and separation of religion from politics are in tension with dogmas and rules of Islam. According to Weiffen (2004: 356) "Although religious doctrine itself is malleable and might after some readjustments and corrections of interpretation become fully compatible with democratic rule, so far the way the religious sources have been interpreted and the traditions prevalent in Islamic societies since the Middle Ages promote autocratic rule".

However, firstly, cultural-essentialism is guilty of homogenizing 'Islam' and culture and ignores the diversity of interpretations of Islam as a religion and as a political ideology (see Amineh 1999: Ch 12–13). Secondly, empirical research shows (Tessler 2002) that strong Islamic attachment does not discourage support for democracy. It is therefore unsurprising that democracy also emerged in many non-Arab Muslim countries. For example, Muslim countries such as Bangladesh, Mali, Niger, Senegal, Indonesia, Turkey and Albania, out of twenty-seven non-Arab countries with a Muslim-majority, are relatively experienced democracies (Diamond 2003: 10–12). Thirdly, the Mediterranean European countries have proven that clientelism and patriarchalism do not have to be unsolvable obstacles to democracy and democratic transition in the Middle East.

Ahistorical and cultural-essentialist assumptions prevent an understanding of the roots of the problems in current global- and domestic affairs of Middle Eastern states and societies.

We perceive Islam and other religions not as homogeneous but as heterogeneous and as such there is not one Islam that can explain the democratic deficit in the countries of the Middle East. Contrary to cultural-essentialism, we argue that the main fault lines are socio-economic, not geo-cultural, in nature. We assert that capitalist industrial development or long-term processes of economic, socio-political and cultural modernization, produce the structural and societal conditions that make democracy possible. Except for a few anomalies—such as Russia, Singapore, China and Iran[4]—empirical evidence shows a direct

---

[4] Iran in comparison with China, Singapore and even Turkey is less-developed and its economy is still dependent on natural resources (see Karshenas & Hakimian 2005).

correlation between successful industrial development[5] and the level of democracy (Lipset 1959; Inglehart & Welzel 2009). This does not mean that the cause-effect relationship between capitalist industrial development and democracy is linear, as there are several intermitting stages or conditions for democratization. The path from development to democracy is not a deterministic one. Democracy does not logically follow when industrial capitalist development emerges. Political elites and the nature of the civil society with related forces and organizations are among the many factors that have an impact upon the occurrence of democratization. It is therefore unsurprising that capitalist industrial development partially occurred in some states and societies of the Middle East, but that political rights and civil liberties are still denied to citizens.

This chapter consists of three sections. In the first section, we will explore the origin of political Islam and its various interpretations as result of exogenous and indigenous developments. In the second section, we will analyze the question of 'Islam', authoritarian persistence and the lack of democracy in the Middle East. In the final section, we will draw our conclusions.

European Expansion and Muslim Responses

Islam as political ideology emerged in response to the expansion of Europe and the decline of the Islamic empires (Ottoman-Turkey, Safavid-Persian, Mughal-India) in the nineteenth century. In the twentieth century post-colonial societies of the Muslim world it was a reaction to the failure of sustainable development and modernization. As a result of sequential capitalist industrial development, Western Europe turned into the dominant region in the world system. Sequential capitalist industrial development refers to the sequence in time in

---

[5] The industrialization process is an expression of complex forces that are already rooted in the more general processes of modernization (see Berg 1979). Thus, industrial development refers to a series of interrelated changes, such as urbanization, rationalization, and secularization, which sets comprehensive social processes in motion of changes in state, society and international system. In this chapter we are concerned only with the period of attempted transition to developed industrial society, with its new social groups, classes and their demands. The particular transition entails economic, social, and political questions and challenges on a scale incomparable with less far-reaching processes of change.

which some societies succeeded in making the transition to capitalist industrial development and began to close the productivity-power gap with those that initially took the lead in moving away from agricultural politics and society (Senghaas 2002; Houweling 2000: 14–15; Amineh & Houweling 2004/5; Amineh 2007). Sequential development, in other words, entailed the socio-economic and political transformation from agricultural-based (or pastoral-tribal) society into industrial-based society of, sequentially from first to last, Great Britain and its colonies (America, New Zealand, and Australia), Western Europe, Eastern Europe, and finally a number of so-called Third World countries.[6] At the same time, the era in which sequential development took place is the period of reactive state formation, nation building,[7] and efforts to close the productivity-power gaps with the developed countries. In the nineteenth century, the Islamic empires failed to imitate or adjust to the power-wealth-generating machinery of an industrial capitalist development and, as a result, were threatened with colonization, peripheralization and exclusion.

When traditional cultures are confronted with exogenous pressures and indigenous modernization, they face a structural and consequently mental transformation that makes them vulnerable to deep internal conflict. As Senghaas has shown (1988), this happened in Western Europe with the emergence of capitalism, continued through the industrial revolution, and is now a global phenomenon. Nothing has shaped the modern world more powerfully and persistently than capitalist industrial development. It destroyed old patterns of economic, political, and social life, creating conditions that spawned conflict, wars, and revolutions between the modern and the traditional.

---

[6] Capitalism as a social relation created conditions for defeudalization, industrialization, development, democracy, and increasing wealth and power in some countries, but also conditions for inequality and income polarization on a global scale. According to the UNDP 20 percent of the world's population account for 86 percent of total expenditure, while the poorest 20 percent account for 1.3 percent. Three-fifths of the 4 bn people in developing countries lack basic sanitation (Financial Times 10 September 1998, in Halliday 1999: 117).

[7] Nation state-building is a process intimately linked with the rise of industrial capitalism. The nineteenth century, from the French revolution to the Treaty of Versailles, was the age of nation state-building, particularly in Europe but extending to the New World (South and North American civil wars can be placed in this context). European regions formerly consisting of city-state federations (the Low Lands, Germany, and Italy) and Japan were also caught up in this process of nation state-building and industrialization (see Overbeek 1993).

It made dynamism and progress its cornerstones. Capitalist industrial development is necessary for the development of civil society with corresponding modern social classes and institutions and crucial for democratization to occur (Moore 1966: 418). These modern social classes benefited from capitalism, the rule of law, a free market, the rise of professionalism and meritocracy, therefore they were the main engine behind gradual reforms, and drove the process of modernization.

At the beginning of the development and modernization process, it is unclear whether traditional culture can be sustained in the context of further development. The return to tradition and the emphasis on a real or imaginary cultural heritage are obvious attempts to preserve identity, while participating in technological progress. In the long-term there is no alternative to imitation and/or innovation. The complexity of politics, society, economy, and culture is not restricted to Europe and the Western sphere, and in order to avoid "chronic conflicts" (civil war), this new complexity must be matched by complex institutional arrangements and mentalities.

Political rivalry within the different traditional forms of European culture developed into a political elimination contest, occasionally leading to victory for the stronger party, if not a consensus. In a way, this political rivalry had positive effects on the innovative potential of Europe. As Dieter Senghaas points out, "Innovation was encouraged by the subsequent development of a competitive economy [industrial capitalism], that extended over whole territories and was later to become a global phenomenon, making economic competition the quintessential logic of social systems" (Senghaas 1988: 3). It eventually led to the kind of modern society that today determines life throughout the West.

In the non-European world, the exogenous modernization pressures of colonial and imperial expansion in the nineteenth and twentieth centuries were followed by indigenous economic and societal modernization processes. Indigenous attempts at political, social, and economic modernization were responses to the pressures of marginalization and peripheralization generated by empires of the impending European-based modern world system.

Attempts at modernization in Islamic empires have taken place intermittently from the mid-nineteenth century, driven first by their political elites and then, after the break-up of empires into smaller states and regions, by the post-colonial secular nationalist elites in parts of the Muslim countries.⁸

External pressures and internal attempts at modernization resulted in different counter-reactions within societies of the Muslim Middle East from the early twentieth century onwards:

(1) a modernistic imitation of the West in order to catch up with European development and to keep the West at bay by using its own weapons: Failed modernization, accompanied by external pressures, led to further decline and additional crises of the Islamic Empires. Crises within the Persian and Ottoman empires climaxed in the early twentieth century with two modern constitutional revolutions: the Iranian Constitutional Revolution of 1906 and the Young Turk revolt of 1908. These events created a backdrop for nation state-building and state-led secular-modernization. The experiences of the Turkish Republic under Kemal Atatürk and of Iran under Reza Shah from 1925 and its continuation in 1950s–1970s by his son Mohammad Reza Shah are examples.⁹ (2) reconsideration of traditions and attempts at revitalizing them: This type of anti-modernist and anti-Western reaction can be observed all over the world, where non-European traditions are confronted with ideas of modernity. Sometimes, movements that urge a return to past values are accompanied by a moderate endeavor to reform, as in the cases of late nineteenth and early twentieth century Islamic modernist/reformist movements in the Ottoman and Persian empires (e.g. Sayyed Jamal al-Din Afghani [1838–97], Mohammad Abduh [1849–1905], Ayatollah Muhammad Hussein Na'ini [1860–1936]); (3) imitation of Western modern ordering principles and reconsideration of traditions: Important representatives of this position, which accepts industrial and technological modernization while upholding traditional values, were Ayatollah Ruhollah Khomeini (1902–1989) in Iran and a segment of his followers in the current Islamic Republic of Iran; and Hassan al-Bana (1906–1949), the founder of the Muslim Brotherhood (*al Ikhwan al-Muslimun*) in Egypt; (4) innovation as an

---

⁸ For modernization and reform in the Ottoman and Persian empires see: Findley (1980); Lewis (1969); Pamuk (1987); Islamoglu-Inan (1987); Ayubi (1995); Owen (1992); Zürcher (1993); Abrahamian (1982); Amineh (1999) and Amineh & Eisenstadt 2007.

⁹ For the experiences of modernization in twentieth century Iran and Turkey, see Amineh, M.P. ibid.; Zürcher et al. (1981); Abrahamian, ibid.

unprecedented response to an unparalleled challenge: Despite internal differences, the new generation of Islamic intellectuals, such as Iran's Abdolkarim Soroush (1945–) and Mohammad Mojtahed Shabestari, Algeria's Mohamed Arkoun (1928–), or Egypt's Nasr Hamid Abu Zeid (1943–), believes that to meet the challenges of modernity, Muslims should not seek to change their religion, but rather should reconcile their understanding of religion with changes in the outside world. This necessitates a conception of religion that accepts the predictability of change in the human understanding of religion.

Authoritarian Regimes and Development in the Muslim Middle East

In resisting marginalization and exclusion, the political elite of late-industrialized countries tried to achieve an autonomous "catch-up" development process, through industrial development or modernization from above. This involved state-led, socio-economic and political modernization by authoritarian patterns of political domination, partially supported by rival powers at the centre of the capitalist system. This can be observed as an aspect of what Antonio Gramsci (1971) called "passive revolution":[10] the development of mimetic political and economic structures in subordinated portions of the world. The consequence of a fragmented society was an amalgamation of social and political powers within the embrace of political elites. Although the ruling elite may have powerful forces on its side, it has to deal with the conflict between traditionalist and modernist forces within society (see above). Here, modern social forces are not strong enough to act independently from the state. In a number of peripheral countries, this process impeded the self-organization of domestic modern social forces and a self-regulating civil society. The modern history of late-industrialized countries and regions is rife with sequential attempts to modernize from above. Eighteenth century France and late nineteenth and early twentieth century Germany, the United States and Japan were successful in their attempts to catch up to the development process.

---

[10] According to Gramsci, passive revolution refers to sets of situations: a revolution without mass participation that is often promoted by external forces. This type of revolution often followed a "war of movement" or a rapid overthrow of a regime. A slower, more capillary or "molecular" social transformation occurs where the most progressive forces must advance their position more cautiously through a long-term "war of position" (see Gill 2003: 52–53).

In the twentieth century much of the world experienced state-led modernization *attempts*: first, those European countries which were late to industrialize (e.g. Spain, Portugal and Greece), then a portion of the Soviet bloc (Russia and Eastern Europe) and a portion of the so-called Third World such as South Korea, Taiwan, the Philippines, Malaysia, China, Singapore, Turkey Brazil, Argentina, and Chile have undergone profound socio-economic development by a variant of authoritarian state-led development. Other parts of the world, such as most of the Muslim countries of the Middle East, are experiencing what Senghaas (2002: 6), calls a "chronic development crisis", a mutually reinforcing combination of a deep economic crisis and cultural frictions, which become entrenched in the public domain, leading to militant confrontations between cultural groups within society.

Successful state-led development, or socio-economic and political modernization from above, requires the creation of a political system in which authoritarian rule is transformed through formal legal guarantees that permit the different social classes and groups to legitimately express their interests, and that places the struggle between contending political forces in a legal and constitutional framework made visible to all and guaranteeing public control over important decisions. This means that in order for modernization from above to be successful, it has to allow the business, middle, and working classes—the social forces created by modernization—to act independently of the state. In bargaining with these social forces, the state becomes less repressive and arbitrary in its actions and more rule-oriented and responsive to society's needs.

In general, since the colonial period, developing countries have been confronted with a dilemma: they could either spurn their own culture and start a "catch-up" program to become equal in wealth and power with the West, or adhere to their own culture and religious traditions while remaining materially weak (see Gellner 1992). In the years following independence, many countries resolved the dilemma of identity and development by choosing the first option. After the disintegration of the Islamic empires, the first generation of their elite to gain power, beginning in the early 1930s—Atatürk in Turkey, Reza Shah followed by his son Muhammad Reza Shah in Iran, Gamal Abd al-Nasser in late-1940s Egypt and, later, the ruling elites in Iraq, Syria, and Algeria—began an authoritarian path to modernization. Authoritarian modernization in most Muslim societies embraced "economic welfare," "democracy," "secularism," "democratic socialism," and "non-alignment" in international relations. In general, the political elites of these Islamic societies were convinced that "developmental or authoritarian states" could promote political stability and economic development and that this process would be threatened if religion, ethnicity, or caste dominated politics.

Even more importantly, some Muslim countries of the Middle East, such as Iran and Turkey in the 1970s and 1980s, succeeded in creating a relatively modern economic structure and made relatively successful attempts at modernizing a part of the state and society. In the case of Iran under the Shah, the regime was unable to ideologically legitimate the newly introduced secular institutions, create a space for political participation, and foster a basic level of economic welfare for the citizenry (see Amineh 1999: chs. 10 and 11).

Elsewhere, political strategies such as secular nationalism or Arab-socialism (e.g. Iraq, Syria, Algeria, Libya, and Egypt) were unable to create a balance between economic development and the political participation of the rising modern, urban-based populations, particularly the urban-middle class that was a product of modernization.[11] From the 1970s onwards, the unsuccessful state-led development and modernization project of the post-colonial secular state and the conflict between religious nationalism and secular nationalism were the subjects of intense dissatisfaction in vast sections of the Muslim countries of the Middle East. The failure of secular state-led development gradually led to the rise of a politicized Islam as an 'alternative' dynamic social force in the Muslim countries of the Middle East, which even developed a transnational orientation and influence. In the next section, we will discuss the various manifestations of modern Islamic political ideology.

Variations of Islam as Political Ideology

"Islam" is not a concept that should be reified but, like other religions, it has altered with time, place, social class, ethnicity, gender, individual experience as well as other variables. The variety of Islamic currents before Western imperial expansion and colonial conquest and influ-

---

[11] More recently the introduction of a "Structural Adjustment Program" of neo-liberalism (i.e. free markets and open economies) in Muslim countries led to economic inequality rather than economic development.

ence differed from that which developed afterward, and both differed from the variety that developed after independence. As a gross generalization, pre-colonial Islam stressed law and practices led by *ulama* (Islamic clergy), who normally, in general alliance with their governments, aimed at maintaining the status quo. With Western influence and expansion in the late nineteenth and early twentieth centuries, a tendency developed to reformulate Islam in terms of political ideology, using elements of modern Western philosophy, science, and technology (Keddie 1995). From this period onwards, political Islamic thinkers and movements proclaimed an Islamic order as an alternative to the European-based state and social order and its corresponding civilization.

The expansion of capitalism around the globe created not only structural globalization (e.g. modern political, economic, and cultural institutions and the enlargement of the nation state), but also social and international cultural fragmentation (Amineh 2003: 168–69). Intellectual and political counter movements to the historical episode described above created two main political ideologies and their related social forces: (1) modern/secular and (2) Islamic-oriented social forces. Secular forces advocated "constitutionalism," "secularism," and "nationalism", as three main elements for the development of a strong nation state. For Islamic-oriented forces an adaptation of Islam to the modern world was the only way to make these developments acceptable.

Since the late nineteenth and early twentieth centuries, Islam as political ideology has manifested itself in various political discourses and social movements that developed as a response to both global and national socio-political and economic conditions.

The first ideal type of modern Islamic political ideology (so-called "Salafism" or Islamic reformism/modernism) and its related movements emerged gradually in the late nineteenth century. Its main representatives were, among others, Sayyed Jamal al-Din Afghani (1838–97, Iran) Mohammad Abduh (1849–1905, Egypt), Ayatollah Muhammad Hussein Na'ini (1860–1936, Iran/Iraq), Namik Kemal (1840–1888, Ottoman/Turkey) and Sayyed Ahmad Khan (1817–1898, India).[12]

---

[12] For an interesting book on the thoughts of al-Afghani see Keddie (1968); for Abduh see Abduh (1897); Kerr (1966); for Na'ini see Na'ini (1909); Hairi (1977); for the life and ideas of Ahmad Khan see Graham & Zaituna (1975).

These new, politicized Islamic ideas emerged as a result of the Persian and Ottoman empires' structural crises, their failure to modernize and reform from above, in order to catch up to the Europeans, and their internal decline.[13] They were also the result of the direct confrontation of these empires with European expansion, mainly from Great Britain, from the mid-nineteenth century to the early twentieth century.

This new type of Islamic thinker criticized domestic rulers (the Sultan and Shah) as despots and traditional religious leaders or *ulama* as fanatics. They all shared the opinion that Islam as practiced by *ulama* was unable to resolve Muslims' material and intellectual problems. Instead they advocated, like the secular forces, independence and constitutionalism and oscillated between pan-Islamism and the nation-state as a political model, against both European colonization and their own weakening domestic empires. Ideologically, Islamic reformists, or the early variant of politicized Islam, aimed to make Islam compatible with Western scientific, economic, and political concepts, in order to bolster Islamic society against the West and adapt Islam to the needs of the modern world. This trend was centered in different geographical areas (e.g. Egypt, Turkey, India, and Persia) and among different social groups and classes—especially the urban intelligentsia and the small modern middle classes. Islamic reformists opposed Western materialism and secular culture but also believed that, only by imitating and naturalizing both Western technique and thought, strong independent politics and society could be achieved in the Islamic world. They reinterpreted early Islamic injunctions, so as to make them compatible with Western liberalism on matters such as a constitutional parliamentary system. These Islamic thinkers had a prominent role during the Western-inspired Constitutional Revolutions in both Iran (1905–06) and Turkey (1908).[14]

The second ideal type of Islamic political ideology (known as Islamism, Revivalism, Radical Islam, Fundamentalism, and Wahhabism) developed in the inter-bellum and carries on until today, despite its crisis in the late 1980s and 1990s. Its main ideological representatives were Hasan al-Banna (1906–49, Egypt), Rashid Rida (1865–1935,

---

[13] For studies on attempts at modernization in Iran under the Qajar Empire (1786–1906) see Amineh, M.P. 1999 op. cit., ch. 4; in the Ottoman Empire see Issawi (1982)

[14] On the Iranian Constitutional Revolution and the role of religious elements and the adaptation of sha'ria to the parliamentary system, see Browne (1910).

Syria), Sayyed Abdullah al-Mawdudi (1903–79, India/Pakistan), Sayyed Qutb (1906–66, Egypt), Ayatollah Ruhollah Khomeini (1902–89, Iran), Mohammad Baqir Sadr (1935–1980, Iraq), and Ali Shari'ati (1933–75, Iran).[15] Some important related organizations are the *al-Ikhwan al-Muslimun*, or the Muslim Brotherhood Organization in Egypt (founded in 1928) and later in Syria and other Arab Muslim countries; *Jama'at-I Islami* in Pakistan (1941); *Hizb ut-Tahrir al-Islami*, the Islamic Liberation Party, in Lebanon (1953); *Tanzim al-Jihad* in Egypt (1979); *Mujahideen-e Khalq* in Iran (1960s), the Supreme Council for Islamic Revolution of Ayatollah Mohammad Baqir Al Hakim (1939–2003) in Iraq; Lebanese *Hezbullah* (1970s); and Osama Bin Laden's *al-Qaeda*.[16] Islamism can be considered as a radical reaction to the intensification of Western capitalism and civilizational expansion, mainly after World War Two, and its socio-economic, political and, most importantly, cultural influences in the Islamic world.

Generally, despite great political ideological differences between these thinkers and related movements, these organizations were a response to westernized and modernized authoritarian regimes and their socio-economic and cultural modernization programs in the Islamic world. In contrast to the East Asian countries of today, modernization processes in most Muslim countries failed, or were fragmented, leading to a chronic developmental crisis that posed an obstacle to successful socio-economic development and prevented an appreciation of the pluralization of value orientations. Under these conditions a profound defensiveness developed against overdue cultural innovation, not only among the lower classes, but also among the middle classes, who tend to be much more socially mobile and thus more susceptible to frustration owing to prevailing circumstances. Only a small circle of careerists and *nouveaux riches* accepted cultural innovation. The middle classes, meanwhile, became a fertile social strata for Islamist recruitment, which led to the emergence of radical Islamic movements in the 1960s

---

[15] See Mitchell (1969); Qutb (1981); Qutb (1980); Binder (1988); Khomeini (1979); Khomeini (1981); Shari'ati (n.d); Shari'ati (1979).

[16] The notion that al-Qaeda is a transnational network of so-called Islamic terrorism operating under a single leadership and through a coordinated regime of programs, strategies, and tactics "is an illusion." But, it exists as a powerful set of ideas inspired by Qutb. For a documentary on the roots and activities of the Taliban and the organization of Osama Bin Laden and Ayman Zawahiri, see "The Power of Nightmares," presented over three nights from Tuesday 18 to Thursday 20 January, 2005 at 2320 GMT on BBC Two.

and 1970s. Such ideas and movements can by no means be reduced to a common denominator, since they are characterized by different features, whether gaining political power by using religion, rallying the religious community for reasons of solidarity, revitalizing one's own traditional values, struggling against the Western "devil," or a mixture of all these motives. These movements do not appreciate the pluralism of values but rather perceive it as the core problem, as an expression of cultural decadence and a repetition of pre-Islamic "ignorance" and moral rottenness (*jahiliya*), according to Sayyed Qutb (1906–1966). As an alternative to the capitalist pluralistic social order, this stream of political Islam and its related social forces (despite its variations) calls for the creation of a non-secular Islamic state order by radical means, namely, the use of violence.

By creating a complex political ideology and organization, Islamism has been able to compete with secular and Westernized trends and forces—especially through translating Islamic tradition and symbols into a popular language and thus securing the support of the urban-based poor social classes and groups all across Iran, Egypt, Pakistan, Lebanon, Palestine, Iraq, Afghanistan, and Algeria. The Islamic tradition has played a key role in Muslim countries, a fact that cannot be denied by even the most secular politicians. Islamism (in all its forms) and its concept of social order is based on a hostile attitude towards the globalization of some Western-based institutions, such as nation-states and, more importantly, trends towards the universalization of their secular and modern normative structures.[17] Some Islamist worldviews,

---

[17] Capitalist expansion as social relation or globalization was accompanied by the emergence and spread of the nation-state worldwide. Norms and values, however, are not included in this process as they relate to the cultural production of meaning. As Clifford Geertz (1973) rightly states, the cultural production of meaning is always local. But, if norms and values spread beyond the local cultures in which they are rooted, they could gain a universal character or become universalized. This means that the concepts of globalization and universalization refer to different domains: while globalization has a structural and institutional connotation, universalization has a normative character. The contemporary world structures have to deal with processes of a simultaneous success in universalization; there is a parallel development of structural globalization and cultural fragmentation. Cultural revival manifests itself in political strategies that call for a return to allegedly authentic, indigenous, cultural roots. In the non-Western world the nation-state is severely affected by this disharmony: while it is globalized, it lacks a necessary cultural basis. Islamists consider the nation-state as an "export from the West" and thus question its legitimacy. Islamism, therefore, can be considered as the challenging "milestone on the road" towards a de-Westernization in world politics of "total revolt against the West."

such as the ideas of Sayyed Qutb (Qutb 1980; Qutb 1981; Khomeini 1979), or the political ideology of al-Qaeda, are not compatible with European concepts of social order. Islamists—based on Sayyed Qutb's ideas and influenced by Wahhabism[18] and Deobandism[19]—target the secular state/society, because they despise its basis in popular sovereignty. Even nationalist ideologies like pan-Arabism, pan-Turkism, or pan-Iranism are perceived to be influenced by secular tendencies.

The global resurgence of a fundamentalist variant of political Islam is mainly a response to unsuccessful attempts by secular-authoritarian regimes of Muslim countries to modernize politics and society, spur socio-economic development, and create democracy.

Many scholars have focused primarily on radical Islamic thought and movements in analyzing political Islam. Many Muslims, however,

---

[18] Wahhabism was founded by the Saudi Abd al-Wahhab (1703–91) in the peripheral and tribal region of the Ottoman Empire. Highly influenced by the writings of the fourteenth century cleric Taqi al-Din Ibn Taymiyya (1263–1328), the leading voice of the Hanbali School of Islamic thought, Al-Wahhab preached that the true version of Islam could be found within the writings of the Qur'an and the Sunnah. Wahhabism takes the literal interpretation of the scriptures to an extreme and refuses any compromise with anything not strictly Islamic. The Qur'an and the Sunnah are the only true sources of Islam, and later developments are to be dismissed. Al-Wahhab rejected any interpretation of the resources. Wahhabism developed in opposition to some other schools of Islam but not to the West, with which it established links at the instigation of the Saudi Royal family. However, it remains obsessed with the influence of Western culture on Islamic culture. Wahhabists believe that nothing man-made, not even a prophet's grave, should be sacred. They did not allow oaths or vows in the name of the Prophet Muhammad or his descendants, and they dealt harshly with anyone caught using alcohol, smoking, listening to music, or playing games. Wahhabists characteristically persecuted wealthy Muslims and called for a return to a puritanical form of Islam. Today Wahhabism is the official religion of Saudi Arabia, whose rulers have become fabulously wealthy from oil. Osama Bin Laden's supporters hate the Saudi monarchy. Madrassas (religious schools) in the northwestern province of Pakistan and many Islamic institutes in Saudi Arabia and the Gulf are responsible for spreading the Wahhabist ideology, producing preachers who open mosques in the West or are called in by local communities.

[19] The Sunni Deobandi sect was founded in 1851 by Muhammad Qasim Nanautvi (d. 1880) and Rashid Ahmad Gangohi (d. 1908) in the city of Deobandi in India as an Islamic revival movement. Its aim was to unite the Muslims against British expansion and colonization of India. It later developed into an opposition movement against its own "neo-colonial" political elite. It aims at purifying Islam, excluding everything non-Islamic, rejecting all other religions, and forbidding Western-style education and any education not directly related to the Qur'an. The movement shares the Taliban's view on women and sees Pakistan's Shi'a minority as non-Muslims. It seeks a pure leader to reconstruct the Pakistani society based on the model of the Prophet Muhammad. President Musharraf, himself a Deobandi, was actually born in the city from which the school took its name. Most of the Taliban leadership attended Deobandi-influenced seminaries in Pakistan.

relate to principles that could be described as "Liberal Islam," e.g. an interpretation of Islam that acknowledges modern institutions such as democracy, pluralism, women's rights, freedom of thought, and promoting human progress. They proclaim a reformation of Islam and a more open society. These ideas can be compared to liberal movements in other cultures and religious faiths (Kurzman 1998).

These new Islamic ideas gradually increased in popularity from the late 1980s. Their main intellectual origin can be traced to Mohammad Iqbal (1875–1938, India/Pakistan),[20] Mehdi Bazargan (1907–95, Iran), Abdolkarim Soroush (1945–, Iran),[21] S.M. Zafar (1930–, Pakistan), Rachid Ghannouchi (1941–, Tunisia), Muhammad Shahrour (1938–, Syria), Chandra Muzaffar (1947–, Malaysia), Mohamed Talbi (1921–, Tunisia), Yusuf Qaradawi (1929–, Egypt/Qatar), Mohamed Arkoun (1928–, Algeria/France), Abdullahi Ahmed An-Na'im (1946–, Sudan/U.S.), Nurcholish Madjid (1939–, Indonesia), and Nasr Hamid Abu Zeid (1943–, Egypt).[22] One of the main characteristics of this current is its criticism of Islamism, Islamic radicalism and, most importantly (and at least by some of its representatives) criticism of Islam as political ideology. It tends towards pluralism and democracy, manifested in its defense of civil society, human rights, and secularism—secularism not according to the French experience of exaggerated laicism, but rather as implemented in Germany, Scandinavia, or Britain. States where the basic secular right of the freedom of religion prevails and a strict separation between state and religion does not exist could inspire modern solutions in the Islamic region.

Internationally, "liberal Islamic" ideas and related movements emerged in the age of what is called globalization. Besides its marginalizing and polarizing implications, globalization also creates opportunities for democratization in developing countries. This means the eruption of pluralism that involves the re-emergence of historical forces, manifesting themselves in different cultural expressions, such as liberal-religious movements, ethnic identities, and linguistic differences. Nationally, the liberal oriented Islamic project is both a response

---

[20] Iqbal (1930/1934); Esposito (1983).
[21] Soroush (1994); for an introductory essay to the ideas of Soroush see Cooper (1998).
[22] A list of Islamic organizations devoted to discussions or promotion of liberal themes (with links to their sites) can be found at: http://www.unc.edu/~kurzman/LiberalIslamLinks.htm.

to the authoritarian regimes in the Muslim world, and a result of the growth of civil society and its related modern social forces in some parts of these countries. This project attempts to find an answer to the chronic developmental crisis of Muslim countries and movements, particularly in the wake of Iran's failure to build a viable Islamic state and society following its 1978–79 Islamic Revolution. The social revolt in the aftermath of the 12 June 2009 elections, led by lay and religious oppositional liberal oriented Islamic forces and elites in Iran, can be considered as the climax of the structural crisis of the Islamic Republic of Iran. It is interesting to note that the current political crisis in Iran is partly a reflection of a clash between contradictory Islamic interpretations and interests, or Islam against Islam.

What does this mean for understanding the lack of democratization in Muslim countries of the Middle East? In discussing variants of political Islam, it becomes clear that Islam (as a religion) is not hindering democratization, rather it is the way Islam has been interpreted.

The history of political Islam shows that there exist and have existed many and diverse interpretations of Islam. Whereas some interpretations might indeed impede democratization, others might actually spur a democratization process in Muslim countries of the Middle East. What, then, are the causes of authoritarian persistence in this region? To find an answer to that question, we need to turn to the debate on the cause of authoritarian persistence and the failure of democratization in Muslim countries of the Middle East.

Authoritarian Persistence in the Muslim Middle East

As we have discussed above, the majority of Middle Eastern countries remain authoritarian and have shown no signs of a shift away from authoritarianism toward democratization. Cultural essentialists perceive Islam as the cause of this authoritarian persistence, but, as argued above, religion (Islam) is not the cause of the lack of democracy in Muslim countries of the Middle East, although (as we have discussed), some interpretations can definitely impede a democratization process and contribute to the persistence of authoritarian regimes.

We argue that an important cause of the lack of democracy in the Muslim Middle East is the chronic developmental crisis in some countries of the region, a consequence of multiple failed attempts at state-building, sustainable development, and democratization.

The process of capitalist industrial development is generally the precondition for democratization. It creates modern social forces demanding political influence and it produces the structural and societal conditions that make democracy possible. If, in the process of development, modern social classes and the private sector gain autonomy from the state, they can emerge as powerful actors, pushing for state accountability and political participation. The key to understanding democratic transition therefore lies in the nature of state/society-relations (that are the result of development or underdevelopment), rather than the nature of society's norms and values per se (see Kamvara 2007: Ch. 7; Amineh 2007: Ch. 1).

In fact, by looking at the processes of state-building and socio-economic development[23] and its political implications from a com-

---

[23] For efforts at capitalist industrial development from above and the role of the states and the local and international conditions in late industrializing countries and the Middle East, see the following works: Trimberger (1978); Owen (1992). In the case of the oil-producing countries of Iran, Algeria, and Nigeria, see Skocpol (1982, 265–83).In the case of selected Latin American countries' strategies towards authoritarian industrialization and possibilities of transition from authoritarianism to democracy see Malloy (1977); O'Donnell et al. (1986). In the case of successful East Asian industrialization from above, see Chang (2002). For an analysis of efforts to industrialization in Iran, see Amineh, M.P. (1999). The basic purpose of state intervention during the early stage of capitalist development is to eliminate constraints and draw on the opportunities existing in the world economy at a particular point in time. Therefore, states have played a crucial role in late development by attempting industrialization from above. The success and failure in such instances depends on specific factors operating in the global economy at a particular time, but also the historical and social forces that influence the patterns of state formation within particular spaces. The local therefore reacts back on and influences the global. Attempts at industrial development in the majority of so-called Third World countries after World War Two were characterized by import substitution industrialization (ISI) and export oriented indtrialization (EOI). ISI as an ideal type can be summarized as follows: (1) the promotion of a domestic industrial base to serve the home market; (2) a substantial reduction in the widespread dependence on importing expensive manufactured goods and exporting relatively cheap unprocessed goods, and (3) the protection of domestic industries through tariffs or import controls. EOI can be summarized as follows: (1) industrial production is oriented towards the world market, rather than the protected domestic market; (2) industrial protection takes place in the context of (more or less) free trade, so that firms must be efficient or suffer the consequences (see Kiely 1998: 83, 98). Only a small number of peripheral countries that applied the development strategy of ISI and EOI reached a relatively high level of development in the late twentieth century. Foremost among them are: Argentina, Brazil, Chile, and Mexico in Latin America, and Korea, Taiwan, Hong Kong, Singapore, China, Malaysia, and Thailand in Asia. These countries accounted for 30 percent of total exports from developing countries between 1970 and 1980. In 1990 this figure increased to 59 percent and in 1992 to 66 percent. At the same time these countries, except for Korea, received most FDI in the developing world, accounting in the period between 1981 and 1991 for 66 percent of

parative perspective in the context of global politics, we can see why most Muslim countries of the Middle East remain largely authoritarian while, for example, a number of Latin American and East Asian countries have become largely democratic.

Let us now discuss the waves of sequential democratization and the debate on authoritarian persistence and lack of democratization in the Middle East.

Certain historical periods appear more conducive than others in facilitating democracy. Samuel Huntington (1991) readily recognized this when writing his work on the *'three waves of democratization'*. Huntington shows how the historical process of global democratization is not linear but sequential; democratization appears to occur in waves (often followed by a temporal reverse course).[24]

Empirical evidence shows a direct correlation between successful development and the level of democracy, and in our notion, the global sequential process of democratization largely corresponded with the sequential capitalist industrial development discussed in the first section. We perceive sequential development as an underlying cause for the global waves of democratization; however, without implying that capitalist industrial development automatically results in democracy. Sequential industrial development only created the necessary condition for the waves of democratic transition, it was not sufficient of itself to bring about democracy, as there are additional factors that facilitate or impede the democratization process.

In order to investigate what these (additional) factors are, we must first turn to the debate on the causes of authoritarian persistence and the failure of democratization in the Muslim countries of the Middle East.

An interesting classification of approaches on the causes of democracy is offered by Eugene Mazo (2005), in his article *What Causes*

---

the average annual inflows (Nayyar 1998: 25). The most marginal areas in this process are sub-Saharan Africa, much of the GME, and many countries in Latin America, Asia, and the Pacific. For failed or fragmented modernization in Arab countries see UNDP 2003 *The Arab Human Development Report: Building a Knowledge Society*. Geneva: UNDP-Arab Fund for Economic and Social Development.

[24] Huntington tries to explain these 'waves' on the basis of the 'snowballing effect' and emulation. The former refers to the process in which the democratization of one country makes other countries follow the example set, especially after democracy proved to be successful. Emulation means that states search for respectability and international funds and as such compromise and adjust to internationally accepted forms of governance.

Democracy? Mazo categorizes the causes of democracy along a continuum from structural theories to agency theories. Structural theories emphasize the 'conditions' for democracy. Agency theories emphasize that the actions and decisions of social actors determine whether democracy emerges.

Some research traditions were characteristic for some periods in the history of the democratization debate. The historical shift from structural theories to agency theories largely reflects the debates spurred by the first, second and third waves of democratization. The first wave of democratization ignited a debate in the aftermath of World War Two. This debate converged around the preconditions of democracy (see for example Weber 1946 or Lipset 1959). The second wave of democratization created a new type of debate which focused on the qualities of the state and political institutions (see Rustow 1970; March & Olson 1984; Rose & Shin 2001). The third wave of democratization altered the democratization debate once again. This time, the emphasis was on agency, considering the deliberate actions and decisions of actors in the political system as the cause of democracy to emerge (or not to emerge) (see for example Rustow 1970; O'Donnell & Schmitter 1986; Robinson 2006). Secondly, emphasis shifted from the characteristics of the state and political system toward the characteristics of civil society (see for example: Gill 2000, Tilly 1975).

We will now address the scholars examining the causes of the failure of democratization in the Middle East in line with the above mentioned continuum[25] from structural theories to agency theories.

Many scholars have argued that it is limited economic development that is responsible for the lack of democracy in the region.[26] However,

---

[25] Important theoretical contributions to the debate on democratization are Weber (1946), Lipset (1959), Inglehart & Welzel (2009), Almond & Verba (1971), Moore (1966), Rueschemeyer et al. (1992), Huber et al. (1993), Rustow (1970), Binder (1988), March & Olson (1984), Rose & Shin (2001), O'Donnell & Schmitter (1986), Haggard & Kaufman, (1997) Collier (1999) Robinson (2006), Tilly (1975), Przeworski & Limongi, (1993), Gill (2000), Skocpol (1979), Diamond (2003), Owen IV (2006). For a depiction of the general scientific debate on democratization, see M.P. Amineh (forthcoming) *'Global System, Authoritarian State/Society—Complex and Democracy in the Middle East'*.

[26] Modernization theory argues that economic development creates the preconditions necessary for democracy: industrialization, urbanization, dissemination of education, wealth, and a healthy independent middle class; which demands political representation and accountable governance. Early Modernization Theory (i.e. Lipset 1959) argued that a certain level of development would irreversibly lead to democracy. At the same time modernization theory failed to identify the threshold beyond which

some Middle Eastern countries had income levels that elsewhere had led to democratization and as such economic growth did not seem to provide an answer to the democratic deficit. However, economic growth is not the same as development. Furthermore, as Przeworski and Limongi (1993) postulate, it is *sustainable* capitalist development that is here the key factor.[27] Oil-producer countries of the Middle East have experienced economic growth and increasing per capita income based on surplus from scarce natural resources (oil and gas) but not from sustainable development (among others a diversified sectoral economy). Capitalist industrial development partially occurred in some countries of the Middle East, even though political rights and civil liberties are still denied to citizens (Mesquita & Downs 2005).

Brigitte Weiffen (2004),[28] in her article '*The Cultural-Economic Syndrome: Impediments to Democracy in the Middle East*', raises an interesting premise: that the income derived from the sale of oil producer-countries hinders democratization in the Middle East. This 'rentierism' reduces the dependency of the state on its citizens for collecting taxes; and in fact, citizens become dependent upon the state for subsidies paid by oil revenues. This reduces demands for accountability and representation (ibid.: 359). At the same time, oil revenue diminishes the need to industrialize and modernize the economy, other than the oil sector itself (Ross 2001; Karl 1997 in Weiffen 2004: 359). The countries that are *both* oil-wealthy and have a Muslim majority are likely to be even more resistant to democracy. Weiffen asserts that Islam and rentierism mutually reinforce each other.[29]

---

democratization would occur. The case of India (democratic but economically 'undeveloped') and the existence of fascist regimes in Europe (economically developed, but non-democratic) proved that modernization theory was wrong.

[27] Additionally, modernization theory does not identify the preconditions necessary for economic development, nor external influences upon the nation-state. It also tends to pay no attention to the political change in the process of transition to democracy. Additionally, the path toward democracy surely cannot be as direct and linear as depicted; change only comes forth out of struggle.

[28] Weiffen, B. (2004: 353-375).

[29] The level of democracy is measured by combining data of the Polity IV Project database of Marshall and Jaggers (in Weiffen 2004: 365) (focusing on institutional attributes of regimes) with the scores from Freedom House (focusing on political and civil rights of citizens). Based on this empirical data, Weiffen shows that in countries where the cultural-economic syndrome is present, its negative impact on democratic performance attains strength beyond the obstruction to democracy found in countries where only one of the barriers exists (Weiffen 2004: 371). Weiffen makes a distinction between 'neither Muslim nor oil wealthy', 'predominantly Muslim without oil wealth',

Following Barrington Moore (1966), Behdad & Nomani (2009) perceived the persistence of traditional forces and the lack of large modern classes (especially a modern middle class and capitalist class independent of the state) to be the most important determinants for explaining authoritarian persistence in Iran. In *What a Revolution! Thirty years of social class reshuffling in Iran'* (ibid.) they argue that it is a weak middle class and a weak private sector, in combination with the strong presence of a traditional conservative class, that hinders democratization. In their case study, they find that a large share of the middle class is employed in the public sector. These people are supportive of the incumbent regime and resistant to change, due to their dependency on the regime. Additionally, the middle class in the private sector is not professionally organized, as labor unions are heavily suppressed by the Islamic regime (ibid.: 102). The private sector is almost non-existent, as the largest private companies were nationalized in the revolution of 1979. Additionally, most capitalist enterprises are very small and can hardly compete with the large state-controlled companies (ibid.: 101). That means that the forces that are expected to push for democracy are weak and disinclined to bring about a democratic transition.

Following Rustow (1970), some scholars have argued that national unity is a crucial condition for democracy to emerge. The lack of national unity in parts of the Middle East (caused by the colonial legacy of state borders and/or immaturity of the nation-state) is deemed catastrophic to democratization. The Middle East is characterized by a multitude of weak states and irredentism, and persistence of sub- and supra-state identities in the Middle East might impede democratization (see Hinnebusch 2006: 378).

Rather than examining the social forces dominant in society, institutionalists examine the characteristics of the state, regimes and political institutions. Following Heydemann (1999),[30] Raymond Hinnebusch

---

'oil wealthy countries without Muslim predominance' and 'predominantly Muslim and oil-wealthy' countries. Weiffen shows that oil wealthy countries and Islamic countries have, on average, lower levels of democracy. Most importantly, "the joint effect of oil wealth and Islamic cultural influence is stronger than the two single variables and has an own predictive power beyond the sum of the two effects" (2004: 366). Theoretically she argues that regimes in such countries have both a sound ideological and economic base (ibid.: 360). Even if regimes pursue economic modernization (because oil is finite) and allow steps toward democracy, fundamentalist Islam still might block that process.

[30] Heydemann, S. (1999). In: Hinnebusch (2006: 380).

(2006)[31] in his article *'Authoritarian Persistence, Democratization Theory and the Middle East: An Overview and Critique'* argues that authoritarian persistence is the result of the emergence of a new *durable* type of authoritarianism in the Middle East: Populist Authoritarianism. "PA regimes originate in the early-middle stages of development in plebeian rebellions against old oligarchies and seek to mobilize and incorporate the masses in the name of redistributive reform (a path that ended up sacrificing economic growth) (Hinnebusch 2006: 380). Because Populist Authoritarianism (as exists in Baathist Syria and the Islamic Republic of Iran) is economically very vulnerable, Middle Eastern PA regimes are forced to make a transition towards Post-Populist Authoritarianism. "[In Post-Populist authoritarianism] economic liberalization was seen as the key to regime survival as it was expected that it would make the private sector a new engine of growth to supplement the stagnating public sector and generate a new bourgeois class with a stake in the regime" (Hinnebusch 2006: 384). Post-Populist Authoritarian regimes try to create and to incorporate the private sector; by liberalizing the economy, public sector assets are passed into the hands of political elites.[32] Secondly, policies that favor the newly created state-class (such as subsidies, lower taxes, roll-back of labor rights) are introduced.[33] As a result, populism is transferred to Islamic movements. So where the state incorporates the private sector, it alienates itself from a major part of society.

Ellen Lust-Okar (2003), in her paper *'Why the Failure of Democratization? Explaining 'Middle East Exceptionalism'*, explains the democratic deficit in countries of the Middle East and North Africa by emphasizing that authoritarian regimes successfully pursued a divide and rule strategy (2003: 2; 4; 12).[34] Lust-Okar describes how in

---

[31] Hinnebusch, R. (2006) 'Authoritarian Persistence, Democratization Theory and the Middle East: An Overview and Critique', *Democratization*, 13(3): 373–395.

[32] Thus, economic liberalization does not result in a competitive capitalist class independent of and needed by the state as an engine of growth, employment or taxation, willing to promote democracy (ibid.: 385).

[33] To appease the middle class, some party pluralism, political participation and greater freedom of expression is allowed.

[34] This was done by pursuing one of four strategies: Hegemonic Islamic Inclusion (Morocco, Saudi Arabia, Oman, Qatar UAE, Bahrain), Non-Hegemonic Islamic Inclusion (Bangladesh, Senegal, Malaysia, Jordan, Kuwait, Iran), Islamic Exclusion (Algeria, Tunisia, Iraq, Syria, Egypt, Mali, Albania) and Neutralism (Lebanon) (see ibid.: 19–20; 31). It were the bitter experiences with the Iranian revolution of 1979, the wave of violence in Algeria and the failed attempt of the Egyptian regime to incorporate

different countries of the Middle East the incumbents managed to exacerbate splits *between* and *within* the secularist and Islamist opposition.[35] The incumbents instilled fear in the opposition by arguing that radical Islamist forces would take advantage of political instability to push for theocracy rather than democracy[36] and that secularists would be better off with the status quo (Lust-Okar 2003: 13).[37] Additionally, Thomas Carothers & Marina Ottaway (2005), Graham Fuller (2005) and Daniel Brumberg (2005) all argue that certain strategies of the incumbents of authoritarian regimes impede a democratic transition. Carothers & Ottaway (ibid.) argue that legislatures often promote underrepresentation, pseudo-representation and misrepresentation. Fuller (2005) asserts that authoritarian regimes in the Middle East often make use of semi-democratic techniques such as referenda (rather than wide-scale elections), a veto to electoral lists, gerrymandering, and manipulation of the mass media. Brumberg (2005) argues that one of the goals of these initiatives is to blow off political steam. Liberal autocracy (as distinguished from full autocracy) is not a step towards democracy; he contends that it actually hinders democratization demands, by appeasing and misleading democratic forces. As such it is a strategy to deal with the paradox of authoritarianism.

In *The Middle East's Democracy Deficit in Comparative Perspective* Kamrava (2007) asserts that it is the absence of a strong vibrant civil society, rather than the presence of a strong political elite, that is key to explaining authoritarian persistence in the Middle East.[38] Due to deep

---

moderate Islamists, that created this opportunity. Iran and Syria represented the failure of secular and Islamist forces to cooperate in overthrowing their authoritarian regime. In Iran, shortly after the revolution, the secularists who had fought alongside the Islamists were eliminated from power. In Syria, the opposition failed, and secularists were targeted by Islamist terrorism. Egypt learned that when moderate Islamists cooperate with secularists, radical forces (such as *al-Takfir wa-l Hijra*) would undermine this cooperation (Lust-Okar 2003: 13–14).

[35] Firstly, the secularist and Islamist opponents failed to form a coalition pressing for democratization. That means it created a split between secularist and Islamists. Secondly, because secularists often disagreed about the potential threat of cooperating with Islamist forces, a split within the secularist opposition emerged.

[36] A similar strategy has been used by South American leaders, they were supported by the middle class because they instilled fear of radical socialist revolution (Rueschemeyer et al. 1992, chapter 5).

[37] That means that Islam plays a key role in the democratic deficit in the Middle East, but in a very different way than is suggested by cultural-essentialists.

[38] The key thing about civil society organizations is that they work independently and autonomously from the state. As such they can provide a platform to the middle

suspicion and intolerance of the state toward civil society organizations on the one hand, and rentierism on the other hand,[39] resulting in unsuccessful economic development and dependency of society on the state, no significant civil society initiatives have occurred.[40] Thomas Carothers and Marina Ottaway (2005) in *'Uncharted Journey: Promoting Democracy in the Middle East'* argue that civil society[41] is far from a blessing for democratization in the Middle East, but that it can, in fact, hinder a democratic transition. Civil Society actors often have a clientelist (mutual dependent) relationship with the state. Incumbents of the regime manipulate and use civil society to strengthen and sustain their power (Carothers & Ottaway 2005).

More recently, some scholars (Resul 2004; Perthes 2008) argue that core powers in the global system are responsible for the democratic deficit in the Middle East. Ali Resul (2004) in *'Democracy and Democratization in the Middle East: Old Problem New Context'*, argues that the US hinders democratization, or is at least reticent in promoting democracy in the Middle East. According to Resul, the US has an interest in preserving Israel's security, securing the flow of oil and gas, and ensuring regional security (ibid.: 390).[42] The Arab-Israeli dispute

---

class for self-empowerment and actualization. Yet, Kamrava is keen to stress that 'by itself civil society does not lead to democratization' (Kamrava, 2007: 207).

[39] Kamrava identifies two main reasons for a weak civil society in the Middle East: (1) Due to the role, nature and agenda of the state, which manifests itself in deep suspicion, mistrust and intolerance of any manifestation of an autonomous civil society. 'Fear that any manifestation may seriously erode their ability to maintain their coercive relationship with society' (Kamrava, 2007: 208). Within the Middle East, the high levels of state coercion of civil society and political activity have left many ordinary citizens radicalized. This has resulted in the rise of extralegal, often religious, organizations, such as the Gama's Islamiyya in Egypt, the Muslim Brotherhood in Syria and the Islamic Salvation Front (FIS) in Algeria. Without the ability to practice normative political discourse, terrorism comes to be regarded as the only alternative left. (2) Unsuccessful economic development due to rentierism, resulting in a society marked by financial dependency and autocratic patronage. Within these societies, the middle class is not independent and, therefore, unable or unwilling to demand political accountability and representation.

[40] At present, within the Middle East, civil society organizations, in the form of *ulama* merchant guilds, informal religious groups and professional associations; i.e. doctors, lawyers, engineers etc., do exist. However, these groups have failed to form a coherent and powerful civil society; rather they have been largely fragmented and unable to institutionalize or to create powerful mutually reinforcing relationships.

[41] Carothers & Ottaway define civil society as a form of political activity in which the citizenry join groups and associations that enable them to participate politically.

[42] Hinnebusch (2006: 391) has similarly argued that democracy is not in the interest of the US. "Access to oil and the security of Israel have trumped the desire for human rights and democracy in US policy toward the region".

has enabled Middle Eastern regimes to legitimize the militarization of the country, with the effect that domestically, societal forces face a strong state coercive apparatus. To ensure regional security and the flow of oil and gas, authoritarian but friendly regimes in the region have been the primary strategic choice of the US (ibid. 390). The fear for instability and Islamic regimes make the US (and to a lesser extent the EU) reticent of promoting democracy in the region.

By contrast, Volker Perthes in his article '*Is the Arab World Immune to Democracy*', perceives the US as *promoting* democratization in the region rather than hindering it. According to Perthes (2008),[43] there is yet another interesting international factor that impedes democratization in the Middle East: that it is not the prominence of the US in the international system, but the resurrection of China and Russia, which is to a great extent responsible for the absence of democratization in the region. Perthes (ibid.: 152) asserts that "the lesson for the political elite in other world regions, especially in the Middle East, is that one need not be democratic, but merely economically open and liberal, to achieve success". Thus, Perthes argues that the US foreign policy model of democracy promotion faces a crisis. The US' export of democracy[44] by meddling in the domestic affairs of authoritarian countries is increasingly met with skepticism, suspicion and resistance by countries of the Middle East. Western countries have become skeptical as well. Perthes (ibid.: 154) argues that it was primarily the recent victory of Hamas in the Palestinian elections of 2006 that marked the end of enthusiasm for the promotion of democracy.[45]

Some International Relations scholars argue that globalization is causing a transfer of power away from the state, towards transnational corporations and international regimes. As a result, regimes end up responsive to global rather than domestic demands. "As citizens are de-mobilized, international networks of political elites listen to each other increasingly and ignore their citizens" (Huntington 1968: 389,

---

[43] Perthes argues that the West faces a dilemma. Western government must cooperate with authoritarian regimes, given their mutual economic and security-policy interest; to have access to oil, to fight terrorism and to find a solution to the Israel-Palestinian conflict. At the same time, by cooperating with authoritarian regimes, bad governance increases, political participation of the citizens diminishes and as such creates a breeding ground for extremist or terrorist groups.

[44] Explicitly stated in Bush's freedom campaign and part of the 'war on terror'.

[45] Furthermore, in our opinion, the difficulties with establishing democracy in Afghanistan and Iraq, has strengthened the hands-off approach to the Middle East.

see Castells 2004, chapter 5). Jerry Harris (2009) in *'Statist Globalization in China, Russia and the Gulf States'* argues that, with the emergence of a globalized economy, a coalition of Transnational Capitalist Classes (TCC) of the authoritarian regimes of the Gulf States, China and Russia has emerged.[46]

The emerging state class in the authoritarian states of the Middle East, which controls the energy resources, increasingly started to associate itself with the state classes in other authoritarian regimes, on a global level. Local state classes, that have become part of the TCC, are primarily preoccupied with creating a global system of production, finance, competition and accumulation, as they believe that national development can only occur through integration in the global capitalist economy (Harris 2009: 154; 159). "[As such] blocs emerge where developing countries that share a desire for a bigger role in the global economy find solidarity in their opposition of Western dominance. But at the same time they are part of an integrated chain of finance, production and accumulation in which, overall class interests are merged with the West" (ibid.: 160). That means a shared transnational class consciousness emerges, which reduces attachment to the nation-state.[47] This reduced attachment makes the state class in Middle Eastern countries less vulnerable to democratic pressures. At the same time, the inclusion of state classes of developing countries into the TCC puts pressure on further global capitalist integration, as some Western leaders and intellectuals fear that these authoritarian regimes will succeed in the development of the domestic economy, depriving the West of its dominant position in the neoliberal global order.

Having reviewed the debate on authoritarian persistence and the failure of democratization in the Muslim countries of the Middle East, the question is how to move forward, both when researching the causes

---

[46] Harris does not make a distinction between the nature of the capitalist class in liberal democratic and non-democratic states and societies. Contrary to the capitalist class in advanced capitalist liberal democratic states, the ruling and governing classes of authoritarian states are identical and form a state-class, The sovereign state, rather than the self regulating market ultimately determines the status of social actors and the constraints for their capacity to articulate their interests in the transnational space dominated by advanced industrialized actors [Amineh 1999: Ch. I].

[47] 'They have business relationships to maintain, investments to protect, houses in the south of France, children at school in Britain... people with international business interests tend not be nationalists. They cannot afford to be' (Rachman 2008: 11 in Harris 2009: 154). As such, this capitalist class does not necessarily promote democratization at home.

of authoritarianism or democracy in particular countries in the region and when aiming to improve the current state of theoretical debate on democracy and democratic transition.

Democratization and the persistence of authoritarian regimes should be understood as the outcome of a complex interaction between both structural- and agency factors. Thus, by focusing only on structural conditions (that means ignoring the role of political actors or focusing only on the choices, actions and decisions of elite- and civil society actors, without taking into account structural constraints or opportunities), we will hardly increase our understanding of democratization. Actors do not function in a vacuum. Structural factors influence democratization indirectly, by shaping the preferences, ideas and possibilities for action of political agents. At the same time, these very actors can change the structure under which they act. None of the structural (culture, economy, or global system) and agency factors (preferences, political actors, decision making, and actions) should ultimately be understood to act in exclusivity of the others. We need, then, to overcome the agency-structure dualism, ahistorical structuralism and determinism on one side and ahistoric voluntarism on the other side, in the analysis of both global and national politics, and provide an ontological and epistemological foundation for a non-deterministic yet structurally grounded explanation of democracy and democratic transition. Agency and structures, ideas and material conditions are bound together and mutually influence each other. This means research should focus on the *interplay* between both agency and structures.[48]

The key to understanding democratic transition lies in the nature of state/society-relations rather than the nature of society's norms, values,

---

[48] Cox observed that structures are prior to individuals, but they are created by collective human action: "[Structures] are already present in the world into which individuals are born [...]. But structures are not in any deeper sense prior to the human drama itself, as some structuralist theory would have us believe." [...] "Structures are not 'givens' [data], they are 'made' [constructions]-made by collective human action and transformable by collective human action" (Cox 1987: 395). This means a rejection of structural determinism, and a confirmation that the social world is formed by collective human action. "A nation, a class, a religion, are not real physical objects, yet they give real form to the human situation. They are ideas shared in the subjectivity of innumerable individuals who are real physical beings. In being so shared, these ideas constitute the social world of these same individuals. They attain objectivity in the structures that circumscribe human action. These structures are as much a part of the material existence of people as the food they eat and the clothes they wear" (ibid.: 395).

or religions, as argued by cultural essentialists. The nature and causes of the democratic transition are shaped and influenced by the changing powers of the various actors who are directly or indirectly involved in it. To better understand the underlying causes of the failure of sustainable development, democratization and authoritarian persistence in the majority of the Muslim countries of the Middle East and its neighbors, therefore, we must examine the strength and institutional capability of these regimes and the ways in which they interact with and rule over society. A strong independent middle class, with related civil society organizations and a strong autonomous private sector are forces expected to be crucial for democratization to occur (see Kamrava 2007).

One of the main reasons for the failure of democratization and persistence of authoritarian regimes in a great number of Muslim countries is weak or fragmented civil society with related forces and institutions. Let us look, then, at the foundations of the survival of the authoritarian oil producer countries of Iran, Saudi Arabia and, to a lesser extent, Syria. The power structures of these countries rests on two pillars: the repressive apparatus and the state-controlled key economic sectors, mainly the oil industries. State revenues from these sectors make ruling political elites independent of society. The revenues are exchanged for support and furthermore administered to buy political loyalty and obedience. The regime can distribute these revenues in combination with repression to essentially pacify the majority of the populace. At the same time, independent state revenues create possibilities for the ruling class to finance the repressive apparatus in order to suppress oppositional forces and maintain order, In this way, independent and non-taxed revenues enable the regime to persist. Via state-controlled socio-economic and political institutions, the regimes are able to control and mobilize people from above through a clientelistic mode of rule. Additionally, powerful international allies—in the case of Iran, China and Russia and in the case of Saudi Arabia the United States—provide them with diplomatic, military and economic support.

It is interesting to look at the chances of social revolt for democratization in Iran after the elections of June 12th 2009. Like Turkey, Iran did achieve a 'substantial' level of capitalist industrial development[49]

---

[49] The creation of democracy and democratic social order is not impossible but difficult without a strong civil society with related forces and institutions. What are the modern forces of a civil society? The working, middle, and business classes. These

in the twentieth century. However, unlike Turkey, the effort toward democracy and democratization collapsed. So, although Iran experienced substantial development and the creation of new social forces under authoritarian rule, Iran has, contrary to many other countries, not experienced a democratization process. Whereas some nation states had sufficient capacity to promote development and eventually democratization—such as some Latin American and East Asian states—why has Iran so far failed to democratize, despite a substantial level of development? To replace an authoritarian regime with democracy a strong civil society is necessary. For a strong civil society, two key interconnected factors need to occur: (1) The rise of a strong and modern independent middle class with related organizations (2) the emerging of an autonomous private sector. With regard to these two factors, two bottlenecks come to the fore in Iran. A large part of the middle classes is not detached from the public sector. Because the oil and gas sector does not provide enough jobs, unemployment is skyrocketing. A huge public sector, state-owned companies and *bonyads* (Islamic foundations) created jobs for a great portion of the middle classes. As such, the middle class is dependent upon the state, and refrains from making demands for radical change. The same goes for the private sector, the size of which is almost negligible. Most companies are state-owned or controlled by Islamic *bonyads*. These foundations are estimated to account for 35 percent of Iran's gross national product (GNP) and the state-controlled oil sector accounts for 27 percent of the GDP (Rakel 2006). Previous policies of Ahmadinejad to

---

modern social forces are a product of state-led development and a successful industrial revolution. The making of a sustainable democracy in a fragmented society (e.g. a society only partially developed) without the appearance of these forces is impossible. The tragic experiences of the failed democratization in Iran in the early twentieth century after the Constitutional Revolution of 1905 and second efforts during the "democratic" government of Prime Minister Mohammad Mossadeq (1951–53)—among others—were caused by a fragmented civil society and limited urban middle and business classes. It was not surprising that a third attempt at making a democratic state/society after the Iranian Islamic revolution of 1979 also failed. This was mainly the result of extremely uneven socio-economic and cultural development. Although the political elites of the Shah's regime were able to rapidly modernize and industrialize a portion of the society, economy, and culture, they were not able to integrate the traditional economic sector, concentrated in the bazaar with its traditional alliance with the *ulama* as representatives of traditional culture. These factors, accompanied by unsuccessful land reforms, the emigration of peasants to urban areas, and an inability to integrate upcoming modern social forces into the political process, created socio-economic and cultural imbalances that polarized society.

privatize state-owned companies resulted in passing private property into the hands of the dominant political and recently military elite and institutions. The private sector, parallel and autonomous of the government, therefore, is not strong enough to build up the required economic power and organizational and financial strength of its own, for it to defect from an allegiance with the autocratic regime. However, it is at that point that democratization efforts are likely to advance exponentially.

Conclusion

The Middle East is often regarded as an 'exceptional' region where democracy and democratization struggle to take hold. The lack of democracy, the persistence of authoritarian regimes and the radicalization of political Islam in the region give rise to the question, what are the causes and conditions of authoritarian persistence and the lack of democracy in the countries of the Muslim Middle East? We have argued that ahistorical and cultural-essentialist assumptions prevent an understanding of the roots of the problems in current global and domestic affairs of Middle Eastern states and societies. Contrary to cultural-essentialism, we argue that the main political fault lines are socio-economic, not geo-cultural, in nature.

We assert that capitalist industrial development, or long term processes of economic, socio-political and cultural modernization, produce the structural and societal conditions that make democracy possible. If, in the process of development, modern social classes and the private sector gain autonomy from the state, they can emerge as powerful actors, pushing for state accountability and political participation. However, capitalist industrial development is not sufficient in itself to bring about democracy, as there are additional factors that facilitate or impede the democratization process.

As a result of capitalist industrial development, Western Europe turned into the dominant region in the world system. In the non-European world, the exogenous modernization pressures of colonial and imperial expansion in the nineteenth and twentieth centuries were followed by indigenous economic and societal modernization processes. Attempts at modernization in Islamic empires in response to European expansion, have taken place intermittently from the mid-nineteenth century, driven first by their political elites and then, after the break-up of empires into smaller states and regions, by the post-colonial secular nationalist elites in parts of the Muslim countries. When traditional cultures are confronted with exogenous pressures and indigenous modernization, they face a structural and consequently mental transformation that makes them vulnerable to deep internal conflict. Islam as political ideology emerged in the context of this process.

Fundamentalist Islamic interpretations and social movements gradually developed in the inter-bellum and continue today. In response to the failure of development and modernization in most countries of the Muslim Middle East, this stream of political Islam and its related social forces (despite its variations) call for the creation of a non-secular Islamic state and societal order by radical means, in some cases by the use of force. Many Muslims, however, relate to principles that could be described as "Liberal Islam," an interpretation of Islam that acknowledges modern institutions such as democracy, pluralism, women's rights, freedom of thought, and promoting human rights. These new Islamic ideas gradually increased in popularity from the late 1980s. One of the main characteristics of these ideas and social movements is their criticism of Islamism, Islamic radicalism, and to some extent, of Islam as political ideology. It is interesting to note that the current political crisis in Iran, in the aftermath of the 12 June 2009, is partly a reflection of a clash between Islamic Fundamentalism and "Liberal" interpretations of political Islam with related social forces: "Islam against Islam".

What does the above mean for understanding the lack of democratization in Muslim countries of the Middle East? In discussing varieties of political Islam, it becomes clear that Islam (as a religion) is not hindering democratization, but that it is the way Islam has been interpreted. Whereas some interpretations might indeed impede democratization, others might actually spur a democratization process in Muslim countries of the Middle East.

The key to understanding democratic transition lies in the nature of state/society-relations rather than the nature of society's norms, values, or religions, as argued by cultural essentialists. The nature and causes of the democratic transition are shaped and influenced by the changing powers of the various actors who are directly or indirectly involved in it. To better understand the underlying causes of the failure of sustainable development, democratization and authoritarian persistence in the majority of the Muslim countries of the Middle East and its neighbours, therefore, we must examine the strength and institutional capability of these regimes and the ways in which they interact with and rule over society. A strong independent middle class, with related civil society organizations and a strong autonomous private sector are forces expected to be crucial for democratization to occur. Capitalist industrial development is necessary for the development of civil society with corresponding modern social classes and institutions

We argue that an important cause of the lack of democracy in most countries of the Muslim Middle East is a chronic developmental crisis, a mutually reinforcing combination of a deep economic crisis and cultural frictions, which become entrenched in the public domain, leading to militant confrontations between cultural groups within society. This crisis is the consequence of multiple failed attempts at state-building, sustainable development, and democratization.

CHAPTER NINE

FROM MEDINA TO THE *UMMAH*: MUSLIM GLOBALIZATION IN HISTORICAL AND CONTEMPORARY PERSPECTIVE

Peter Mandaville

There has been a strong cosmopolitan impulse in Islam since the time of the Prophet Muhammad in the seventh century CE, and in this sense the history of Muslim transnationalism significantly predates the formal establishment of nation-states. The Qur'an itself resonates with an injunction for Muslims to engage in international relations: "We...made you into nations and tribes, that ye may know each other."[1] The word quickly became social reality in the early years of the Muslim community as Islam rapidly spread from its humble origins in the western Arabian oasis town of Medina to encompass virtually the entire modern Middle East, Persia, Northern Africa and even Spain. Over successive centuries, the religion would spread to West and East Africa, into the Indian subcontinent and across to the archipelagoes of Southeast Asia. The notion of the *ummah*—or world community of believers—was hence central to the theory and practice of Islam from the very beginning.

Globalization Then

Yet we should not overestimate the extent to which this concept expressed the existence of a meaningful polity. Political factionalism emerged in the Muslim community soon after Muhammad's death, and although the *ummah* enjoyed a period of unity under the first four caliphs ("successors" to the Prophet), dynastic politics soon took over as the lands under Muslim control grew by several orders of magnitude. Although the caliphate system existed formally until its abolition in the wake of World War I, it had ceased to name a single political

---

[1] The Holy Qur'an 49:13.

community by about the tenth century CE. Despite this political fragmentation, transnationalism flourished in the medieval Islamic world. Where formal relations between Muslim polities were often characterized by competition, rivalry and external invasion, there emerged at the level of the *social* a rich cosmopolitan milieu of merchants, travelers and itinerant scholars. Janet Abu-Lughod (1989) for example, speaks of the maritime trading routes linking the Middle East and Asia in the 14th century as a nascent "world system." The Indian and Mediterranean oceans became the conduits of a vibrant commercial and intellectual exchange over the next centuries (Risso 1995, Fawaz et al. 2001). With African Sindis in India, Hadhrami merchants from Yemen in the Malay peninsula, and Dagestani scholars in Arabia, Muslim multiculturalism emerged as something of a norm along the littoral coasts of these vast seas. While mercantile life was certainly the driving animus behind much of this transnationalism, the emergence of centers of excellence in Islamic education—in Cairo, Bukhara, and Samarkand, for example—also gave rise to a strong measure of scholarly nomadism. And as the pilgrimage (*hajj*) that constitutes one of the religion's five pillars came to encompass more and more cultures, annual gatherings in Mecca served as a living testimony to the diversity of the *ummah* (Eickelman and Piscatori 1990).

Muslim transnationalism assumed a more overtly political character again from the mid-18th century when, in response to European colonialism, various Muslim scholars and political activists began a program of religious reformism to modernize Islam—one which also sought, in part, to bridge differences between various Muslim sects and factions. Beginning with Shah Wali Ullah in India, this trend reached its zenith in the mid-19th century in the figure of Jamal ad-Din al-Afghani. Al-Afghani, a Persian who, throughout his active career, spent periods of time in Egypt, France, and Turkey, best embodies the political dimension of this reformist impulse. Afghani observed that by the mid-1800s, Muslims the world over were subject to colonial occupation by various European countries. His solution was to combine a drive to modernize Islam so as to render it compatible with the norms of Western science and technology with an appeal to a new transnational political activism among Muslims—a program that became known as 'Pan-Islam' (Landau 1990). Although Afghani managed to exert certain influence over the Ottoman Sultan Abdul-Hamid II, he eventually fell out of favor and the nationalist agenda associated with the Young Turks and later Mustapha Kemal came to dominate the political agendas of most Muslim countries. It is worth noting, however, that key Islamic reformers and Islamist ideologues such as Muhammad Abduh (a disciple of Afghani's) and Abul Ala Mawdudi in Pakistan were both, at times, associated with Pan-Islamic ideals. With the secular nationalism of Kemal on the rise, the political dimension of Muslim transnationalism once again entered a period of decline. No event better captures this crisis than Kemal's abolition of the caliphate in 1924. The future of Muslim polity became a subject of heated debate among scholars and various attempts to regenerate global forums for Muslim discourse in the interwar years, such as the various Muslim Congresses failed to take hold (Kramer 1986). Over the next thirty years, political Islam became increasingly oriented along national lines, with individual movements—such as the Muslim Brotherhood founded in Egypt in 1928—seeking to counter the secularizing trends associated with modern nationalism in the Middle East. The loss of Jerusalem in the Six Day War of 1967, the oil crisis of 1974, and Iran's Islamic Revolution in 1979 prompted short periods of renewed Islamic globalism in the political arena. Nevertheless, and despite the efforts of Muslim intergovernmental groups such as the Organization of the Islamic Conference (OIC) founded in 1969, national interests have tended to predominate over geopolitical unity in relations between Muslim nations (Husain 2002).

Despite the relative lack of co-operative transnational politics at the official, inter-state level in the Muslim world, the last twenty years has witnessed an enormous growth in the number and density of transnational linkages between sociopolitical movements operating at the sub-state level. It would be useful to note here that one of the earliest and still enduring—indeed, thriving—forms of cosmopolitan Islam today centers around the Sufi, or mystical, tradition. Variants of mysticism, often highly personal and emotive in nature, emerged within a century of Muhammad's death. They soon assumed a more institutional character in the form of orders or brotherhoods (*tariqa*), usually organized around a central figure (*shaykh*) who gave his name to the order. So popular and widespread a phenomenon was Sufism that it came to form a strong component of the urban social order by the Middle Ages—so much so, in fact, that even orthodox scholars opposed to Sufism on theological grounds (such as the 14th century jurist Ibn Taymiyya—often portrayed as the historical ideologue for many contemporary radical groups) found it socially expedient to affiliate themselves with one or more *tariqas*. These brotherhoods would often assume a transnational aspect when itinerant followers established subsidiary branches in new countries. One source, for example, lists nearly two hundred *tariqas*, many of which are regional or country branches affiliated with a central *shaykh*. Despite a relative decline during the 19th and early 20th centuries in the face of the orthodox revivalism and reformism discussed above, Sufism has enjoyed a huge resurgence in recent years, most notably among Muslim communities located in Europe and North America. Various waves of postcolonial migration and transnational labour patterns associated with increased globalization have transplanted various Sufi orders and their followers. The Naqshbandi order associated with the Cyprus-based Shaykh Nazim, for example, can claim a widespread global following. A rich set of transnational practices linking Britain and Pakistan has emerged around the cult of the living saint Zindapir (Werbner 2003). It is these more fluid, personal and informal linkages, then, which provide an entry point for our discussion of contemporary transnational Islam.

Contemporary Muslim Transnationalism

The scope and diversity of the Muslim world, combined with technologies of communication and travel, produce enormous variety in transnational Islam today. This runs the gamut from highly personalized intellectual linkages between individuals to the high diplomacy of Islamic intergovernmentalism in the OIC and state-sponsored *da'wa* (propagation) work via organs such as the Muslim World League (Schulze 1990). When it comes to the question of transnational social movements, there is not only a wide range to contend with, but considerable variation in scale, style and activities. I have already, for example, touched on several of the many Sufi connections, a topic to which we will return below. There is also the enormous Tablighi Jama'at, a largely apolitical faith movement whose annual conferences in India represent the second largest world gathering of Muslims after the *hajj*. Transnational *da'wa* work is one of the group's main pursuits, and to this end it maintains coordination centers in South Asia, the Middle East, Europe and North America (Masud 2000). Other groups are oriented towards social and economic development issues. Women Living Under Muslim Law and Sisters in Islam, for example, style themselves as international solidarity networks. Muslim Aid is a leading global charity. Far flung diasporas, such as the Chinese Uygar community in Turkey, organize on behalf of Muslim kin and brethren back home, while new media spaces provide opportunities for discussion and debate among Muslim youth groups in the European Union and the United States.

The political forms of contemporary Muslim transnationalism—i.e. those groups whose explicit aim is the establishment of Islamic polities—are somewhat less diverse. Olivier Roy identifies two major networks that encompass many of the nationally-oriented Islamist movements: one affiliated with the Muslim Brotherhood and covering mainly the Arab Middle East (e.g. Hamas in Palestine, al-Nahda in Tunisia) and the other organized around Pakistan's Jama'at-i Islami (Roy 1994). It is more accurate, however, to say that these connections, for the most part, are ones of general ideological orientation and intellectual lineage rather than active, coordinated sponsorship and coordination. It should be emphasized again that these groups are, in the main, working locally to establish Islamic states in particular countries. Their political aspirations do not extend beyond national borders, and in this sense I do not regard them as transnational movements *per se*. However, this does not mean that certain of these groups—particularly the more radical among them—are not at times implicated in the agendas and activities of actors whose political aspirations extend beyond the state. Ayman al-Zuwaihari, for example, former leader of Egypt's Islamic Jihad, effectively folded his group into Usama bin Laden's al-Qaeda in the mid-1990s.

When we move on to deal with transnational political movements whose goals are more global in scope, things become murkier still. Linkages and relationships can be highly informal, nebulous, and rather ad-hoc, contributing to an aura of uncertainty in terms of scale and breadth of geographic coverage. That groups such as al-Qaeda appear to be constituted by cells on virtually every continent, cropping up in such seemingly unlikely locales as South America, lends their activities an aura of omnipresence. By cultivating this image of ubiquity, and through a careful public relations strategy involving media soundbites that seemingly appear out of the ether, a relatively small number of such groups have managed to catapult themselves to the forefront of transnational Islam in the eyes of the public. The spectacle of September 11 and a series of smaller scale attacks in multiple countries have all served to reinforce this image in recent months. Since these events, the public discourse on transnational Islam has focused almost exclusively on shadowy militant networks, many of which are described as inspired by Wahhabism, a hardline variant of Islam usually seen to emanate from Saudi Arabia. In the wake of the October, 2002 bombing in Bali, Indonesia, for example, significant attention focused on Jemaah Islamiah, described as an al-Qaeda "franchise" seeking to establish a Pan-Islamic state encompassing Muslims in Indonesia, Malaysia, the Philippines, Singapore and Brunei. Much is made of the fact that ideologues associated with the group had studied Islam in Saudi Arabia or other parts of the Middle East, supposedly confirming a transnational Wahhabi agenda.

Globalization Now

But endless terrorism conjecture gets us little way in terms of understanding the mainstream Muslim experience of today's globalizing processes. Insofar as changing migration patterns have been one of the hallmark characteristics of more recent globalizations, there is a sense in which the most innovative and dynamic aspects of contemporary Muslim transnationalism are to be found not in those non-Western regions usually considered to be the heartlands of the Muslim world, but rather within the new Muslim communities of Europe itself. The notion of a 'European Islam' has gained considerable currency in recent years, both within academic literature and in popular discourse. Although there exists considerable debate as to the features, parameters, and significance of this concept, it can undoubtedly be said that the term expresses the fact that Islam has well and truly found a place for itself within the social fabric of contemporary European society. No longer perceived solely as an 'immigrant religion,' Islam is claiming the right not only to exist but also to flourish within the boundaries of the European Union. Social responsibility, active participation, and civic engagement are the hallmark characteristics of an emerging trend amongst Europe's younger generation of Muslims. A telling episode occurred in the summer of 1994 when a group of ulama meeting at Château-Chinon in France issued a fatwa in which they declared that Europe could no longer be considered *dar al-harb* ("the domain of war"), a term from classical Islamic political thought used to designate lands outside the political and moral pale of Islam. While these scholars were not willing to go so far as to label Europe *dar al-Islam* (which would have implied the presence of a Muslim sovereign and the pre-eminence of shari'a law), they nevertheless realized that Islam had, over the past two decades, become exceedingly prevalent in Europe. The continent became in their eyes, and in a subsequent text, *dar al-ahd*, the domain of treaty or unity, implying a form of community based on the coexistence of multiple faith systems, mutual respect and sociopolitical responsibility.

This 'upgrading' of Europe serves as a telling metaphor for the changing relationship between Islam and the region right across the board. Just as Muslims are increasingly a part of Europe, so does Europe find its way into Muslim discourse more and more today. The aim of this chapter will be to examine some of the ways in which this relationship is evolving within the realm of Muslim intellectual activity—particularly among those thinkers and activists concerned with the politics of Islamic identity and community in Europe. The picture that emerges from this analysis is one of a rich symbiosis between Islamic and European culture, and one that flies in the face of popular accounts of a "clash of civilizations" or of some inherently adversarial contest (Huntington 1996). Like others, I note that the true nature of the complex relationship between Islam and the West cannot be understood by working with static, stultified categories in which particular innate features are assigned to each side. Instead, an appreciation of this relationship can only accrue through taking account of the great diversity inherent within both traditions and the fact that in an increasingly globalized and transnational world, no cultural forms—or their concomitant intellectual output—can be understood as a preformed given.

I will begin by providing some background context that will help throw light on the changes that Islam in Europe has undergone over the past twenty years. This section will look mainly at intergenerational issues—in short, the Islam of the parents versus the Islam of their children. I will also identify a shift in the locus of leadership within Muslim communities in Europe, particularly as regards the question of where the current generation is looking to find new ideas and new interpretations of Islam that are compatible with the day to day realities of European life. It will be suggested that young Muslims have been turning increasingly to thinkers and writers who stress a more universalist (or, at the very least, a 'polycentric') interpretation of the religion. This is in contrast to the Islam of their parents which they often see as rather 'local' and tainted with sectarian or ethnic overtones. This new breed of Muslim intellectual rejects the dogmatism of centuries old fiqh and seeks instead to engage critically with the traditions and prescriptions of Islam. Furthermore, these figures—highly attuned to the specific issues faced by Muslims in Europe—offer a creative vision that urges their audience to view life in the West as a condition that allows Islam to flourish. Active participation and engagement with the wider society is also encouraged. I will illustrate these trends by highlighting new organizations and practices among European Muslims, by examining some of the innovative ideas espoused by European-based Muslim intellectuals, and by considering the role played by new media and information technologies in the creation of a Muslim public sphere in Europe. It will be part of my argument that these new discourses do not exist in isolation within particular national contexts, or within some kind of 'fortress Europe.' Rather, they are premised upon an engagement with ideas circulating in the wider Muslim world—hence the focus on what I term 'transnational religious discourse.' The new formulations produced within Europe, I will argue, also have the potential to travel beyond the confines of that continent, sparking and animating new debates within the transnational *ummah*. Before I begin, however, I should like to make some comments which will help to clarify the parameters of my discussion and also to hopefully elucidate my usage of the term 'critical,' which appears throughout the text.

Estimates of the number of Muslims in Europe vary considerably, ranging generally between 9 and 15 million. Even with the lower figure, however, Muslims still constitute the largest religious minority group on the continent. The problem here is only partly one of counting methodology (and the question of whether Muslims in Eastern Europe are included), it is also a problem of definition: who is a Muslim? There are some authors who use the category 'cultural Muslim,' meaning anyone of an ethno-national background for which Islam is the majority religion (i.e. Pakistani, Bangladeshi, most Arab countries) (See Dassetto 1993). This is a problematic labeling, however, because a great number of those Muslims in Europe who fall into this category do not see Islam as a large part of their lives. They may self-identify as Muslims, but not necessarily as a primary component of their identities. They may observe prescribed religious practices up to a point, but without holding too much to be at stake in so doing. Further scrutiny of this question reveals, however, that it is also far too simple to just posit two distinct categories such as 'active Muslim' and 'passive Muslim.' To do so is to ignore the element of contingency that is so vital to understanding how and under what circumstances particular identities (or components of identity) become activated. For example, I have had numerous Muslims of South Asian background in the UK tell me that until the Rushdie Affair of 1987, they had never thought of Islam as a large part of their lives. Then suddenly they found themselves marching in front of a rally, demanding that a book be burned. In short, Islam, for them, became politicized for a time. It is thus, in part, the impossibility of sharply defining and categorizing Muslims in Europe that I want to stress here.

That said, the analysis I will offer in this chapter, does confine itself to a particular group. When I speak of 'Muslims in Europe' or 'European Muslims' I am referring not just to anyone who is nominally Muslim by virtue of his or her ethno-national heritage, but rather to those who consider Islam and its regular practice to be a primary (although, as we will see, not necessarily exclusive) component of their self-identity. Suffice it to say that these are Muslims for whom Islam is clearly in the fore- rather than the back-ground. This is a point that may strike some as verging on the tautological, but which I think, helps to gesture towards differentiation between various modalities of Islam in Europe. The borders of this group are, however, quite porous and I would never try to make immutable claims about its characteristics. What I am trying to capture is simply the common sense value of the following analogy: Most Europeans are "Christian." We would not, however, try to say something about the changing nature of European *Christianity* by talking about all nominally Christian Europeans. Likewise with Islam. I have therefore focused my research on individuals, organizations, and practices with a primary, overt and consistent affiliation to Islam.

Something that features heavily in this chapter is the development of what I have termed a 'critical Islam' in Europe. By using this concept I am trying to describe a particular orientation towards Islam, one that is marked, above all, by a willingness to historicize the normative import of particular religious interpretations. It recognizes that to some extent Islam is, and always has been (at least since the death of the Prophet), a product of its times. In other words, the meaning of Islam and its bearing on various social realities is not fixed once and for all. Even the elaboration of *fiqh*, according to critical Islam, must be viewed as conditioned by the social and political contingencies of the social and cultural settings in which it occurred. The substance of this approach derives from the critical theory of the

Frankfurt School—Theodor Adorno, Max Horkheimer, Herbert Marcuse, Walter Benjamin et al.—and more recently, Jürgen Habermas. In a seminal essay, Horkheimer made a distinction between 'traditional and critical theories (Horkheimer 1972).' The former (uncritical) kind of theory takes the world as it finds it and assumes the presence of certain underlying and eternal structures that determine all social outcomes. Change is possible only insofar as one learns to work within this given framework. Critical theory, on the other hand, comes to the world with a rather different perspective. It starts by asking questions about how what is accepted as 'natural' came to be so. What are the historical conditions—and particularly the relations of power—which gave rise to the present world? Furthermore, it wonders, what deficiencies have accrued from this process, and how might things need to be changed so that people can emancipate themselves from the resulting constraints? How might human agency be brought to bear upon what, in the eyes of traditional theory, seem to be structurally determined circumstances?

When we look at Islam in the context of Horkheimer's distinction, it becomes a way to describe the difference between those Muslims wedded to the dogma of, for example, jurisprudential frameworks developed in the medieval period ('traditional theory') and those Muslims who believe that Islam can only be made relevant to the present day by understanding these seemingly rigid doctrines as products of history, culture and power. The point is not that these understandings of Islam are necessarily correct (or incorrect), but rather that we recognize the fact that certain people at specific times possessed the capacity to define their particular interpretations of Islam as somehow universal and valid for all time—thereby giving rise to what we might call 'Islamic hegemonies.' The way forward, according to critical Islam, would therefore be to reinterpret and reformulate the central precepts of the religion such that they speak directly to the contingencies of today rather than by receiving them through the distorting filters of history. A cognate to Horkheimer (albeit not an exact one) can be found in the work of the late Pakistani intellectual Fazlur Rahman. Rahman made a distinction between 'normative' and 'historical' variants of Islam. By normative Islam he meant the originary, 'pure' essence of the religion as it is found in the Qur'an, the sunna of the Prophet and the period of the rightly-guided caliphs. Once we move beyond these confines, according to Rahman, we enter the age of historical Islam, in which this initial purity is lost and the religion becomes subject to the subjective and distorting influence of countless middlemen (e.g. *ulama, fuqaha, qadis*, etc.). Regardless of how well-intentioned and wise they might have been, Rahman points out, such intercessions inevitably produced over time more and more distance between the subject and the object of submission (*Islam*). His claim is that these sources "were misconstrued by Muslim scholars in medieval times, made into rigid and inflexible guides—for all time, as it were—and not recognised as the products of their own times and circumstances" (Fazlur Rahman 1982: 36–39). Other Muslim intellectuals who represent this trend towards a critical Islam include figures such as Mohammed Arkoun, Hasan Hanafi, and Fatima Mernissi. Each has, in their particular areas of speciality—philosophy, theology (*kalam*), and gender discourse, respectively—demonstrated how it is that prevailing conventional wisdoms in the Muslim world have been established throughout history (see Arkoun 1984, Hanafi 1987, Mernissi 1991).

It should be noted that despite all of its emphasis on the intersubjective nature of Islamic meaning and on modes of textual production, critical Islam is not to be mistaken for a postmodern orientation towards Islam. A postmodern Islam would embrace what Jean-François Lyotard (1985) termed a "skepticism towards metanarratives." That is, it would mean the rejection of any grounds upon which to found something like a pure and authentic Islam. Rahman's normative Islam would simply not be possible under such premises. Critical Islam, however, does not go this far. It believes that there is such a thing as an eternal core to the religion, albeit one that Muslims have lost over time. Just as the critical theory of Adorno and Horkheimer ultimately had faith in the emancipatory potential of the Enlightenment—believing only that the project of modernity had gone astray—so does critical Islam yearn for the (re)achievement of the spirit embodied in the early Medinan period. The challenge, in other words, is to triumph over history—or, rather, to achieve Islam despite history.

The New Terrain of European Islam

The 1980s was a period of intense socioeconomic and religious marginalization for Muslims in Europe. The South Asian immigrant populations of northern England, for example, bore the brunt of Thatcherism in the form of widespread unemployment and widespread

'Islamophobia.' Arabs in France and Turkish *Gastarbeiter* in Germany found themselves subject to the same exclusionary and discriminatory policies and attitudes as their religious kin in the United Kingdom. In other countries on the continent, Islam had yet to even establish a meaningful foothold. Something like the Rushdie Affair—and particularly the reaction of Muslims in British cities like Bradford—therefore has to be understood as the culmination of many years of social disenfranchisement rather than as an isolated 'religious' incident.

By the early 1990s, however, substantial changes in the position of Muslims in Europe were afoot. The worst of Islamophobia was over and there had been some appreciable change in the socioeconomic fortunes of Muslim communities. Also very important was the emergence of a critical mass of young second generation Muslims—born and raised in Europe—ready and eager to enter mainstream society. The numbers certainly boded well for this new generation. Britons of Pakistani and Bangladeshi descent, for example, almost doubled between 1981 and 1991, with nearly half now born in the UK. The age dispersion compared with white Britain is also striking. There are almost twice as many under-16s among the South Asian population and only two percent of this community is over the age of 65 compared to 17 percent among the majority population (Lewis 1994: 15). The rising profile of European Islam in the 1990s is undoubtedly linked in part to this population and the Muslims who constitute the subject of this study draw largely from these communities.

When we examine these demographic changes in the context of Islam, a number of issues arise, the most important of which, perhaps, is a clear generational divide between the older and younger generations of Muslims in Europe. Understandings of Islam and the role it should play in one's life have been subject to considerable change within the current generation of European Muslims. For their parents, growing up in Turkey, Pakistan or another Muslim majority country, Islam was a taken for granted part of the social fabric. But this 'Islam of the parents' does not necessarily translate into an idiom that speaks to the problems faced by Muslims in Europe today. Some writers note that when Islam is 'transplanted' in this way, "the religious symbols and rituals...are no longer affirmed by the social environment, and they thus lose [the] character of certainty which underpinned their existence [in the homeland]" (Thomä-Venske 1988). It is not only the social environment that fails to affirm them, but also the next generation that fails to find much of use in this Islam—and subsequently rejects it. Often, much of what the older generation regards as Islam is dismissed by the younger generation as somehow tainted, or as a vestige of cultural practices specific to their parents' countries of origin. This leads many young Muslims to complain that the older generation tries to live according to the religious norms of their homeland, as if Europe were a place where Muslims were still in the majority: "They would talk about Pakistani politics constantly, but never neighbourhood politics...they didn't want to engage with non-Muslims."[2] This question of isolationism features heavily in intergenerational debates. With most (particularly young) European Muslims seeking actively today to establish a place for themselves within mainstream society, the apparent ambivalence of their parents in this regard is an intense source of frustration. When it comes to religion, watching their parents' generation engage in endless and seemingly petty debates about proper prayer technique did nothing but alienate younger Muslims. They sought an Islam that had something to say, for example, about how to properly live one's life in a non-Muslim society and the particular challenges posed by those circumstances. Mosque leaderships tended to be of the older generation and, again, representative of 'local' Islam from the villages of South Asia or Morocco. Many religious organizations would even 'import' imams and ulama from Pakistan and Bangladesh for regular tours of duty—thus preventing the first generation of Muslim immigrants from ever leaving the relative safety of Islam in the homeland. Young Muslims often found this religious leadership to be particularly dogmatic and narrow minded in its conception of Islam. Questions and challenges in the mosque were not tolerated and the younger generation grew increasingly frustrated at being told, when querying certain aspects of Islam, "that's just the way it is."

It is therefore not surprising to find that the current generation of young Muslims in Europe has turned away from traditional sources of religious leadership and authority in droves. Most of this younger generation is highly educated and looking for a more sophisticated idiom of Islam. Intellectually they have tended towards major figures within the wider Muslim world such as, initially, Abu Ala Mawdudi and Fazlur Rahman, and today writers such as Abdolkarim Soroush

---

[2] Dr. Ataullah Siddiqui, Research Fellow, The Islamic Foundation, Personal Interview, Leicester, 29 July 1998.

in Iran, Malaysia's Chandra Muzaffar, and the Qatari-based Sheikh Yusuf al-Qaradawi. Simultaneously, there has emerged within Europe itself a new breed of Muslim leadership, often focused around highly-educated, relatively young, professionals and intellectuals. Some of the key figures here are Ziauddin Sardar, Yusuf Islam (formerly the pop singer Cat Stevens), Shabbir Akhtar, and Tariq Ramadan—whose ideas will be considered further below. Akhtar captures the spirit of this movement (and that of the aforementioned critical Islam) well when he writes:

> *Within the House of Islam, there is today a great need for self-criticism and introspection, both severely jeopardized by the emphasis on a purely external, somewhat legalistic, religious observance. Muslims are religiously obliged to turn inward, to take the full measure of their own failings, and try to effect social and personal criticism...(Shabbir Akhtar 1990: 213)*

Others emphasise the importance of language and the development of a new Muslim public sphere—that is, the emergence of new spaces in which such critical discouse can emerge and flourish. The importance of European Muslim publications such as *Q-News* and *The Muslim News* is therefore difficult to underestimate. *Q-News* "appeals to young, educated Muslims, impatient of sectarianism, and is able through an international language, English, to access innovative and relevant Islamic scholarship (Lewis 1994: 207)". This publication has also contributed enormously towards the availability of sound religious advice through a column by the late Dr. Syed Mutawalli ad-Darsh, a prominent religious scholar in the UK. Every fortnight in *Q-News* he would dispense fatwas on a vast range of issues relevant to Islam in European society. Many of these were answers to questions sent in by readers on marriage, sexuality and contraception—topics which young Muslims often find it difficult to raise with traditional ulama in local mosques. Several Islamic publishing houses in the UK have also dedicated themselves to producing useful materials for English-speaking Muslims. Among them are Ta-Ha in London and the publishing wing of the Islamic Foundation in Leicester. This latter organization generates a wide range of literature ranging from children's books to treatises on Islamic economics and the translated works of Mawdudi. "We try to make our coverage general," they say, "so that any tendency or movement—and especially their children—can use our books."[3]

---

[3] Siddiqui, *op. cit.*

The Foundation also produces literature targeted at non-Muslims in public life in order to help them understand the beliefs and circumstances of their Muslim employees, colleagues, constituents and pupils (see for example McDermott and Manazir 1993). There is also, of course, the role of new media such as satellite television and, especially, the Internet to be considered (see Mandaville 2000). Innovative websites emphasize progressive, critical Islamic scholarship.[4] Sites focusing on the work of intellectuals popular with young Muslims—such as Yusuf al-Qaradawi and Abdolkarim Soroush—also play a prominent role.

In the eyes of young Muslims today, then, the traditional scripturalism (or "village Islam") of their parents holds little hope of providing resources for the issues and problems they face in their day-to-day lives. What is needed, rather, is a renewal and reinterpretation of Islam—a reorientation towards religion—such that it speaks directly to the circumstances of being Muslim in 21st century Europe.

Defining a European Islam for the 21st Century

Now that we understand some of the forces which have animated recent shifts in Islamic discourse, the characteristics that define these trends can be examined in greater detail. As I have argued already, a new type of Islamic intellectual—often born and educated in the West—is leading the current generation of Muslims to feel comfortable taking Islam into their own hands. They emphasize the importance of reading Islamic texts directly and making moral choices based on responsible and rational interpretations of these texts. This is, in essence, a rejection of dogmatism. Shabbir Akhtar, for example, quotes Qur'anic verses forbidding compulsion in religion and advising tolerance for other views both within and outside one's faith. For him these suggest "a specifically Islamic manifesto on freedom of conscience and conviction (Akhtar 1990: 76–7)." For such thinkers, one's life in the West is therefore not to be lamented, but rather embraced, offering as it does the opportunity to reread, reassess and reassert the validity of Qur'anic teachings in new contexts. Indeed, there are a number of Muslim leaders who firmly believe that it is from Muslim contexts

---

[4] Http://www.islam21.net/

in Europe and the West that the most radical and innovative Islamic thought will emerge in the years to come.

Many contemporary thinkers, as we have seen, urge Muslims to go back to the sources and read for themselves, exercising good judgement and trusting in their own personal opinions as to what the texts mean for Islam today. I have mentioned Fazlur Rahman's injunction to young Muslims to read the Qur'an and the Hadith without relying on bulky, medieval commentaries. Another prominent religious scholar, writing specifically for Muslims in Europe, urges them to undertake "a fresh study of the Qur'an... not with the aid of commentaries but with the depths of your hearts and minds... You should read it as if it were not an old scripture but one sent down for the present age, or, rather, *one that is being revealed to you directly* (Nadwi 1983: 190, emphasis added)." Young Muslims are hence told to imagine themselves as Muhammad (a controversial proposition in itself), and to recognise that just as the Qur'an was revealed to the Prophet in a particular setting in space and time, so must its message be made to speak to the particular circumstances of European life.

There are indications that this call is being heeded. Young Muslims in Europe often meet informally to discuss the Qur'an and other textual sources, attempting to read them anew and, as much as possible, without the prejudice. There is hence no reluctance to delve into the usul al-fiqh, but there has been a shift as to what Muslims are hoping to find there. Gone is the obsession with the minutiae of prayer technique and obscure points of medieval theology. The emphasis now is on wider questions concerning Muslim identity and relations between Muslims and non-Muslims. Also less frequent now are intersectarian debates on points of *fiqh*. Some organisations, such as Young Muslims UK, have decided that one's choice of *madhhab* or school of jurisprudence should be a personal choice. Where the organisation needs to take a public position on some issue, however, this is decided by a process of *shura* (consultation) in which the views of various *madhahib* are considered. Again, this ethos reflects the style of education which many young Muslims have received in Europe. Reflection and comparison allows them to develop their own responses to the situations and challenges of life in the West; through this activity they are able to develop an emancipatory theology that "allow[s] them to be European without breaking with Islam (Nielsen 1995: 115)." This amounts to a strong reassertion of the principle and practice of *ijtihad* ("independent judgement") as a competence possessed by all Muslims and not simply an elite (albeit socially detached) group of ulama. For many young Muslims today, a legitimate promulgator of ijtihad is anyone who speaks to a particular question or cause with morality, perspicacity and insight. Pnina Werbner notes that:

> For a younger generation of [Muslims] growing up in Britain the definition of what is Islam is and means may well come to be increasingly constituted not by the Qur'an and Hadith, but by dissenting political ideologies... [Their] texts increasingly fuse a multicultural rhetoric of anti-racism and equal opportunity with the ethical edicts of the Qur'an and Hadith (Werbner 1996: 115).

Young Muslims today are hence seeking to create an Islam that addresses the social predicaments and daily experience of life in the modern West. They have neither the time nor the patience for South Asian idioms of Islam from the last century. "The need now," as Phillip Lewis (1994: 208) notes, "is for a critical and constructive exchange both within these traditions and with the majority society."

It is in the cosmopolitan, transnational spaces of cities such as London and Paris that this kind of exchange is taking place. The myriad range of cultures, ideas and people that flow through these spaces produce rich sites of hybridised intellectual activity. The syncretisms and interminglings which inhabit these cities also constitute the cutting edge of critical Islam. It is also an environment in which such conversations can be openly expressed, assessed and reformulated. In this sense, Western transnational space stands in stark contrast to the situation in many Muslim majority states where the capacity to stray publicly from officially-prescribed doctrine is heavily circumscribed. Western settings, on the other hand, offer the aspiring Muslim intellectual the opportunity both to *express and encounter* alternative readings of Islam. It is no wonder, therefore, that so many exiled and diasporic Muslim activist-intellectuals choose to make their homes in the global city (Lebor 1997: 101–2).

A hallmark dimension of the new Islamic discourse in Europe has been a tendency towards greater activism and community participation. The refiguring of Europe as *dar al-ahd*, as mentioned above, is a case in point. If we elaborate this shift in thinking we can see that it has some very serious implications for the ways in which Muslims in Europe orient themselves towards the societies in which they live. Jacques Waardenburg (1996), for example, identifies a new approach to Islam in Europe that emphasises active participation in community life rather than the political introversion which characterised the early phase of Muslim immigration and settlement. Muslims will no longer hold themselves apart from the majority society but *will* continue to distinguish themselves from it by offering an alternative order, Islam. These claims are to be seen as addressed both to state authorities and to society at large. "The Muslim community in Europe is searching for a new idiom through which to express itself," says Ataullah Siddiqui (1998: 27). This takes the form of seeking a recognised and legitimate place in the public sphere. Muslims are hence constructing new frameworks for the practice of Islamic politics in response to the conditions of life in Europe. But what do these new strategies imply? My claim is that this shift represents a new Muslim disposition towards political engagement and the emergence of an 'active' approach to the theory and practice of Muslim politics in the public sphere. This is also therefore a new discourse on Muslim participation in and responsibility towards the wider communities in which they live. Some, such as Jocelyn Cesari, argue that through the new associations formed by young Muslims in France, "a new form of citizenship is emerging, [one that refers] to concrete and local action rather than voting or involvement with political parties. In other words, the *civil* dimension seems to be more relevant than the *civic* one (Cesari 1997: 8, emphasis added)".

Many young Muslims would hence like to see Islam as something political, but not necessarily as political Islam or Islamism in the sense of seeking to establish Islamic states. Hence we find a number of leading European Muslim intellectuals today seeking to reassert aspects of Islamic thought in a contemporary light. The work of Tariq Ramadan, a professor of philosophy in Switzerland and one of the chief architects of the new Islamic discourse in Europe, provides an excellent example. In his *To Be A European Muslim*, which can be read as a veritable manifesto for the discursive changes highlighted in this chapter, he cites the importance of the concept of *maslaha* ('public interest'), seeking to reframe it as an important feature of contemporary Muslim life in Europe (Ramadan 1999: 76–82). The great medieval theologian al-Ghazali, he points out, once claimed that maslaha was the end goal of the entire body of shari'a (holy law); Ramadan believes this to be particularly true today. For him an emphasis on public interest means that the question of whether a particular practice should or should not be permitted needs to be viewed in the context of its effect on the entire community rather than simply deemed *halal* ('permissible') or *haram* ('forbidden') by a religious scholar with his nose buried in a collection of *fatwas* (religious edicts) from the tenth century. Dilwar Hussain, a fan of Ramadan whose own research probes the concept of maslaha even further, points out that:

> This is particularly relevant in cases where Muslims are living in circumstances where the situations of daily life are not covered clearly by the texts. When things are changing so quickly, one cannot rely exclusively on analogical deduction (qiyas) from the sources... [so] we need to find a new flexibility when dealing with juridical issues.[5]

Hussain wants to invert the classical conception of maslaha, which sees it primarily as a means of 'closing the gates to evil,' and to concentrate instead on maslaha refigured as 'opening the gates to good.' "For example," he says, "there's the idea of opening the gates for women to play a role in public life, and seeing this as a 'good,' as something in the public interest: maslaha." The question arises, however, as to who holds the keys to these gates—a question to which Hussain, as yet, has no answer. "That's what I'm working on now," he says optimistically.

We see, then, the importance that Muslims today are laying on rereading and reassessing the textual sources of Islam in new contexts. In this regard there would appear to be some degree of discursive overlap between these new intellectual trends and recent thinking in Western critical theory. The notion of dialogue and some form of 'communicative action,' to invoke Habermas, within a public sphere seem to be intrinsic to both (Habermas 1990, 1992). Figures such as Tariq Ramadan, in his creative readings of the core sources of Islamic law, have begun the crucial process of developing the contours of what might be termed a 'minority fiqh'—a jurisprudence designed specifically for Muslims living in situations in which they are not a majority. The challenge, as Ramadan sees it, is to find a way for Muslims to protect and uphold the core of their religion without resorting to isolationism; to participate, in other words, without diluting the essential meanings of Islam:

> To promote and to advocate such involvement in Western society is not only new, and thus difficult, but also necessitates that some sensitive legal questions and ethical issues receive, as essential prerequisites, clear answers and solutions (Ramadan 1999: 102).

---

[5] Dilwar Hussain, Research Fellow, The Islamic Foundation, Personal Interview, Leicester, July 29, 1998.

Many Muslims in Europe who are part of this new trend see themselves as playing a role within the context of a much wider picture. "Muslims in [Europe] have a more global sense of Islam," says one religious scholar, "and hence have a role to play in the globalisation of the religion."[6] This means articulating Islam in terms that non-Muslims can understand, but it also means re-articulating Islam to *Muslims* in new ways. Europe offers a unique context for the reassessment of theories, beliefs and traditions, while increased transnationalism enables these new reformulations to travel the world. For some Muslims this offers the greatest hope for rethinking Islam:

> *In order to have ijtihad [independent judgement] you need freedom of thought. This does not exist in most Muslim countries. We Muslims in the West should debate, discuss and disseminate our ideas because this will encourage Muslims living where there is not freedom to do the same, or at least to make use of the materials and ideas we produce.*[7]

We can meaningfully speak today about the existence of something like a global infrastructure for the maintenance, reproduction and dissemination of Islam. This 'regime' possesses no central authority and there is very little co-ordination between its various constituitive elements. Nevertheless, through a diverse range of organisations, technologies and transnational structures the contours of a transnational Islam are beginning to emerge. We have already mentioned several of the institutions which collectively form this infrastructure such as the 'imported imams' who travel back and forth between homeland and diaspora, and the myriad regional and transregional Muslim organisations which mediate daily life for believers in a variety of national settings. In addition, we can also point to the role played by various communication and information technologies, from the circulation of a wide range of English-language books on Islam via international publishing networks linking Washington, D.C. with Durban, London and Karachi (Metcaff 1996: xv) to cyberspace debates between Muslims of various madhahib in Internet chat rooms. Diaspora television programmes also play a role in the sustenance of long distance communal and religious ties (see Naficy 1993), as does the live broadcast

---

[6] Abdul Kadir Barkatulla, Director, Islamic Computing Centre, Personal Interview, London, July 21, 1998.
[7] Siddiqui, Interview.

of the hajj in many Muslim countries and its subsequent availability on video (Metcaff 1996: 11).

Migratory spaces and global cities also figure heavily in transnational Islam. With their culturally diverse and highly mobile populations, cities such as London are important nodal points for networks of discourse and often serve as factories for the production and import/export of (reformulated) ideology. As Adam Lebor puts it, "Positioned halfway between the Middle East and the United States, with easy access to Europe, the hub of a global communications network, and with decade-old ties to Islam's lands, London has now become the *de facto* intellectual capital of the Middle East (Lebor 1997: 101–2)." It is therefore not surprising that a number of transnational movements have chosen to set up premises in Europe. We can think here of the Tablighi Jama'at, an eminently transnational organization, whose European 'headquarters' in Dewsbury co-ordinates and despatches da'wa tours to destinations all around the world. Travelling Tablighis of many ethno-national backgrounds—although mainly from the Indian subcontinent—pass through the centre on their way to Canada, Malaysia, South Africa and Mecca. As Barbara Metcalf observes, "Dewsbury…looks more like Pakistan than does Pakistan itself. Tabligh participants are part of this contemporary world of movement even as they transcend cultural pluralism by the re-lived Medina their actions create (Metcaff 1994: 721)." In the time of transnationalism the Muslims of Europe thus have a vital role to play. It is they who are in the best position to engage in a sustained critical renewal of their religion; and it is also they who can most effectively speak this new Islam to the world.

Conclusion

The discourses of European Muslims have contributed significantly to the development of a critical Islam. I have argued that Europe provides an environment conducive to the development of alternative Muslim discourses. As we have seen above, Muslims encounter a diverse range of interpretations and schools of thought in Europe today. As dialogue is enabled between these different tendencies, the differences between them are often attenuated. Most crucially, however, this is a space in which no particular conception of Islam is *negated*. Difference is negotiated, rather than eradicated.

That is not to say, however, that European Islam is a model of sectarian harmony. There are always forces working to narrow the boundaries of political community and seeking to monopolize the discourse of political legitimacy. There still exist within Europe certain tendencies seeking to promulgate a conception of Islam that impels radical political activism. What does one do, for example, about more extreme groups, such as Hizb ut-Tahrir and al-Muhajiroun, who demand that Muslims work towards the establishment of Islamic states in Europe and who refuse to engage with pluralistic conceptions of Islam? For this group, Europe—and 'the West' in general—still serves as an enemy figure which must be subverted. One possible strategy is to turn the tables on the extremists and to construct a discourse in which *they* become the unwitting victims of Western hegemony rather than its great resistors. This is accomplished by observing that a large proportion of their own discourse is devoted to anti-Western rhetoric; so much so, in fact, that they end up neglecting to address the problems which most Muslims in Europe face on a day-to-day basis. That is to say, they are so obsessed with denouncing Western hegemony—and, in fact, have managed by and large to define the political field in relation to this very issue—that they do not engage with the substantive issues facing their constituency. Some Muslim thinkers, more notably in the West, have started to problematise the methodology of the extremists by pointing out that in many ways it simply serves to reproduce Western hegemony. "As long as Islamic political thinkers are locked in a (one-sided) conversation with western political thought," writes Bobby Sayyid, "they remain locked in a logic in which there is no space for anything other than the West (Sayyid 1997: 114)." This sentiment is echoed by Akeel Bilgrami, who argues that "[a] failure to come out of the neurotic obsession with the Western and colonial determination of their present condition will only prove [to Muslims] that that determination was utterly comprehensive in the destruction it wrought (Bilgrami 1995: 218)."

That said, we still at this point need to be wary of the claims we make about the prevalence and reach of the tendency towards a critical Islam in Europe. Many Muslims still know that the pressures for greater 'unity' are often nothing more than demands for greater 'uniformity.' Ever wary of this predicament, independent-thinking Muslims often have difficulty finding like-minded peers, preferring instead to go it alone. For them, safety in individuality is more important than safety in numbers. And there are always those schools of thought and mosques which simply refuse to come out of their shells. But many Muslims *are* reconciling themselves to Islam's heterogeneity and seeking dialogue with other traditions. They realize that this internal diversity can only be a good thing, and that it in no way threatens the integrity of Islam; rather, they see it as an intrinsic aspect of their religion. As the leadership of European Islam passes to the next generation, all signs are that a greater sense of unity will emerge among young Muslims;[8] but this will be a unity based on difference, an awareness that it is only through recognizing plurality within that Islam can adapt to life in the West. Encounters and debates with other (even more narrow-minded) Muslims have hence played a central role in defining Islam's political agenda. In this sense, being part of European society can actually contribute towards the development of critical thinking in Islam: critiques not only of the West, but also—and more importantly—of Islam itself. As emerging members of European society, Muslims face new questions, and these require new answers. Critical Islam has thus become an imperative for Muslims in Europe.

---

[8] In institutional terms, an important step in this direction was taken with the formation of the Muslim Council of Britain in late 1997.

PART FOUR

ASIAN RELIGIONS

CHAPTER TEN

ESTABLISHMENT OF BUDDHIST SACRED SPACE IN CONTEMPORARY INDIA: THE AMBEDKARITE BUDDHISM, DALIT CIVIL RELIGION AND THE STRUGGLE AGAINST SOCIAL EXCLUSION

Knut A. Jacobsen

Introduction

Although there were hardly any Buddhists in India at the time of independence in 1947, the two main symbols of the nation of India have strong Buddhist associations. The lion-capital of the Ashoka pillar from Sarnath is the national emblem of India and the Ashokan wheel from the base of the same Ashoka pillar from Sarnath is in the centre of the Indian flag. The main reason for the use of these symbols with strong Buddhist associations for the national emblem and the national flag is that it was suggested by the great leader of the Dalits, Bhimrao Ramji Ambedkar (1891–1956), who was one of the six members of the flag committee constituted in June 1947.[1] Ambedkar was already at that time an admirer of the Buddha and his teaching. Ambedkar lobbied for the adoption of several other Buddhist features to become part of the Indian state between 1947 and 1950, not only the wheel of dharma in the flag and the Ashoka lion as the emblem of the nation, but also the inscription of a Buddhist aphorism on the pediment of the Rashtrapati Bhavan, the residence of the President of the Republic

---

[1] Ambedkar proudly recalled that he got the lion capital and the Ashoka wheel adopted without anyone in the Constituent Assembly opposing it. That the Sarnath lion capital became the national emblem and the Ashoka wheel (*chakra*) as national symbol in the flag due to Ambedkar is a not often recognized fact. In a recent monograph on the national flag, the author does not note the potential Buddhistness of these symbols. She just notes that the second flag commission recommended the replacement of the spinning wheel of the Congress flag with the Ashoka *chakra* and that Nehru justified it on aesthetical grounds (Virmani 2008: 148). She does note that the press reported that the chakra could have a double meaning, it kept one part of the spinning wheel and conveyed gratitude to that idea of Gandhi as well as recalling the Buddhist emperor Ashoka's emblem.

(Jaffrelot 2003) and for the Buddha Jayanti (the Birthday celebration of the Buddha) to feature in India's official calendar. At that time, Ambedkar had not yet converted to Buddhism, and there was no sizable Buddhist community in India. The symbols were perceived as reflecting India's past as a Buddhist civilization. Ambedkar's understanding of Buddhism was shaped by a new type of Buddhism, often called modern Buddhism, which interpreted Buddhism as a rational and secular philosophy and primarily a teaching of ethics which was identified with a postulated non-sectarian early Buddhism, that is, a non-sectarian Buddhism of early India (Lopez 2002).

Ambedkar did not convert to Buddhism before 1956, but his personal preference for Buddhism was well known much earlier. In speeches he gave in 1936 he already encouraged all Untouchables to leave Hinduism and convert to another religion, as that was their only chance of being treated as equal by Hindus (Ambedkar 2004). In one of these speeches in which conversion to Christianity, Islam and Sikhism were discussed as possibilities, he ended his speech by telling the story of Buddha's *parinirvana* and quoting his last words in his own retelling: 'Believe in yourself, don't be dependent on others. Be truthful. Always take refuge in the truth and do not surrender to anybody' (Ambedkar 2004: 32). He then concluded: 'I also take refuge in the Buddha' (Ambedkar 2004: 32). As early as 1943 Ambedkar visited Buddhist shrines and discussed plans for the revival of Buddhism in India (Ahir 1994: 7). When he established his first educational institution in Bombay, he named it Siddharth College (Ahir 1994: 7). In 1948 Ambedkar arranged the translation into Marathi of P. Lakshi Narasu's book *The Essence of Buddhism*, a book that influenced his interpretation of Buddhism as the religion of reason, so that people thinking about converting to Buddhism could read it. In the 'Preface' he noted that he was writing a book on Buddhism (which was published in 1957 under the title *The Buddha and his Dhamma*). In 1950 Ambedkar, in an article 'Buddha and the Future of His Religion,' concluded that 'Buddhism is the only religion which the world can have' (quoted in Ahir 1982: 25). Ambedkar taught that the three jewels which he himself believed in—liberty, equality and fraternity—were derived from Buddhism and the teaching of the Buddha. Ambedkar created a new form for Buddhism often called New Buddhism, Navayana Buddhism or Ambedkarite Buddhism. It began with Ambedkar's conversion to Buddhism in a public meeting in Nagpur on 14 October 1956. Several hundred thousand members of the Mahar caste, an ex-untouchable caste to which

Ambedkar himself belonged, converted in the same public ceremony. This event marked the rebirth of Buddhism in India. Today almost ten million Buddhists belong to the Ambedkarite movement in India and the dominant form of Buddhism in India today, to which more than 90 percent of Buddhists belong, therefore, is Ambedkarite Navayana Buddhism.

Ambedkar was a leading politician before and after India's independence: he was the leading spokesperson for the untouchable/ex-untouchable castes and 'by far the greatest figure ever born to the untouchable communities' (Deliège 1999: 175). As the father of the Indian constitution he had a great impact on the shaping of the Indian state. However, it is a curious fact that he was more or less forgotten in the national history of India until a few years ago. The past ten years have seen a remarkable growth of interest in Ambedkar in India and in scholarship. There is a new awareness of his influence and his contribution to India and the Dalits. However, as late as 1995, Upendra Baxi could write that 'Ambedkar remains a totally forgotten figure' (Baxi 1995). By that he meant that there was no academic discourse about Ambedkar's life, thought and impact on Indian society. This was partly because of his conflicts with Gandhi and the Indian National Congress. Ambedkar was considered a villain in nationalist history since he was opposed to Gandhi, the father of the Indian nation. But Baxi thinks that the neglect of Ambedkar may also have something to do with his background as an untouchable. The Congress party was dominated by upper caste politicians. Jawaharlal Nehru was a Brahman, Mahatma Gandhi a Vaishya. Another reason might be that for a long time many viewed Ambedkar's main influence as limited to the Mahar caste, the caste to which he belonged, or to the state of Maharashtra. The Buddhism of Ambedkar and the Mahars was also considered as more a political identity than a religious practice so this tradition of Buddhism did not attract the interest of Buddhist scholars. Ambedkar's new interpretation of Buddhism was not well received by other Buddhists who thought that his interpretations were based on serious misunderstanding. And consequently, the Ambedkarite Buddhists were often not considered 'real' Buddhists. The Buddhists who follow Ambedkar consider him a *bodhisattva*, an enlightened being. For Ambedkarite Buddhism, Ambedkar is perhaps more important than Buddha, and many look upon Ambedkar as the saviour.

While Ambedkar was still a totally forgotten figure in 1995, Gail Omvedt, one of the foremost scholars on Ambedkar and Ambedkarite

Buddhism, concluded in 2004 that there are more statues of Bhimrao Ramji Ambedkar in India than of any other historical person (Omvedt 2004). It is to be noted though that these statues, although erected in public places, are often of poor quality. Nevertheless, there are statues of Ambedkar in many villages of India, in Dalit urban residential areas and at crossroads, and in front of educational and official buildings throughout India. In the state of Uttar Pradesh, after the political party Bahujan Samaj Party (BSP) based on the Ambedkarite movement won the election in 2007 and the leader of the party Mayawati Kumari (born 1956) became Chief Minister, erection of large-scale monuments has become a main item on the agenda. What characterizes the Ambedkarite movement's interpretation of Buddhism and what is the significance of the statues and monuments of the movement?

Ambedkarite Buddhism as Modern Buddhism

The first characteristic of the Ambedkarite Buddhist movement is that it is a product and expression of modern Buddhism. Buddha's teaching is defined as a rational and logical teaching comparable to modern political philosophies. What is not rational and logical can not be the teaching of the Buddha (Omvedt 2003: 7). Ambedkar gave new interpretations of the teaching of the Buddha and many of his interpretations are typical of modern Buddhism. His interpretations were shaped by the rebirth of Buddhism that had already happened in India, and by the Western Orientalists' creation of a homogeneous Buddhism. Ambedkar was in contact with the Mahabodhi society, the Buddhist revival society that was founded by the Sri Lankan Buddhist modernist Anagarika Dharmapala for the re-conquest of the Buddhist monuments in India.

Typical of modern Buddhism is the claim that it represents a recovery of a postulated 'real' Buddhism. Buddhism is understood primarily as a system of rational and ethical philosophy, and modern Buddhism rejects many of the rituals and magical elements of Buddhism, characterizing them as superstition. Typical for modern Buddhism is that early Buddhism and the teaching of the Buddha are seen as the most modern and rational, resembling the ideals of the European Enlightenment. Modern Buddhism is often removed from contemporary Buddhist practices, and tries to create a form of Buddhism that has never existed before, a homogenous tradition that is non-sectarian, non-ethnic, a form of pure Buddhism unpolluted by cultural influences. Ambedkar well understood the difference between historical Buddhism, contemporary forms of Buddhism, and the Buddhism to which he himself converted. His term for the Buddhism which he founded, therefore, was the 'new vehicle' (Navayana) which he, however, understood to be a return to the real teaching of 'early Buddhism'. Modern Buddhism typically also emphasizes meditation, but this was without significance for Ambedkar.

Ambedkar saw Buddha as a social reformer and rationalist philosopher. For Ambedkar, Buddhism was totally oriented around building a just and happy society. Suffering was caused by poverty and caste, not ignorance, and the message of the Buddha was how to get rid of poverty, caste and the injustice done to the marginalized. The supernatural attributes of the Buddha, meditation, ideas of karma and rebirth were not part of Ambedkar's Buddhism. The ritualism of today's Buddhism is not real Buddhism, according to Ambedkar. The role of the monks is not to dominate, but to serve society (Ambedkar 1992 [1957]). The notion of rebirth did not mean reincarnation but transformation. Ambedkar also denied that the four noble truths were part of Buddhism. The reason for the Buddha's renunciation was not the sight of a sick man, an old man, and a dead man, but a clash between the Sakyas and the Koliyas. Ambedkar excluded those parts of Buddhism that did not support his own egalitarian social democratic philosophy. In his interpretations, Buddhism becomes a modern materialist philosophy that incorporates a critique against the Indian caste society. 'The function of religion,' wrote Ambedkar (1987 [1956]), 'is to reconstruct the world and make it happy, not to explain its origin and end.' This statement is obviously inspired by Karl Marx and his well-known thesis (in *Theses on Feuerbach*) that the point of philosophy is not to interpret the world but to change it. Ambedkar reconstructed the Buddha as an ideal social reformer and the teaching of the Buddha was about the necessity to transform society. When monks renounce the world, they do not leave it, but dedicate themselves to serving the marginalized and the poor. 'Dhamma is not concerned with life after death, nor with rituals and ceremonies; but its centre is man and relation of man to man,' wrote Ambedkar in *The Buddha and his Dhamma* (p. 83). The salvific goal of Buddhism, *nirvana*, was reinterpreted to mean a just society.

Buddhism as the Untouchables' Religion

Ambedkar was from an untouchable caste, as were most of the converts. The Ambedkarite movement mobilized mostly Mahars from Maharashtra. Jatavs from Uttar Pradesh later joined in larger numbers. The second characteristic of Ambedkarite Buddhism is that Buddhism has become a religious identity for groups and persons in India that are identified as scheduled castes (S.C.), Untouchables (or ex-Untouchables, since considering anyone untouchable is prohibited by the Indian constitution), Harijans (a term popularized by Mahatma Gandhi), and Dalits.[2] Dalit is a political term and for the Dalit political activists, considering oneself a Dalit implies a political identity. In contemporary India, Buddhism and the Dalit movement are two sides of the same coin. The Dalits in India are not a homogenous group, they do not form a uniform community but are divided into numerous castes and sub-castes (Deliège 1999).

The caste hierarchy is based on an ideology that promotes a dualism of purity and impurity: the Brahmans at the top are the purest, and the untouchables the most impure. However, while the untouchables are well aware of caste ideology, they subscribe to it only up to a point, and not in order to legitimate their own economic depravation (Deliège 1999). Untouchables do not accept that their caste is inherently low. 'The model of caste hierarchy held by Harijans is that of a humanly instituted order in which they find themselves in an undeservedly low position as a consequence of misfortune, historical accident or trickery' (Deliège 1999: 63). There have therefore been several eman-

---

[2] Deliège (1999) has noted that of all the generic terms used for "Untouchables" none are entirely satisfying. See Deliège 1999, 10–22 for a critical discussion of the terms. Among other terms used are *antyaja, adi-dravidas, adi-andhras, adi-hindus, achchuuta, achut,* Depressed Castes, Exterior Castes, Outcastes, Backward Castes, Scheduled Castes. The term Harijan ("children of God"), popularized by Mahatma Gandhi, has become widespread. Ambedkar rejected Gandhi's term in favour of "Scheduled Castes". Deliège notes that many of those who reject the term Harijans belong to the politically active communities close to Ambedkar (p. 15). The author also stresses that an originally neutral term can with time take on pejorative connotations. In Maharashtra "many Mahars who followed Ambedkar and converted to Buddhism demanded to be called 'Neo-Buddhists'; today, however, this expression has become practically synonymous with Untouchable" (p. 15). The term Dalit ("downtrodden") which has become popular in North India and in all of India among intellectuals, comes from the political movement Dalit Panthers, that was founded in Bombay in 1972, but later disintegrated. Deliège notes that Dalit is now the politically correct term to use.

cipation movements among the Dalits. Some of the most important are the Satnami movement among Chamars in Chhattisgarh, founded in the 1820s by Ghazi Dash; the Ad-Dharma movement in Punjab started in the 1920s by Mangoo Ram; the Ravidas movement in Uttar Pradesh; the Dalit Panthers founded in 1972 which organized mainly Ambedkarite Buddhists; and the Ambedkar movement in Maharashtra and Uttar Pradesh and other states. These emancipation movements show that the Dalits do not accept their social position as fate, and the movements have done much to spread the idea of equality in India. The ideology of hierarchy is no longer acceptable in India and there are hardly any figures or movements who defend it in public. Caste is nevertheless a social reality.

Ambedkar argued that Buddhism was the religion of the ancestors of today's Dalits. As part of providing a new social and religious identity for the Dalits, Ambedkar connected the untouchables to early Buddhism. Buddhism was transformed into an ideology of justice for the marginalized, and the early Buddhists were identified as the ancestors of today's untouchables. It was Brahmanism who transformed these Buddhists to untouchables, he argued. Untouchability was a punishment for not becoming Hindus. Ambedkar held that the untouchables were original Buddhists who had been given the status of untouchable when Hinduism became established. In his book *The Untouchables: Who Were They and Why They Became Untouchables* (Ambedkar 1990 [1948])? Ambedkar explains that when the Hindus came to power, those Buddhists who were not willing to become Hindus, were segregated and had to live in separate quarters outside the villages and they became the untouchables. This is a modern myth that Ambedkar fashioned, and there is no historical evidence at all to defend this thesis. The caste system, he argued, solidified after the defeat of Buddhism by Hinduism, and the Buddhists were redefined as untouchables.[3] Ambedkar's view is summed up by A.K. Narain:

> Untouchability was born out of the struggle between Buddhism and Brahmanism. According to him [Ambedkar] the Untouchables were originally Buddhists and their untouchability was a punishment for sticking to Buddhism. He called them the 'Broken Men' who were forced to live outside

---

[3] Here Ambedkar based himself also on the earlier thinkers of the anti-caste movement such as Jotirao Phule and Iyothee Thass. Omvedt writes: "By the 1920s this identification with early Buddhists was an underlying theme among many Dalit movements" (2003: 18).

the village from the very beginning. He further believed that the root of their untouchability was beef-eating and that Untouchability became intimately connected with the ban on cow-slaughter which was made a capital offence by the Gupta Kings of the fourth century and thus he could say with some confidence that Untouchability was born sometimes about 400 A.D. (Narain 1994: 85).

That the Dalits were the original Buddhists, as Ambedkar asserted, meant that when the present-day Dalits converted to Buddhism, they did not really convert, but simply returned to their original religion. Ambedkar's primary aim of conversion to Buddhism was to gain a new religious and social identity for the Dalits. For the Hindus, Ambedkar thought, when interacting with Untouchables who were also Hindus, the identity of being Untouchables was most important, while when interacting with Christian Untouchables, their identity as Christians became foremost. Religion overwrote caste in a sense. Changing religion, therefore, argued Ambedkar, offered a way out of untouchability. Buddhism, however, has become identified to some degree with Dalit culture.[4]

Buddhism as a Critique of Hinduism

Ambedkar's main belief was that the Dalits were not part of Hindu society. A principal purpose of his conversion to Buddhism was to abandon his Hindu identity and to lead the Dalits towards another religion, which he saw as necessary for the Dalits to attain equality, liberty and fraternity in India. Ambedkar's experience with growing up untouchable in a Hindu-dominated society and his political opposition to Gandhi are at the foundation of his conversion to Buddhism. He experienced serious discrimination especially in his childhood and youth. That Gandhi defended the *varnashramadharma* or the Hindu system of caste hierarchy, in his conflict with Ambedkar about a separate electorate for the Untouchables, led Ambedkar to declare that he would leave Hinduism. Gandhi thought *varnashramadharma* too

---

[4] Fewer than 5 percent of the Dalits are Buddhists. Around 75 percent of the Mahars are Buddhists, the majority of the Jatavas (a Chamar caste) in Uttar Pradesh are Buddhists. Small groups of Dalits in Gujarat, Punjab, Rajasthan, Karnataka and Madhya Pradesh have also become Buddhists (Lobo 1996).

central to Hinduism as a religion to be given up,[5] but Ambedkar then pronounced that although he was born a Hindu, he would 'not die a Hindu'.

More than twenty years before Ambedkar actually converted to Buddhism, he had announced his intention to renounce Hinduism. He had decided that renouncing of Hinduism was necessary to give the Mahars a different identity that was not based on caste. Ambedkar saw traditional Indian religious culture as constituted by two co-existing religious traditions, the Brahmanical Hindu and the Buddhist. Ambedkar understood these two traditions to be in a relationship of permanent moral conflict. Ambedkar's understanding of this conflict is summed up in the following way:

> When today's Untouchables' ancestors—described as a single tribe separated from other communities only on tribal grounds—adopted Buddhism, they did not revere Brahmins or employ them as priests. They even 'regarded them as impure.' The self-imposed isolation of these Buddhists angered the Brahmins, who responded by preaching 'against [them] the contempt and hatred with the result that [they] came to be regarded as Untouchables.' At this stage then, presumably pre-Ashokan (although Ambedkar's chronology is unclear), untouchability was assigned to an isolated tribe of Buddhists on the basis of religious competition (Blackburn 1993: 6).

Hindu temples were closed to untouchables. Ambedkar was active in the action for gaining access for Untouchables to the Hindu temples, but Hindus opposed the idea. This reality of exclusion is behind his later conversion to Buddhism. Why should he want to be integrated into a religious community that fought against integrating them? In 1935 he became convinced that Hinduism could not offer the untouchables anything. Ambedkar clashed with Mahatma Gandhi on the issue of Untouchables and he doubted the will of Gandhi to put an end to untouchability even if Gandhi claimed to speak for them. Ambedkar wanted to use the possible independence of India as a way to end untouchability. At the Round Table Conference in London in 1930, Ambedkar demanded separate electorate to the Untouchables and representation, similar to the demands made by the Muslims for the Muslim communities. When Gandhi met Ambedkar in 1931, Gandhi claimed himself as representing the Untouchables in India.

---

[5] For the Gandhi-Ambedkar debate, see Omvedt 2003: 248–253; Omdvedt 2004: 56–72; Jaffrelot 2003: 52–73.

Gandhi recognized only Muslims and Sikhs as minorities. For Gandhi, to accept the Untouchables as a separate community meant that the Hindus would be divided and he thought the British would exploit it in their 'split and rule' policy. In 1932 Gandhi did a 'fast until death' to stop the untouchables from gaining separate electorate. Ambedkar had to accept Gandhi's claim from fear of retaliation against Dalits. Deliège has suggested that Ambedkar's subsequent conversion to Buddhism was a reaction in particular to Gandhi's Hinduism (Deliège 1999). His debate with Gandhi on caste had proven to him that Hinduism could not be separated from caste.

Several arguments are used to understand Ambedkar's choice of Buddhism, but Ambedkar's resentment and anger against Hinduism was one important reason. An aspect of Buddhism that made it attractive for Ambedkar was the traditional Buddhist intolerance of Hinduism. Buddhism is often celebrated as a religion that is particular tolerant, but this is based on a selective reading of Buddhism. Buddhism is a polemical tradition that arose as a critique of other religions, and especially as a protest against certain elements of Hinduism. A central doctrine of Buddhism, the *anatman* doctrine, is formulated as a denial of a Hindu doctrine, the idea of *atman* or a self, often understood as a principle of pure consciousness or the passive witness to the mind and body, that does not die when the body dies. Buddhism also was opposed to the Veda, the revealed texts of the Brahmanical tradition, opposed to the status of the Brahmans and opposed to their sacrificial religion. Thus Buddhism undermined the legitimacy of the Brahmanical ritual power. When Ambedkar converted at the rally in Nagpur on 14 October 1956, he took 'refuge in the Buddha, the Dhamma and the Sangha' from a Burmese monk, U. Chandrtamani, but when he thereafter turned to the masses gathered there and administered the vows to them, he added 22 vows as well. Many of them are directly directed at Hinduism:

(1) I will not regard Brahma, Vishnu or Mahadev as gods and I will not worship them.
(2) I will not regard Ram or Krishna as gods and I will not worship them.
(3) I will not honour Gauri, Ganapati or any other god of Hinduism and I will not worship them.
(4) I do not believe that god has taken avatar.

(5) I agree that the propaganda that the Buddha was the avatar of Vishnu is false and mischievous.
(6) I will not do the *shraddhapaksha* ceremony (for the departed) or *pandadan* (gifts in honour of the deceased).
(8) I will have no rituals done by Brahmans.
(19) I renounce the Hindu religion which has obstructed the evolution of my former humanity and considered humans unequal and inferior.[6]

The 22 vows can be divided into two groups, those that break with the Hindu identity and those that affirm Buddhism. Ambedkar did not want the converts to simply add some Buddhist features to their Hindu religious practices. It was necessary, he thought, to make a total break with Hinduism.[7]

Buddhism as a Political Vision

Ambedkar's conversion to Buddhism was obviously a critique of Hinduism. But it is unclear to what degree his conversion was to a personal faith or more an imagined civil religion for the Dalits. For Ambedkar, religion was necessary as the foundation of a moral society. This was his main criticism of Marxism. Ambedkar did not think that religion had to be based on anything supernatural.[8] Buddhism for Ambedkar seems to be a holistic political and moral system. Ambedkar's main interest was in social change and the reconstruction of society, and his interpretation of Buddhism saw Buddhism as a social vision which promoted the goal of ending social injustice. For Ambedkar, Buddhism was not a renunciant tradition aiming at individual salvation. Ambedkar had no interest in meditation or in establishing an institution of monks.

---

[6] See Omvedt, 2003: 262 for a list of the 22 vows.
[7] Most Dalits in India have been attached to Hinduism and have remained so. They were denied to use the temples but were not excluded from all aspects of religious life. That they were denied access to temples meant that they had little knowledge about the Hindu gods and central Hindu concepts. The concepts of karma and rebirth are often totally unfamiliar.
[8] From his studies in the United States, Ambedkar was well-acquainted with Durkheim's theory of religion.

Ambedkar considered Buddhism a religion in the Durkheimian sense, with a focus on the sacred as a binding force for social relationships (Omvedt 2003). 'Religion,' wrote Ambedkar, 'means the rules imposed for the maintenance of society' (Ambedkar 2004: 12). Without sacredness there would be no morality. Buddha, argued Ambedkar, taught that 'Dhamma is morality and as Dhamma is sacred, so is morality' (Ambedkar, quoted in Omvedt 2003: 260). Ambedkar's understanding of Buddhism was quite different from most other interpretations. The root of all suffering in the world, argued Ambedkar, is the conflict between the classes. The search of the Buddha therefore started with the problem of social exploitation. Ambedkar denied that the four noble truths (all is suffering, suffering has a cause, etc.) were part of the teaching of the Buddha. Far from arguing that suffering was an inherent part of the worldly existence, the point of the Buddha was that it is possible to create a world free from suffering. The message was that humans are able to create a society based on righteousness by their own effort. He did not accept the common interpretation of karma and rebirth, since it seemed to be based on an idea of the self. The idea of karma was contradicted by the doctrine of *anatta* (non-self) and the idea of karma seems also to legitimate untouchability. He also argued that the Buddhist monks can be the hope of Buddhism only if they are social servants (Omvedt 2003).

Religion in the sense of civic religion was necessary for society, according to Ambedkar, and Buddhism could give the Dalits a religion that was free of caste. It gave the Dalits a religious tradition for their intellectual development, religious rituals without Brahmanical supremacy and without the concepts of impurity and untouchability. Buddhism also created a distinct identity that Dalits who converted to Islam and Christianity did not get.

From Exclusion to Inclusion: Processions, Statues and Monuments

A characteristic of the Ambedkarite Buddhist movement is the use of processions and the erection of Ambedkar statues, Ambedkar monuments, Ambedkar parks and the naming of institutions after Ambedkar. When I watched the Ravidas Jayanti procession in Varanasi in 2008, it was impossible not to be struck by the blending of the political and the religious that seemed to characterize the procession, and which is a characteristic of the Ambedkarite movement as a whole.

The trucks, tractors and the people were much more prominent in the procession than any religious symbols. It seemed to be a procession that put people on display, that presented a political statement about Dalit power. The celebration was of the birth of saint Ravidas (Raidas) who lived in the fifteenth century and is remembered as a leading poet in the medieval Hindu Bhakti and Sant tradition.[9] Ravidas was from the Chamar caste, a community of leather workers, a caste that was considered untouchable by caste Hindus. The procession was a political mobilization of people on the margins of Indian society that to an increasing degree have been using processions as a means to contest the marginality (Jaoul 2007). Similar processions on Ravidas Jayanti take place in many other cities in Uttar Pradesh. The images on display in the procession were those of Ambedkar, Buddha and Ravidas. All three are celebrated as leaders of the Dalit communities. Celebrating these religious figures gives opportunities for affirming and gaining acceptance for a public presence. Analyzing the Buddha Jayanati Dalit procession in Agra, Owen Lynch argues that the procession is a civil ritual and not political although local politicians participate and that the procession represents to the residents as a whole the accomplishment of inclusion in the civil society of the Dalits (Lynch 2002). The increasing number and importance of the Dalit processions in contemporary Uttar Pradesh can be explained by the aspirations of this community and new political power.

An important organization of the Ambedkarite movement is the political party Bahujan Samaj Party (BSP) that was founded by Kanchi Ram in 1984 on the anniversary of Ambedkar's birth. This Ambedkarite and Dalit-led political party has been in power in Uttar Pradesh several times under the leadership of Mayawati, the current leader of Bahujan Samaj Party who is a Dalit from Uttar Pradesh and an Ambedkarite Buddhist. Mayawati's family converted to Buddhism in 1980. Uttar Pradesh is the state with the highest population in India, close to 200 million, and after Punjab the state with the highest percentage of population of Scheduled Castes (around 21 percent; in Punjab around 26 percent).

During the rule of Bahujan Samaj Party (BSP) in Uttar Pradesh, the Chief Minister Mayawati has named a number of institutions after

---

[9] For an overview of the Sant tradition see the volume edited by Schomer and McLeod (1987).

Ambedkar and has started construction of several grand-scale monuments celebrating Ambedkar, Buddha, Kanchi Ram, and herself and some other Dalit leaders. These are means for Dalits to attain their proper place in Indian society. They signify the public recognition of the importance of Ambedkar for the nation of India and his contributions to the modern state. They symbolize a conquest of public space by the civil religion of the Dalits. Mayawati's rule in Uttar Pradesh supported the building of monuments in honour to the Dalit contribution to Indian society.

The most important monuments being built by the Uttar Pradesh government under Mayawati are the Ambedkar Park (Ambedkar Udyan) in Gomtinagar in Lucknow, the Kanchi Ram Memorial Sthal (Kanshi Ram Smarak) in Lucknow, the Buddha Sthal, Prerna Bhawan, and a giant Dalit memorial Noida. The monumental Ambedkar Park (Ambedkar Udyan) in Gomtinagar in Lucknow is described in the following way: 'Spread of 130 acres, the compound matches London's St Paul's Cathedral, Cambodia's Angkor Wat and Egypt's Karnak temple in terms of sheer scale. You might call this the new Rome.'[10] Responding to criticism of the expenditure and scale of the projects, Mayawati commented: 'Had memorials for eminent persons belonging to the Dalit community and OBCs [Other Backward Classes] been built by the government that ruled the country after Independence, the BSP government would not have felt the need for the task.'[11] One journalist commented: 'But when they, even you and I, walk through these memorials after they are ready, the one message that no one will miss is that it was Dalits themselves who successfully overturned the humiliation and oppression of thousands of years. Those statues, including Mayawati's, will speak.'[12] The establishment of Dalit Buddhist space is important for the process of demarginalization. Building monuments is about symbolic power and they are attempts to create sacred centres celebrating Dalit power. The building of monuments is part of the same process that Ambedkar started by giving the Dalits a Buddhist past: to rid India of its conceptions of untouchability and the idea that some human beings are worth less than others.

---

[10] http://vinodksharma.blogspot.com/2009/07/mayawatis-memorials-mark-epochal-change.html. Downloaded October 5, 2009.

[11] The Hindu, 27.6.2009, downloaded October 5, 2009.

[12] http://vinodksharma.blogspot.com/2009/07/mayawatis-memorials-mark-epochal-change.html, downloaded October 5, 2009.

The tallest statue of Buddha in the world (152 meters) is now being constructed with the support of the Uttar Pradesh government. Originally to have been built in Bihar, it was moved to Uttar Pradesh because the Mayawati government was in support of Buddhism. The statue is to be installed in Kushinagar, the place of Buddha's *parinirvana*, in a park of 600 acres along with a university, hospital and museum.[13] The statue confirms the Buddhist Dalit interpretation of Indian history and contemporary society and culture. It is a statue of the Buddha but it is also an emblem of the Dalit community since the Dalit community lays claim to the Buddhist tradition of the Indian past as well as of contemporary India. What started with the erection of the first Ambedkar statues in Uttar Pradesh in the 1970s (Jaoul 2007) has by 2009 developed into the process of constructing the world's tallest Buddha and a number of enormous monuments to the Buddha, Ambedkar, Kanchi Ram and the Dalit movement.

Exclusion, separation and segregation characterized the situation for the untouchables in traditional societies in India, and in many places still do. In the Sanskrit literature untouchables were called *candelas* and this term designated 'those who were not allowed to dwell in a town or a village but had to live in special quarters outside the village or town limits' (Deliège 1999: 11). They were set apart from the rest of society. The Dalits were an integral part of Indian society with economic and ritual roles, but they were also at the same time excluded from society. They lived both inside and outside this society, their 'spatial isolation reflects this relative ostracism' (Deliège 1999: 67). They lived in separate localities segregated from everyone else in the village, they were denied access to temples, denied access to the wells, temples streets, Brahman neighbourhoods and education. Deliège writes: 'While the temple and the Brahmin quarters are located at the centre of the village space, the Untouchables live on the periphery, as far as possible from the residence of the principal gods' (1999: 99). Ambedkarite Buddhism is attempting to move the Dalits from these margins of the Indian society to the centre. The Dalits are reinventing their own history and are creating a better past in order to carve out a better future. The purpose of this reinvention is demarginalization.

---

[13] http://www.thaindian.com/newsportal/uncategorized/uttar-pradesh-to-have-worlds-tallest-buddha-statue_10031050.html (downloaded 9.9.2009). For a video presentation of the project see http://www.videosift.com/video/The-Worlds-Tallest-Statue-Bronze-Buddha-in-Uttar-Pradesh (downloaded 9.9.2009).

In this process the boundaries of history are expanded beyond the empirical-analytical to include myths of the subaltern communities in the past (Narayan 2008). A main characteristic of the Dalits is that they have been an excluded group, and the conversion to Buddhism, the conversion of history, and the conversion of sacred places, are efforts at attaining social inclusion. This characteristic of the movement is understood as a strategy of social demarginalization, using the symbolic means. The spatial and social exclusion of the Dalits in traditional Hindu society stands in contrast to the social inclusion symbolized by the Ambedkar statues, monuments, parks and institutions. For the Dalits, this visibility is a way to move from the margins to the centre. Untouchability was about denial of access and expulsion to the margins; statues, monuments and processions symbolize the refusal of marginality.

Ambedkar has increasingly become the unifying symbol of the 'imagined community' of Dalits in India. The conquest of public space with statues and symbols of Ambedkar points to a particular strategy of the Dalits. An important aspect of untouchability was the denial of access. These processions, statues and monuments become symbols of the Dalit community, of a rational religion focused on Buddhism as a social vision, and the celebration of Dalit leaders as leaders at the centre of the Indian nation.

Conclusion

An important part of the rebirth of Buddhism in India was the discovery of the ancient Buddhist monuments and the Buddhist takeover of those monuments and traditions of place. Establishing new Buddhist temples at ancient sacred places, settlements of monks, and the re-establishment of the Buddhist pilgrimage were part of that process. The conquest of Buddhist space is an important part of the rebirth of Buddhism in India. In the case of the Ambedkarite Buddhists, building monuments in places associated with Ambedkar represents the creation of Buddhist Dalit spaces. Recently, the building of grand-scale monuments of the Buddha, Ambedkar, Kanchi Ram and other figures has become a major strategy of the Ambedkarite and the Dalit Bahujan Samaj Party in Uttar Pradesh. One important aspect of this construction of monuments has to do with the establishment of Dalit Buddhist space in India. Since in the Ambedkar movement early Buddhism is identified as the religion of the Dalits, i.e. the ancestors of the Dalits were Buddhists who were persecuted by the Brahmins, the ancient Buddhist monuments are being redefined as Dalit monuments. New Buddhist monuments such as the Buddha statue in Kushinagar can become symbols of a new Dalit identity that is grounded in a magnificent past. This redefinition is part of the continual process of de-marginalization of the Dalits in Indian society. For the Dalits, not only the Hindu nationalists but also the Indian Congress and Mahatma Gandhi were perceived as supporters of Brahmanical understanding of Indian history and culture that legitimated caste. An important part of Dalit identity reconstruction is to establish for themselves a history outside the Brahmanical paradigm (Narayan 2008). When the Buddhist monuments were discovered, they could not be claimed by any community in India. Since there were no Buddhists in India, they belonged to the past, not the present. With the emergence of Navayana Buddhism, these monuments could be claimed by a community in India. The current construction of new Buddhist-Dalit monuments connects the present Dalit Buddhists to the ancient Indian past, and therefore continues the project of Ambedkar of creating a new non-Hindu identity of the Dalits. The Navayana Buddhists claim to be the original Buddhists, and that means that the ancient monuments are thought to belong to their ancestors. That Buddhism is present in the flag of India and that the emblem of the Indian state is a symbol of Buddhist rule of India, seem also to provide symbolic support for Dalit Buddhists to make the move from the periphery to the centre of India.

As a founder of a new tradition of Buddhism, Ambedkar saw himself as an educator and political leader, not a religious leader (Fuchs 2004). There was also no organizational structure of monks in Ambedkarite Buddhism and Martin Fuchs writes that this state of affairs 'fits very well with [Ambedkar's] conception of religion and its social significance not to have an elite body of spiritual *virtuosi*.' The focal point of the new Indian Buddhists is Ambedkar and the community of Dalits. This is one reason why the statues of Ambedkar are omnipresent in India. He is an emblem for the Buddhist Dalits, the main symbol of their civic religion. This helps to explain why in Uttar Pradesh, the only state ruled by the political party that sees itself as the inheritors of the Ambedkar movement, a number of public building projects were initiated that celebrate Ambedkar and other leaders of the Dalit movement. The building by the Mayawati government of monuments of the Buddhist Dalit political leaders and the establishment of Buddhist Dalit space is an attempt to demarginalize the Dalits, to move the Dalits to the centre of the Indian civilization by using the civil religion that was created by Ambedkar.[14]

---

[14] In September 2009 the Supreme Court of India imposed a legal ban on Mayawati government's construction of the Dalit-Buddhist monuments in Uttar Pradesh. But the Mayawati government changed the names of the building projects, and construction has continued.

CHAPTER ELEVEN

HINDU TRADITIONS IN DIASPORA:
SHIFTING SPACES AND PLACES

Martin Baumann

Maintaining and Adapting: Religions in Diaspora

Hindu traditions have become a global phenomenon in modern times. Hindu traditions were brought overseas by different modes of transference: during 19th century, the British Raj brought indentured workers to East and South Africa, the Caribbean, Fiji Islands and Southeast Asia. After World War II, people from India, the majority among them Hindus, left South Asia for North America, Europe and Australia. They were in search for work as skilled workers such as doctors and technicians and for good educational opportunities. An accompanying trajectory has been neo-Hindu *gurus* and *swamis* (teachers) who spread Hindu ideas and practices in the West since the 1960s. Lately, since the 1980s, more than half a million Tamil people from Sri Lanka fled the war torn South Asian island for Europe and Canada in particular. In Europe, among the approximately one million Hindu people, nine out of ten are Hindus of South Asian descent, i.e. immigrants or descendents of immigrants.[1]

Like any religion in diasporic context, a crucial feature is the simultaneous endeavour to maintain and adapt religious ideas, practices, organisational forms, architecture and much more. Continuing the transplanted religion without acculturation and changes will alienate the very tradition to later generations. As a consequence, sooner or later language used in liturgy and ritual changes to apply to the language of the country of residence; newly constructed buildings for worship align to architectural models of the host society; forms of congregational meeting incorporate elements previously unknown to the

---

[1] For the global spread of people of Hindu faith see Rukmani 1999, Vertovec 2000, Baumann 2003, Jacobsen and Kumar 2004. See also the online bibliography "Global Hindu Diaspora" by Baumann 2004.

tradition; religious specialists need to respond to new duties, necessities and responsibilities. These processes are common to all immigrant religions, facing new demands and challenges.[2]

A brief example may illustrate the facet of adaptation: Jews in early 19th century USA introduced a regular weekly synagogue sermon in the vernacular, added an organ and mixed choir, and abandoned separate for mixed seating.[3] Likewise, the very space for performing Jewish religion shifted: "For many Jews in the nineteenth century, the synagogue now became the locus of religion, replacing the home, where fewer and fewer ceremonies were observed. Indeed, traditional home ceremonies like candle lighting, *kiddush*, and *sukkah* were increasingly shifted into the synagogue." (Sarna 1995: 222) And, similar to observations subsequently discussed with regard to Tamil Hindus, changes in gender relations came to the fore: Jewish women, "whose domain formerly had been the home [...] flocked to the synagogue, just as Protestant women flocked to church, and synagogues had to find ways of meeting their needs. Suddenly, and perhaps for the first time in history, some synagogues had more women in attendance on Saturday morning than men." (Sarna 1995: 222)[4]

Migrated religion over time develops into a re-constructed and re-established religion. Though for the first generation the cultural and religious bonds have become disembedded from their previous larger socio-cultural background as prevalent in the country of emigration, children and grandchildren of the (im)migrants strive to re-embed the religion in the new context. Changes and innovations get introduced to line up to mainstream ideas of the host society. These processes and dynamics are not confined to modernity but took place likewise in antiquity and pre-modernity (Schiffauer 2005, Baumann 2009, for antiquity see Auffarth 2007).

During the past 20 years, social and cultural studies to a growing extent subsumed the analysis of continuity and change of a migrated religion under the notion of diaspora. Two millennia ago, the translators of the Septuagint coined the very term to denote the situation of Jews living outside Israel-Palestine in the period of the Second Temple

---

[2] See on this complex, Knott 1991: 100–105; Williams 1992: 232–255; Williams 2000: 277–287; Hinnells 1997: 826–835; Baumann, Luchesi, Wilke 2003: 12–21.
[3] See Sarna 1995: 221–222. Traditional Sephardic liturgy used sermons no more than occasional features, given on special occasions only.
[4] See as well, Diner 2004: 112–152 and Raphael 2008.

(Van Unnik 1993, Cohen, Frerichs 1993, Tromp 1998). Newly 'discovered' as a useful and encompassing notion, "diaspora" developed to apply to any group and nation living far away of its country of origin. The state of a people being in exile, displaced or forced to emigrate was taken as sufficient to speak of a diasporised nation and a people staying in diaspora. The rapid broadening of the term subsumed people such as immigrants, guest workers, refugees, expatriates, as well as overseas and ethnic communities.[5]

As a consequence of this semantic expansion, however, the term lost any usefulness to demarcate specifics of a situation characterised by a (at least) triangular, certainly not static interrelation of diaspora group, country of origin, and country of residence (Hettlage 1991: 7-10, Baumann 2003: 228-248). The interrelations of dependence, influence, exchange and separation between these poles take on different and changing ranges of intensity. The range of communication takes on forms of strong to weak and intense to low interrelation, depending on the very situation (Saint-Blancat 1995: 13-16).

To provide an example from antiquity, Alexandrian Jews in Egypt during 2nd and 1st century BCE maintained strong bonds with Palestine and Jerusalem by way of pilgrimage and annual paying of the contribution and donations. In reverse order, Jews in the diaspora received the Jewish calendar and laying-down of festival days as well as instructions from the undisputed religious center, i.e. Jerusalem. At the same time, Jews in Alexandria structurally to a large extent had adapted to the country of residence, i.e. Ptolemaic Egypt: they spoke Greek, dressed the same way, behaved like Greeks, and shared Greek education ideals and much more (Safrai 1974, Delling 1987: 35-40). However, this "external Hellenisation" (Hengel 1976: 140) came to an end with regard to religious observances: they did not participate in festivities and holidays of Greek Pagan gods and Egyptian gods. In contrast, they honoured no god other than JHWH and observed the law of the Torah. This example illustrates divergent ranges of reserve (e.g. distancing of diaspora Jews towards Pagan cults) and intense exchange (adopting Greek way of life), a structural analysis applicable to many other religious communities in diasporic environment.

---

[5] Tölölyan 1991: 4. For a reconstruction of the disciplinary and object-related enlargement of the diaspora term see Baumann 2000a, Krings 2003. For a critical reappraisal, see Tölölyan 1996: 4-6, Cohen 1998, Mayer 2005.

In line with such an analytical perspective, applicable for empirical research, we suggest a working definition of diaspora and diasporic setting. The definition aims to retain the comparative heuristic and analytical potential of the term (dislodged from its religious semantics) to study immigrant groups and communities. We suggest that a diasporic situation shall be qualified by a group of people which perpetuates a recollecting identification with a fictitious or faraway existent geographic territory and its cultural-religious traditions. Emphasis is placed on the enduring, often glorifying identification with a cultural-religious point of reference outside the current country of living. Prototypically, i.e. in most, but not all cases, this situation came about by a migration process and involves an identificational difference of the diaspora group to the dominant cultural and religious norms and orientations of the host society. Importantly, this difference constitutes the fundamental tripolar interrelatedness of diaspora group, country of origin and country of residence. Thus understood, the notion "diaspora" also clarifies when not to speak of a diasporic situation, i.e. when the rudiments stated are missed. The term thus fruitfully and in comparative way is applicable to study topics of the dynamics of religion, i.e. processes of continuity and change of a religion (Vertovec 1997, Cohen 1997, Baumann 2000a: 313–337, Baumann 2003: 64–71, McLoughlin 2005: 529–533).

Based on these theoretical considerations, this chapter aims to analyse a specific aspect of religious change and continuity by way of a heuristic neologism, i.e. that of *templeisation*. The term was invented by Vasudha Narayanan to bring to attention the growing importance of the Hindu temple among Hindu immigrants in the USA (Narayanan 2006). According to her observations, to a growing extent the temple develops to become the main site for biographical rituals (Skt. *samskaras*), for being introduced to Hindu tradition and for celebrating festivals. A decisive shift takes place from the home to the temple, accompanied by a shift in authority away from women and mothers to men and priests. Following, we shall employ Narayanan's study as a heuristic hypothesis to scrutinise afresh the data on Tamil Hindus from Sri Lanka in Germany and Switzerland. Thus, the chapter asks to what extent processes of "templeisation" are observable among Hindus, in particular among Tamil Hindus in continental Europe.

Following, in part 2 the chapter provides a sketch of Tamil Hindus in Germany and Switzerland, providing information also with regard to their socio-economic situation and processes of religious institution-building. Part 3 gives a sketch of ritual spaces of Hindu traditions, i.e. rituals performed in the domestic and the public spheres. Part 4 concentrates on the increased importance of the diaspora temple as multifunctional site. Finally, part 5 applies the heuristic perspective of templeisation and analyses exemplary areas and shifts. The conclusion discusses to what extent incipient processes of templeisation may be observable among Tamil Hindus in Germany and Switzerland.

Tamil Hindus from Sri Lanka in Germany and Switzerland

The currently most visible and numerically strongest Hindu population in Germany is formed by Tamil people.[6] Since the escalation of the Sinhalese-Tamil war in Sri Lanka in 1983, about 300,000 Sri Lankan people left for Canada and 200,000 for Europe. In Germany, up to late 2002, about 60,000 men and their families have taken refuge as asylum seekers. In line with German policy of distributing asylum seekers all across the country, the refugees from Sri Lanka were settled in small numbers in a multitude of towns and cities. Nevertheless, due to pragmatic reasons such as a less restrictive jurisdiction, the permission to work legally while still being subjected to the asylum proceedings, and the fact that relatives lived there already, a numerical concentration of Tamil people in the Ruhr area (situated in the mid-northern part of Germany) came about. It is in this region that a small Tamil infrastructure with shops, cultural and political societies and the founding of Hindu temples has evolved. Tamils organise language and music courses as well as dance classes. The legal status of Tamils in Germany varies: overall about half of the Tamil population is comparatively safe and an increasing number has acquired German citizenship, the status of the other half varies between different levels of allowances to stay for six months to a year, to be renewed regularly.[7]

Despite their insecure legal status, since the late 1980s Tamils have started to open small places of worship with permanently installed statues of deities (Skt. *murti*; Tam. *murtti*). Two thirds of Sri Lankan Tamils are Hindus, approximately 40,000 Hindus, almost all Saivas

---

[6] For the about 30,000–40,000 Hindus from India see Oesterheld, Günther 1997 and Goel 2006, for the about 6,000 Afghan Hindus see Hutter 2006.

[7] Baumann 2000b: 93–116. For the social, economic, and legal situation see in detail, Salentin 2002, Baumann 2003a: 44–54.

and Saktas (Baumann, Salentin 2006: 307). Both the sharp increase of the number of refugees and the arrival of women and children played a decisive part in the creation of new places of worship. In addition, those Tamils, having lived for several years in Germany by then, had acquired financial resources and administrative skills to get a temple functioning.

Whereas in 1989 only four small temples, situated in poor basement rooms existed, in 1994 the number had climbed up to ten temples. And again, five years later, in 1999, the number of temples had doubled to 20. In mid-2000, Tamils maintain some 25 Hindu temples of different sizes: A few are situated in cellars and flats, some in former industrial storerooms and halls. There is one purpose-built temple, the Sri Kamadchi Ampal temple in Hamm/Westphalia, while the construction of another newly built temple is under way in Berlin (to be finished in 2010). A clear concentration with eleven temples is observable in the industrial Ruhr valley, the city of Hamm (east fringe of the Ruhr valley) being home to three temples alone (Baumann 2000b: 149–151, 161–165; Baumann 2003a: 65–69).

A few temples have started to celebrate the annual temple festival with a public procession, thus bringing the gods and Hindu tradition to wider notice. The first to have done so was the Sri Kamadchi Ampal temple in 1993. The attendance at the festival grew from a few hundred rapidly to 4,000 participants in 1996. In 2002 already some 12,000 to 15,000 participants and visitors came to take part in the festival. These public processions also enable Hindu participants to perform bodily austerity practices known from South Asia, such as women carrying a heavy fire pot or doing prostrations, and men rolling on their sides around the temple or performing the *kavati* dance (Tam. "austerity based on a vow", enacted by dancing with a bow on the shoulders, decorated with peacock feathers). Some of these dancers have been pierced with hooks in their backs and a spear pricked through their cheeks (Baumann 2006, Luchesi 2008b).

Since its inception, the 14 days lasting festival of the Sri Kamadchi Ampal temple has grown nearer established South Asian patterns each year. Strikingly visible, the temple's head priest, Sri Paskarakurukkal, succeeded in building a huge South Indian style temple in the industrial outskirts of Hamm. Financed by donations from devotees and bank loans, the inauguration ceremony took place in July 2002, generating an enthusiastic interest from the media and many German people. The temple has a 50 feet towering *kopuram* ("temple tower", Tam.) and covers a ritual hall of some 700 square meters.

In 2007, Sri Paskaran was able to sanctify a monumental, 27 feet rising procession card, the acquisition also indicating the self-attributed importance and supremacy of his temple (Luchesi 2008 "Mobile Tempel"). The annual festival grew year by year, attracting some 25,000 to 30,000 visitors and participants in 2008 from Germany, the Netherlands, Denmark, Great Britain, France and Switzerland. For many Tamil Hindus, the Sri Kamadchi Ampal temple has developed into a major pilgrim site in Western Europe.[8]

In Switzerland Tamil Hindus make up the majority of Hindu people as well. According to statistics, in 2005 some 42,000 migrants from Sri Lanka resided in Switzerland: 30,000 Sri Lankan citizens, 7,300 Sri Lankan people having acquired Swiss nationality, and about 4,500 asylum seekers provisionally admitted.[9] Since the late 1990s, the number of Sri Lankan immigrants securing a stable status and those receiving Swiss citizenship has grown steadily. Nevertheless, about half of the people face a potential drive back to insecure and war-torn Sri Lanka.

According to the Swiss Census 2000, the educational and economic situation of Sri Lankan Tamils is plainly under average: 65.5% obtained primary education, 17.5% secondary education and 17% an advanced education.[10] The less advanced education and the provisional legal status of admittance limit chances for upward mobility. These relegate Tamils to take up jobs in less-prestigious sections: 38.2% of them work in the poorly-paid sector of restaurant kitchens and 11.9% in the likewise inadequately paid sector of health care, i.e. as nurses as well as floor cleaners.[11] In particular the insecure legal status puts constrains

---

[8] For the temple see, Baumann, Luchesi, Wilke 2003b: 147–168; for the diversity of regional and Sanskrit tradition practices at the three different temples in the town of Hamm see, Wilke 2003. Numbers of the festival 2008 stated in the newspapers *Die Welt*, 23.06.2008 and *Westfälischer Anzeiger*, 16.06.2008. The festival 2009 was visited much less due to the many losses of relatives during the escalation and end of war in Sri Lanka in Spring 2009 (in case of the death of a family member, relatives should not visit a temple for 30 days).

[9] Numbers according to Bundesamt für Flüchtlinge 2006, Bundesamt für Statistik 2006, 2006.

[10] Bovay 2004: 40, 117. The total Swiss national education is: 29.5% primary education, 51.3% secondary education, 19.2% advanced education.

[11] Bovay 2004: 117. In comparison, among the total Swiss populations, 5.4% work in restaurants, 10.9% in the sector of health and social care.

on Tamils to take on any job, at times two jobs parallel. Only a job, regular income and own social security provides the chance to obtain a more secure and lasting stay in the host country (Markus 2005, Baumann 2007: 230–232).

Despite this unfavourable situation, since the 1990s Tamils achieved to gain a positive image in wider society, due to their diligence, industriousness, reliability, willingness to adapt and eagerness to learn. The second generation advances in educational level, speaks the vernacular (German, Swiss German and French in west Switzerland), identifies with Swiss life and Switzerland, and many obtained Swiss citizenship. Indicators like these point to an improvement in social status and professional opportunities.

According to a study by Christopher McDowell, 87% of the Tamil refugees arriving in Switzerland during the period 1983 to 1991 had been Hindus (McDowell 1996: 119). The Swiss Census 2000 specifies the number of Hindus living in Switzerland as 27,800 people, 92.5% of them of non-Swiss nationality (Bovay 2004: 12, 126–127). The real number of Hindus most possible is quite higher, coming up to some 40.000 to 45.000 Hindus in Switzerland (Baumann 2007: 226). This sum includes also some 8,000 Hindus from India and a few thousand converts to neo-Hindu groups such like the Krishna community (ISKCON), Divine Light and several others. The number of Tamil Hindus can be estimated to 30,000 to 34,000 people.[12]

As in Sri Lanka, Tamils in the diaspora strongly keep to endogam marriages, i.e. to marry not outside the ethnic group but to have a Tamil husband or wife. Both in Germany and Switzerland, among all ethnic groups Tamils score highest regarding the rate of endogam marriages (Bovay 2004: 67, Baumann 2000b: 104). This observation is significant regarding the handing on of the religious and cultural tradition to the next generation. Generally speaking, marriages between like religious and ethnic partners to a high percentage rate socialise their children in the same religious tradition and secure its maintenance, while religiously mixed marriages make the keeping of the religious tradition much less likely.

---

[12] C. Baumann 2003, Baumann 2007: 226. For the Indian Hindus see, Wächli 2008. A proper Indian Hindu temple does not exist. Most of the Indians are either for a short stay only in Switzerland (students and exchange workers), others staying for long are highly skilled and well established and express no need for a temple.

Similar to the developments in Germany, the 1990s were a time of temple proliferation. Up to 2008, Tamil Hindus have built 18 temples of varying size, the majority located in the conurbations of cities in the German speaking cantons. Spacious temples in converted factory buildings evolved in the outskirts of Zurich, Basel and the capital Bern, also staging public processions, attended by several thousand participants. Similar to the circumambulation festival at the Sri Kamadchi Ampal temple in Germany, devotees perform various kinds of bodily demanding and severe practices. Also, a new temple is designed to be built in 2010 in Olten (mid-Switzerland), aiming for a similar monumental and visible temple as the "model" of the Sri Kamadchi temple in Hamm/Germany.[13]

Hindu Ritual: Spaces and Places

The reconstruction of the histories of temple institutionalisation in Germany and Switzerland should not undermine that importantly Hindu religiousness and ritual are practised at home as well. In very broad terms and emphasising spatial categories, the vast complex of Hindu ritual can be categorised in domestic rituals, the *grhya* rites (Skt.), and solemn, public rituals, the *srauta* rites (Skt.) (Flood 1996: 41, 198–223). Domestic rituals involve importantly rites of passage, the *samskaras*, in particular birth, initiation, marriage and death. Rites of transition form an important part of Hindu ritual activity and accompany a person (in particular higher castes) through his and her life:

> Rites of passage are also classified as 'bodily rites' because of their central concern with the body—the imposition of cultural meanings upon the biological body and its transitions from conception to death. Rites of passage are expressive of, and transform, a person's identity, an identity which is personally or psychologically important and which is recognized by the wider community: they are the formal imposition of an identity and its recognition by a social group (Flood 1996: 201).

Commonly, a household asks a Brahman to come and perform these 'occasional rites'. The various prenatal, birth and childhood rites usually take place at home, while for reasons of space marriage has to be

---

[13] Information provided by Rafaela Eulberg, Ph.D. student at the Dept. for the Study of Religions, University of Lucerne, completing a study on Tamil Hindus' temples and emerging visibility of Hinduism in Switzerland.

performed in larger locations like a community hall and a celebration hall attached to the temple. Predominantly, marriages are arranged, paying attention to compatibility of caste (Skt. *jati*), both in South Asia and the diaspora.[14]

Domestic rites also encompass 'daily rites', in particular the *puja* ("homage", worship) (Flood 1996: 55). In very many Hindu households there is a shrine of varying size with *dharma* pictures and small statues of the preferred gods and goddesses. *Puja* similar to life transition rites, involves sacrifice as a series of formalised bodily acts offering flowers, incense, light and vegetarian food to the venerated deities. In more elaborated terms, *puja* also forms a part of temple worship. Another form of Hindu religiosity, in particular practised by women, but also by men at home, is fasting. At certain so-called auspicious times of the religious cycle of weeks, months and year, women fast for a period of several days, from one to ten days or more. They do not abstain from food totally, but follow specific diet regimes. Fasting usually is based on a vow (Skt. *vrata*, Tam. *nertti*), promising the god or goddess fulfilment, either to thank for a given boon or to beg for a wish (Pearson 1996).

Solemn, public rituals take place at different sites: inside and outside the temple, at specific places in nature (e.g. trees, junctions, rivers), and during pilgrimage. Rituals in the temple (Skt. *mandir*, Tam. *koyil*, *alayam*) comprise basically the rite of bathing, collective worship, followed by individual or family based worship. Bathing (Skt. *abhiseka*, Tam. *apicekam*, "consecration") involves the worshipping of the installed deity's statue, the *mūrti*, with various substances such as milk, honey, rose water, yoghurt, fruits and sandal wood paste. The icon symbolising and 'embodying' the deity is dressed and decorated, and receives food offerings such as boiled rice and sweets. The deity's meal later is offered as blessed food (Skt. *prasada*, Tam. *piracatam*) to the people attending. Traditionally, according to the sacred texts only Brahman priests are entitled to perform this ritual (Flood 1996: 209, Fuller 1984, 1992).

---

[14] Flood 1996: 200–208, McGilvray 1998: 37–49. The *Grhya Sutras*, *Dharma Sutras* and *Sastras* as well as regional oral traditions provide the text bases for the different rituals. The number of *saṃskāras* varies according to the textual source, though 16 rites evolved as a standard number. Good differentiates as well rituals in southern Saivite temples between "'public worship' [...] benefiting the whole cosmos, or 'personal worship' [...] for oneself," see Good 2001: 241.

The collective worship, *puja*, is carried out by the priest in front of each deity. He offers flowers, water, sacred speech (*mantras*), music (with a bell), incense, and light. We call this worship collective as the visitors to the temple closely watch the priest and performance. After a few initial *mantras*, the priest draws back the curtain in front of the shrine and the visitors are able to see the deity. They have the 'auspicious sight', *darsana* (Skt., Tam. *tricanam*), see and are seen by the deity. Diana Eck in her by now classic study *Darśan: Seeing the Divine Image in India* (1998) holds:

> *The central act of Hindu worship, from the point of view of the lay person, is to stand in the presence of the deity and to behold the image with one's own eyes, to see and be seen by the deity. [...] Since, in the Hindu understanding, the deity is present in the image, the visual apprehension of the image is charged with religious meaning. Beholding the image is an act of worship, and through the eyes one gains the blessings of the divine (Eck 1998: 3).*

While this central ritual takes place in the temple, festivals of the Hindu year may also take place outside the temple. These religious festivals commonly are addressed to specific deities and their special days. Most prominent and a celebrated highlight of a temple's calendar is the carriage festival. The deity so-to-speak is brought out of the temple in a big procession circumambulating the temple compound. "To witness the icon is to have the auspicious 'vision' (*darsana*) of the deity and so to receive blessing."[15]

The Diaspora Temple as Multifunctional Site

This sketch of ritual spaces in Hindu traditions underscores the religious importance of both domestic and temple ritual. A *Saiva, Sakta* or *Vaisnava* do not regularly need to visit a temple in order to be a pious person, some might very rarely have *darsan* in a temple. Christopher Fuller emphasises:

---

[15] Flood 1996: 211. The numerous festivals, their occasions and specifics cannot be described here, see for example, Younger 1980, Fuller 1984, Fuller 1992. We leave out the important topic of pilgrimage to so-called "auspicious sites", see Bhardwaj 1973, Eck 1984, Feldhaus 2003.

> *It needs to be borne in mind that temples, and what goes on in them, are but one part of Hinduism as a whole. Much Hindu religious practice takes place in the home, or in the fields or on the riverbanks; some Hindus hardly ever visit temples at all and many certainly engage in as much religious activity outside temples as in them (Fuller 1988: 50).*

Furthermore, Hindu religiousness as practised in South Asia importantly is non-congregational and it is misleading to speak of a "Hindu community" or "Hindu congregation".[16] Nevertheless, as mentioned, Tamil Hindus in Germany and Switzerland had been eager to found collective places of worship, starting with small sites in basement and private rooms, developing to much more specious halls for worship and social gathering. As temple priests and members of temple committees repeatedly expressed in interviews, Tamil Hindus flocked to the provisional temples and thus space soon proved to be too limited and cramped. The search for larger premises thus was a necessity in order to accommodate the growing number of people. Importantly, the temple as a locality and as an institution developed to a central place and space of religious maintenance as well as social meeting. Diaspora studies underscore that living away from home awakes a growing self-awareness of one's religious belonging. Research among Hindus in Great Britain underscores "many adults reported that they had become more aware of their religion in Britain" (Logan 1988: 124) and that the minority status "forced them into self-awareness and into strategies for the protection and preservation of their self-identity." (Thomas 1993: 187). Kim Knott concludes in her timely study *Hinduism in Leeds*:

> *Temple practice [...] has become of crucial importance in the retention of tradition and its transmission from one generation to the next. Attendance at the temple provides an opportunity for the strengthening of social relationships and cultural ties between members of like kin, caste and language groups (Knott 1986: 115).*

Definitely, these observations and results are not restricted to Great Britain in particular and Hindus only. Recent research reiterates the importance of newly founded places of worship for Sikhs, Jains, Buddhists, Parsi, Christians, Muslims and Hindus as well as other immi-

---

[16] Brockington 1981: 202; Fuller 1984: 14. Public discourse, however, more often than not attributes the terms of "community" and "congregation" to the population constituted by Hindu families.

grant groups in diasporic setting (Coward et al. 2000, Jacobsen, Kumar 2004). With regard to the case of the Hindu temple, in addition to serving as a place to regularly please the deities and have *darsan*, the diasporic temple developed into a physical and psychological focal point of a Hindu population in a certain region. The temple may also serve as a supplementary school, a community centre, sometimes as a sport activity centre for the youth such as the 1992 built Shree Krishna temple in Coventry (Great Britain), and generally a social place to meet other like migrants (Nye 1995: 98–101). Strikingly, the above mentioned Sri Kamadchi Ampal temple calls itself explicitly a "cultural religious centre" and it plans the construction of a "Kultur Zentrum" (cultural centre) with a spacious hall to perform weddings and a separate building for cultural and educational activities.[17]

In addition to qualitative studies, we have quantitative empirical data regarding the personal and social importance of the Hindu temple among Tamil people in Germany. The results are based on the large scale study "Living Together in Germany" conducted among seven migrant populations in Germany in 2001.[18] The study generated data for 874 people of Sri Lankan Tamil origin, constituting a 23% respond rate for Tamils. Among others, the study asks for the range of sympathy towards an organisation and institution (such like a political party, Greenpeace, Hindu temple, Catholic Church, LTTE, and others).

Table 11.1: Sympathy for a temple among Hindu Tamils in Germany

Sympathy for temple	%
very unsympathetic	3.1
rather unsympathetic	2.0
indifferent	10.2
rather sympathetic	19.3
very sympathetic	65.4

---

[17] See the website of the temple, www.kamadchi-ampal.de/Deutsch/deutsch_index.html --> "Projekte" (accessed 19.06.2008). Baumann 2000b: 153. In similar line, a number of temples in Germany and Switzerland have attached special cultural and wedding halls.

[18] The questionnaire study with 95 items was carried out in 1999–2001 by Kurt Salentin at the Department of Sociology, University of Bielefeld, Germany, see Salentin, Wilkening 2004.

We are able to assert that two thirds (65.4%) of Tamil Hindus feel very sympathetic towards a temple, added by a fifth (19.3%) feeling rather sympathetic towards the temple. The percentage of having indifferent and less sympathetic interests in the temple comes up to some 15%. That is, some 85% percent share sympathy for a Hindu temple, underscoring the previous outline of a temple's importance in the diaspora (Baumann, Salentin 2006: 304, 308).

In addition, another item asked how often the respondent visits an event and function of the listed organisation or site (such as a cultural society, German or Tamil party, a temple, a Catholic service in Tamil/in German, and others). Though temple attendance certainly takes less importance for Hindus than for Christians or Muslims as an indicator for religiousness, the variable, nevertheless, is instructive. At least, temple attendance is a visible marker and expression of religiousness. Frequencies of visits to Hindu temples are shown in table 11.2.

Almost a fifth of Hindu Tamils in Germany visit a temple at least once a week (14.8%) or more often (4.5%). One third visit a temple or attend a related festival at least once a month and almost 50% go to a temple only once a year or less often (Baumann, Salentin 2006: 304, 309).

Unfortunately, comparative data do not exist with regard to the range of sympathy towards the temple and temple attendance in South Asia and Sri Lanka in particular. Thus, it is not possible to state whether the temple achieves *more* importance than in back home Sri Lanka and whether it is more or less visited in the diaspora than in the former home country (depending also on accessibility, distance, caste restrictions, etc.). Viewed from a comparative perspective, however, this finding—high sympathy for the religious institution and high scoring of temple attendance—is typical for most first generation immigrants, irrespective of their religious traditions. As pointed out

Table 11.2: Attendance of a temple among Hindu Tamils in Germany

Temple attendance	%
less than once a year or never	17.5
at least once a year	31.0
at least once a month	32.3
at least once a week	14.8
daily or about daily	4.5

above numerous diaspora studies confirm the strong tendency among immigrants to establish religious sites in order to worship a god or gods, celebrate festivals, meet fellow émigrés and reconstruct a social space defined in one's own cultural and linguistic terms (Vertovec 1992, Warner 1998).

It seems safe to conclude that the importance of the diaspora temple is based on new meanings with regard to social and cultural as well as religious identity maintenance. The attributed meaning of a temple's function and raison d'être was enlarged. It has a broadened significance compared to temples in the country of origin. In brief, the temple provides an institutionalized home away from home for diaspora people, pointing to a significant shift in meaning.

Shifting of Ritual Spaces and Places

In order to evaluate the transferability of the heuristic of templeisation it needs to be asked, whether we also observe a shift in the ritual sphere. In the above was outlined a basic differentiation in spatial terms and were explored main Hindu domestic and solemn, public rituals. Does the Hindu temple, in contrast to the domestic sphere, become the main site to socialise Tamil Hindus in religious practices and ideas? Does it introduce to devotional acts, rituals and Hindu gods and concepts? In the following, we provide an account of exemplary areas to examine whether a shift from the home to the temple, likewise a shift away from women and mothers to male priests is observable.

Rites of passage (samskāras): Certainly Tamil Hindus in diaspora celebrate a number of rites of passage at home, as formerly in Sri Lanka. These may be prenatal rituals, the birth rite, the giving of the name. However, we observe that some *samskaras* now primarily take place in the diaspora temple. Among these is the child's first feeding with solid food, the first cutting of the hair and the introduction to writing, i.e. drawing the first letter of the alphabet.[19] Also, the important rite of initiation (*upanayana*), practised by high-caste or 'twice-born' Hindus to receive the sacred thread, usually takes place at home. In

---

[19] See, for example, the picture of the ritual of writing, performed in the Sri Sivasubramaniar temple Zurich at www.murugantemple-zh.ch/eng/engindex.php -> "services" (accessed 19.06.2009).

the diaspora, high-caste boys may undergo the *upanayana* ceremony also in the temple. Importantly, marriage rites primarily take place in the temple, though in South Asia, depending on space and financial resources available, marriages usually took place at home and the adjacent ground. The trend to celebrate marriages in the temple was introduced in South India since the 1940s, enabling low caste people to stage a wedding without life-long indebtedness.[20]

On first sight, a trend towards templeisation among Tamil Hindus in Germany and Switzerland seems to take place, i.e. a shift of life transitory rites from the home to the temple. However, as mentioned the socio-economic situation of the majority of Tamils in Germany and Switzerland needs to be taken into account. More often than not, families live in rented flats of multiple dwellings. Such flats cannot serve larger numbers of people, certainly not for a wedding. Additionally, the Tamil asylum seekers and immigrants are eager not to disturb neighbours in the dwelling who might complain about both the noise of the ritual (bell ringing etc.) as well the smell of incense and camphor. In this case, the temple provides a welcome alternative to the limited space of the private home: larger numbers of invited guests can be served and due to the temple's locality in industrial areas (often), restrictions regarding noise and smell do not exist. Also, food served, in particular while performing a marriage, is much cheaper cooked and provided for by a temple. Usually a temple has cooking facilities at its disposal.

A second main reason is of importance: In continental Europe, a scarcity of Tamil Hindu priests is notable and at times temple boards have severe difficulties in finding a priest to perform the required regular rituals for the deities installed in the temple. Temple boards employed different methods to solve the problem: a Brahman who in Sri Lanka or South India was educated in performing temple rituals, but now works in another profession, is convinced to serve part time as temple priest. Also, temple boards aim to import a priest from South Asia so that the hired *pujari* (temple priest) performs the rituals for the deities regularly (Baumann 2004b). Immigration regulations

---

[20] Good 1987: 15. Funeral rites are neither connected to the temple nor to the home as death is considered inauspicious and highly polluting.

and restrictions though may prevent the entry of the priest to Switzerland or Germany, however.

A consequence of the shortage of priests is that visits to families in their home to carry out a *smaskaras* rite provide organisational problems. The few priests available, most of them employees with shifts or regular job times, simply cannot visit the many families, living in small units ("Kernfamilie") scattered across a number of towns and villages. As such, families need to come to the temple to have the rite performed. The often noticed diasporic limitations apply both to the situation of the family and the priest.

However, a visit to the temple has an advantage of its own for the family: a temple as a place of attributed authenticity and purity lends authority to the rite performed. The striving for legitimization and authority leads Hindus, in particular younger families with no elder family members, to the temple. Though currently this situation predominates, future developments may reverse the shift away from the temple back to the home: it may be assumed that with the likely socio-economic uplift of the next generation, with more spacious living conditions and better income, accompanied by an increase of temple priests (*pujari*) and domestic priests (*purohit*) more life transition rites will be celebrated at home. In the Netherlands, Surinamese Hindu priests contest for clientele and rituals to perform at the families' home.[21]

In line with the idea of templeisation, a shift is observable amongst young women and children. Though women do their daily practice in front of their home shrine, regular visits to temples, in particular to goddess temples (Tam. *amman alayam*), have acquired a strong significance in the diaspora. Visits to such goddess temples are done with great favour. Johanna Vögeli who studied the religiosity of Tamil Hindu women in Switzerland states: "In particular *amman* temples enjoy a high popularity among women as the *shakti* is perceived strong and because of this they would receive a lot of energy." (Vögeli 2005: 67, translation MB). In the temple, the young women are introduced

---

[21] Commonly in South Asia separate practitioners specialised as a religious teacher, domestic priest, temple priest, ritual specialist, funeral priest, astrologer or healer. In the diaspora, the residential priest often has to carry out a range of the different duties and services, see Knott 1986: 73–75; for Surinam and the Netherlands, see instructively van der Burg, van der Veer 1986.

and taught how to practise special rituals at festival days. More often than not, it is the male priest who gives the instructions and explanations. Apart from some elderly women, often it is the priest who explained the arrangement and the procedure of the ritual to the younger women. The priest leads the function and it is him who is the main reference of authority. No more the elder women at home serve as examples and teachers, but the male priest in the temple. Though more in-depth research is in need, in this respect the hypothesis of templeisation appears to apply.

Finally, a significant shift from home to the temple takes place with regard to introducing children to Hindu devotional practices and ideas. In particular, this is the case when no elder family members live with the family and when the mother and the husband both work. On average, both in Germany and Switzerland the Tamil population is comparatively young, with few elderly people. In South Asia, the grand-mother introduces and teaches the children, a person of knowledge, experience and authority often absent in the small diasporic family. Thus, primarily on Friday evenings and festival days, the whole family visits the temple. Here children learn to venerate the gods and to pay respect; the priest may give a general introduction to the festival day and its specifics.

In addition, of particular importance is the introduction of Hindu classes, either on Saturday afternoon or Sunday morning. The priest teaches the children Hindu key ideas and narrates prominent stories. The importance of scripture and authoritative text is stressed. This development deserves much attention as standardisation and conceptualisation of what "Hinduism" is and what its key teachings are meant to be. For example, the Sri Kamadchi Ampal temple in Hamm/Germany already published a booklet called *Hinduismus für alle* ("Hinduism for all", Srinivasan 2007)), and the priest of the Sri Thurkkai Amman Tempel near Lucerne/Switzerland is about to launch a booklet on *Hindu Rituals* (Sarma 2009). We may observe the same trends as studied in the Netherlands a decade ago: in the mid-1990s: Alphons van Dijk stated that with regard to Hindu tradition this "lived and experienced religion develops to a believed, considered and systematized religion." (van Dijk 1996: 193, translation MB). Again, not women and mothers introduce children to Hindu practices and ideas, but the male priest. And, the introduction takes place in the temple or in a communal room by formal teaching, not by informal practice at home.

Religious Dimensions: Shift of Importance

In the mide-1980s, Kim Knott observed with regard to Indian Hindus in Great Britain:

> Temple practice [...] has become of crucial importance in the retention of tradition and its transmission from one generation to the next. Attendance at the temple provides an opportunity for the strengthening of social relationships and cultural ties between members of like kin, caste and language groups (Knott 1986: 115).

This observation is also true for the Tamil Hindu diaspora in Germany and Switzerland, now also about two decades in place. The process of templeisation applies as Tamil Hindus attribute new meanings and an enlarged significance to the diaspora temple. The temple signifies a culturally and religiously own defined space in foreign lands, forming a home away from home with known rules and, to some extent, re-established power regulations of caste and status. In addition to providing ritual space and, in Hindu terms, 'bringing the gods to the new land', the temple also functions as a maintainer of cultural and religious identity.

Templeisation as a decisive shift of ritual and authority from the home to the temple needs some qualification. The diasporic shortages with regard to the marginalized socio-economic situation of many Tamils as well as the scarcity of ritual specialists lead many families to perform the domestic rites of life transitory rituals (*samskaras*) in the temple. This shift is a pragmatic response to limitations, based on current external factors. The basic distinction between domestic rites, *grhya* rites, and the solemn, public rites, *srauta* rites, nevertheless remains. The pragmatic shift of space and place might get reverted as soon as enough domestic priests will be available and Tamils have gained sufficient sources to move to larger flats and own houses.

Importantly, the shift of authority, i.e. who introduces and teaches Hindu practices and ideas to the upcoming generation, increasingly aligns to predominant features of the countries of residence (Germany, Switzerland): media like books and verbal explanations as well as teachings in the temple to children and young women, done by the 'multifunctional' priest, point to an important shift. Rather than performative ritual and devotion—characteristics of a Hindu temple—cognitive conceptualisation and considered systemisation become increasingly important for the continuation of diasporic Hinduism. In the long run, this shift may appear decisive, turning thus standardised Hinduism from a practised and experienced tradition into a considered and systematized religion. In this way, in a few generations to come Hinduism may develop into a "Hindu denomination" with set confession, service times and teaching courses.

CHAPTER TWELVE

RELIGIONS IN INDIA AND CHINA TODAY

Peter van der Veer

Introduction

When politicians in India or China say that they want to bring Hindu identity or Confucian harmony back into social life one can be certain that they want in fact to bring about change instead of returning to the past. When American politicians want to spread religious freedom all over the world one may at first see this as part of a global expansion of human rights, but also assume that it is connected to the expansion of evangelical networks that find their political and financial support in the US. At the most general level one may assert that there is a religious revival in many parts of the world, but not without wondering where religion has been all the time when it was not yet "revived". At the same time one needs to be very cautious with the notion of the politicization of religion, since religion is always political, always concerns power, including the defintion of power. When Buddhist monks in Sri Lanka, Burma, Tibet come on the streets to resist the state they are doing politics and I would suggest that it is wrong to see that as something that does not fit their renunciation, that is against their religion brought about by extreme circumstance. Rather, I would argue that Buddhism has always been just as political as all the other religions.

Departing from this cautionary note about religion and politics I want to focus on two elements of the current situation in Asia and their historical genesis, the nation-state and religious movements. The first deals with the governance of religious difference and the nature of state intervention in society. Its main theme will be the violent production of national identity in the religious field. The second deals with the development of religious movements within a political field that stretches beyond the nation-state. Its main theme will be the spread of spiritual movements within and beyond the nation-state. I will limit my discussion by focusing on India and China within a comparative framework without developing a systematic comparison. Let me first introduce this framework before I discuss the two elements that I mentioned above.

To understand the connections between religion, power, and identity one needs a comparative framework. In my view comparison is at the heart of cultural analysis. I should make clear at the outset that I see comparison not primarily in terms of comparing societies or events, or institutional arrangements across societies, but as a reflection on our conceptual framework as well as on a history of interactions that have constituted our object of study. One can, for instance, say that one wants to study church-state relations in India and China, but one has to bring to that a critical reflection on the fact that that kind of study already presupposes the centrality of church-like organizations as well as the centrality of Western secular state formation in our analysis of developments in India and China. That critical reflection often leads to the argument that India and China (and other societies outside the West) should be understood in their own terms, and cannot be understood in Western terms. However, Indian and Chinese terms have to be interpreted and translated in relation to Western scholarship. Moreover, such translation and interpretation are part of a long history of interactions with the West. In the Indian case it is good to realize that English is also an Indian vernacular and in the case of China it is good to realize that communism is not originating from the Song dynasty. Today this field of comparison has been widely democratized by modern media, so that everyone is in a mediated touch with everyone else and has views on everyone else, mostly in a comparative sense. Comparison, as I understand it, is thus not a relatively simple juxtaposition and comparison of two or more different societies, but a complex reflection on the network of concepts that both underlie our study of society as well as the formation of those societies themselves. So, it is always a double act of reflection.

Religion is central to the analysis of civilizations, like those of India and China and everything that belongs to the cultural sphere of these great civilizations, like Vietnam, Thailand, Korea, and Japan, to mention a few. And, at the same time it is central to the analysis of their modernity. But it is very hard to understand exactly how the generic term 'religion' can be applied in the analysis of civilization and modern societies.

It is precisely the emergence and application of the generic term 'religion' as purportedly describing, but in fact producing a distinctive social field that shows the value of comparison or, perhaps better, the need for comparative reflection. It shows the central importance of the interactions between Europe and its civilizational Others in understanding the emergence of this social field. This is not an argument for the centrality of Europe in world history, but one for the centrality of the interactions between the West and its Others despite the obvious marginality of Westerners in Asia in terms of numbers and otherwise. What I have been arguing for in previous work is an interactional approach in which the interactions between Europe and Asia are seen as central to the emergence of modernity in both Asian and European societies (van der Veer 2001). To understand religious and political developments in Asia today one has to start with the nineteenth-century imperial formation. This is a phase of globalization that continues to be absolutely fundamental to the reformulations of religion in global arenas today. While it is undoubtedly true that the current phase of globalization has enhanced virtual communication in a global network society, the global system of nation-states that has been developed in the nineteenth century is still very much in place. Moreover, many of the debates about secularism and religion are carried on from this period.

It is in the period of empire-building that the interactions between Europe and Asia are most significant and that the concept of religion comes to play such a central role in the understanding of modernity. In the nineteenth century Asian religions like Confucianism, Daoism, Buddhism, and Hinduism are manufactured, constructed, invented in interactions between China and Europe as well as between India and Europe, while at the same time Christianity and Islam are being re-imagined in their image. It is of course not the case that these civilizational traditions did not exist before, but that they are inserted in emerging global understandings and thereby fundamentally changed. In that sense religion both in Europe and in Asia is a modern phenomenon, despite the long existence of the Catholic Church in Christianity and the authority of the scriptural tradition and its interpreters in all the other religions mentioned. All these religions are gradually nationalized and become part of national identity as well as globalized and part of world culture. This is a crucial part of becoming modern. Nationalism is an important social and political force everywhere that transforms the traditions that are found in the nation. As both a cultural and political force nationalism is the most important connection between religion and politics. Nationalism itself is never self-sufficient, but always relates to an emerging world order of nation-states, even in the imperial phase.

The transformation of traditions in the construction of national identity is such a radical rupture in history that it justifies my suggestion that we have to understand religion today as a modern phenomenon. Religion and secularity are simultaneously produced as connected aspects of modernity. Previous scholarship has often opposed the secular and the religious as modern against traditional, but this perspective should be recognized as secularist ideology, as an ideological claim within a particular historical configuration. In that sense it may have quite real and significant effects, not from the unfolding of a Rational World Spirit but as produced by historical movements and institutions like the state. The secularization-thesis, a progressive history of the decline of religion and the gradual secularization of society, does not pay attention to the deep connectedness of secularity and religion and thus cannot account for the contradictions in that progressive history and its lack of empirical evidence in most parts of the world. Still, like other elements of modernization theory, it is still part of the worldview of modernizing elites everywhere.

The encounter of Western power with Asian religions in the modern period is one that has been preceded by pre-colonial missionary and political encounters, but also by a long history of the expansion and spread of religious formations within the Asian region. The presence of Christianity, Islam and Judaism in Asia long precedes European expansion. Moreover, there is a long history of expansion and spread of Asian religions, like Buddhism and Hinduism. One could, of course, mention that Judaism, Christianity, and Islam, all originate in West-Asia and that they are also Asian religions, but then we would also have to ask from which period "Asia" is a meaningful category. Obviously, the encounter of Christianity with Islam is of very long standing, as Pope Benedict XVI has recently reminded us when he referred to hostile comments made by a 14th century Byzantine Emperor about Islam, but the encounter of Hinduism and Buddhism with Islam is just as old.[1] There is no objective reason to see Islam and Christianity as not indigenous in Asian societies as against Buddhism and Hinduism, although there is a strong nationalist urge in India, for example, to

---

[1] Lecture given by Pope Benedict XVI at the University of Regensburg on 12 September 2006.

argue for such a fundamental difference. These ideological claims are far from harmless, as we know from the history of communalism in India as well as from the history of anti-Semitism in Europe.

However long and important the history of religious encounters in Asia may have been the modern period of imperialism and nationalism provides a specific rupture with the past, because of the externality of imperial power and the ideological emphasis on the difference of modern society from both its own past and from other, so-called backward societies. Comparison and an evolutionary perspective on difference became crucial in the high days of the empire. As Edward Said (1978) has rightly argued, the new scientific knowledge of Orientalism also provided the colonized with a new understanding of their traditions. Hinduism, Buddhism, Confucianism, Daoism were discovered and evaluated by philologists, archeologists and other historians while traders, missionaries and colonial officers tried to deal with the contemporary forms of these traditions. It is this apparatus of imperial knowledge that has created an archive that is still crucial for any understanding of Asian traditions. It is this archive that needs to be understood if one wants to understand the nature of the modern transformation of religion, both in Asia and in the West.

Buddhism is a good example. It came to be recognized in nineteenth-century scholarship as existing in various parts of Asia and thus as transnational. In contrast to the old enemy Islam it was also regarded as an ethically high religion with universal pretensions like Christianity. Besides such discussions on the essence of religion, whatever their importance, there were also crucial developments in Asia. Above all, there were archeological attempts to find ancient Buddhism under layers of Hinduism in India in the same period. Major General Alexander Cunningham (1814–1893), the founder of the Indian Archeological Survey, found Buddhist sites in India, such as the famous Sarnath. These findings were an important element in establishing ancient Indian history in which Buddhism was portrayed as the enemy of Brahmanism, came to be destroyed by Islam and ultimately supplanted by Hinduism. This was essential to the grand narrative of Indian history in which Buddhism was also seen as an alternative to caste-ridden Hinduism and taken up as such by egalitarian reformists like the Untouchable leader Ambedkar. It is this simultaneous production of Buddhism as native to India and as a world religion that could be universally respected for its modern, egalitarian message that becomes so important in the Indian location.

In Sri Lanka something else happens. Here Buddhism comes to be reframed first by the Pali text Society of Rhys Davids, then by Theosophists like Colonel Olcott who designs the Sri Lankan Flag and creates a Buddhist catechism, and most importantly by the reformist monk Anagarika Dharmapala. It is precisely because of the reconfiguration of Buddhism in Western scholarship as a world religion within the imperial framework that enables it to become such an important element of religious nationalism among the Sinhalese in Sri Lanka. The dialectics of orientalism and nationalism is of great importance on both sides of the imperial imagination. On the side of the metropole it is the development of a universal spirituality, of which Buddhism is seen as a prime example that fits the marginalization of institutional religion in a secularizing society.

The modern idea that we can characterize a society or set of societies by its civilization in order to make it available to universal understanding is exemplified by calling Sri Lanka a Buddhist society, India a Hindu society and China a Confucian society, as well as Europe a Christian or Enlightened Modern Society. To analyze the relation between religion and the state as well as the development of religious movements in Asia one needs a comparative framework that highlights the historical transformation of discursive traditions into the modern category of "religion".

The State and National Religion

The notion of civilization, as Norbert Elias (1978) has argued for Europe, is directly related to the emergence of national consciousness, but, I would add, also to seeing the nation as part of larger regional and global configurations. To illustrate this let us look briefly at the idea that China is a Confucian society. In the context of an assumed worldwide religious revival we seem witness to what many observers call 'the revival of Confucianism'. President Hu Jintao and other Chinese leaders have reevaluated the Confucius tradition. They now concede that harmony as the central value of Confucian teachings is something to be cherished. Worrying about growing economic disparities amid rapid economic growth, the Chinese Communist Party (CCP) focuses on Confucian harmony as a form of societal consensus and solidarity. For the first time in 66 years the Party organized a lavish worship ceremony at Tianjin's Confucius Temple in November

2004. In the town of Qufu, the birth place of Confucius, the official ceremony of commemorating his birthday has since 2004 become an important public ritual, broadcast live on state television. The Ministry of Education is encouraging numerous courses in Confucian culture by establishing Confucius Institutes all over the world following the model of the Goethe Institute or the British Council.

But what is being revived and whether it is secular or religious remains very unclear. Political attempts to make Confucianism the secular morality of Chinese civilization today are historically similar to debates at the end of Qing to make Confucianism a national religion (guojiao). Both state officials and major intellectuals were involved in this project, but it is precisely the intellectualism and distance from popular belief that has prevented to make Confucianism into something akin to Japanese State Shintoism before World War II. The attempts to transform Confucian traditions into a civil, national religion were extremely interesting as a form of social engineering, but ultimately failed, largely because Confucian teachings could encompass Daoist and Buddhist teachings but not the social energy that local Daoist and Buddhist cults could mobilize. Although Confucianism can provide a legitimating ideology for state authoritarianism that enforces social harmony, as one sees for example in Singapore, its proponents will face great difficulties in making it into a national religion.

The current position of the Communist Party towards Confucianism is quite a departure from its long-term secularist project. Not so long ago to be accused to be a Confucianist was to be branded a reactionary feudalist. But Confucianism with its civilizational morality is much more palatable for atheists than Buddhism, Daoism, or the wide-ranging category of popular religion. Long before the Communist Party came to power in China there had been a number of secularist campaigns attacking religion, supported by both intellectuals and state officials. Already in the last phase of the Qing period such campaigns were initiated. "Smash temples, build schools" *(huimiao, banxue)* is a particularly telling slogan that was used in a campaign against temple cults and religious specialists during reforms in late Ching at the end of the 19th century. According to the reformists, led by Kang Youwei (1858–1927) and supported by the emperor, China had to modernize quickly and this had to be done by promoting education and by getting rid of religious superstition. These two elements belonged together, since education should train people in modern, rational thought while superstition and magical thought should be discouraged. Before the Communist victory in 1949 a number of campaigns, first in late imperial China and afterwards in the Republic, destroyed or "secularized", according to one estimate, half of a million existing temples (Goossaert 2006). What the Communists did after 1949 was, to a very great extent, a continuation of these campaigns. While one might have expected that the nationalists in Taiwan with their Confucian nationalism would have had a fundamentally different policy towards religion than the Communists, the opposite is in fact the case. Till the late 1960s the nationalists kept religious activities under a very tight control. All these campaigns against religion should have produced a secular China, but the contrary is true. In Taiwan religious activities are all over the place and with the loosening of the tight controls over religion in the PRC we see religious activity flourishing in large parts of the country.

While secularization has not really happened secularism in China has been and continues to be a very significant project, buttressed by state power. Chinese secularism is, ideologically, a form of scientism and rationalism. From a 19th century enlightened and evolutionary perspective it pitches scientific rationality against magical superstition. Secularism is thus a battle against the misconceptions of natural processes that keeps the illiterate masses in the dark and in the clutches of feudal rulers and clerics. The term for superstition (mixin) comes from Japanese as many other terms that are employed in the discourse of modernity, like indeed the term "religion" (zongjiao) itself. In using these neologisms it makes a distinction between religion that contributes to the morality of the state and superstition that is detrimental to modern progress. These views are shared by intellectuals of all persuasions, including the nationalists and the communists, but also by many reformist religious thinkers. This is both a discursive and an institutional shift as an aspect of the transition from the ancient regime of the Qing empire to the modern Republic. The traditional system of three teachings (sanjiao), Confucian, Buddhist and Daoist, in which Confucian state ritual defined the framework for the other two was transformed in the Republic by the notion that there were five acceptable world religions: Buddhism, Taoism, Catholicism, Protestantism, and Islam. Confucianism was kept outside of this arrangement, because it was considered to be both national instead of global and in essence secular rather than religious. These religions that are officially recognized till today are being organized along the models of Christianity in nation-wide associations that are ultimately controlled by the state.

What remains outside of this is what is often called popular religion (minjian xinyang), namely all those cults that are in fact closely connected to Buddhist, and Taoist ideas and practices but are not part of these associations. Moreover, many of the Buddhist and Taoist local cults are hard to transform into nation-wide associations. Especially Taoism had been deeply intertwined with local cults. The opposition between officially approved religion and local forms of superstition gives authorities a great space for controlling and repressing all kinds of religious expressions.

Anticlericalism and scientism together were deeply connected to Western, enlightened ideas about progress, in which magic had to be replaced by scientific rationality and by moral religion as basis of national identity. Major currents of western thought, like social Darwinism, neo-Kantianism, and Marxism were absorbed in China. Not only prescriptive thought about society came to stand in the light of rationality, but also descriptive social science, such as sociology and anthropology lost their ability to describe the effects of these ideologies on society since they could not distance themselves from them. Intellectuals played an important role in the secularist projects of nationalizing and rationalizing religion and, crucially, they were part and parcel of large-scale state interventions to produce a modern, national identity.

I do not want to detail the sordid history of state persecution of clerics and destruction of temples both before and during Communist rule. I only want to draw attention to the fact that under communism the anti-superstition and anti-clerical campaigns were combined with anti-feudalism campaigns. The 1950s not only saw the brutal elimination of millenarian movements like Yiguandao, but also the destruction of feudalism and thus the redistribution of temple land and temple property, secularization in its original sense. Mao, as a good Marxist, predicted the decline of religion as part of the creation of a socialist China in the following words:

> *The gods were erected by peasants. When the right time comes, the peasants themselves will throw away these gods with their own hands.*

However, as matter of fact, Mao and the Party did everything to destroy the gods but the peasants did everything to rescue them.

In Communist China atheism or a form of historical materialism became the official ideology of the country and religion came either under outright attack or was brought under the tight control of the

Party. The liberalization of China from 1978 onwards has also brought a liberalization of the religious field. It is very hard to assess the direction of developments today, since a century of persecution has severed the chains of oral and ritual transmission in many parts of the country, destroyed the lives and livelihood of clergy and therefore much of the infrastructure of religion. Building this up requires economic support that is mainly coming from tourism, since many of the shrines are in places of touristic interest. The rebuilding of religious infrastructure is thus related to new forms of consumption and will be closely dependent on them.

In India we find quite a different development of the religion-nation-state relation, revolving mainly around the majority-minority issue. Hinduism in India, on the one hand, has both been as difficult to define as Confucianism in China, but nevertheless has proved a suitable candidate for national religion since the late nineteenth century. Religion in India has been harnessed to anti-colonial nationalism in the struggle for Independence and both Hindu and Muslim communities have been mobilized along these lines. This has led to India's Partition in 1947 in which Pakistan, a homeland for Muslims, has been separated from India, a secular state with a Hindu majority and a considerably diminished Muslim minority. This historical rupture has been followed by the separation of East-Pakistan or Bangladesh from West Pakistan in 1971. Furthermore, it has led to regular confrontations between Pakistan and India about the contested area of Kashmir.

Relations between Hindus and Muslims and especially attempts to make Hinduism the established religion of India determine our understanding of religions in India today. The dangerous mix of religious nationalism led by Hindu religious leaders, organized in the Vishva Hindu Parishad (VHP) or World Hindu Congress, with anti-Muslim (as well as anti-Christian) politics, organized by the Rashtriya Swayamsevak Sangh (RSS) or National Volunteers Corps and its political wing, the Bharatiya Janata Party (BJP) or Indian People's Party, has led to a very volatile political situation in India. It seems that the Gandhian project to use religious discourse for fostering communal harmony has lost much of its influence, while the secular state cannot be counted upon to be the guarantor of that harmony. In fact, it is precisely the political process that leads to the disturbance of that harmony. The political scientist Paul Brass has convincingly argued that some cities in India that are prone to communal rioting have 'institutionalized riot systems'. In the city are organized networks of activists in the service of political parties who stage riots aimed at ethnic and religious minorities. Brass calls these activists "riot specialists" (Brass 2003). Of special interest here is the nefarious relation between politicians, riot specialists, and law enforcement. Since the assassination of Mrs Indira Gandhi by her Sikh bodyguards the state at local, regional, and central levels has become increasingly involved in communal violence. Although the processes involved here are primarily political they are intimately intertwined with religion, since religious issues are often used to mobilize people along communal lines. Analytically, a sharp distinction between secular politics and religious worldviews cannot be easily made, since political boundaries overlap with ethnic and religious ones. One of the major issues today in India is the declining socio-economic prospects of the Muslim population due to discrimination in all sectors of public life. This is not a religious issue per se, but the discrimination of Muslims is often legitimized in terms of their 'not belonging' because of the 'foreignness' of their religion, to their 'hyper-masculinity' as a result of the fact that their religion allows them to have four wives, and so on.

A paradigmatic case for the understanding of religion and the state in India today is Gujarat where a major pogrom on Muslim citizens in 2002, killing around 2,000, has been supported by the state. Ahmedabad, the scene of the worst violence, had witnessed communal riots before in which the police had abated the violence, for example in 1969, but conditions changed dramatically in the 1980s with the emergence of the BJP as a major political player and the decline of the Congress Party. In this period a normative secularism gave way to an empirical Hindu majoritarianism. At the central level politicians, such as R.K. Advani (Home Minister from 1998–2004), launched a number of campaigns to promote Hindu nationalism, focusing on the issue of removing a sixteenth-century mosque from the site of the alleged birthplace of the Hindu God Rama in the North Indian pilgrimage centre Ayodhya. This sort of campaigns led to pogroms on Muslims in 1992 and 2002. It is this intensification of communal politics in India that has changed periodic communal violence, related to elections, into a more structural and permanent antagonism between Hindu and Muslim communities. In this climate non-state actors can still refer to the normative secularism that is enshrined in India's constitution and fight for a better treatment of Muslims but the institutions of the state respond to these justified claims mostly by selective action and inaction.

The worsening of the relations between Hindus and Muslims over the last decades has certainly influenced religious experience and religious organization in India. Islam is an arena of great debate and conflict among Indian Muslims who have to formulate their attitudes towards a secular state that fails to protect them and is inefficient in delivering welfare to them in a context in which powerful Hindu political groups want to culturally marginalize them. This comes at a moment that Islam-inspired terrorism is an object of international concerns and politics. The volatile development of foreign relations between India and Pakistan (with Afghanistan looming large in the background) undoubtedly affects the position of the Muslim community in India deeply, since they are constantly summoned to "choose" between their nation and their religion. Alternatively, outsiders distinguish between 'good' and 'bad' Muslims depending on their religious orientation within Islam. This often concerns so-called syncretistic Sufi practices that are seen to cater for both Muslim and Hindu communities and are thus seen to be part of "good Islam" as against "bad, fundamentalist Islam". These external views are related to internal debates about correct practice which are much more complex than the external views allow. Islam is a discursive tradition in which there are a great number of different viewpoints and debates that are not so easily reducible to Indian Islamic syncretism versus Wahhabi (foreign) fundamentalism.

Similarly Hinduism as a discursive tradition can also not be reduced to the political ideology of Hindutva (Hindu-ness) that equates Hindu with Indian and thus places everyone who is not a Hindu beyond the pale. Nor can it be made into the orientalist myth of all-embracing tolerance, exemplified by the notion of the manifold paths to salvation. Again, we see a much more complex picture in which Muslim saints are important for many Hindus, in which the rise of backward castes undermines the hegemony of Brahman castes, complicating the unity sought after by Hindu nationalists, in which untouchables and tribals are targeted by Hindu missionization and come to play an important role in communal violence. Hindu culture is not only open to straightforward Sufi saint worship, but also to popular expressions, such as Bombay film lyrics dependent on Urdu love poetry. Some of the greatest Bombay movie stars in the era of Hindutva mobilization were Muslims: Aamir Khan, Salman Khan, and Shahrukh Khan, suggesting a rejection of this mobilization of communal sentiments in Mumbai, a city terribly hit by anti-Muslim pogroms and later revenges and retaliations by Muslims.

Important for the future development of Hindu and Muslim discursive traditions is obviously how people are educated. According to the economist Amartya Sen (1999) education and especially literacy is perhaps the most important resource for creating equal opportunities and enhancing human potentiality and freedom. Education, however, also furthers class distinctions, as Bourdieu argues, as well as ethnic and religious antagonism (Bourdieu and Passeron 1990). Since state education fails to service large sections of the population the field is wide open for religious organization. On the Hindu side it is the VHP with its Vidya Bharati subsidiary that promotes at the end of higher education Hindu astrology and Vedic knowledge (supported by the government during the reign of the BJP) and at the end of primary and middle schools Hindu textbooks that especially in their portrayal of the history of Muslims and Christians in India are decidedly fostering a communalist worldview (Froerer 2007). On the Muslim side it is the proliferation of madrasas with primarily religious education that produce generations of religious students (Taliban) who can hardly be used for secular jobs and may be prone to radicalization, although there is considerable debate about the latter suggestion (Vicziany 2007). Middle Class Hindus and Muslims often choose secular schools and universities for their offspring, but even there the prospects especially for Muslims to gain appropriate employment are not bright. It is for these reasons that education is so much a battleground today between secular and different religious forces. Christianity is very much part of this struggle, especially in tribal areas and among untouchables where it is often one of the very few channels of social mobility. The attacks on Christians and Christian missionaries in various parts of India form an indication of the seriousness of this battle for the mind of the future generation. Especially the inroads of the RSS and VHP in tribal areas and among untouchables have made these parts of the populations susceptible to the ideas that they have a possible future as respectable Hindus if they take part in the pogroms against Muslims and Christians. At the same time radicals reject religion altogether and strive for recognition as racially oppressed dalits. Interesting is that all these demands and struggles are couched in a fully modern, and in fact secular idiom of national heritage, freedom of ideas and expression, as well as sovereignty. It is also important to note that the global discourse of human rights that is employed not only by the United Nations but also by the USA is an important element in the violent and non-violent negotiations of conversion and education, unwittingly reinforcing the idea of foreignness and national defense.

Religious Movements, National and Transnational

If we would limit our view of religion to the relation with the state and the attempts to create a national religion we may miss a widely varying panorama of competing Buddhist, Christian, and Daoist groups with all their own transnational networks supported by resources that cannot be controlled by the nation-state. It is possibly rewarding to compare this expansion of religious movements with the creation of a pop culture that is helped by television and the creation of consuming audiences over a wide variety of societies. Whatever the state's ambitions of total control it is the transnational character of these movements that will put a limit to the state's abilities. That is not to say that these movements are anti-state, since in most cases they are not. They can even be seen as constructive in developing civil society, as Richard Madsen has been arguing for Taiwanese Buddhism (Madsen 1998). However, in my view, they should not be understood merely in terms of their relation to the state, but rather in their own terms, with their own objectives that may or may not clash with the state.

Most scholarship here is, rightly, focused on the expansion of Christianity in the region. The missionary expansion of Christianity all over the world in the nineteenth century brought with it a completely new, modern relation between existing religious tradition on the one hand and education, social welfare, and health on the other. This missionary expansion of Christianity transformed Christianity but also all the religions it encountered. Scripturalism, church-like associations, the rise of the laity and so on are all part of what I have called "conversion to modernity" (van der Veer 1996). Christianity, however important, is only one of the religions that are part of the conversion to modernity. It is instructive to look at the transformation of Hindu, Buddhist and Daoist movements in the context of nationalism and transnationalism. Instead of giving an overview of the entire range of religious movements in India and China I want to focus on two particularly interesting instances of what is often called 'Asian Spiritualiy', namely Chinese Qi Gong and Indian Yoga.

Although in 1917 Mao had written negatively about qi exercises as promoting tranquility and passivity, while he himself wanted to promote activity as essential for the survival of China, qi exercises did survive the attacks on traditionalism and feudalism by being aligned to science (Jian Xu 1999: 972). In the 1950s qi exercises were more and more part of a state-sanctioned medical science. In this way qi exercises came to be practiced by acknowledged physicians rather than by spiritual masters. Qigong therapy was thus taken out of the realm of superstition into the realm of scientific clinics. Not only medical science but also physics and biology produced experiments focusing on the existence of qi. However, this scientific sanctification and purification of qigong did not result in total state control. This is partly inherent in the fact that traditional Chinese medicine, while claiming to be 'scientific', simultaneously claims to transcend the limitations of 'Western' science. At the same time it is a nationalist claim of a superiority of "Chineseness" that is difficult to attack by a state that promotes socialism with Chinese characteristics, as Deng Xiaopeng called it. Outside of the control of the state was the spontaneous qigong craze of the 1980s in the aftermath of the Cultural Revolution. People started to do qi exercises everywhere and to some extent this can be read as setting the body free from the constraints imposed by the state and signifying a transition to greater individual freedom and interaction (Chen 2003). The state tried to channel this spontaneous outburst of qigong activities into qigong institutions and movements, but some of them, most notably the Falun Gong or Falun Dafa, as it is called later, turned out to be a real challenge for state control (Palmer 2007).

On 25 April 1999, more than ten thousand Falun Gong adherents from all over China gathered around Zhongnanhai, the capital's political heart, setting the stage for the most serious political case since the pro-democracy demonstrations of 1989. The reason for this gathering was to request from the government the official recognition of the Falun Dafa Research Association, the lifting of the ban on Li Hongzhi's latest publications and the release of Falun Gong practitioners detained during previous demonstrations. According to the People's Daily (June 15, 2000) the government never had forbidden the practice of normal exercises:

> *People have the freedom to believe in and practice any kind of qigong method, unless when people use the banner of exercises to spread superstition, create chaos and organize large scale gatherings which disturb the social order and influence social stability.*

Three months after the demonstration in Beijing, the Central Committee of the Communist Party of China issued a circular that forbade members of the Communist Party to practice the Falun Dafa. Three days later, on July 22, the Ministry of Civil Affairs issued the decision to outlaw the Falun Dafa Research Association (Chang 2004).

What is the Falun Gong? It was founded by a man with the name Li Hongzhi who was born according to the authorities on 7 July 1952, but according to his own autobiography on 13 May 1951 which would be the date of birth of Sakyamuni, the Buddha and allow him to claim that he is a reincarnation of the Buddha. In 1991 he joined qigong activities. In 1992 he started giving lectures to a growing audience and in the following years he registered his Falun Gong association with the official China Society for Research on Qigong Science. This association is quite typical in its claim to be scientific, connected to health, but it seems to go further in its moral teachings and connection to Buddhist and Daoist cosmology. It connects to the ancient idea that through physical qi exercises one also cultivates one's moral character. There is a messianic streak in the teachings of Li Hongzhi with an emphasis on all kinds of evils that threaten the world (now including the Communist party) and the position of li Hongzhi as saviour. When the state cracked down on the Falun Gong it claimed that it had outnumbered the 55 million-strong Communist Party in April but this was revised down to a mere 2 million in November of 1999. It is impossible to say how many followers have gone underground, but it is probably substantial. Moreover, the Falun Gong has become very active transnationally among the diasporic Chinese communities, especially since its founder has fled China and lives in New York. However, again, it is hard to say how important the Falun Gong has become since it is only one movement in a global spread of taiji, qigong, and forms of martial arts under the rubric of Wu Shu, like Qiaolin and Kungfu. Although the practitioners emphasize the differences between these practices and traditions, from a historical and sociological viewpoint they form one tradition with a number of variations.

In India one direction is the same as taken by the Chinese, namely yoga mainly as a physical exercise (hatha-yoga) and a health practice that can be experimented with by medical science. Yoga is seen to be extremely healthy for the body and for the mind. Another clear direction is the creation of the healthy, strong masculinity for the Hindu nation. This is primarily the field of martial arts to which yoga practices can be linked. Like the Falun Gong in China the religious organization of bodily disciplines in India can gain a political meaning. This is true for organizations like the RSS and the related Vishwa Hindu Parishad that is organizing the various spiritual leaders and their movements under a common nationalist platform. These organizations are anti-secular and, since India is a democracy unlike China, they are allowed to be both cultural and political. A particularly interesting development in yoga is its alignment with the development of global capital. Since yoga was never seen as subversive by the powers that be it became a recognized element in middle class religiosity. As such it followed the trajectories of this class that became more and more transnational in its orientation during the 1960s. Its older connection with nationalism was not thereby forgotten or marginalized but utilized in identity politics in the countries of immigration, especially the USA. Indian spirituality is something to be proud of since many non-Indians are also attracted to it. The global reach of yoga was stimulated by groups, such as the Divine Life Society, founded by Sivananda, but can be best understood by the fact that its origins lie in an imperial modernity, mediated by the English language. From the English speaking world yoga, however, has spread to the rest, making for 4 million yoga practitioners in Germany and 13 million in the USA (Strauss 2005). In the 1960s yoga became part of the youth revolution that shook Western culture. Promoted by popular music-groups like the Beatles Indian spirituality became a lifestyle element that could be commodified and marketed in a variety of ways. In the West it became part of a complex of alternative therapies based on lifestyle and bodily exercise. In light of the therapeutic worldview that is part of global capitalism it has now also come back to India in the new perceptions of the urban middle class of Indian tradition. Due to the opening up of the market for Eastern spirituality not only yoga has benefited, but a variety of Chinese spiritual exercises such as taiji quan and qigong have also gained a transnational market.

In both India and China movements that propagate religious traditions and especially alternative utopias can have a political impact. While in India such movements became part of an in principle legitimate nationalist project, although some offshoots were quickly de-legitimized as 'extremist', in China such movements were under constant attack from both the Kuomintang and the Communists. The reason for this significant divergence can perhaps be found both in pre-colonial and colonial histories of the Chinese and Indian polities. The Chinese imperial state constantly fought peasant rebellions that were inspired by a religious cosmology and Chinese intellectuals were brought up in a framework of Confucian distrust of popular religion. The failure and bloodshed of two major religious rebellions against Christianity and imperialism in the 19th century further promoted the idea of secular science as an answer to China's backwardness. In India religious movements seem to become gradually part of a spiritual resistance against imperial power and, as such, a major element in the formulation of anti-colonial nationalism.

In the postcolonial period it is really the liberalization of the Indian and Chinese economies under the impact of global capitalism that frees the energies of spiritual movements to organize civil society. This is very clear in the Chinese case where liberalization first gives space to a spontaneous qigong and later to the rise of movements like Falun Gong that connect qigong to older ideas of a moral and political nature. In India one can see this especially in the rise of a Hindu nationalism that rejects an earlier secular and multicultural project of the state by emphasizing Hindu traditions as the basis of Indian civilization, thereby excluding other contributions by religious minorities. It is especially a new-fangled urban religiosity that is both interested in yoga and in a strong nation that supports this kind of politics.

Indian spirituality has been formulated by Vivekananda during a trip to Chicago and has been further developed in constant interaction with the rest of the world. A political figure like Mahatma Gandhi fits seamlessly in this history. When in the 1970s and 1980s till the present day highly educated members of the Indian middle class migrate to the USA for medical and engineering jobs they are confronted with a quite aggressive marketing of Indian spirituality in a market for health, for exercise, and for management practices. This, in turn, is brought back to India where especially successful new movements like the Bangalore-based Art of Living with Guru Ravi Shankar cater for a mobile, transnational class of business entrepreneurs. China's isolation between 1950 and 1980 has ensured a belated entry of Chinese spirituality on this market, but nevertheless it is quickly catching up with products like taiji quan and qigong. In the Chinese case there is a stronger connection with sports and especially martial arts, which are also promoted by Hong Kong and mainland movies. In both India and China one finds a similar appropriation of spiritual traditions to cater for the newly emerging middle classes. These newly manufactured spiritualities have a tenuous relationship with textual traditions, guarded by centers of learning and spiritual masters. They are creative in their response to new opportunities and anxieties produced by globalization and are, as such, comparable to Pentecostal and charismatic varieties of Christianity.

Conclusion

An analysis of the nature of the nation-state continues to be of primary importance when one tries to determine how religious formations in Asia develop today. In China the Communist Party, though still atheist in orientation, is developing a more accommodative relation with Chinese religions. Especially at the level of the "moral state" it tries to align itself with a particular form of Confucian morality as an essential part of national identity. In its relation with religious institutions and movements it has opened the field for more religious expressions as long as they further commercial society and do not threaten the status quo. In India the normative secularism of the state has slowly given way to assertions of Hindu majoritarianism. Especially the failure of the state to provide adequate secular education allows for the socialization of communalist attitudes. This has led to a very volatile situation in which both the international (Pakistan) and the regional (Kashmir) political developments contribute to the radicalization of religious identity politics.

The nation-state is part of a global system of nation-states and religious formations are also both national and transnational. While one can study the spread of global spirituality from the second half of the nineteenth century the current phase of globalization does enhance the importance of transnational connections for all world religions as well as for forms of spirituality that are not tied to religious institutions and doctrines. This is immediately obvious when one examines the current spread of Pentecostalism and Evangelicalism across Asia, but it is also striking when one looks at Buddhism and Islam as well as at spiritual movements like Qi Gong and Yoga. To some extent these expansions of religious and spiritual formations are tied to patterns of migration, but more in general they both connect ethnic groups and transcend them. They are part of an emergent network society in which the state is still the major player but can be challenged from across its borders.

PART FIVE

JUDAISM

CHAPTER THIRTEEN

ONE PEOPLE? CONTEMPORARY JEWISH IDENTITIES

Eliezer Ben-Rafael

Identity and flow

This chapter delves into the multiplication of Jewish identities, since the dawn of modernity. Seeing the diversity of directions taken by these identities, we ask whether one may still speak these days of something common to all formulations of Jewishness and if it is still appropriate to speak of 'One Jewish People'.

This issue is actually tackled by a large body of literature which proposes a variety of paradigms intended to distinguish forms and contents of modern Jewries. In a general manner, the distinctions focus on a number of topics that are strongly interrelated. On the one hand, there is an evincing of the confrontation of Judaism with modernity, and on the other, consideration of the specific contexts that Jews encounter over the globe—especially Israel as opposed to the Diaspora. Jacob Katz (1973), for instance, focuses on the deep crisis experienced by European Jewry in the nineteenth century and reviews the various attitudes that emerged in those circumstances. Katz especially emphasizes the relation between secularization and individualization, which is not too far from Michael Meyer's (1999) analysis which distinguishes four basic attitudes—straightforward rejection of modernity, compartmentalization of areas subjected by modernity and traditional Judaism respectively, adjustment of Judaism to modernity, and subordination of the first to the second.

In a more substantive perspective, Daniel Elazar (1999) underlines that in the modern era—and according to circumstances of time and place—we find religious, ethnic and national aspects of Judaism emphasized at diverse degrees by various formulations of the Jewish identity. Elazar insists that this process of differentiation is anchored in the fact that Jewry has become an essentially subjective phenomenon and is by no means a definitive given of the Jewish condition anymore—as it was in the traditional setting. This understanding is, in turn, close to Charles Liebman and Stephen Cohen's (1990) when they insist on the fact that Jewishness is now a 'personalistic' and 'voluntaristic' matter. On this ground, the authors contend, we witness the growing importance of the question of 'identification' to Jewishness, in contrast to the question of the contents themselves of Jewishness. Answers to that question take on, of course, most diverse contours according to circumstances. Hence, between Israeli and American Jews, one finds substantial differences regarding the significance given to, and the identification expressed with, the notion of the Land of Israel, or, in a same vein, between the different approaches to the 'relevant other', that is, the notion of the 'non-Jew.'

In contrast, Pierre Birnbaum and Ira Katzenelson (1995) evince the continuity of cultural orientations among Jews beyond the variety of reactions to modernity. This perspective finds support in the work of Shmuel Eisenstadt (1992) who speaks of a 'Jewish civilization' whose roots are to be found in Jewish religious traditions and which have been conveyed throughout the transformations of Judaism over the centuries. At the centre of this civilization stands nowadays a notion of cultural-historical community most often labelled 'peoplehood' which, however, does not prevent intra-Jewish cleavages—as abundantly documented in the work of Jonathan Sacks (1993). Sacks, indeed, shows three lines of cleavages in the contemporary Jewish experience: between the religious and the secular, between the Orthodox and the liberal, and between Israel and the Diaspora. Close to him, David Vital (1990) rather sees a dichotomy which, in his own view, is doomed to allow room for a one-polar picture where Israel is the only setting where the continuation of Judaism is somehow warranted for the generations to come.

Our own discussion is inspired by these works and the preoccupation which they express regarding the prospects of survival of 'one people'. Our approach, however, also aspires to consider all existing Jewish identities as building up a space of possibilities and the extent to which they illustrate sufficient consistency to warrant some kind of unity. An approach that, of course, requires us to assume that they all share, in one measure or another, given common criteria, which alone renders pertinent their sharing the same space of formulations. It is this structuralist perspective that guides our study of Jewish identities.

Our discussion stems from the Levi-Straussian perspective (Levi-Strauss 1958, 1961) which deals with collective identity as embedded in aspects dictated by the very significance of the notion. In our own formulation (Ben-Rafael 2002), a collective identity consists of the way individuals see themselves as 'members' of a given group of people and thus necessarily implies the three following facets. The first facet is the self-image carried by individuals of their commitment to a given social entity and its affiliates, in whom they consider themselves members; the second facet concerns individuals' perceptions of what makes this collective a 'singular' entity, meaning its symbols, norms and other aspects; the third facet consists of the impact that membership in the collective carries for individuals' positioning vis-à-vis 'others' or 'non-members'. These facets, to be sure, are not necessarily understood identically by everyone who sees him or herself as a member of the collective. Versions of the collective identity may fluctuate among different individuals and milieus both diachronically and synchronically—according to life experiences and conditions. Furthermore, and from a substantive point of view, not only may each facet be phrased differently in these different versions, but they may also receive different emphases in the overall assessment of the collective identity. Accordingly, it is less appropriate to speak of one permanent formula of collective identity applying to one collective than of a space of possible identities. This does not however gainsay that the more remote the different versions from each other, the greater the probability that the unity of the identity space is endangered and susceptible to fractures up to a stage where parts of the collective no longer recognize themselves in each other. Following here Wittgenstein (see Schatzki 1996), we may formulate this perspective with the notion of 'family resemblance'. By this notion, the philosopher designated the unequal resemblance of given features that appear in different combinations among individuals belonging to a same family network and grants them this *'air de famille'* which they possess.

It is with these preoccupations in mind that we analyze here the numerous forms of Jewish identity that started to emerge in the eighteenth century with the growth of modern secularism. Though very different from one society to the other, modernity has meant wherever it took root that man and society stand at the centre of the social order, and traditional truths have seen their influence drastically reduced— except as far as they are shouldered by ideologies of the 'good society' carried by factions and individuals. With the coming of this era, traditional Judaism found itself in the eye of a storm of revolutionary ideas, and soon lost much of its influence over the Jews. The Emancipation widened the rift. Many then chose to express their Judaism in new ways, until eventually traditionalists came to represent a small minority. In fact, even prior to the Emancipation, many Jews, sensing the imminent cultural revolution, championed the notions of equality and personal freedoms (Russell 1996). They were convinced that economic and technological developments would bring down the barriers between the groups and sectors in society, leading to a modification not only of their status, but of Jewish society and religion as well. Indeed, the processes that took place in the course of the nineteenth century triggered a radical change in relations between Jews and non-Jews, bringing them closer together on the one hand, but spawning modern anti-Semitism on the other. At the same time as the Jews were allowed to return to England and make their home there, for example, it became the fashion in elite circles to try and persuade them to convert to Christianity (Ragussis 1995). Similarly, while Jews were admitted into the French army, the Dreyfus affair which implicated a Jewish military officer sparked a wave of anti-Semitism. Above all, the transformation of the Jews was spurred by their internal dilemmas, which were cast in a new light by Europe's revolutions.

The search for new formulations of Jewish identity and their multiplications would not decline ever since. Looking for some notion of order, we delve into this diversity by clustering the various formulations according to the particular facet of collective identity which they are primarily attached to. Because these clusters are dynamic and witness developments and ramifications over time, we find it helpful here to view them as 'flows'. We take this notion from the work of Appadurai (1996) who uses it as a key concept for analyzing the variety of global processes that dominate our present-day world—from flows of technologies and goods, to flows of ideas and ideologies. We find this analogy appropriate for our own purpose, seeing that versions of Jewish identities emerging in given places and circumstances have always tended to expand throughout the Jewish world and to contribute everywhere to the versatility of Jewishness.

As a starting-point, we first describe pre-modern Jewishness that dominated communities for centuries. From there we move to a focus on the different flows of Jewish identities that brought about the complex space of identities that Jews have come to illustrate over the years.

The Caste Model as Codifier

From Biblical to Rabbinical Judaism, one can by no means speak of one Jewish identity (Schmueli 1980). The differences between versions concerned varied and numerous topics—the nature of man, the notion of 'sin' or the future world. Until Mendelssohn's innovations at the end of the eighteenth century, the definitions of the three facets of the Jewish identity were shared by thinkers of Judaism everywhere. The first facet was enounced as commitment to the 'Jewish People' and the exigency of comprehensive solidarity with the Jews—as assessed by the command of 'All Jewish people are responsible for each other'. At the heart of the facet focusing on the singularity of the collective, there was the belief in the 'God of Israel and His Teaching' which requested the acceptance of an extended set of commands which gave shape to well-defined models of behaviours and life styles. The third facet concerns the positioning vis-à-vis 'others,' consisted in the principle that 'Jews are in exile everywhere outside the Land of Israel'. This assessment meant that Jews should not see themselves as belonging to their diaspora environment, but as coming from and expecting to return to, the Land of Israel. Out of these three facets, it is the principle of the faith that was the principal element that determined the significance of the other two. This emphasis on the collective's particularism, however, was tempered by a universalistic-monotheistic assessment of the source of Judaism. Accordingly, imposed on the Jewish People is the duty of saving itself from the diaspora by a religious fervour calling for the coming of the Messiah. By the same token, however, by saving themselves, it was also firmly believed that Jews would actually save the entire world. This is the essence of what is meant by the 'election' of the Jew who is primarily commanded to practice God's commands 'between himself' (Katz 1987). The sociological concept that is most appropriate to this kind of collective identity is the notion of 'caste' which, as we know requires keeping to purity and minimizing contacts with 'others' (Smith 1994).

These three assessments of the traditional Jewish identity lost their ultimate status among Jews with the advent of modernity. In view of the new realities, many Jews came to consider the caste model archaic. The post-traditional outlooks regarded those basic assertions as leading questions that could be given new answers. Because of this status as a referent for further formulations of the Jewish identity, those assertions should still be seen as codifiers—in Levi-Strauss' terms, as 'deep structures'—of the Jewish identity while, by the same token, these formulations should be understood as their 'surface structures'. Hence, with respect to the 'commitment' facet—the concept of the 'Jewish People'—this assertion must now be questioned; does this notion still point to a collective whose definition is primarily religious, or is it now indicative of just a social, cultural, or ethical—loosely defined—community? The 'singularity' facet, the concept of the God and Torah of Israel, now invites the question as to what Jewishness consists of in a new secular and individualistic reality—a culture, a collection of symbols, a history, or a shared fate? The 'positioning' facet, the concept of the 'Land of Israel', raises now the issue of its real versus metaphoric significance at a time that Jews are becoming or already are full citizens of the societies they live in.

Each new formulation of Jewish identity represents answers of its own to these three questions that make up another set of surface structures of Jewishness; and altogether, these formulations make up the variety of contemporary Jewishness. This 'forest', so to speak, can however be somehow ordered when looking at it by clustering the various formulations according to the specific deep structure to which each one first refers. Hence, the ultra-Orthodox flow stands out by the paramount importance its constituent formulations grant to the faith; all formulations grouped in the ethnocultural flow emphasize above all the notion of 'Jewish People' as a culture-producer collective; the national flow is primarily turned toward the notion of 'Land of Israel' and the building, on this territory, of a new Jewish nation. In the following we consider these flows and their ramifications in this order, before discussing their convergences and divergences.

The Ultra-Orthodox Flow

When we speak of the ultra-Orthodox flow, we mean those versions of Jewishness that aspire above all to the perpetuation of the traditional identity. A close examination shows, however, that we have here a subdivision into two camps: the first aspires to be the direct continuation of the East European tradition; the second camp sees itself wholly associated with the first but experiences new—and essential—emphases in the context of its being a part of Israeli society.

Diasporic ultra-Orthodoxy

As mentioned regarding traditional Judaism, the very existence of the Jewish People is grounded solely on its connection with God and His Teaching. Without religion and Talmudic law—*halacha*—the collective called "Israel" is no different from any other nation, and thus has no reason to exist. Beyond all the differences that may exist between schools of thought—from the traditional Lithuanian *Mitnagdim* ('opponents' to Hassidism) to the various Hassidic sects, all subscribe here to the idea that Judaism and religion are one and the same thing. They all accept Hatam Sofer's (Moshe Sofer 1762–1839) assessment that 'there is nothing new from the Bible' and that 'The new is forbidden by the Bible' (Mittleman 1996). Hence, in response to modernity, those schools—Hassidim and Mitnagdim who together make up the ultra-Orthodox flow (the haredim, literally, i.e. 'fearing' or 'anxious')—invest themselves in finding ways to remain faithful to traditional halachic patterns of life at a minimal cost of adaptation (Neusner 1995a). This is the goal of the Haredi party Agudat Israel (founded in 1912 in Katowice, Poland), whose founding as a political party was in itself an indication of the influence of modernity. None the less, when some (mostly German Jews) preached in favour of a more conciliatory attitude toward modernity and accommodation with the non-Jewish environment, the majority (mostly Eastern European Jews) determinedly turned the party against secular tendencies within Jewish communities. They were the ones who crystallized the haredi model around three principles: total devotion to the commandments, a self-perception as an elite enrolled on behalf of the faith, and a heavy use of markers to signify that enrolment. Moreover, this movement was also strongly opposed to the Zionist project, since it remained convinced that the 'Return' to the Promised Land would only be initiated by a divine act, in response to the Jews' dedication to God's Teaching. According to Agudat Israel, Zionism which aspired to bring all Jews to immigrate to the Land of Israel and create a 'normal' nation there, was nothing else than a project intended to bring about the collective assimilation of Jews within the secular Godless world.

It is on this basis that Haredi Judaism expanded in the Jewish world—though the Holocaust decimated their ranks in Europe itself. In England, Belgium and the USA, more especially, Haredim have established strong communities and centres of learning—*yeshivot*—though they tend to remain centred on themselves. They still have a basic reluctance vis-à-vis Zionism but ever since the creation of the State of Israel in 1948 and the concentration there of a substantial portion of the Jewish people, most Haredi sects have developed an accommodative approach, especially in response to the difficulties encountered by the Jewish State vis-à-vis its neighbours. Hence, in times of crisis in the Middle East, the ultra-Orthodox mostly—and this concerns primarily Gur and Habad Hassidic movements—support Israel within the context of local politics—and principally in the context of American politics—without giving up their struggle against secular Zionism. Up to now, Agudat Israel denies that the existence of the State of Israel has any theological significance. Many consider living in Israel a virtuous act only in the sense that the country is a part of the Promised Land and is populated by Jews.

Over time, however, it is the Israeli Haredi community that has achieved prominence in this flow of Judaism.

Israeli Ashkenazi Haredim

Like ultra-Orthodox Jews elsewhere, in Israel too they viewed the national enterprise as a betrayal of Judaism which, they said, requires Jews to work toward messianic Redemption by dedicating themselves to the observance of the religious commands. Yet in Israel, the ultra-Orthodox are less able than their counterparts elsewhere to remain indifferent to the Jewish environment (Friedman 1986). They are a part of the Jewish state and as such are, of course, dependent on it in numerous material and institutional respects. Besides this, however, since by their very tenets they see themselves a sort of 'vanguard' of the Jewish people enrolled to hasten Redemption, in the context of a Jewish sovereign society (and in the Holy Land of Israel especially), they are prompted, willingly or unwillingly, to involve themselves in the general Israeli arena and forward the general impact of Torah commands. Hence, they participate in elections trying their best to gain political power, which inevitably brings them to anchor themselves in the Israeli setting. This is reflected, among other things, in the Haredim's turn to modern Hebrew, which, despite their initial resistance has become their main vernacular; it is a linguistic turn that expresses a relative narrowing of the communication gap between them and the rest of Jewry and which strongly distinguishes them from their counterparts in other countries where they are far less involved in the all-Jewish arena. Another sign is that while Haredim are probably the group with the highest reproduction rate in the country, they have not augmented the share of Ashkenazi Haredi parties in the Knesset for decades. This is apparently accounted for by the tendency of many Haredim to vote for non-Haredi (mostly right-wing) parties—in contrast with rabbis' instructions. Hence, while Haredim in Israel participate fully in the Haredi transnational diaspora, they show, more than Haredi Jews in America, England or Belgium, clear signs of convergence with the local national culture. The price is that they also become open, more than others, to their environment.

Mizrahi ultra-Orthodoxy

Another kind of Israeli contemporary ultra-Orthodoxy (Leon 2005) is the form that has developed among Mizrahim. Its roots are found in cultural codes—reverence for traditions and spiritual leaders—that existed among Mizrahim in the Diaspora and which they imported with them to the new communities they formed in Israel. Mostly a traditional—or partially modernizing—population before their immigration, Mizrahi Jews were never shattered by a Zionist-Traditionalist confrontation comparable to the one that broke out in Eastern European Jewry in the late nineteenth century. In contrast to the Ashkenazi experience, the Mizrahi population as a whole—including its rabbis—never saw in Zionism an ideological issue, for the creation of a Jewish State in Israel was always understood as the concretization of the Biblical promise of Return. In Israel itself, it is true, socially mobile elements were quick to undergo secularization under the influence of the dominant culture, and could then easily find their way to the middle-class. However, those—mostly non-mobile elements—who remained in their communities continued to retain particular rites and customs, though to a declining extent. Their original codes remained influential enough to motivate many youngsters to study in religious institutions of higher learning (yeshivot) and to encourage the formation of a new brand of Israeli Mizrahi rabbis. Yet in actual fact those codes were not influential enough to oppose long-term erosion of many others' loyalty to ancestral legacies and the weakening of their commitment to religion.

This development could not but alarm the new Mizrahi rabbis who, in fact, found themselves in somewhat the same situation as that, about a century earlier, of the Ashkenazi rabbis who forged the model of ultra-Orthodoxy to confront the 'escape from religion' that was then spreading through Eastern and Central European Jewry. Notwithstanding the different circumstances that the new Mizrahi religious elite encountered in the 1970s and 1980s in Israel, they too were spurred to react by zealous bigotry, enrolling themselves in what they saw as the survival of Judaism, and multiplying their distinctive markers. Moreover, they also created a political party of their own—Shas.

Unlike the Ashkenazi Haredim, Shas was able to obtain political successes even among the non-Haredi—which is unthinkable of Agudat Israel among the secular Ashkenazi population. Success was achieved by exploiting respect for the learned and the Rabbi in Mizrahi communities, and the consequent customary feeling of veneration, on the part of many traditional—even non-observant—Mizrahim for religious leaders. That support was reciprocated by the emphasis of Shas on its working for the benefit of underprivileged Mizrahi communities.

In conclusion

In a general manner, a strong flow of formulations of the Jewish identity stems from the reiteration of the primacy of Jews' singularity in terms of loyalty to the Torah and the Halacha. For this flow, Jews are a people only as the People of the Covenant. It is the understanding of this principle's significance that has for many years distinguished between some of the formulations pertaining to this flow. Hence, a major difference—anchored in narrow parochialism—that historically divided Hassidic and Mitnagdim groups focused on articles of faith and attitudes toward holy learning. More recently, it is the understanding of the notion of the Land of Israel that makes the difference between inflexibly anti-Zionist groups like Satmar Hassidim and others like Gur and Habad Hassidisms who are more eager to recognize Israel as a worthwhile contribution to Jewish history. Still more recently, one notices that Israeli Haredim are tending to adopt major symbols of Israeli culture and to develop patterns of involvement in wider society, while further on, Mizrahi Haredim clearly state that recognizing Israel as a Jewish state is not an issue for them at all.

It may be assumed that this permeability, to some extent, reflects the all-Jewish solidarity and commitment anchored in the credo of Judaism, including ultra-Orthodox Judaism. Basically, as mentioned, Haredim see themselves as a kind of 'vanguard' of the Jewish people on behalf of a Judaism which, they believe, should become the ground for a vast 'return to religious observance' by world Jewry as a whole.

It is also undeniable however, that by this very token tendencies can be found among extremist Haredim to see themselves not only as a vanguard but also as the only 'genuine' Jews. This explains the presence of Neturei Karta (the 'Guardians of the Wall') in Jerusalem—as well as other small groups in the Diaspora—which continue to deny the legitimacy of Zionism and Israel's very existence. Such groups, in opposition to the general attitude of the Haredim worldwide, do not hesitate to join forces with Israel's enemies, on behalf of Judaism, actually denying Zionists the right to consider themselves Jews.

The Ethnocultural Flow

While the Haredi flow grants 'the God of Israel and His Teaching' the principal role in the Jewish identity structure, the ethnocultural flow consists of versions that primarily emphasize the dimension of the 'People of Israel', and see it as the carrier of singular symbols and a peculiar history but also of essentially universal cultural values. The supporters of these versions seek submersion in modernity and aspire to crystallize the contribution of Jewishness to the contemporary civilization. These definitions tend to distinguish Jews from non-Jews in given respects while in others, universalism and resemblance are insisted upon. Supporters of ethnocultural forms of Jewry actually insist that they are integral segments of their present-day national society. The many formulations which pertain to the ethnocultural flow are best set in relation with each other by dividing them into sub-flows according to their relation to the religious principle—i.e. religious versus non-religious ethnocultural versions.

Religious Ethnocultural Versions

Modern Orthodoxy

Besides the flow of ultra-Orthodoxy, and as a part of the ethnocultural flow, modern Orthodoxy basically accepts modernity but aspires to reconcile it with the retention of Halacha Judaism. This form of Orthodoxy emerged in Germany in the first half of the nineteenth century, and maintained its belief in the divine source of the Commandments and the ban on altering them in any way. Its leading thinker was Samson Raphael Hirsch (1808–1888) for whom the Torah represented the truth even in modern times. Modernity itself, he claimed, comes from God, which requires Jews to undertake secular learning in addition to religious studies. Haim Hirschensohn (1857–1935), a follower of Hirsch, tried to associate their school of thought with the creation of Agudat Israel and to imprint it with an aspiration to reinvent the concept of the 'Jewish People' to suit modern individualism (Mittleman 1996). However, he was soon left out as the majority opposed compromising 'too far' with modernity as advocated by Hirsch, Rosenheim and others who held that Judaism was, above all, a humane religion propounding the message of universal redemption. The German 'modernists' believed that Jews should become integrated into society as observant Jews and they were unable to avoid harsh confrontations with the ultra-Orthodox over several questions—especially the readiness to find flexible solutions to the halachic problems that constantly arise in all areas of modern life, such as sex, the status of women, medicine, dress, Sabbath observance, and so on. The confrontation, however, has not prevented the flourishing of important present-day communities that are declaredly 'modern Orthodox' and have generated important thinkers like Soloveitchik and Lévinas.

French Jewry

An extreme example of this flow is the case of French Jewry. Ever since the French Revolution of 1789, this Jewry has been under the pressure of a 'republicanist' dominant culture that requests every group in society to literally 'dissolve' into the main stream, and is determinedly opposed to the development of any cultural pluralism. In this context, Jews were led to understate their Jewishness, and overstate their 'Frenchness'. Hence, throughout the entire nineteenth century and a good part of the twentieth—in fact until the 1970s—the synagogue was almost the only legitimate framework where Jews could lead a community life. That was also the era when many Jews presented themselves as 'Israelites' or 'French believers in Moses' (Birnbaum 2003). In principle, Judaism was defined as a religious allegiance without any wider significance and which firstly involves individuals. Being Jewish was thus moulded, in this perspective, on the same pattern as those defining Catholic or Protestant identities. This meant no little difficulty for Jews, especially since many of them were influenced by the *'laïcité'* conveyed by the dominant culture and found themselves outside the scope of activity of Jewish institutions. In actual fact, frameworks like

Zionist youth movements or cultural Yiddish circles existed and represented a kind of counter-culture vis-à-vis both the Jewish religious institutions and the official republican ideology. It is in this context that Judaism became there a fertile ground for philosophical and intellectual developments feebly sustained by community structures.

It is only in the 1970s that things changed with the arrival of numerous Jews from Morocco and Algeria. These newcomers who had experienced in North Africa symbiotic social and religious community life inserted themselves in their new environment along with models that tried to accommodate both their own drive for a Jewish communitarian setting and the requests of republicanism to understate their '*communautarisme*'. Jewish institutions, both religious and non-religious, developed—community centres, cultural clubs and coordinating frameworks—while a version of Jewish identity gradually appeared, that blended all-Jewish solidarity, an aspiration to retain elements of Jewish singularity within and without religion, and the assertion of the primacy of the French national identity.

Since the late 1960s, moreover, French official policy toward the Israeli-Palestinian conflict, tends—with the support of major media and many intellectuals—to be pro-Palestinian and critical of Israel, which causes French Judaism undeniable discomfort. No few Jewish intellectuals are then led to defend themselves from leaning towards Israel. What exacerbates matters is the fact that the past two decades have also seen the growth of an important Muslim minority in France—ten times larger than the Jewish community—that often reflects the events of the Middle-East in hostile attitudes toward French Jews. These circumstances incline many Jews to assert with still more vigor the collective dimension of Jewishness, up to the point of questioning the official 'anti-communautariste' republicanism already weakened—at least de facto—by the straightforward socio-religious 'communautarisme' displayed in the open by large segments of the Moslem population.

Haskala and Reform Judaism

Both modern Orthodoxy and secular forms of Judaism like France's have their common source in the Haskala (Enlightenment) movement and in-depth changes in the understanding of Judaism which it promoted. Initially a small circle of intellectuals led by Moses Mendelssohn (1729–1786), this movement was the first in modern times to attack traditional Judaism (Neusner 1995a). Stating that the Bible represented nothing else than the law of the early Israelites, this group aroused furore in the Jewish public at that time. Though, the new attitude soon spread to larger milieus while thinkers like Naphtali Herz Wessely, Naphtali Herz Homberg, and David Friedlander, all followers of Mendelssohn and his philosophical rationalism, bypassed their leader's example and did away with traditional ways of life. Attached to the cultural and educational modernization of Jews, they saw in Judaism a culture on a par with other world cultures. In Eastern Europe, the movement's adherents, such as Mordecai Aaron Guenzburg (1795–1846), were less negative vis-à-vis the validity of the Halacha, focusing mainly on its 'practices' and advocating its study concomitantly with general education.

Moved by the aspiration to make Judaism a fully fledged culture, Enlightenment—in Eastern as well as Central Europe—sought to reinstate Biblical Hebrew as a language of literature and culture. Jacob Emden, for example, defined it as the 'natural' language of the Jews, and Jonathan Eybeschütz waged a battle to sustain the 'Hebrews' language'. From Joseph Perl to Abraham Mapu, Moshe Leib Lilienblum and Judah Leib Gordon (Yalag), authors saw it important to write at least some of their works in Hebrew.

As seen later on, many Eastern European participants in the Haskala finally turned to Jewish nationalism. At the same time, in Central Europe, this movement rather encouraged the development of ethnocultural models. Leopold Zunz (1794–1886) and others founded in Germany the *Society for the Scientific Study of the Jews* (*Wissenschaft Des Judentums*) which sought to combine the study of 'historical Judaism' with modern science. The great historian Heinrich Graetz, who followed that approach, stated that the object of study for a Jewish historian was the Jewish People. This was also the starting-point of the emergence in Central Europe of Reform Judaism, one of whose founders, Abraham Geiger (1810–1874), was both a rabbi and an outstanding scholar of Wissenschaft des Judentums. The new shift in Jewish thought would first be reflected in creating a house of worship now called a 'temple' which opened its doors in Hamburg in 1818. All references to the Return to Zion were removed from the prayers (Sacks 1993) as the choice of the term 'temple' indicated that the congregation no longer yearned to rebuild the Temple of Jerusalem; Hamburg or any other place, it was assessed, would do just as well. By the same token, the word '*Galut*' (exile) was understood metaphorically, taking on a positive meaning indicating the moral mission of the Jews wherever they made their home. Within a short time, the movement revoked the traditional dietetic laws (kashrut) while some went as far as advocating the banishing of the ritual circumcision of male babies.

These ideas served as the foundations for the structuring of Reform Judaism in the U.S., where it was given a systematic definition at the first conference of rabbis, held in Pittsburgh in 1885. The participants declared themselves the Central Conference of American Rabbis and endorsed a program (the Pittsburgh Platform) which, inter alia, claimed that the Torah is primarily a source of ethical precepts and should be seen as the cradle of universal culture. The Jews of today are not a nation, it was assessed, but a cultural-religious community carrying a universal message. It is in the frame of this legacy that Reform Judaism, in the twentieth century, illustrates strong activism in American society and demonstrates its deep aspiration to fight for social and political causes.

The Reform movement was also the first to grant women the right to serve as rabbis and cantors, and in recent years, has gone so far as to afford recognition to homosexual congregations. Paradoxically, the movement is also resurrecting some of the traditional rituals it previously renounced: greater emphasis is being placed on Hebrew, and men are again required to cover their heads in the temple. Some Reform rabbis have even renewed the observation of kashrut. In addition, increasing stress is being laid on Israel and solidarity with world Jewry. All of these issues have naturally aroused considerable controversy, ultimately spawning an array of factions (such as Progressive Reform Judaism). In brief, over the years, the Reform Movement has shown signs of moving in two opposite directions simultaneously. It has no qualms about instituting changes even when they clearly conflict with Halacha and Orthodox Jewry, and on the other hand it evidences a trend to renew some old rituals. This duality, it may be suggested, reflects the attempt to gain legitimacy for its 'daring' moves, in return for evidence of fundamental loyalty to Judaism.

Conservative Judaism

It was, in fact, this dilemma that led to the establishment of the Conservative Movement, a stream of Judaism that occupies the space between Orthodox Judaism and the Reform Movement. As a distant echo of Zecharya Frankel in the mid-nineteenth century, Conservatism is a haven for those who are put off by the extremism of the Reform Movement, who wish to maintain a certain degree of uniformity and unity among Jews, and who look favourably, in principle, on Halacha, yet are unwilling to forego the right to change it when 'commanding.' The Conservative Movement was established in New York in 1886 by graduates of the Jewish Theological Seminary influenced by Franz Rosenzweig (1886–1929). For Rosenzweig, even in the modern era, there could be no Judaism without commandments. Modern life was a new challenge the Jews had to confront, with the obligation to observe the commandments as far as they are still 'relevant'. Another theologian with a profound influence on the Conservative Movement was Emil Fackenheim (1916–2003), who in grappling with the question of commitment to Judaism in the modern era maintained that it was of utmost importance to preserve Halacha as a collective fact. Adopting an 'objectivist' approach, he stressed the principle of peoplehood as the condition for ensuring the survival of the Jewish identity. Aware of the fact that different people observe the Jewish law in different ways at different times in their life, he claimed there was no single 'true' pattern of Jewish life (Fackenheim 1974). Spurred by these ideas, the scholars of the Jewish Theological Seminary formulated an approach that encouraged critical examination of the Scriptures in order to clarify what was 'truly' essential to the Jewish faith (Neusner 1995a). While they did not categorically question the majority of commandments, they were closer in spirit to the Reform Movement than to Orthodox Judaism. Hence, Louis Ginzburg attributed overriding importance to the continuity of Jewish lifestyles, yet endorsing freedom of choice and selectivity in respect to Talmudic Law.

One subject of contention among American Conservatives in later decades was whether or not women could be counted in a *minyan*, the quorum of ten individuals required for communal prayer. This controversy developed into the question of whether women could perform ritual duties, up to and including the office of rabbi. In the 1980s, new works were published which contain a re-evaluation of Halacha from a historical-dynamic perspective, leading to the nullification of numerous religious laws. The new approach welcomes Jewish pluralism and gives legitimacy to different attitudes toward the authority of Halacha. It denies that the Jews are a Chosen People, and asserts an openness of mind to 'non-Jewish wisdom' (Wertheimer 1993).

The Conservative movement was also host to the emergence of a new trend, the Reconstructionists, led by Mordecai Kaplan, who aspired to forms of religious experience unfettered by institutionalization. This trend views involvement in the congregation as a central value of Judaism. Under the heading of *havura* (intimate community), it encourages the sharing of responsibility of all members of the congregation for any matters on the collective agenda, and deems the religious experience to be both individual and collective.

Non-religious Ethnocultural Formulations

While the former ethnocultural formulations do adhere to the religious principle—under a variety of interpretations—other formulations are willing to free themselves from it. No few individuals, as we know, and sometimes the most famous, have gone here as far as to convert to Christianity—among the most famous cases, Mendelssohn's sons themselves, Karl Marx who was converted by his father at the age of 6, Heinrich Heine and many others. Even when the severing from Jewry did not result in conversion, we also know of numerous Jews who embraced general causes and removed themselves from Jewish milieus. Hence, socialist and communist movements, ever since the nineteenth century have been strongly tributary to Jews, who often rose to the ranks of their leadership. These movements were especially attractive to Jews not only because of their sensitivity to social problems inherent to the Jewish culture but probably also because of these movements' declared aspiration to a society where particularistic identities would lose any discriminatory meaning. It is notable that Ferdinand Lassalle (1825–1864) created the first socialist party ever, and that in Russia, the strong presence of Jews among revolutionaries was already visible in the anarchist parties, and became most salient among the social-democrats—both Mensheviks and Bolsheviks. Among the latter, there were no less than four Jewish members among the seven that made up the all-powerful politburo in the aftermath of the 1917 Revolution. In Hungary, Bela Kuhn led the short-lived communist revolution of 1919 and there were no less than 14 Jewish members in his government. After World War II, we again find numerous Jews in the various ruling communist parties of Eastern Europe—most of them to be liquidated by Stalin. Moreover, from

Leon Blum (1872–1950) in France to Harold Laski (1893–1950) in England, Jews were among the leaders of Western socialist parties.

It is in this context that the history of socialism and communism belongs to the contemporary history of Jews. However, many of these Jews—from Lassalle and Marx to Trotsky and Rosa Luxemburg—who chose to embrace universal causes were also moved by a desire to remove themselves from their Jewish roots. As such, they do not belong to the discussion of Jewish identities. This is definitely not the case of others who were no less sensitive to the contradictions of society but opted for an alternative—Jewish socialism.

The Bund

The constitutional congress of the Bund took place in 1897. The Bund aimed at a redefinition of Judaism that rejected both the religious and the territorial perspectives on the desirable Jewish condition. Instead, it offered a Jewish Socialist ideology (Neusner 1995a). With its power base mainly in Poland and Russia, the Bund was attached to the principle of class struggle within the Jewish community, striving to unify the Jewish 'proletariat' that would join the revolutionary socialist camp springing up throughout Europe and the rest of the world. Nevertheless, alongside its Marxist calling, the Bund recognized the singularity of the Jews and was determined to remain faithful to and foster Jewish culture. For the Bund, Jewish culture was the culture of the Jewish popular masses, that is, in Eastern Europe, the Yiddish culture. The preservation of this culture requested, in the eyes of the Bund, that wherever they resided, Jews would be granted cultural autonomy in the future socialist society. To achieve this aim, the Bund did not hesitate to argue with its 'sister' movements, the Communists and Socialists, who were unwilling to acknowledge the 'special' requirements of the 'Jewish question.' This was particularly difficult a challenge, as at the head of revolutionary movements one could often find young educated Jews who expected to solve their 'Jewish problem' by merging into non-Jewish forces. This challenge did not hinder the Bund's fight on behalf of, at one and the same time, a universal utopian society and a Jewish culture (Gorny 2006).

The conflicting forces that shaped the Bund and its philosophy are aptly demonstrated by the figure of one of its most prominent thinkers, Vladimir Medem (1879–1923), a man who was raised in the Russian Orthodox Church but returned to Judaism as a Jewish Socialist. Speaking for the Bund at the Russian Social-Democrat Party convention in 1903, he introduced the idea of Jewish autonomy in Eastern Europe, thereby clashing head-on with the Leninists who labelled this notion a 'bourgeois nationalist aberration'. Medem insisted on the right of the Jewish proletariat to constitute an independent revolutionary force unwilling to renounce its culture. Chaim Zhitlowsky (1865–1943), who championed Medem's approach, had no qualms about speaking explicitly of a national Jewish identity. At a certain stage, he actually suggested that the Jewish Socialism of the Bund was a continuation of Jewish tradition and Biblical prophecy. These attitudes had an impact even beyond the framework of the Bund. The historian Simon Dubnow, for example, drew his inspiration for a program of cultural autonomy from the ideas propounded by the Bund. Yet despite its strength among Jewish communities at the turn of the twentieth century, the Russian Bund and its activists fell victim to the Russian revolution and the Bolshevik regime. For twenty years, it was the turn of the Polish Bund to raise the banner of Jewish socialism, but it too was fated to disappear, this time as the victim of the Nazis in the tragedy of the Holocaust.

Ethno-secular Judaism and Secular Humanistic Judaism

The Bund, however, by no means exhausts the topic of secular Judaism in the diaspora. A major fact, indeed, that is bound to the entry and evolution of Jews in the era of modernity is that many of them dissociated themselves from religion and ancient customs without denying their being Jews, creating thereby the notion of 'free Jew', a notion that indicates a secularization of the Jewish identity that is short of a total abandon of anything Jewish. This attitude stands outside the system of Jewish beliefs but remains marked, in one way or another and to differing extents, by the acceptance of some rituals which are now interpreted as expressions of membership in the Jewish People and of concern for its history and culture. Free Jews, indeed, would often attend a synagogue on high holidays—Rosh Hashana (the Jewish New Year) and Yom Kippur (the Day of Atonement), when they would even fast,—have their male children circumcised at eight days of age, and celebrating a bar-mitzvah at 13. Many would also hold a religious wedding, in addition to a civil one, and a yearly family gathering on

Passover eve. Some of these Jews would also be responsive to community organizations, show interest in publications dealing with Jewish affairs, and eventually attend clubs intended for this kind of public.

Among the wide range of frameworks attached to this Jewishness which attempt to disconnect Jewish cultural markers from affiliation with the synagogue, a prominent example is the Movement for Secular Humanistic Judaism. This movement was founded in 1965 in Detroit and has counterparts in France, England and many other countries (Cohn-Sherbok 1996). As a rule, these groups' ideology assume that no divine force intervenes in this world, and believe in the human mind, the power of the individual, and the supreme value of human dignity. According to this perspective, Judaism represents a constant battle to ensure identity and survival, and consists of a culture, languages of its own, ethics, traditions, and historical memories. At the same time, the movement champions democracy, freedom, and the separation of religion and state. In this formulation of Jewish identity, the collective memory of the Holocaust, all-Jewish solidarity, and commitment to the welfare of the State of Israel, carry particular significance. The Torah is regarded as Jews' major contribution to world cultures, but the movement by no means invalidates other experiences and contributions. Pluralistic in essence, the movement rejects the absolute authority of Halacha, and is disturbed by the notion of the Jews as a Chosen People. It holds that belief in the coming of the Messiah should be interpreted as the aspiration of humankind at large. All in all, the Jews should see themselves as a particular historical-cultural entity carrying universal values.

Conclusion

What is common to all these different ethnocultural formulations— religious and non-religious—is the importance they grant to 'Jewish peoplehood' as carrier of a history, values and symbols. In comparison with the importance of peoplehood, the singularity of the collective, which is defined with many nuances by the various schools, comes second. In addition, the positioning vis-à-vis 'others' is by no means expressed in unambiguous terms, as the holders of these versions of Judaism see themselves fully integrated in non-Jewish national societies. As a whole, these formulations concur with the influence of liberal Western civilization which sustains the openness of social boundaries among communities, and thereby encourages Jews to evince the universalism of their values and legacies.

This ethnocultural flow, as a whole, which primarily concerns non-Haredi diaspora Jewries, gives an essentially cultural-historical interpretation of what Jewishness means. A major feature of this kind of Jewishness is its voluntary aspect, the fact that its specific forms are a function of individuals' own choices—how to reflect their Jewishness, to what degree, and in what areas of life. This is a kind of Jewishness that shares many features with the way a large number of Israelis also express their collective identity, but with the difference that in the diaspora it is not supported by a national Jewish environment. In a diasporic context where expressions of, and concerns with, Jewishness starts from essentially individual decisions, Jewishness might remain superficial for those who do not feel sufficiently interested to invest themselves in it.

The analysis of this flow of Jewish identities, it should still be added here, shows that for many ethnocultural Jews, religious or non-religious, two axes now primarily symbolize the Jewish experience: the memory of the Holocaust, and all-Jewish solidarity. For them, the memory of the Holocaust was the ultimate event that more than any other singularizes Jewish history. They see here a moral obligation vis-à-vis the Jewish People, compelling until the 'end of generations', a memory that awakens every time another anti-Semitic act takes place somewhere in the world. This feeling of responsibility accounts for the multiplicity of Holocaust museums throughout the world and the status of the Holocaust in other Jewish museums.

On the other hand, but not unrelated, for many ethnocultural Jews, one of the major aspects of their link to Judaism consists in their transnational sentiment of solidarity with Jews wherever they are, and especially, where they encounter 'trouble' as Jews. This solidarity which is embedded in old Talmudic sayings—*Kol Israel Haverim* ('All Children of Israel are friends') and '*Kol Israel Arevim ze la-ze*' ('All Children of Israel are responsible for each other')—led them to show the strongest interest in the plight of Russian Jews in the 1960s and 1970s and, since its creation, in Israel and its turbulent history. Israel serves here as a catalyst for all-Jewish solidarity and while opinions may be divided among intellectuals regarding the justification of the Jewish state's 'realpolitik', numerous diaspora Jews consider it as some sort of 'original homeland'. Which leads our discussion of Jewish identities to the national flow.

The National Flow

The national flow refers to these versions of Jewish identity that share in common the importance they grant to the third facet of the original basic structure, i.e. the reference to the Land of Israel, and which draw from this assessment the aspiration to a non-diaspora Jewish reality. However, this flow, like the others, consists of a variety of formulations. Some of these formulations stem directly from Zionist ideology and others are generated by the Israeli reality which, in some cases, may question essential statements of the original national program.

Zionism

Zionism was founded in the late nineteenth century in the midst of a far-reaching crisis throughout Eastern European Judaism. The national solution of Zionism to this crisis put forward a secular program drawn from the very core of traditional Judaism itself. It defined, in secular terms, as 'abnormal', Jewish life outside the Land of Israel that has always been interpreted in religious terms as 'exile'. Against traditional Judaism which pinned its hopes for messianic redemption on the observance of the commandments, secular Zionism feared for the Jews' future at the hour of persecutions and disillusion from emancipation. Zionism was actually influenced by the winds of nationalist ideology that blew throughout Europe and wanted to duplicate at the intention of the Jews, the model of a nation-state that was being erected there on the principle of national territory. It thus called for a 'territorialization' of Judaism, whereby the ethno-religious identity would be converted into a national identity by mass immigration to the very piece of land that was traditionally asserted to be the origin of the Jews as well as their target when Redemption would come. It is to be noted here that the term 'Zion' from which derives the word Zionism is an indication that this kind of nationalism, Jewish nationalism, holds the geographical element to be more significant than the collective or its cultural singularity (see also Buber 1994). This shows how far the Zionist revolution intended to transform religious tradition without repudiating it, by giving new meaning to familiar symbols.

The notion itself of 'Zionism' appears for the first time in an article by Nathan Birnbaum (1890) but the concept of 'Return' was already articulated in many works and under different forms by writers and publicists like Nachman Krochmal, Moshe Hess, Peretz Smolenskin, David Gordon, Moshe Leib Lilienblum and others. Support for the idea was boosted by Pinsker's 'Auto-Emancipation' (1882) which prepared the ground for Herzl's political Zionism as elaborated in 'The Jewish State' (1896) and officially inaugurated at the First Zionist Congress of 1897, in Basel.

As mentioned, a major element in the Zionists' capability to enlist power among the Jewish communities is their 'nationalization' and secularization of traditional symbols. The adoption by Zionist immigrants to Palestine of Hebrew, as the language of everyday life, is the best example of their approach in this respect. Plucking it from the sacred texts and 'tossing it out onto the street' to be used for the most prosaic of activities might have been considered iconoclastic. It is particularly surprising in view of the fact that those who reinvented Hebrew as a spoken language already had a common tongue—Yiddish. This is the only case in history of its kind and its only explanation is that Hebrew was engraved on the collective memory as a symbol of Judaism, even among those who had no knowledge of it. To bring these people to adopt Hebrew was thus seen by them as 'the thing to do' when re-settling in the 'ancestral land'. It expressed the renewed contact with the legacy of Ancient Israel, and at the same time, distinguished the new population from all other forms of Jewishness. A transformation that could be set in motion thanks to the fact that its carriers—during the first waves of immigrants—were convinced Zionist militants. By their dedication, these individuals succeeded to breath new life into old Jewish symbols and endow them with new 'relevant' significance. The symbolic framework that came out was to constitute decades later the foundation on which worldwide Jewish solidarity with the State of Israel would be built.

From another perspective, however, Zionism was at a disadvantage vis-à-vis traditional Judaism. The caste model, we should remember, linked the redemption of the Jews to that of the whole world, and this axiom was conveyed to all forms of contemporary ultra-Orthodoxy. Zionism, on the other hand, aspired to Jewish redemption alone: wherever they came from, Zionists wanted to create a homeland for Jews that would first guarantee them security and the possibility of building a new Jewish national culture. In other words, engineering the 'normalization of the Jewish people'. This very positioning granted, of course, weight to the ultra-Orthodox' argument against Jewish nationalism: while modernization in the Diaspora, they contended, favoured the individual assimilation of Jews, Zionism, in the Middle-East, was achieving their collective assimilation, that is, their becoming a national collective 'like all others' having lost its specific worldly mission.

It is in this context that one may account for the utopian overtones that marked the Zionist endeavour in the Land, during the first decades, especially, but not only, among the various socialist groups. Leaders like David Ben-Gurion, Moshe Sharett, Berl Katznelson, Zalman Shazar and others invested their best to elaborate on the unique character of Zionism and Socialist Zionism as aspiring at the creation of an 'exemplary society' that will not only solve the "Jewish question", but be a 'light for the peoples of the world'. This society, they claimed, will be grounded in social justice and equality that are at the heart of both the socialist ideology and Ancient Judaism. In other words, they presented Zionism as a scheme articulating in secular terms a kind of universal mission counterpoising religious messianism.

Israeli Jewishness

The cultural revolution represented by Zionism served as the basis for implementing the Jacobinian ideology of national integration (*mizug galuyot* or the 'fusion of exiles') when, after the creation of the State, mass immigration arrived from tens of countries. Though, the desire for linguistic and cultural unification did not always result in unity. The very call for unification implied recognition of the special status of those portrayed as the worthy role models—i.e., the first and second generation 'pioneers.' Furthermore, as in any immigrant society where the newcomers are striving to put down new roots, here too being 'native-born' was a source of social prestige. It is the children of immigrants who fulfil their parents' lofty ambitions that ensure the success of their endeavours. In the case of Israel, the native-born also carried the bulk of the security burden and the armed struggle, reinforcing their image as the 'salt of the earth.' In addition, the sons and daughters of the pioneers were highly conscious of being the children of people who had adopted a new national Jewish identity, and of themselves representing a 'new kind' of Jew who had never known life in the Diaspora. The fact that they were also a minority group for a long time added to their lustre. As an 'elite' which prided itself on this status, they created their own symbols, the most conspicuous of which was a typically nonchalant use of Hebrew that could be acquired only by being born 'within the language', that is, in the country (Katriel 1986). A laconic style of speech which abhorred euphemisms and high language in general, underscored the connection to the Middle East by incorporating numerous Arabic words. For a long time, entry into this elite was not easy. Acceptance, when it was offered, never dulled the patina of 'nativeness,' if only on the symbolic level.

These nativistic attitudes are to be set in relation to the wider question of the place and status of the new Jewish collective in respect to 'others' who refer here at the same time to two contradictory horizons. On the one hand, there is the orientation toward the Jewish world where Zionism was born and to which it still refers when claiming to represent the nationalism of the Jew—though it conferred higher moral status to those who answered the call to 'return to Zion'. On the other hand, there is the environment, the Middle East, which the new entity aspires to become a part of. This dilemma between two opposed orientations already appeared in the 1930s, when several intellectuals took this contradiction to its extreme, advocating that Jews who had immigrated to Israel should cut themselves off from the Diaspora. They went so far as to renounce the label 'Jew,' declaring themselves 'Hebrews'. This 'Canaanite' ideology—as it was called—was first formulated by Yonatan Ratosh and insisted that the 'Hebrew nation' should get divorced forever from Jewish tradition (see Amir 1997). This trend, however, remained on the fringes of public life, though later it fuelled the anti-Zionist left, whose major claim is that as long as Israel is defined as a Jewish state, the Arab minority will inevitably rebel and the Israel-Palestinian conflict will remain insoluble (Evron 1995). The 'solution' as phrased by Joseph Agassi (1990), is that the Jews in Israel belong to the Israeli nation in the same way that those who reside elsewhere belong to other nations. This position assesses what postzionism is about (Silberstein 1996); focusing on the Israeli-Palestinian conflict, it places the blame for the hostility on Israel and Zionism, advocating the elimination of the reference to Judaism as the basis of national identity. In this respect, postzionism draws itself out from the discussion of Jewish identities.

These Canaanite and postzionist attitudes have, however, remained marginal and have had but little influence on 'Israeli' culture, which, despite its nativistic overtones has remained basically attached to the Zionism of the founders and was perceived as 'mainstream'. This culture, however, has undergone profound change. The collectivistic mind that prevailed prior to the establishment of the state and in the first years of statehood was gradually replaced by a more individualistic model following demographic, economic and political developments. The statist ideology that gained in strength in the 1950s and 1960s stressed the need to move from utopia to nation-building. 'Pioneer' was redefined to relate to anyone who 'contributed' to the state: not only farmers and settlers as in the past, but also professionals, public functionaries and business people. Moreover, the country—born out of war and still afflicted by security concerns—reserved a place of honour for the armed forces, and now placed great stock on a military career.

Though, mass immigration which tripled the population within a few years, brought to the country a broad array of cultural groups that diffused new perspectives and perceptions, and a new—widely unplanned—social order came into being. Numerous myths were now to be shattered, among them the superiority of physical labour, which had been central to the pioneering ethos, while higher education and professionalism became legitimate pursuits. At the same time, immigration and wars resulted in a constant strengthening of Israel's relations with the Jewish world, now viewed as the country's 'natural partners', in contrast to the anti-diaspora mood in vogue among Zionists years before.

These economic, social, and cultural processes also had an impact on the drastic change that overtook the leading forces of society. Along with a constantly growing middle-class, came the features of Western consumer society while the '1948-generation' (the generation of the War of Independence) had become bureaucrats, financiers, politicians, and businesspeople. As this elite came to be defined in terms of achievements, the meritocracy adopted a more formal standard language. The disdain for 'foreign' languages disappeared, as new sources of communication gained in importance. English became virtually a second language at all levels of education, professional life and business, and fluency in English was now an attribute of status.

Even in this context, some signifiers of native culture persist today and can still be discerned in patterns of speech, dress, and behaviour, but their sources are now mainly the army, high school, the university, or pubs. While many of those identified with this culture at the start of the twenty-first century belong to the middle or upper class, 'nativeness' has inevitably lost a considerable chunk of its appeal as it now characterizes a relatively large sector of the population, and no longer a restricted cohort. Paradoxically, this very fact is encouraging some groups to preserve their own features.

Mizrahim

In Israel today, Jews who immigrated from North Africa and the Middle-East (called by generalization Mizrahim, plural of Mizrahi or Oriental Jew) constitute about 43% of the population; they themselves or their parents arrived in Israel from traditional or quasi-traditional Muslim societies. Originally, as mentioned in our discussion of Mizrahi ultra-Orthodoxy, the majority among this population understood Zionism and the creation of the Jewish State as the concretization of the Divine project of Redemption. On the other hand, it was also the case that when they arrived in Israel, these Jews experienced a feeling of crisis in the face of the secular character of society and its major institutions. Exposure to this culture was to cause an erosion in these groups' traditionalism, which was the direct context of the expansion of the kind of Israeli Jewishness known as 'traditional Jewishness' which applies principally to Mizrahim and implies a positive attitude toward religious institutions, together with a readiness both to leave behind numerous religious symbols and to accept new norms in family and occupational life. However, those whose access to social mobility was impaired, often adhere still today, to the conviction that they were discriminated against originally by the 'establishment'. In any case, they remain at some distance from the dominant culture, continuing to form low-class communities that exhibit ethnic traditional symbols. This is the constituency of Shas, and sociological research (Ben-Rafael and Peres 2005) also shows that people in these communities do strongly interiorize the Jewish-Israeli identity, giving special emphasis to the Jewish component and its primordial attributes. These Mizrahim had a profound—though unintended—effect on the immigrants from the former Soviet Union (hereafter: the 'Russians') when they arrived in the 1990s.

Russian immigrants

The Russians firstly learned from the Mizrahim how ethnicity could become a basis for multicultural claims in Israel. It is of acute importance for them, seeing their velleity to retain cultural and linguistic values and symbols which they had brought with them to Israel and which they consider an integral part of their identity. As these Jews are no less secular than those who had come from Eastern Europe long before, they do not speak of a 'sacred legacy.' They do, however, view their original culture and language as markers of their being 'cultured'. Viewing this ambition as entirely natural, they do not hesitate either to familiarize themselves with the culture of their new homeland, and become 'Israelis' in the way they perceive this notion. In point of fact, after three generations under a hostile Marxist-Leninist regime, these immigrants have a very limited knowledge of Judaism. Many learned whatever they know after arriving in Israel, when they were exposed to the Hebrew language and the calendar of Jewish holidays, both of which are signifiers of Jewish identity in Israel. From this perspective, immigrants from the former Soviet Union have joined the Mizrahi sector as a force for multiculturalism in Israeli society, although the marks of their singularity are non-Jewish rather than Jewish.

On the other hand, also of determinant significance is the fact that many of them have considerable cultural and educational resources, and, according to their own self-image, belong to the middle class. This feature is reflected in their ambition for social mobility and their willingness to invest in the human capital of their children. If they maintain their desire to enhance their status as a distinct cultural group, they may become the first successful example in Israel of the American model of 'white ethnicity', that is, a middle-class community that sees itself as an integral part of society, while at the same time highlighting the singularity of its culture and identity in various symbolic contexts.

In brief, while one may expect that quite a few socially mobile Russians will assimilate totally into Israel's middle-class milieus, others may well be willing to retain a form of symbolic ethnicity. In contrast to the Mizrahi model which offers its own definitions of Israeli-Jewish identity, Russian 'retentionists' would be prone to continue seeking a formulation of identity that enables them to strengthen their Jewishness, develop their Israeliness, while at the same time retaining aspects of their Russian culture, and opportunities for using their Russian language. As a group, their primary desire is for the dominant culture to come to terms with the growing phenomenon of multiculturalism that they themselves best exemplify.

Religious-nationalist settlers

Another group that has developed in recent decades has also become a major actor of Israeli multiculturalism—the religious-nationalist settlers in Judea and Samaria (in Hebrew abbreviation '*Yosh*') on the West Bank. This group originates from the religious-national sub-flow which, at the beginning of Zionism, was inspired by emblematic figures. One thinks here of Yehuda Alkalai, Zvi Hirsch Kalischer, Shmuel Mohilever and Yaakov Reines who were all prominent figures in the Zionist movement and observant Jews. Followers of these figures formed the national-religious parties—Mizrahi and Hapoel Hamizrahi which unified in 1956—that stood at the centre of the political map, took on themselves the task of providing religious services to the Jewish population at large, while at the same time developing frameworks that duplicated, under religious forms, those that emerged from the secular sectors: kibbutzim (collective settlements), moshavim (cooperative villages), a university, and so on. Abraham Isaac Kook (1865–1935), the first Chief Ashkenazi Rabbi in pre-statehood Israel (elected in 1924), is the one who first broke the pragmatic and moderate approach of religious Zionists by endowing Zionism with a religious meaning. He saw in the Zionists—who generally were not religious—a kind of involuntary tool in the hand of Jewish Destiny leading to Salvation.

For several decades, Kook's radical nationalism did not prevail in the national-religious camp where the central leadership was firmly attached to the retention of their party's cooperation with the dominant party at the time, that is, the Labour Party (formerly Mapai). However, in the 1960s, a group of national-religious activists (known as the 'Youngsters') appeared as an opposition to the established leadership of their movement and its efforts to maintain the status quo in religious-secular relations. The Six Day War (1967) and the occupation of areas such as Samaria and Judea, which are part of the Biblical concept of the 'Land of Israel,' propelled the Youngsters onto centre stage. Citing sacred texts that spoke of the 'divine promise' of the land to the Jews, the new leadership claimed it a religious duty to hold onto and settle these areas at all costs. This should now, they believed, be a central principle of national policy. This attitude gave birth to the Gush Emunim (Bloc of the Faithful) movement which worked feverishly to establish new settlements on the newly conquered land. With the rise to power of the right-wing parties in 1977, their endeavours gained momentum, as dozens of new settlements were created across the pre-1967 border. With the start of Israeli-Palestinian negotiations and the demand for the establishment of a Palestinian state alongside Israel, political contention with the national leadership intensified over withdrawal from the Occupied Territories. This led to the emergence of extremist groups within Gush Emunim, some of which became involved in underground activity. The crisis point was reached in November 1995 with the assassination of Prime Minister Yitzhak Rabin. In parallel, aside the radicalized National-Religious Party, a new religious-national party, the Ihud Leumi (National Union) was created that attracted the largest part of the ballots of Yosh settlers. These parties constitute now the militant right-wing of the Israeli polity, opposing any territorial concession to the Palestinians in the West Bank.

The political ideology of the national-religious camp indeed considers the singularity of the collective to lie in its overriding duty to fight to maintain control of the 'holy land.' Here the concept of the Land of Israel is not merely the most important of the three aspects of Jewish identity—a hierarchy found in all varieties of Zionism—but takes on mythical uncompromising meanings that redefine the singularity of the collective in both cultural and spiritual terms (Ravitzky 1993). The advocates of this approach are unwilling to accept any limitations whatsoever on Jewish settlement in the territories, a stance that inevitably engenders conflict with the national leadership. To some extent, this radical religious nationalism comes up to a position close to Canaanites when it states the ultimate importance of the territorial concept of Land of Israel. On the other hand, it is also quite close to the postzionists, since it does not mind to incorporate within the Jewish State a non-Jewish population that, if effectively implemented, might bring to an end the dream itself of national Jewish society.

In conclusion

This flow of Jewish identities sets at the centre of its discussion the notion of Land of Israel and on this basis positions the collective vis-à-vis 'others'. Most contenders here are secular, but some formulations are dictated by religious faith or by loyalty to traditions. This flow started with an ample elaborations of Zionist formulations that shared in common the assessment that a new Jewish nation is to be build on the national territory, grounded in a new Hebrew culture. Hence, 'Israeli-Jewishness' has effectively become reality on the basis of a 'nationalization' of traditional symbols and a self-awareness to constitute a distinct segment within the Jewish world. None the less, within some groups, the acquisition of the national identity has been added to the one shared a priori, and leaving room for new forms of multiculturalism. To this is still to be added that forms of Israeli ultra-Orthodoxy—Ashkenazi and Mizrahi—discussed in relation to the Haredi flow, as well as the presence of Israeli Arabs and Druzes which cannot be tackled in the frame of a discussion of Jewish identities, still contribute to the complexity of Israel's patchwork.

Tensions and 'Family Resemblance'

A conceptual framework based on the notion of the 'space of identity' has been used above to clarify the distinctions between and within different formulations of Jewish identity. Using this framework, we have considered the different models of identity and how they evolve, converge, and diverge. We have seen that beyond the differences between eras and schools of thought, all traditional attitudes share three basic principles, or deep structures. The first is the primordial sense of belonging to a single collective with common patriarchs and matriarchs, embodied in the concept of 'the Jewish people'. The second is the perception of the singularity and purpose of the collective, or loyalty to what we have called 'the God and Torah of Israel'. The third principle relates to the place or status of the collective vis-à-vis 'others', which in this case defines everything outside 'the Land of Israel' as 'exile.' While these three principles give rise to basic dilemmas, interpreted literally, they delineate a sort of 'superior caste' with a destiny whose realization depends solely on the actions of the members of the collective itself.

These principles of traditional Jewish identity have served in our discussion as criteria for examining the new streams in Judaism that emerged when traditional society began to crumble. The unequivocal assertions of the caste model became questions that could be answered in many different ways: what is the nature of the collective commitment of those who now define themselves as members of 'the Jewish people'? How do these Jews interpret the meaning of 'the God and Torah of Israel,' or more generally, how do they view what it is that makes them a 'special' entity? What image do they hold of their connection to 'the Land of Israel' and the status of the collective in relation to 'others'? The responses have been framed by moral attitudes, life experience, and historical circumstances, all of which may be given different weight in different times, places, and circles. Clearly, then, Jewish identity is not a uniform pattern, and each of its formulations is relatively closer to or farther away from the others. This is what is meant by 'space of identity' to which the different formulations belong as long as they share, to whatever extent, what Wittgenstein (1961) labels 'family resemblance.' Even if they do not furnish similar answers to the basic questions of identity, they must at least address the same questions. Provided they do so, they cannot be considered totally alien to each other.

When we apply this principle to the formulations of Jewish identity that emerged with the disintegration of traditional society, we find that the 'post-traditional' definitions are still grappling with the same dilemmas: affiliation with the Jewish people versus affiliation with general society; cultural universalism versus particularism; longing for the Promised Land versus loyalty to the country of residence. Although certain groups continue to struggle to preserve traditional Judaism, new groups appear alongside, or in opposition, to them, and gain in strength.

We have discerned three distinct flows of Jewish identity. These flows, to be sure, are not exclusive and diverse formulations may belong simultaneously to more than one flow. That said, it is still possible to speak of three flows that are distinct from each other in the way in which they perceive the three facets of identity, and mainly according to the facet that they emphasize more. The ultra-Orthodox flow—inside and outside Israel—sees religious faith as the central element of Jewish identity. Its various formulations evidence rigidity and sternness. At the same time, there is a kind of rapprochement—among the major groups—to the State of Israel, if not to Zionism itself. This is particularly emphasized among Ashkenazi Haredim in Israel. Regarding the Mizrahi Haredim, this question does not come up at all as they never confronted the issue of the illegitimacy of Zionism on religious grounds. The ethno-cultural flow is propounded by numerous diaspora formulations who, save for the ultra-Orthodox, represent the whole spectrum of attitudes to religion, including the large cohorts of secular Jews. The anchor of this flow is the definition of Judaism, as a culture indicative of the experience of 'the Jewish people'. The national flow is advocated mainly by the non-ultra-Orthodox Zionists and Israelis. This flow's central element is 'the Land of Israel' as the necessary territorial foundation of the new Jewish 'nation,' thereby creating a dichotomous image of world Jewry—Israel on the one hand and the Diaspora on the other—with Israel occupying the position of leadership over the Diaspora. Here too, however, one may speak of diverse formulations according to the attitude to religion and ethnic culture.

These distinctions were reflected in linguistic preferences. The ultra-Orthodox, insisted on preserving the holy tongue as the language of study, prayer, and ritual. The Ashkenazim among them, especially in the Diaspora, have remained faithful to Yiddish as the language of everyday life in the community, along with the local language for communication with their surroundings. At the same time, and ever since the Enlightenment, ethnocultural formulations emphasize the importance of learning the language of the nations in which Jews reside. The Reform and Conservative movements, in turn, represent varieties of Judaism that resolutely turned to local non-Jewish languages. Although followers of the Enlightenment were also among the first to promote Hebrew as a language of secular Jewish culture, it was the Zionists who fought to make Hebrew a national language. Each of the three flows also constitutes a basic challenge to the others. The ethno-cultural flow clashes sharply with the other two because of its tendency to accept far-reaching innovations regarding the boundaries of the collective, changes that are anathema to the ultra-Orthodox flow. The ultra-Orthodox flow stands out for the many Jewish signifiers it preserves, which are very different from the civil or secular styles of the proponents of other formulations of Jewish identity. The national flow, unlike the others, focuses on a specific territorial reality and distinguishes Israeli Jews from those anywhere else in the world.

Related to these essential differences, each flow also tends to clash with the others over leadership ambitions. For the ultra-Orthodox, it is clear that they are the most robust guardian of Judaism, in their own eyes at least, and should thus be seen as the true leaders of the Jewish world. For the tenets of the national formulations, it is no less obvious that since Israel is the only sovereign Jewish community in the world, where preoccupation with Jewish issues and Judaism is a matter of central policy and concern, it is Israel that should be seen as the centre of the Jewish world. For those who identify with ethnocultural formulations, it is no less patent that they represent the segment of the Jewish world standing at the forefront of innovations in Judaism and of activism on behalf of universal causes, which should warrant their role in Jewish affairs.

Alongside these sources of contention, and simultaneously, the three flows converge in major respects. All formulations that pertain to the three flows draw their symbols and myths from the same trove of customs and narratives; they are distinct mainly in the way in which they interpret them. Consequently, the symbols of each flow are familiar to the others, and all three participate in the same discourse. Finally, all or nearly all relate to 'the Land of Israel,' or at least the State of Israel as well as to Jewish communities worldwide, out of a sense of solidarity. Last but not least, the dynamism of Israeli society as a compact Jewish setting excelling in the creation of cultural symbols, accounts for its impact on Jewish communities worldwide. One knows, for instance, that Israeli Hebrew—originally created to distinguish the Jewish population in Israel from the diaspora—is now returning to New York, Paris and Moscow where it penetrates Jewish schools and is taught as the contemporary first Jewish language. The same is true of Israeli folklore, rock music or forms of secular rituals that have become part of the distinctive markers of the Jewish diaspora vis-à-vis non-Jewish environments, and in fact these common denominators somehow counterbalance the tensions in place between the three flows.

All in all, and since its traditional formulation lost its authority, the Jewish identity has undergone drastic transformation and has generated dilemmas that have eventually become its most essential features. Our analysis reveals the immense diversity of this Jewish identity throughout time and until this day. The major finding is that the three flows—ethnicity, nationalism, and ultra-Orthodoxy—channel the wide variety of models of Jewish identity that emerged with the disintegration of traditional society. To be sure, it is difficult to pinpoint the common denominator that unites the space comprised by the numerous formulations of Jewish identity which we encounter in the investigation of those flows.

What we have found is a relative and uneven proximity and resemblance exhibited by the different formulations vis-à-vis each other. This picture is best described by the Wittgensteinian notion of 'family resemblance' (Wittgenstein 1961). Wittgenstein elaborated on this concept when analyzing the structure of languages. Like his analyses of 'word games' that make up distinct codes, we have also found within the space of formulations constituted by Jewish identities, very different ones which still display a certain resemblance. The diversity is manifest in a plethora of dissimilarities as well as points of resemblance that are inconsistent and clearly asymmetric, despite the fact that they all derive from the same sources, and are dressed in the same symbols drawn from the same founts and the same narratives. In other words, like word-games, the different phrasings of Jewish identity are similar to each other in that complex sense that a family is made up of closer and more distant relatives who resemble each other in a variety of ways and to varying degrees. The distances we have discerned among Jewish identities indicate how those formulations converge into clusters, as well as how distinct they are from each other. All relate to the same social entity and contend with the same basic questions, and it is as such that their differences and similarities can be contained under the heading of 'family resemblance'. Only in these terms can we find any commonality between Shas in Israel, Secular Humanistic Judaism in the USA, and the Bund in Europe. In the 'family' of Jewish identities, these formulations are indeed 'cousins', although very distant ones. Like the members of an extended family, these formulations are likely to develop a differential or asymmetric sense of solidarity with or hostility toward their many 'relations'.

These different formulations, however, cannot be entirely estranged from one another as long as they ask the same questions, even though they do not provide the same answers.

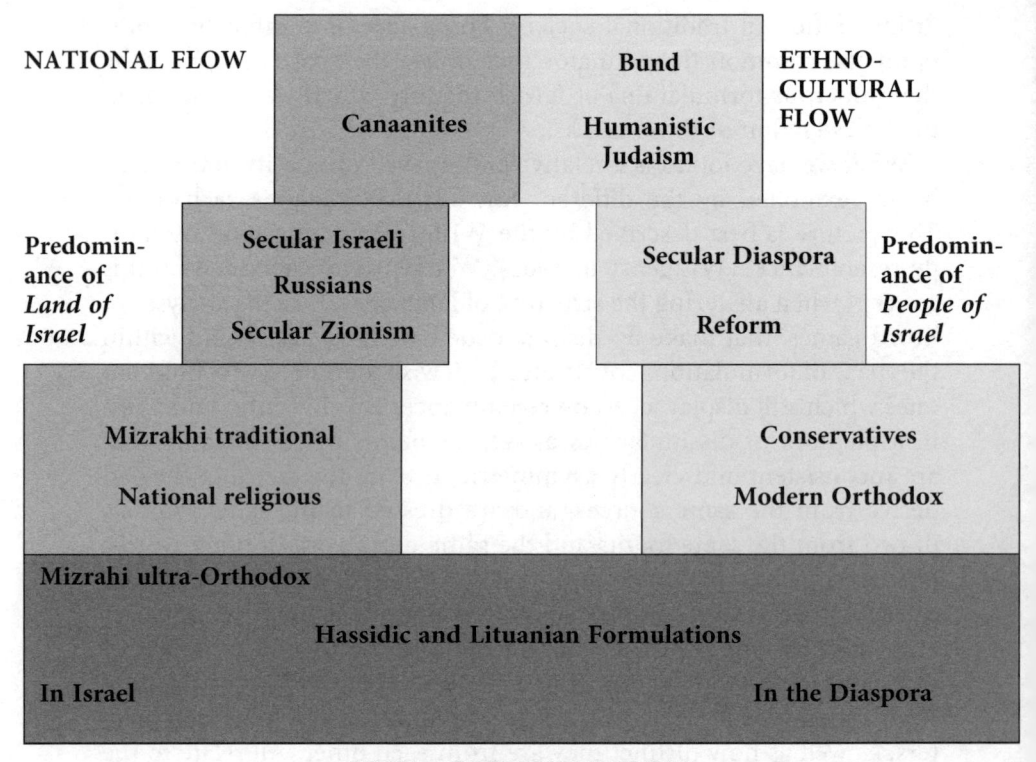

NATIONAL FLOW			ETHNO-CULTURAL FLOW
	Canaanites	Bund / Humanistic Judaism	
Predominance of *Land of Israel*	Secular Israeli / Russians / Secular Zionism	Secular Diaspora / Reform	Predominance of *People of Israel*
	Mizrakhi traditional / National religious	Conservatives / Modern Orthodox	
Mizrahi ultra-Orthodox	Hassidic and Lituanian Formulations		
In Israel			In the Diaspora

ULTRA-ORTHODOX FLOW

Predominance of *God and Torah of Israel*

Figure 13.1: The space of Jewish identities by "family resemblance"

CHAPTER FOURTEEN

JUDAISM AND GLOBAL RELIGIOUS TRENDS: SOME CONTEMPORARY DEVELOPMENTS

Shlomo Fischer

In this chapter I will describe several salient trends pertaining to the Jewish religion today. In my description I will focus upon the largest Jewish communities in the world—that of the United States and Israel. Even with respect to these communities I shall not be able to cover all contemporary developments and trends, especially in regard to the various sub-communities. I shall rather focus upon those trends which seem to reflect or echo global trends as regards religious adherence or participation, religious belonging and the relationship that religion has to other social spheres and to social life in general.

I shall argue that the Jewish religion partakes of three different trends that characterize religion today, globally. These tendencies are not total, nor do they exhaust the religious picture today, but they are salient enough that they have attracted significant scholarly attention. These trends consist of:

1) The focus upon the individual and his/her personal or intimate experience, meaning or realization. The attachment that one has to religion, very often centers around the individual, the personal and the intimate. Sometimes, this takes place with a reduction in certain communal commitments, belonging and identities. In other cases it goes together with strong collective commitments.
2) A disjunction between Jewish belonging and personal belief or behavior. This points to two related phenomena: a) "Belonging without believing." Belonging to Jewish organizations and especially Jewish religious organizations does not necessarily imply adherence to traditional Jewish religious belief in God, revelation, the commandments, life after death etc. b) "Vicarious religion"—This implies that membership in a (the) Jewish religious collective does not require that one carry out or perform religious behaviors by oneself. On the contrary, it seems to free one from carrying out

such behaviors on the grounds that they are performed *for one*, by specially designated or official role incumbents—be these clergymen or the Orthodox population as a whole.

3) An increasing abstraction of Jewish religious practice from Jewish culture or Jewish "life" in general. This development characterizes mainly fundamentalist groups, yet as we shall see it constitutes a continuation and enhancement of the social differentiation that characterizes modern society as a whole. This process, among Jewish ultra-Orthodox, as among Islamic fundamentalists. seems to be responsible for some of the recent expressions of "religious extremism" especially in regard to separation of the sexes. According to this line of thought Islamic and Jewish fundamentalists are becoming increasingly radical because of their increasing modernization and globalization.

Some of the ideas advanced in this chapter are new suggestions which call for further research. I am raising them here in order to show the possible fruitfulness of comparing religious Jewish phenomena with trends in worldwide religion.

The Centrality of Personal Experience

The American Case

The most salient development in Jewish religious attachment is the centrality of personal experience, meaning and realization. This trend was identified first in regard to American Jewry by Steven Cohen and Arnold Eisen in their book *The Jew Within* (Cohen and Eisen 2000). Cohen and Eisen initiate the summary of their argument as follows:

> *The starting point of our analysis was and remains the sovereign self: confidant of its unalterable Jewish identity by virtue of birth to at least one Jewish parent and asserting an unquestionable right to choose how, when and whether it will enact that identity in practice. The self—albeit in negotiation with others, particularly other family members—is the ultimate arbiter of Jewish expression...* (p. 185).

Cohen and Eisen stress that communal or collective expressions of Jewish attachment are much less salient than they used to be: "...relative to the parents' generation, today's Jews in their thirties, forties and early fifties are finding less meaning in mass organizations, political activity, philanthropic endeavor and attachment to the State of Israel..." (p. 184).

Cohen and Eisen emphasize that this characteristic of American Jews pertains to American religion as a whole and that the centrality of personal experience and meaning is also key to the religion of non- Jewish Americans (see Luhrmann 2004, Wuthnow 1998). While the centrality of personal experience and meaning in American Judaism is certainly appropriate to the American context, we also find it in Israeli Judaism, not only in the "transplant movements" of Reform and Conservative Judaism (which are still minor on the Israeli scene[1]). It has also become a significant motif among Israeli Orthodox Jews. These are divided into two major "streams" or sectors—a religious Zionist sector and an ultra-Orthodox (*Haredi*) one. For each of these respective divisions personal experience and meaning and individual self-realization has achieved a new saliency, though in different ways. In the following sections I will briefly explore these developments.

Self Expression and Personal Meaning in Israeli Jewish Orthodoxy

One of the major changes in Israeli society in the past forty or so years has been the shift from collectivist to individualist orientations. While this change has not affected equally all sectors of Israeli society (as we shall see), nevertheless, it has to one degree or another affected many elite sectors and it certainly characterizes the discourse of the mass media and several more specialized professional discourses such as economics and the law. This change has been registered by Israeli social scientists of various theoretical orientations ranging from Critical Theory (Shafir and Peled 2002) to what had formerly been the mainstream functionalist one (Almog 2000). The major manifestations of this change have been the introduction and dominance of a "liberal citizenship discourse" with an emphasis upon civil liberties (Shafir and Peled 2002), a consumerist orientation in consumption and culture, a neo-liberal orientation in economics (at whatever extent) which has accompanied the breakup of the governmental, quasi-governmental and Labor Federation economies (Shalev 2000, Shafir and Peled 2002: 231–259); and a general change in cultural ambience which is best captured perhaps by linguistic changes such as the shift from *hagshama atzmit* (self-fulfillment through contribution to the collective)

---

[1] The Reform movement in Tel Aviv has taken some hold among the Greater Tel Aviv (upper) middle class and the Beit Daniel Synagogue in north Tel Aviv has become a favored venue for life cycle rituals for this group.

to *mimush atzmi* (personal self-realization) and the disappearance of such terms as *halutziut* (acting as a vanguard).

This change has been related to the entrance of Israel into the world market economy, the emergence of material prosperity for many sections of the middle and especially upper middle class and the growth of a post-materialist society in which mere survival is no longer the major concern but rather self-expression and the quality of life (Inglehart 1997). Part of the shift in orientation away from mere physical survival and economic well being to a concern with self-expression has been a renewed interest in spirituality and New Age religion. In Israel, as in other parts of the West, this interest has been for the most part with religions that do not have a historic association with the Jewish people such as Buddhism and Shamanism. The New Age religions are largely concerned with individual well being and fulfillment and in many cases involve meaning systems that individuals construct in the manner of *bricolage* from components of several religious traditions and belief systems. In certain cases, elements of the Jewish tradition (Kabbalah, Hasidism) have also been reinterpreted in the spirit of the New Age.

Expressivist Individualism in Radical Religious Zionism

This emphasis upon the personal and the individual has also manifested itself within the radical religious Zionist community. In this community though, the new individualist emphasis displayed itself in and through the existing cultural frame. As we shall see this cultural frame also proved receptive to the individualist orientation.

Thus, before we discuss the new individualist and personal orientation in radical religious Zionism we will briefly describe the cultural frame of this community which underpins its theology, politics and culture.

Radical religious Zionism like other resurgent political religious movements in Southeast Europe and the Middle East has strong links to Nationalism. This link to nationalism has resulted in a new transformed Jewish theology. At the center of this theology is the granting of religious meaning to the material, secular, mundane world and to bring this world under religious regulation. Initially, this meant especially the granting of religious meaning to the secular mundane realms of nation-building—politics, settlement, economic and cultural production.

In order to achieve this, the major stream of radical religious Zionist theology employed an intellectual structure that the philosopher Charles Taylor has called expressivist (Taylor 1989). According to this structure, spiritual phenomena such as Divine ideals and perfection find their most complete realization by being expressed in the material, mundane world and conversely, phenomena of the material world find their most adequate self-realization when expressing their spiritual "inner form." According to the expressivist conception of the *Emuni* community, within all finite created material creatures there is an inner will to become united again with its source in God.

Initially, in the generation from the 1960s through the 1990s this expressivist approach, as indicated, manifested itself mainly upon the collective political level—the mundane Israeli state is to be the vehicle for the realization of Divine ideals mainly through the project of settling the Greater Land of Israel including the West Bank and Gaza. At the same time, these ideals and this project was not understood as something—a divine commandment—coming from "outside." Rather it was conceived of as expressing the general popular will of the Israeli Jewish people. This Jacobin democratic popular will was understood as a manifestation of the underlying inner will to return to God . Because of its expressivist character, radical religious Zionist ideology gave great prominence to notions such as self-expression, self-actualization, freedom, authenticity and self-recognition. As indicated, in the first decades of radical religious Zionism's hegemony it emphasized these themes in regard to collective subjects such as the Jewish nation and the Israeli state (Fischer 2007).

From the Collective to the Individual

Since the mid 1990s this expressivist structure began to become increasingly applied not only to the collective/political level but also to the individual, private and intimate planes. Religious thinkers, writers and artists have emerged who seek to realize religious meaning and ideals in individual experience, in the routines and minutiae of everyday life, in the body, sexuality and aggressive drives, in artistic creativity of all sorts and in the free development of the personality through "open" education. In the pages that follow, I will describe very briefly some of these developments (Fischer forthcoming).

I will start my remarks with a description of developments in theology. The first of these developments is textual—the challenge to the canon of R. Abraham Isaac Kook's writings which started to crystallize in the late 1990s. R. Abraham Isaac Kook (1865–1935, first Chief Rabbi of Palestine) laid the theological and ideological groundwork for radical religious Zionism through his ramified theological and philosophical writings. The accepted canonical version of R. Kook's thought that had been promulgated by R. Kook's son and disciples and had been hegemonic until the end of the 1980's, presented R. Kook's philosophy and theology as being wholly collectivist and concerned with the nation, history and the national redemption. From the mid 1990s onwards, various radical religious Zionist groups began to publish new collections highlighting passages of R. Kook's thought which were very individualist and personal in nature. They also began to publish R. Kook's writings in their original state, before they underwent editing by his son and disciples. These passages preserved the individualist, mystical and even antinomian passages in his writings (Rosenak 2000).

This trend towards the expressivist inward individual in theology is complemented by other trends in radical religious Zionist religion such as the new interest in Hasidism and other streams of Jewish thought which emphasize individual salvation and the individual's relation to God. Some of the most favoured texts emphasize that faith in God is an individual existential leap. Other texts, like Kierkegaard's *Fear and Trembling*, argue that an individual through an inner existential decision can disregard the general law in his attempt to achieve closeness to God (R. Mordechai Yosef Leiner and his followers). This focus upon Hasidism and with it, Kabbalah and mysticism, has resulted in something of a New Age ambience in some Yeshivot (rabbinical seminaries) and settlements.

In connection with these developments, some writers in *Nekuda* and other publications around the turn of the millennium formulated a new religious ideal of taking the Torah out of its ritual and grand collective contexts and realizing it in everyday life and its concrete details (e.g. shopping in the mall, double parking and personal and sexual relations within the family) (Sorek 1998). Through the turn from the Nation, History and the State to the everyday, these writers have attempted to open up a space for personal and intimate experience. Some of these writers have even explicitly made use of post-modernist thought in order to free themselves from the exclusive domination of the religious Zionist grand narrative of Eretz Yisrael, the Nation and Redemption (Shagar 2004).

Another area in which the new individualist trend has manifested itself is that of art and artistic creation. Interest in artistic self-expression has become widespread in recent years in West Bank settlements, in yeshivot (rabbinical academies) and in the religious Zionist community at large. This development has manifested itself in poetry and creative writing workshops being held in yeshiva high schools and even more in *Yeshivot Hesder*[2] and within the settlements. Similarly, classes and workshops in sculpture, drama and modern and creative dance also dot these communities (*Nekuda* 2006). There are fourteen religious womens' dance and theater groups active today (Retlinger-Reiner 2007). One of the most important journals for young poets in Israel is associated with young radical religious Zionist poets from the West Bank. Perhaps the most widespread and visible engagement of radical religious Zionist young men and women with the arts is in the realm of cinema. Twenty years ago a special school for religious Zionist filmmakers was founded. Today scores of young men and women are currently engaged in filmmaking. In all of these literary, performing and plastic arts, religious young people explore the most sensitive themes concerning, religious faith, the body, erotic and sexual orientation and personal identity (Kaploon and Berekowitz 2000, Ha'aretz 2003, Sheleg 2000: 59–63).

This is a complete departure from, not only traditional Orthodox Judaism, but from life in the settlements as recently as 15 years ago. The discourse concerning this artistic creativity involves the application of the expressivist structure to new realms. The practitioners of this creativity talk about exploring language or the body and its movements so as to create works "with the quality of prayer." They focus upon exploring the materiality of the media of their expression so as to create new artistic languages which will express faith and religious ideals. At the same time they also view artistic expression as a means of self-discovery and they emphasize greatly spontaneity and even play.

---

[2] Rabbinical academies (for age 18 and up) which combine rabbinical studies with military service.

Young poets and writers speak about meeting their authentic selves which is also a meeting with God.

This new artistic creativity opened up new themes. One of the most important of these is the relationship of the individual to his religious tradition and commitment. Young radical religious Zionist creative writers and artists, especially by means of poetry and film discussed their doubt, alienation, disappointment and conflicts vis-a-vis their religious tradition and religious faith. They also discussed how they constructed religious meaning and attachment for themselves in personal, even idiosyncratic ways (Jacobson forthcoming).

Another central topic that radical religious Zionists emphasize in poetry (Jacobson forthcoming), fiction (e.g Greenberg 1997) and film[3] is that of sexuality—1) the centrality of sexuality to experience and identity and 2) the meaning and the experience of the religious restrictions on sexual expression imposed by Orthodox Judaism. Since 1997 one of the central themes of Emuni poetry and fiction is that of sexual desire and sex itself. A new literature written by men concerning straight sex mainly with girl friends and wives focuses on desire and sex. Sex is not treated only as a need or a constraint or something you do in order to procreate—it is a legitimate part of the religious identity. As such it is a pathway to God.

This idea receives elaboration in theological writing. Here again the focus is on the legitimacy of sex conducted "naturally"—out of desire and for its own sake. This writing emphasizes human and sexual spontaneity and argues that the natural union of man and woman represents and is part of, the union of God and his creation (Maor 2005). To what extent does this emphasis upon spontaneity and "naturalness" extend to practice? It's hard to tell, but undoubtedly there has been a loosening of boundaries. Even more tellingly there seems to be some indications that at the edges of both literature and life, the stress upon spontaneity is testing the normative sexual restrictions of Orthodox Judaism. One of the more telling developments of late is that a new cable television series, "*Srugim*" ("crocheted skullcaps"), devoted to the personal (and sexual) relations of young urban religious singles has become a huge hit in religious Zionist circles.

---

[3] Films from Ma'aleh.

Experiments in education has been a field in which practice has outpaced systematic theory. Again in the past 15 years we have witnessed the growth of experimental radical religious Zionist frameworks which have placed the student's autonomy and authenticity at the center of the educational endeavour. The concept which has been key here is that of student choice and responsibility. Vanguard Emuni educators have established a number of leading secondary schools in which students can (indeed must) choose their curriculum and their teachers, can attend classes upon their cognizance and can choose and take responsibility for their religious lifestyle including various degrees of non-observance (Avichail 2004). A much wider circle engages in such practices in a more limited way, and the concept has been the subject of books, conferences and in-service training programs.

The rationale behind such steps has been that the educational process must take into account the individual and idiosyncratic aspects of the student so that she can recover and express her authentic self a la Rousseau (Avichail 2004). Secondly, that the student must engage in genuine creative learning experiences involving his whole self.

The most radical area in which these new trends assert themselves is in regard to instinct and violence. Here, one of the most radical theologians, R. Yitzchak Ginzburg has elaborated a theology of the material. The material, as opposed to the spiritual—can fully express the full existence—the full "Whatness"—of God; the absolute solidity of his being. Material objects in their sheer ontological self-sufficiency can express God's ontological self-sufficiency. In the area of human relations the act that most affirms the ontological solidity of my own being is that of revenge. Violent revenge does not allow my being to be negated or denied. By affirming one's being through revenge one can connect to the ontological solidity of God's being, especially if it is defence of the Jewish people who have a special connection with God.

Most startlingly, Ginzburg employed this theology of revenge to justify the massacre of 29 praying Muslims in the mosque in the Patriarch's Tombs in Hebron in 1994 by Dr. Baruch Goldstein. Again, Ginzburg very much emphasizes the spontaneity, the unthinking "naturalness" and even the "animality" of the act which transcends conventional, petit bourgeois definitions of good and evil (Ginzburg 1994, Fischer 2007b).

In regard to these ideas R. Ginzburg did not remain an isolated thinker. An entire culture of nationalistic, anarchically violent bohemian settlements has grown up in the last 15 years. This nationalist bohemianism has begun to manifest itself in a new kind of settlement that has begun to dot the landscape, especially in the inner hilltop reaches of the Shomron, deep in the densely populated Palestinian territory. These are the "illegal" outposts and farms. A number of these settlements are the result of personal initiative and are not linked to the sponsorship of the Regional Council of Judea and Samaria, the religious Zionist Amana settlement organization, the Ministry of Agriculture or the Jewish Agency and they in large part do not receive subsidies from them. A good many of the younger members, especially, are alienated from the state and its symbols and structures including the educational system and the IDF. This alienation has greatly increased since the Disengagement from Gaza and Northern Shomron and may lead to violent encounters with the police and the IDF, partially in connection with attempts to evacuate these illegal outposts. In fact most of the concern regarding violent resistance to evacuation centers around this "Hilltop Youth". Normative rabbinical authority is not accepted either while many of these outposts are also engaged in endemic violent conflict with their Palestinian neighbors showing that violence is part of their ethos (Shulman 2007). Some of their alleged activities include uprooting olive trees belonging to Palestinians and poisoning Palestinian sheep.

The men and women of the outposts and illegal settlements combine many of the themes that we have discussed above, and they have a counter-cultural and anti-structural (in the sense used by Victor Turner [1974]) ambience about them. They continue the radical religious Zionist theme of imbuing the land (i.e. the Land of Israel) with religious meaning and value, but they give it a new twist emphasising its immediateness and concreteness. The outposts and hilltop settlements are not villages with red roofs all concentrated together as are the classic Gush Emunim settlements. Rather they are spread horizontally over distances so that each farmhouse merges with the rocks, soil and olive trees in its immediate vicinity. They make a point of wanting to be on the land in the most unmediated way; living in direct contact with the elements. Many of them farm organically, they tend to wear homespun clothes noteworthy for their simplicity and build their own homes from materials locally available. Very many of them eschew electrical sources of energy, using wind or solar power (Meir 2003). A few more established settlements such as Bat Ayin also interweave the themes of creative arts, counter-cultural and New Age ambience, ecology and unmediated contact with nature, the earth and its elements and violence (Lavie 2003).[4]

Here too, not only in regard to Goldstein's terrible act, but in the ongoing endemic violence between some of the settlers and their Palestinian neighbors as well as the Israeli security forces we can detect a loosening of boundaries.

To summarize, the culture and theology of radical religious Zionism in regard to a variety of arenas—art, education, sexuality and even violence—gives great prominence to notions such as self-expression, self-actualization, spontaneity, authenticity and the authentic self. This constitutes a long term characteristic of the radical religious Zionist community but in the past decade or so it has very much emphasized *individual* self-expression, spontaneity and authenticity. The emphasis on the personal and the individual is at this point becoming pervasive. One of the indications of this is the popular psychological discourse on family and couple relations which now fills the weekend editions of the religious press and the sheets distributed in synagogues devoted to sermons on the weekly Bible reading. As in the culture at large, the establishment of family and children have ceased to become merely obligations imposed by the religion and the nationalist cause; they have become sources of self-fulfillment to which the application of a therapeutic discourse is appropriate.

These characteristics of personal meaning and self-expression challenge the prevailing picture of radical religious Zionism as a resurgent "fundamentalist" religion solely prone to anti-modern, non-rational religious and political extremism. The emphasis upon the individual and her self-expression and self-realization, the emphasis upon artistic creativity, personal meaning, the body and sexuality and psychological discourse—brings this religious community not only very close to American forms of Judaism but to central themes of modern, Western culture as a whole.

---

[4] In 2003 two residents of Bat Ayin were convicted of planting bombs near schools in the Arab village near Jerusalem of A-Tur.

Spirituality, Radicalism and Personal Meaning in Israel's Ultra-Orthodox Community

The new individualist or personalist developments within Israeli Ashkenzic Haredi religious culture have to be understood, I submit, within the context of the challenges to the boundaries of Haredi society and its culture which have emerged from a variety of sources in recent years. I shall suggest that these individualist developments constitute part of the responses to these challenges.

I shall thus, start off by describing various contemporary challenges to the Haredi way of life in Israel as it crystallized over the past 50 years. I shall then focus upon a number of new developments which I believe are a response to these challenges. A few of these, especially the new women's groups, are quite sensational and have received coverage in the press. After the description and analysis of these developments, I shall close this section with several remarks concerning the Haredi boundaries and their relation to the boundaries in Jewish society in general.

As is well known, Israeli ultra-Orthodox society has attempted, since the 1950's to construct a social enclave, to use Emanuel Sivan's term with high boundaries. The defining characteristic of this society and the major mechanism of its separation from the mainstream of Israeli society is the fact that most of its adult males for the first few decades of their adult lives (until their forties or sometimes more) do not participate in the work force but rather study Torah in Talmudic academies, yeshivot or Kollelim. Some of them continue on as staff in these academies for the rest of their lives, while others join the commercial or vocational work force at the age of forty or more. The large Haredi families (8 children and more are common) are supported by the small stipend that they receive, their wives' salaries (at least until the third child) and government transfers of various sorts. Women are not expected to excel in Torah study, but rather in livelihood and home care. Classically speaking, Haredim are expected to spend their entire time in religious devotion and family and when necessary, livelihood. They are not expected to engage in higher secular education and secular leisure activities had been discouraged. In general, their distinctive dress and life style segregates them from the other sectors of Israeli society. This segregation has been enforced by two sorts of serious sanctions—the first is the stipends controlled by the academies;

improper behavior can result in expulsion from an academy and loss of income. Secondly, since all marriages are arranged, such behavior can also result in severely limiting one's own or one's family members' marriage options. Since Haredim have little secular education, their options in the non-Haredi world tend to be limited.

Since the 1970s the Haredi system has been crowned with success. Its population has grown, due to large natural increase and due to that and other reasons it has achieved considerable political power. Nevertheless, in recent years, this highly bounded enclave has been challenged by a number of factors, some of which are related to its recent success. I shall list some of them.

The first factor is economic. During the Intifada of 2000–2004, the Israeli government, despite the political power of the Haredim, had succeeded to a certain extent in reducing government monetary transfers. Though the Haredi parties had in recent years clawed back some of the payments, there is no question that the average Haredi family today receives significantly less government resources than it received ten years ago. The result of this has been to increase pressure on men to leave the academies and enter the work force. Programs for job training for Haredi men and women have been opened in Jerusalem, Betar and other Haredi locations. Entrance into the work force, of course, decreases Haredi social segregation. This economic pressure also affects Haredi women. Population growth means that there are limited openings in the traditional employment sectors of Haredi women—the ultra-Orthodox school system and the like. Thus Haredi women have been branching out into computer design, programming and even insurance and other businesses. One even reads of Haredi women lawyers, interior designers and film-makers (Rotem 2007a).

Secondly, the changing composition of the Haredi population. There are three important new elements in the Haredi population all of whom bring with them increased openings to, and presence of, the non-Haredi world. The first are the "returnees to Judaism" the *Baalei Tshvua,* these are largely non-Orthodox Jews who have become newly ultra-Orthodox, as part of the world-wide religious resurgence. While they may be fervently religious, they carry with them, in their selves and in their bodies, knowledge, skills and dispositions from the secular world. In addition, and especially in Jerusalem and its environs, ultra-Orthodox Jews from the US and Europe are settling in increasing numbers. Most of the males work and some even have professional careers. Some of them are considerably well off economically and they bring with them new consumption and leisure habits. Furthermore, it is noted that Haredi Sephardic Jews from North African and Middle Eastern countries integrate in those communities. The Haredi way of life, both in Europe and in Israel, had historically been a strictly Ashkenazic affair. However, since the 1980's we are witnessing the salience of a Sephardic haredi community, mainly in connection with the rise of the Shas Party. For the most part, these Sephardic Jews bring with them a more open and relaxed relationship with the non-Haredi world.

A third factor is the internet. Many Haredim have access to computers and the internet, some because of their work or administrative positions. The real issue that the internet raises is not Haredi access to "secular" sites or even to pornography. Such access always existed. What the internet allowed is the creation of free Haredi chat sites. That is the creation of a public sphere in which the inner problems of the Haredi society can be freely discussed. These include not only current problems such as the financial situation and issues in the Haredi community and unseemly rivalries and conflicts over money, power and influence, but also historical controversies and scandals. Furthermore, academic works on Haredim and Hasidism are also examined and discussed. The traditional palliative against such free discussion—repression in the name of communal values doesn't work anymore and incurs ridicule (Rose 2007).

The fourth factor is the very success of the Haredi community itself. The Haredim no longer feel defensive and besieged. Due to their presence, population and political power, they have "domesticated" urban spaces which are not strictly Haredi such as the entire city of Jerusalem and they feel at home in it. Hence today many Haredim are found in the malls and recreational spaces of the city, participating in mainstream consumption and leisure activities, such as going to the Zoo, cafés and bars and movies (El-Or and Neriah 2004).

In recent years a new social category has emerged—the New Haredim—these combine several of the new characteristics such as males engaging both in work and in new patterns of consumption and leisure.

Israeli researchers noting these pressures and changes, have raised a series of questions. In the 1980s, researchers such as Friedman raised the question of the sustainability of the Haredi way of life. Noting the growth in population and the increased family size, Friedman questioned the economic viability of the Haredi lifestyle, given the fact that most Israeli Haredi males do not work. As we have seen, though, in the intervening twenty years, not only have the Haredim survived, they have positively flourished. The new questions that now arise are: Are the Haredim undergoing Israelization? Are they, even despite themselves, joining the Israeli mainstream? Does their presence at shopping malls, in work situations and other areas not represent that—not only in behavior but also in thought and dispositions—they are becoming a bit more like everyone else?

I think that such questions are a little bit simplistic and reflect the concerns of university researchers, not the Haredi population that they are investigating.

It must be stressed that none of these changes described above involves a principled or ideological change. The highest values are still Torah study and strict observance. Haredi males are still expected to spend their lives devoted to these and their wives are to obediently support them. Hence we are not talking about principled, large scale changes. What these changes do represent is erosion at the edges of the Haredi boundaries. That behaviors and thoughts that were looked a bit askance upon several years ago are a bit more acceptable and routine. Does this development have any significance? If it does not represent "Israelization" or principled change does it represent anything at all?

I would like to suggest that the meaning of the new developments can best be appreciated if we juxtaposed them with a different series of new developments in the Haredi community. There seems to be a new spiritual fermentation within the Haredi community which ranges from the high to the low. I will list some of its manifestations. There is a new interest in Kabbalah and mysticism and psychological-ethical literature and exercises. This new interest seems to span all the groups—Hasidim and "Lithuanians" and is remarkable in some quarters for its sophistication and erudition. The new Jewish revivalism represented by the Nach Nachim[5] and the Meshichistim (The Habad Messianic) groups is very visible, especially on the Haredi "Street". They are of course still marginal, but the Breslovers have some support

---

[5] A sect belonging to the Hasidim of R. Nachman of Breslov (Bratzlav, Ukraine) which stresses the holiness of reciting the formula of "Na, Nach, Nachman of Breslov".

from the old-line Jerusalem haredi establishment. We are also witnessing the growth of a new popular religion—centered around tombs of saints and pilgrimages to Eastern Europe. The newly invented (since 1995) Death Anniversary of Rachel the Matriarch, drew huge Haredi crowds to her tomb site in early November. Finally, there are new sects practicing new asceticism and renewal.

I would suggest that the erosion of the boundaries has an effect, but not a simple effect of Israelization. Rather, by putting the accepted roles and boundaries into question it invites a search for new meanings and new legitimation. The changes we described above cannot overthrow Haredi society, but they can subtly undermine its legitimacy, make it less taken for granted. Hence it engenders a search for new meanings, often appealing to the personal and spiritual. These new meanings I further argue, contribute to the restructuring of relations between Haredi society and other groups.

I will relate briefly to two aspects of this spiritual fermentation. The first is the new study of Kabbalah, mysticism and spiritual texts. Yoni Garb, in a series of recent articles (Garb forthcoming a, forthcoming b), noted that this is a new development. From the post-war years to the present century Haredi Torah study focused almost exclusively upon the Talmud and its commentaries and the Halacha and its codes. As opposed to that, Garb details changes in the Hassidic and Lithuanian worlds.

In the Hasidic world Garb describes the growth of a new species of ecstatic Hasidic masters, who are not the descendants of existing Hasidic dynasties. One such master, R. Tzvi Meir Zilberberg conducts ecstatic gatherings for the masses and elite in which he displays far-reaching erudition. These gatherings are attended by scholars from all Haredi sectors including the Lithuanian and even the religious Zionist community. Zilberberg also gives spiritual counseling to scores of people. Garb notes that the flourishing of such spiritual leadership is also accompanied by the growth of a ramified Hasidic and mystical literature, which is not only sophisticated and learned but also innovative and even theologically daring. Garb describes similar developments in regard to Kabbalah proper. Not only is it possible in Haredi bookstores to buy books written by contemporary Kabbalistic masters, identified with the Haredi community (such as R. Gamliel Rabinovitch), which explain abstruse philosophical concepts to the broad public, it is also possible to download files on the internet containing lessons with the same contents. A similar renaissance also affects the world of ethical psychological literature (*mussar*). Garb talks about a growing synthesis between these various worlds of Hasidim which contributes to this spiritual fermentation.

This new renaissance of spiritual writing, study and teaching also involves new social relations with other groups. Recently, Boaz Huss has shown how the new interest in mysticism has rehabilitated a leading medieval mystical author, Abraham Abulafia. Since the 13th century he had been under serious rabbinical interdiction (on the part of the leading Jewish authority of the late middle ages, R. Shlomo ibn Adret—or Rashba) "for messianic and heretical ravings". As a result he had been read out of the canon of Jewish mysticism for over five hundred years. Interest had been renewed in Abulafia, not among traditional Kabbalists but in the academic study of Kabbalah. First, Gershom Scholem devoted a chapter of his classic work *Major Trends in Jewish Mysticism* to him and then Moshe Idel devoted several detailed monographs to this figure. Since the 1990s Abulafia has become of considerable interest to New Age mystic groups (of all denominations), who apparently became aware of him through Idel's writings. The Habad-Breslov revival fringe has brought Abulafia into Haredi mystical circles. They apparently have been influenced by the New Age and also by academic writing. Recently, Abulafia's collected works have been issued in Meah She'arim (the main Haredi neighborhood of Jerusalem) by the Breslover Amnon Gross, but with the approval of the mainline religious authorities, who explicitly wrote that the interdiction had been lifted. Thus we see, that the new spiritual fermentation, while not "modern"—but rather mystical, ecstatic and in some quarters ascetic—has opened new channels between the Haredim and other groups, some of whom are not even Jewish. It should be noted, perhaps ironically, that the new spiritualist development does denote a form of Israelization, but not of the form of adopting the mores and dispositions of the Israeli mainstream of work, army and consumerism. Rather the Haredi spiritualist vanguard resembles the New Age and spiritualist fringe of Israelis with whom they are in touch.

The other two phenomena of Haredi spiritual fermentation are two women's sects which have come into existence in the past few years. Boundary issues in the Haredi world are particularly acute in regard to women. On the one hand, because they work, they are much more in contact with the outside world. On the other, having only marginal access to the Torah, they cannot achieve any religious or spiritual autonomy. In terms of norms and values they are totally dominated by men.

Both sects that I discuss have been seriously tainted by scandal. However in this chapter, I move beyond the issue of scandal and examine the spiritual meaning that these movements had for the hundreds of religious women involved in them.

The first of these movements relates to extreme "modesty" or covering up of women's bodies. This phenomenon has acquired vast importance in the Haredi world in recent years. In this section I will discuss women's movements who voluntarily cover themselves up in extreme ways. Later on, I will discuss the enforcing of this modesty and the separation of sexes by men.

The trend or tendency towards extreme women's modesty and even veiling expresses itself in two different phenomena. The first is that of the "Veiled Women" or as the media sometimes described them, the Taliban Women. This is a group in Beit Shemesh led by Bruria Keren who was imprisoned in the spring of 2008 for child abuse. This group, which consists of about forty women, conceals the outline of their bodies by wearing multiple cloths, skirts and blouses. That is, they wear three or four skirts. They entirely cover their hair with kerchiefs and some of the women cover their faces by putting on kerchiefs which cover their neck, chin mouth and nose and by pulling down one of the hair covers so that it covers their forehead and even eyes. The ideal of this group is not to leave the house at all. When they leave, because they cover their face, they often cannot see and are led on the street by one of their children. This group has a large *Chozer Betshuva* and Sephardic element in it. They would gather in Bruria Keren's house for classes and lectures and the reciting of psalms, late at night, often leaving in the early hours of the morning.

The second phenomenon is deep in Me'ah Shearim and for the most part consists of Jerusalem Ashkenazic Haredi women. The families of these women, for the most part, belong to the Toldot Aharon sect and its breakaway, Toldot Avraham Yitzchak which are extremist Hungarian Hasidic sects which have been active in Jerusalem since the 1920s. A few members belong to Neturei Karta families. These women wear *shals* or shawls—a tentlike garment which conceals the outline of the body and double sided (front and back) aprons which have the same purpose. Again we are talking about scores of women.

Some of the members of this group gather in one of the homes of their members—a Sephardic woman, married to a Breslover Ashkenazi—for mutual reinforcement, prayer and psalm reciting. Some of their gatherings are conducted in Yiddish. Though Bruria Keren is a Baalat Tshuva (previously less religious who "came back" to rigorous religious practice), in terms of Meah Shearim, having come from a religious Zionist background, I have been told that the Jerusalem group holds her in high regard. I have also been told that one or two members of this group cover their faces with a black veil which has small holes in it.[6]

The Beit Shemesh group, especially, was considered as non-normative. They cover parts of the body which the Halacha does not enjoin, and they engage in behaviors which are not part of current Halachic practice among Haredim such as not speaking to, or even in the presence of, men. In the Haredi parts of Beit Shemesh, let alone in the more secular zones of Israeli society, they are routinely insulted as being Arabs or Taliban and stopped by police and security personnel. When one of their members appeared before a rabbinic court in a divorce case, the rabbinical judges demanded that she remove the veil. When she refused the judges ruled that her husband must divorce her because she has adopted the "ways of the gentiles", i.e. the Arabs. Bruria Keren was arrested in May 2008 for child neglect and abuse.

Most journalistic and scholarly writing on these groups has focused on the feminist angle. Here we have groups of women, it is contended, who have taken the religious initiative and instituted new ascetic practices on their own accord, without and even against male rabbinic authority. So the discussion here has resembled the discussion of veiling in the Islamic world and community. Can these practices be considered women's initiative and women's voice, even though the practice itself seems deeply repressive? Other writings focus upon the reaction of the rabbinical patriarchy of the state and religious community.

Particularly in regard to the Beit Shemesh group, I would like to focus upon another aspect of this phenomenon. In interviews the Beit Shemesh women talk repeatedly of the spiritual significance of their

---

[6] I am indebted to Orna Levy who shared with me her fieldwork on these women. See also Zalcberg 2008.

practice, that it brings closeness to God, "inwardness" and spirituality and that it will bring the Redemption. I think that the inner meaning of such statements can be gleaned from how they describe their own modesty. They keep on saying that this or that aspect of their body, is feminine and will entrap men—the wrist or the nape of the neck. or their pretty faces and that it must be covered up (in situations in which the entire body is covered the erotic character of the face or any uncovered part perhaps is enhanced). They seem to be engaged in wholesale eroticization of their bodies, their voices, their being. Parts of the body which in routine social interaction in the workaday secular world lose all erotic meaning, in the discourse of these women becomes charged and cathected. Many of these women have had extensive contact with the secular world; they seem to be very aware of their own sexuality and their discourse is designed to heighten it (Rotem 2007, Erlich 2008, Makover 2008).

Their "spirituality" seems to consist precisely in this—having heightened or charged the erotic potential of my body or my limbs, I radically cover them up. The veiled women of Beit Shemesh speak of modesty as a "task" or as work. By means of this double movement, they impose the victory of purity and holiness over sin and temptation.

This practice has some precedent in the history of Jewish mysticism. Mendel Piekarz describes practices in early 18th century Poland of utilizing the "evil inclination" to achieve holiness. The most radical of these consist of exposing oneself to severe temptation and then overcoming it—such as getting into bed with a naked woman and not having intercourse (Piekarz 1998: 204–269). The holiness thus achieved is held to be of a higher level than purity which was not challenged by temptation. The "task" of modesty by the women of Beit Shemesh seems to have a similar inner logic. First you heighten the erotic—in discourse and consciousness—and then you cover it up.

If the Veiled Women of Beit Shemesh use their bodies to generate holiness, then the Megairot group tries to use housework as an avenue to God. Founded in the Gush Katif settlements in Gaza by Sylvie Dahari, the Megairot group encompassed hundreds of women all over Israel and the Occupied Territories. This movement straddled the religious Zionist and the Haredi worlds. Hundreds of Haredi women attended Megairot seminars in Bnei Brak and Jerusalem while the same or even a higher number attended in Raanana and Ramat Gan, as well as Gush Etzion, strongholds of middle class religious Zionism. Many of these women have advanced degrees and professional careers.[7]

Megairot (which means "drawers") consists of a detailed discipline of how to use housework to approach God. Sylvie says "God has to be in the house". If the Veiled Woman represent contemporary religious radicalism, then Megairot represents the Hasidic orientation of worshiping God through the mundane and the everyday. The point of the Megairot discipline is to become focused and aware so that you can use the activities of everyday housework as a departure for prayer and meditation. Sylvie says: "Everything that happens to me or that I do is an occasion for a conversation with God." At the core of the system are several key concepts. These include "role definition"—Does the acting of the drawer match this definition? Does what I am doing now match my definition at this time period? If the answer is no then you are not well focused and aware. The second concept, not surprisingly, is focus. The third concept is dignity. This refers especially to the fact that I must eat and dress with dignity—not absentmindedly and without thinking. One should not absentmindedly eat leftovers, or eat them in the course of cleaning up. You wish to eat, you set the table and you sit down. It also refers to not dressing sloppily, even in the house, and not torn underwear or stockings. Again the most routine everyday activities have to become deliberate, focused and aware.

It would seem that the Megairot discipline does help women to cope with nine kids, job and husband. But that is not the point. Once you are focused, then everything becomes the occasion for a prayer. As you are deliberately folding sweaters you say a prayer for each child whose sweater you fold. You pray to become more aware and focused and as time progresses you become more spiritually sensitive. You start to see God more in your life.

The Megairot system enjoins traditional roles—the husband remains the authority. In fact "he is the king." However this is so, only because God ordained it so. Your husand is in fact a metaphor for God. You express your fear of God through your relationship to your husband. The result of this, as one Megairot husband put it to me—is that family

---

[7] This preliminary analysis of Megairot is based upon interviews with several women who had been intensively involved in the movement.

relations become abstract. My wife stopped relating to me concretely. I am merely a religious idea to her. This seems to affect in general the way these women relate to their traditional roles. Such roles are sufferable only because they lead to spiritual growth. Unlike Veiled women and like Hasidism, the new legitimacy that Megairot give to traditional roles does not lead to normative confrontation. But again, as Gershom Scholem pointed out in regard to Hasidism, it does tend to empty them of concreteness.

Thus while Megairot is not on the surface scandalous as are the Veiled women of Beit Shemesh they do create an autonomous locus for religious experience and authority. This seems to be the reason why the Jerusalem Ultra-Orthodox religious court placed them under interdiction. It also seems to underpin the scandal that broke out recently regarding Megairot. In the past few months, Sylvie has been accused and condemned for financially, emotionally and even conjugally dominating and exploiting her adherents. Apparently, there is something in these accusations. Viewed sociologically, one might suggest that the rapid and extreme change in status that Sylvie underwent—from kiosk saleswoman to independent spiritual authority—encouraged in her a certain degree of anomie and normlessness.

Conclusion

These phenomena of the new spiritual fermentation in the Haredi world are all focused on the personal sphere or the private spheres. The Megairot women wish to use housework and intra-family relations as a pathway to God. The Veiled women of Beit Shemesh wish to achieve a state of heightened holiness by focusing on their sexual bodies and then covering them up. And the renewal of mysticism, Kabbalah and Hassidism focuses on personal religious experience.

This development parallels the other developments that I have described in American Jewish life and in radical religious Zionism. Furthermore, this common focus on the personal has led to the softening of group boundaries. As we have seen, Haredi Hasidim and religious Zionists together participate in the new renaissance of mysticism and Hasidism; the Breslov-Habad revivalist fringe spans both groups and both groups are to be found in the new mass pilgrimages to Holy Tombs both in Israel and in Eastern Europe. The Megairot group too, spans or shuttles back and forth between both groups. It is the same focus on personal religious experience and individual religiosity which allows for this fluidity. But this fluidity, as we have seen, does not only affect other Orthodox groups. The new interest in Kabbalah involves new relations with New Age groups and academic figures. Thus this theme of personal religious experience and meaning seems to be a global theme of the Jewish religion today, spanning communities from the New Age ambience of California to the ardent and austere religious life in Beit Shemesh and the bohemian nationalism of the hilltop youth.

Belonging without Believing or Behaving

A very different trend that categorizes contemporary Judaism is "belonging without believing." Recent research both among European (post) Christians and among American Jews have highlighted a certain disjunction between membership in religious organizations and adhering to the tenets of the religion that such organizations represent.

In regard to Europe, Grace Davie, and following her, Jose Casanova, have identified a pattern of religious adherence which they call "belonging without believing" (Hervieu-Léger 2004, Casanova 2006b). By this phrase they refer to a situation in which Europeans of Christian background cease to adhere to traditional, institutionalized European religion (whether Catholic or Protestant) and cease to hold traditional Christian beliefs or dogmas.[8] Nevertheless, these churches do continue to play an important role in collective and individual identity:

> From France to Sweden and from England to Scotland, the historical Churches (Catholic, Lutheran, Anglican or Calvinist) although emptied of active membership, still function vicariously, as it were, as public carriers of the national religion...Europeans continue to be implicit members of their national churches even after explicitly abandoning them. The national churches remain there as a public good to which they have rightful access to celebrate the transcendent rites of passage, birth and death...(Casanova 2006b: 14–16).

According to Casanova "cultural" and Christian elements are intertwined in European identity in complex and rarely verbalized ways.

---

[8] Many Europeans, though, hold private religious belief systems assembled from many sources. Grace Davie has termed this "believing without belonging."

Similarly Grace Davie has described the European situation as "vicarious religion." She defines this concept as "the notion of religion performed by an active minority on behalf of a much larger number, who (implicitly at least), not only understand, but quite clearly approve of what the minority is doing" (Davie 2006: 24). She argues that not only are European Christian clergy expected to perform rituals of birth, marriage and (especially) death for the larger population, but they are also expected to *believe* for them and uphold a certain traditional moral code (especially as regards family and sexual relations) (Davie 2006).

Recently, Steven Cohen and Lauren Blitzer (2008) have applied this concept to American Jewry. Noting that religiously American Jews believe in traditional Judeo-Christian faith concepts (God, an afterlife, Heaven and Hell) even less than Americans who are totally religiously unaffiliated; they also showed that American Jews belong to religious Jewish organizations such as synagogues to the same degree that religiously committed Christian Americans do. In other words, religiously affiliated American Jews *believe* in religious beliefs to the same degree that secular Americans do; but they *belong* to religious organizations to the same extent or more than the most devout Christians.

Cohen and Blitzer attempt to explain this pattern by suggesting that religious belonging for American Jews serves other ends than purely religious ones.[9] Given the historic blending of religious and ethnic identity among Jewish populations and given that American Jews seem to reject pressures deriving from their non-Jewish environment to render asunder ethno-national and religious components of identity (Cohen and Blitzer 2008), it would be reasonable to suggest that some of the ends of membership in organizations which seems to be religious (such as synagogues) are in fact those of expressing or fulfilling ethno-national identity.

If we combine the way the concept of "belonging without believing" was used in regard to both American Jewry and European Christians we see that it basically consists of two related components. The first is belonging to a collectivity which is characterized by two components—a national or ethno-national component and a religious com-

---

[9] Some religious attitudes Cohen and Blitzer attribute to the Jew's minority position in society. Thus unlike Christian religious groups they favor absolute separation of church and state.

ponent. We have seen that religious membership can serve as a marker for total membership in the collectivity—it marks both religious and national belonging (membership in the Lutheran Church in Sweden marks members as Swedes both in the religious and national sense). Secondly, apparently, because of such membership in a common collectivity, religious action or belief undertaken by some members can be "on behalf" or "for" other members.

I would like to mobilize these concepts of "belonging without believing" and vicarious religion in order to enable us to understand certain aspects of Israel's "traditionist" or *Masorati* population. This population constitutes more than a third of Israel's total Jewish population. About 80% of those who define themselves as *Masorati* are of Middle Eastern or North African origin, while about 20% are of Ashkenazic origin, that is whose families originally come from Eastern or Central Europe.

"Traditionist" Jews are characterized by substantial observance of the Jewish religious tradition, yet the degree of their observance is much more flexible than that of Orthodoxy. The favored image of "traditionism" is that of going to synagogue or making Kiddush on the Sabbath and then driving to the beach or to a football game. For many years, traditionism was treated as a transitional or residual category. It was assumed that Jews from "pre-modern" (or developing) Middle Eastern or North African countries arriving in the modern, secular state of Israel would first adopt flexible "traditionist' behaviors before abandoning religion altogether. As has been pointed out, for a long time Israeli social science organized itself around the categories of the "secular" and the "religious" (Orthodox). It was assumed that these were two internally consistent ideal types. "Traditionism" was explained in terms of both of these ideal types. It was considered a deficient form of either or both of these types, lacking in inner consistency or coherence. It was further stigmatized by the association with *Mizrahim* who were of low socio-economic status and came from undeveloped or pre-modern societies. For its part, as an incoherent pattern of religious adherence "traditionism" itself contributed to the stigmatization of the *Mizrahim*. In very recent years though, with the rise of self-conscious *Mizrahi* intellectuals and academics and the entrance of most of the Mizrahi population into the middle classes a space has been created for a more balanced examination of the *Masorati* phenomenon.

Using the model of "belonging without believing" I suggest that "vicarious religion" constitutes the inner rationale of *Masorati* religion.

Masoratim believe that as members of the Jewish, the Jewish-Israeli and the *Mizrahi* collectivities, an active minority composed of strictly Orthodox and rabbis performs full Jewish observance on their behalf.

Masorati Jews exhibit all the characteristics of the "belonging without believing" model. They evince significant attachment to collectivities. In a recent study involving open ended interviews very many traditionist Jews evinced strong attachment to their *Mizrahi* identity. These traditionists also tended to see an essentialist connection between their *Mizrahi* and their *Masorati* identity. Thus, for them, the *Mizrahi-Masorati* identity contains both ethnic and religious components. Almost all the interviewees also evinced a strong Jewish-Israeli identity. Indeed some of them were uneasy with their Mizrahi identity because they saw it as divisive and as undermining their overall Jewish-Israeli identity. Here too, they saw their traditionism as connected to this overall identity and they cast doubt upon the strength of the Jewish-Israeli identity of secular Jews who did not observe any Jewish tradition at all.

Academic research in the past 30 years has also connected the Mizrahi-Masorati population to a strong Jewish-Israeli identity Sometimes this connection has been done indirectly, as when articles analyzed the orientations, activities and programs of political parties and movements whose supporters contain a large, sometimes, dominant, component of *Mizrahim-Masoratiim*. Often this research claimed the attachment of the Mizrahi-Masorati community was of an exclusivist, primordial, nature and mitigated against a civic, universalist construction of Israeli identity.

At the same time, the Mizrahi-Masorati population also has very definite worldviews and value commitments. According to the study involving the open-ended interviews, *Masoratiim* identify their traditionist way of life with morality itself, claiming that totally secular individuals cannot be moral, or have primarily instrumental relations with society. They also seem to affirm traditional notions of gender and age roles and sexual orientation. Most importantly, they also seem to acquiesce and even to affirm the legitimacy of the fully Orthodox way of life. This has been affirmed in my own anecdotal experience and in the experience of almost everyone that I know.[10] Nevertheless,

---

[10] One example among many of this sort of acquiescence is that in my basic training company in the IDF, ultra-Orthodox members of the unit easily prevailed upon

this affirmation of Orthodoxy on the part of the *Mizrahi-Masoratiim* somehow does not bind them necessarily as individuals.

I suggest that the religious subject upon whom it is incumbent to observe the religious tradition, is for the *Mizrahi-Masorati*, primarily the collectivity or the public. It is the Jewish and (to a lesser extent) the Mizrahi collectivity that is to hold services in the synagogue, observe the Sabbath etc. The Jewish religion is mainly observed in public or familial settings. Individuals in private settings do not feel that they have to observe the rituals and commandments. The way that the public observes the religious tradition and obligations is through their performance by designated individuals and groups—rabbis and Orthodox. These perform the mitzvoth (religious commands) for the group and hence for all the individuals who are members of the group. Like the Bishops in Europe who must believe in the traditional way (otherwise they are criticized by the press and the general public)—it is expected that religious people and rabbis carefully observe the entire tradition. But the individual non-religiously specialized member of the group does not have to observe in a fully Orthodox fashion. By his (more flexible) observance the traditionist Jew joins in with the public and expresses his own membership in the Jewish (and Mizrahi) publics. But precisely because the meaning of individual observance is not the fulfillment of a religious obligation but the expression of group membership it can be more flexible. Individual *Masoratiim* can choose how they wish to express their membership (by eating Kosher or fasting on Kippur but not necessarily by going to the synagogue; or by refraining from sexual relations the week after menstruation but not refraining from traveling on the Sabbath).

Thus the religious observance of Mizrahi-Masorati Jews cannot be described as incoherent, formless or inconsistent. It carries a very definite inner logic. However, it does offer different guidelines for the individual and the collective or the public in regard to religious observance. Whereas the standard Orthodox approach (including that of the Sephardic Orthodoxy, such as represented by R. Ovadiah Yosef), insists that the acting religious subject is the individual (who is required to pray, wear fringes—*tzitzith*—and meticulously observe the Sabbath), *Masorati* Jews understand the acting subject to be the

---

the Mizrahi-Masorati members to observe the Sabbath in Orthodox fashion inside the living quarters.—not to smoke, turn on lights or listen to the radio.

public or the collectivity. This construction allows *Mizrahi-Masorati* Jews greater freedom and flexibility in regard to individual religious observance, and hence it makes it easier for them to "fit in" and integrate themselves into Israel as a modern, differentiated society. At the same time it does not require them to relinquish their traditional cosmologies vis-a-vis gender and age roles, nor their strong sense of group belonging. This construction, moreover, also seems to be rooted in the historical religious patterns of the North African and Middle Eastern Jewish communities.

Fundamentalist Radicalization among Israel's Ultra-Orthodox: The Abstraction of Religion from Life

As we have seen above, recent years have witnessed a radicalization within some of the ultra-Orthodox groups in the greater Jerusalem area. This radicalization has expressed itself mainly in regard to the place of women and relations between sexes. I have described above the inner meaning that extreme covering up of women's bodies has for the women who extremely cover themselves. In this section I will discuss increased efforts by men to enforce this radical "modesty". This radicalization concerning women's modesty and relations between sexes has involved extending radical demands not only to the members of zealous groups but to other religious groups who live in geographically adjacent areas and to the Haredi society as a whole. The radical groups have also been charged with wishing to impose these demands on the general Israel public at least in areas such as Jerusalem (Zahava Fischer 2009).

Many of these far reaching demands have centered around issues of the place of women in the public space. They concern first the issue of separate spaces on public buses. In regard to this, Haredim in Jerusalem, but also in other places, have demanded the creation of special "*Mehadrin*"[11] buses in which men would sit up front and women would be confined to the back of the bus. These buses are said to serve exclusively Haredi neighborhoods, but they would preserve their *Mehadrin* character during their whole route, even when traveling through the general, non-Haredi parts of the city. In an ad hoc

---

[11] Religiously supererogatory.

fashion (some claim due to unilateral violence on the part of extremist Haredi groups) such buses are already functioning on certain routes. The issue has aroused a certain amount of resistance in Jerusalem and a special committee from the Ministry of Transportation is to prepare recommendations. In addition to Jerusalem, there are *Mehadrin* lines in Beit Shemesh and Beitar and in the inter-city route between Jerusalem and Bnei Brak. They have also been attempted, with mixed success in peripheral and smaller towns such as Yerucham.

Beit Shemesh, a town close to Jerusalem, has also been a focus of radicalization. For the past twenty years or so, extremist ultra-Orthodox groups from Jerusalem have been moving there because of housing shortage in Jerusalem. Some of the more extremist elements among this population have been demanding that women adhere to dress codes of far-reaching modesty including covering up the outline of the body (see above). They also have attempted to prevent women from full access to the public space, demanding that they do not appear on certain streets on Friday night. So-called modesty patrols have been attempting to enforce these restrictions both in the Haredi neighborhood and in areas adjacent to them, including thoroughfares and shopping centers. These adjacent areas contain large non-Haredi populations which use the thoroughfares and visit the shopping centers. The attempts to enforce the modesty restrictions have involved both violence and intimidation and have affected other Haredi groups which have not undergone such radicalization as well as religious Zionist and even secular groups (Sheleg 2009, Zalcberg 2009). There have been similar moves in Jerusalem such as manifested in a recent flyer which requested that on Friday nights women use the north side of a thoroughfare and men use the south side[12] (though in Jerusalem the demands have not been accompanied by violence).

This radicalization could be one response to the challenges to Haredi boundaries that we discussed above. However in this section, I would like to discuss a specific aspect of the nature and spirit of these demands. Once again, I think that an understanding of these extreme demands can be aided by a comparison with other religious groups. Olivier Roy (2006) has argued that Islamic fundamentalism, far from representing a defense of traditional Islamic society in fact represents an attack upon traditional Islamic culture. Contemporary Islamic

---

[12] I have in my possession a copy of the broadside requesting this.

fundamentalism, according to Roy is characterized by an "uncoupling of religion and culture". This is the result of the Westernization and globalization of Islam—of the massive immigration of Muslims to Europe and the fact that very modern people (of Muslim extraction), who had extensive secular education (eg. engineers and doctors) are now teaching themselves Islam. Such people can conceptualize a "pure Islamic religion" that is defined with criteria that are purely religious and totally internal to the religious domain. Fundamentalism vindicates this pure religion and holds it to be superior to the historical Islamic religions which were always embedded in specific Islamic cultures, Arab, Persian, Indian, North African etc. Thus fundamentalist globalized Islam which is conceived of as a pure, essential religion devalues and attacks the achievements of historic Islamic culture—philosophy, literature, poetry, theology, schools of interpretation and law, calligraphy, architecture etc. They reject legacy, transmission and authority in favor of faith, spiritual experience, and individual and personal rediscovery of religion (Roy, p.3).

This process occurs both in European Islam and in the Islamic countries themselves. Roy points out that

> When the Taliban came to power in Afghanistan in 1996, their enemy was not the Western world: they had an excellent relationship with Americans and foreigners... What the Taliban were fighting was not Christianity nor the Western world, but the traditional Afghan culture. They waged a cultural war: they forbade music, poetry, dance, all forms of games, everything resembling spectacle and entertainment (Roy 2006: 4).

According to the fundamentalists, the purpose of the Islamic state is to help the Muslim perform his religious duties and come close to God. Hence the Taliban banned two central Afghan cultural practices: caged song birds and kites. Caged song birds can distract one from his prayer and kites may get stuck in trees. In order to free a kite one may have to climb a tree—you can then look into your neighbor's yard and see a women unveiled, which is a sin. "Why risk burning in hell for a kite. Kites are banned (ibid.: 5)".

One can add that this dis-embedment of religion from its cultural context continues a long term modern trend of social differentiation. As has been pointed out, as part of the general process of social differentiation, religion becomes a separate sphere and institution. Contemporary developments in the Islamic world continue this long-term process and perhaps bring it to an extreme. This process is aided by some of the globalizing trends that Roy mentions, and I may add, the internet. The internet creates a virtual Ummah, abstracted from any concrete, historical community. Thus, Jihadis who have lost specific cultural identity, not only use the internet for its many instrumental virtues but also act in the name of the virtual, global Ummah. It is this on-line Ummah which removed from any concrete community can best embody the community of pure religious Islam removed and abstracted from any cultural or national affiliation.

I will apply a similar analysis to this new Haredi radicalization. In this case though, I will discuss not how religion is embedded or dis-embedded in culture, but how it is embedded and dis-embedded in community life. Just as historically Islam had been embedded in concrete, specific cultures and communities, so Judaism also had been embedded in concrete specific communities whether in Central or Eastern Europe, the Middle East or North Africa. These communities were organized for pragmatic living and their material, economic and political well-being was a prime, legitimate concern both on the collective and individual levels. These were not merely "religious" communities but had a strong ethnic or ethno-national dimension. In other words they were ethno-religious communities. As pragmatic communities, it was taken for granted, that they were composed of men, women and children and that all of these groups had a role to play in both the public and private spheres. In this situation, the religious teaching and law, the Torah and the Halacha *regulate* the pragmatic community but don't abolish it or central aspects of it. The traditional art of halachic decision making is, in fact to balance the needs and orientations of the pragmatic ethno-religious community with the demands of the Halacha. Thus casuistry is employed in order to implement the famous rule of "the power of the permissive ruling is stronger".

The radicalization described above—of restricting the access of women to the public sphere and other strictures—consists of a dis-embedment of religion from Jewish pragmatic communal life which is parallel to the de-coupling of Islam from the historic cultural communities in which it was always found (Arab, Persian, Central Asian, Indian, Indonesian etc.) that Olivier Roy describes. This radicalization consists of the conceptualization of a pure Jewish religion which has no reference to the pragmatic life of a community and its needs and orientations. Thus religious considerations overrule all other considerations without even weighing the latter. If Hasidic men returning from the Friday night *tisch* (Hasidic ritual meal involving sermons and songs) might be distracted from their spiritual contemplation by women on the streets, women are asked not to leave their homes, or to restrict themselves to certain sidewalks. This is clearly parallel to the Taliban banning song-birds and kites.

Because of this attitude of de-coupling, the radicalized *Haredim* ignore and even desecrate Halachic decisions whose aim is to accept the pragmatic exigencies of community life and balance religious demands with the exigencies of everyday life. A good example of this is a halachic decision from the 1950's by the leading authority of the last generation, R. Moshe Feinstein (Belarus 1895–New York 1986). This decision permitted Orthodox men to ride in crowded buses and subways in order to get to work even if that involved proximity to women and inadvertent physical contact with them. In accordance with the long standing Halacha, such contact is not forbidden if inadvertent and not accompanied by affection or sexual intent. R. Feinstein even wrote that if a man was sexually aroused by such proximity to women and such contact then something was wrong with him and it is his responsibility to get help. When made aware of this ruling, radical Haredim calling for the separation of men and women on public transportation derided it and even ripped up copies of it. The difference between the two points of view is clear: whereas R. Feinstein accepts the pragmatic life community and only tries to regulate it while reasonably taking into account its requirements, the radical Haredim de-couple religion from the pragmatic life community, and its demands have no standing whatever in their approach. Thus it is better to enforce strict separation despite the huge inconveniences that it causes.

In certain ways, this trend continues long standing trends in *Haredi* society. David Sorotzkin, in a recent doctorate (Sorotzkin 2007) has shown that the thought of the Maharal of Prague (R. Judah Loew, 1520–1609) is one of the sources of the Haredi ideal. The Maharal argued that the Jews were not a natural community and not subject to nature's requirements and laws including those of pragmatic wellbeing and conduct. Rather Jewish fate depended upon their direct relationship to God. Historical developments, too, expressed and encouraged this de-coupling of religion from pragmatic communal life. One such development was the emergence of the "Holy Community" in the Ashkenazic Old Yishuv in Jerusalem. This community which developed in the course of the nineteenth century on the basis of immigrants from various Ashkenazic communities in Europe was to devote itself exclusively to prayer and Torah study in the Holy city while subsisting on philanthropy from the residents' home communities (the *halukah*) (Friedman 1974). This is clearly not an ordinary pragmatic, ethno-religious community, devoted to workaday economic well being.[13] Another development, was the Ausstrit or secession of the Orthodox communities of Frankfurt am-Main and other places in Central Europe from the historic Jewish communities when these were taken over by Reform and Neology. These historic communities were organic ethno-religious communities (*Gemeinde*) expressing the various dimensions of Jewish existence—communal, economic-pragmatic, ethno-national, religious etc. The seceded communities were (voluntary) *associations* (*Gesellschaft*) devoted to religious observance (Katz 1998). Thus here too, we have an abstraction of religious observance from what had been a full ethnic life community.[14] Finally, Chaim Soloveitchik (1994) and Menachem Friedman (1998) describe the transition from "life-tradition" or "mimetic halacha" to "book tradition" or "textual halacha". The former describes religious practice that is learned by osmosis and imitation within a living community. The latter describes practice that is taken out of texts and books, denatured of a social context and then applied to practice. The transition from "life" to "text" was facilitated by the destruction of traditional Jewish life in Europe by the First World War and the Holocaust, and in North Africa and the Middle East by the rise of radical Arab Nationalism.[15] Here again, religious practice is not something which is embedded in a living social community, but rather comes to it as a "force from outside" and imposes itself upon it.

Despite these long term trends, the tradition that the Jewish religion is practiced in pragmatic ethno-religious life communities dies hard, even among the ultra-Orthodox. For generations, despite these

---

[13] Friedman's analysis shows the fissure in that conception. Precisely because the economic base of the Old Yishuv was uncertain, an unusual amount of energy was spent on economic and material concerns. Similarly, its freedom from the obligation of work and its basis upon philanthropic grants made it attractive for many deviants, both religiously and socially, thus undermining its claim to special holiness.

[14] It was precisely because of this that many venerable rabbis in both Central and Eastern Europe opposed the Ausstrit, including R. Bamberger of Würtzburg and R. Naftali Tzvi Yehuda Berlin of Volozhin (Lithuania).

[15] Which in itself also reacted to Zionism and the creation of the State of Israel.

tendencies of the abstraction of religion from life communities the ultra-Orthodox communities of the Old Yishuv and of Central and Eastern Europe continued in many ways to think and act like ethno-religious life communities. However, in recent years there has been an intensification of the abstraction of religion from life. This seems to be due to some of the factors that I have mentioned above in regard to Islam—the influx of newly religious *Hozrim Betshuva* ("Returnees to Judaism") who come from modern educations, life styles and professions and have lost all contact with traditional Jewish ethno-religious communities and the importance of the internet and other aspects of globalization. Also important in this context has been the integration of Orthodox communities in the United States into American society and the rise of the concomitant need for English language manuals and texts explaining in an abstract and generic way "what Judaism is" and how to practice it. As we have seen, such types of manuals are very important for the development of European Islam and its radicalization.

Conclusion

The Jewish religion today exhibits a significant dynamism and vitality with new developments affecting almost all geographical areas and sectors. What is noteworthy about this dynamism is that it tends to accentuate the salience of, or even to isolate, the various components of social and religious action. Thus some trends accentuate the importance of individual or personal meaning, experience and self realization, with or without reference to collective membership, while others focus upon such collective membership and downplay individual religious observance or belief.

The other aspect that is noteworthy is that all of these new trends reflect, or are Jewish manifestations of, trends that are present in other religions or are global trends in religion. Thus the focus upon personal religious experience and self realization is very present both in contemporary American Evangelism (Luhrmann 2004) as well as in European Islam (Roy 2006). As we have seen "belonging without believing" characterizes the historical European Christian religions, as well as American moderately committed Jews and Israeli *Mizrahim-Masoratiim*. And the abstraction or de-coupling of religion from culture and life in characteristic of both Islamic and Jewish fundamentalisms. Thus while Judaism certainly has its own history and structural features, in the contemporary world it cannot be understood apart from general trends in religious life and belonging.

PART SIX

THE COMPARATIVE DIMENSION

CHAPTER FIFTEEN

RELIGION, TERRITORY AND MULTICULTURALISM

Yitzhak Sternberg

Introduction

In the discussion about the major impacts of the globalization process on recent and contemporary religious life, a prominent place is given to consequences of the increase in various global flows, and especially in migration flows, such as deterritorialization, delocalization, transnationalization and the emergence, in an unprecedented scope, of virtual religious communities (see Hervieu-Léger 2002, 2009; McAllister 2005; Dianteill 2002; Mary 2002; Saint-Blancat 2002). However, as students of globalization have also indicated, this does not mean that the importance of the local and the territorial aspect in human life, in general and particularly in religious life, is necessarily diminishing or fading away. Thus, some scholars emphasize the continuing importance of the local even in a globalizing world and coined the special term 'glocalization' to depict it (Robertson 1995). Furthermore, the continuous importance of territory for religions and religious life should not surprise us, given the historic connection between religion and 'sacred spaces' (Eliade 1954). Hence, in addition to the concepts mentioned above, scholars stress the continuous importance of the local and tendencies of re-territorialization as also characterizing recent and contemporary religious life (Hervieu-Léger 2002, 2009; McAllister 2005; Dianteill 2002; Mary 2002; Saint-Blancat 2002).

In what follows, a comparative approach is applied to some recent and contemporary religious perceptions of and attachments to territory, by looking at several different cases. Moreover, the examination of the differences and similarities manifested by these cases with regard to territory can also be helpful in understanding the possible connections between religions, and world religions in particular, and multiculturalism (Taylor 1992). Multiculturalism relates to the degree of intra-religious and inter-religious tolerance. Each religion, and especially so each world religion, has an endemic aspect of exclusiveness and intolerance. This is echoed in Huntington's words: 'Even more than ethnicity, religion discriminates sharply and exclusively among people. A person can be half-French and half-Arab and simultaneously even a citizen of two countries. It is more difficult to be half-Catholic and half-Muslim' (Huntington 1993: 27). Hence, the cases examined are also compared with respect to the issues of intra-religious and inter-religious tolerance or intolerance, and to the question whether religion is necessarily an obstacle on the way to achieving inter-group or intra-group tolerance or, in other words, to achieving multiculturalism.

The different cases are discussed according to the scope of the territorial unit involved in the religious territorial perceptions and attachments. The sequence of presentation is from larger to smaller territorial units.

The cases compared

(a) The first case presents a religious contestation, which also has territorial aspects, that encompasses the whole globe. According to McAlister (2005), since the 1970s many U.S. evangelical groups have produced a global mapping of territories, and Pentecostal discourse even maps space into unambiguous theological geographies: territories are either Christian or demonic. These mission-oriented groups have mapped the globe into Christian-reached and unreached territories, and have concluded that 'successful church planting in the Pacific, Africa and Latin America has largely reduced the world's prime evangelistic real-estate to a swath of territory from 10 to 40 degrees north latitude, running through Northern Africa and Asia known as the 10/40 Window' (cited in McAlister 2005: 252). The reason these regions are Christian-unreached territories is their ancient pacts with un-Christian powers, usually territorial spirits and deities associated with rocks, trees and rivers.

This theology is characterized by militaristic discourse and spatial imagery as 'prayer teams' of 'prayer warriors' come together for a given 'prophetic prayer action' on the 'spiritual battlefield'. Encompassing the entire globe, these spiritual and territorial battles are also conducted on a smaller scale. Thus, for example, one such battle is over the territory of Haiti. The new wave of evangelical Protestantism announced a 'spiritual war' against Vodou in Haiti over the soul of the nation. In this battle, the spirits of Vodou are described by the evangelicals as demonic beings that possess and control their priests, and the general of this diabolical army is perceived to be Satan himself (McAlister 2005).

As in many parts of Africa and Latin America, Haitian pastors—tutored by American evangelicals in spiritual warfare techniques—launch 'crusade' ceremonies that aim to exorcize the land itself from demonic entrenchment. One series of crusades takes place in a national historic landmark for Haitians: Bwa Kayiman, the site where in 1791 the slaves of colonial Saint Domingue staged a religious ritual and vowed to fight for freedom. According to the Pentecostals, the enslaved religious leader, Boukman Dutty, who had invoked the Vodou spirits for help, had made a 'pact with the devil' and dedicated Haiti to Satan; and this alliance is responsible for Haiti's subsequent 200 years of misery. The pastors intended to exorcise the Vodou spirits who still governed the site, and 'win' the space 'for Jesus' (McAlister 2005). One witnesses in this case transnational evangelical crusades and spiritual warfare over national territory. Territory and place are seen here as central points of religious tension and conflict. For the evangelicals this battle over a specific territory is a zero sum battle. A territory, it is worth mentioning, shared by Vodou and Catholicism.

(b) The second case concerns also what may be considered as a battle over a national territory. In Israel, in the 1970s, one witnesses the appearance of a new Jewish religious fundamentalist movement called Gush Emunim (the Bloc of the Faithful) that strongly emphasized the importance of Jewish settlement on and political control over all parts of the land that God promised to the Jews—Eretz Yisrael (the Land of Israel). This territorial aspect has become central in their visions and perceptions (Lustick 1988; Aran 1990, 1991; Friedman 1990; Feige 2009).

The rabbinical figures whose impact on the development of this settlement movement was immense were Rav (Rabbi) Avraham Isaac Kook (1865–1935), who served as the chief Ashkenazi Rabbi of Palestine, and his son Rav Tzvi Yehuda Kook (1891–1982). In sharp contrast to most Orthodox Jews of the early twentieth century, the elder Rav Kook was not disturbed too much by the rejection of Jewish religious law by secular Zionists. Secular Jews, he argued, had an important contribution to make to the redemptive process even if they were unaware that their actions had a divine meaning. By settling in the Land of Israel, working its soil, and developing its potential for habitation by larger numbers of Jews, the secular Zionists were carrying out the divine plan to redeem not only the Jewish people, through its restoration in its own land and the coming of the Messiah, but, through them, the entire world and the gentile nations as well.

Kook especially emphasized the importance of the Land of Israel for redemption:

> *Eretz Yisrael is part of the very essence of our nationhood; it is bound organically to its very life and inner being. Human reason, even at its most sublime, cannot begin to understand the unique holiness of Eretz Yisrael... The hope for the Redemption is the force that sustains Judaism in the Diaspora; the Judaism of Eretz Yisrael is this very Redemption'* (cited in Lustick 1988: 32).

Furthermore, for the elder Rav Kook, living and working in the Holy Land was a *mitzvah* (divine injunction) equivalent in value to all the other religious commandments combined. Rav Kook (the elder) also emphasized the important role of *tzaddikim* (righteous, charismatic men) for redemptive guidance. And indeed, approximately forty years after his death, the founders and leaders of Gush Emunim saw themselves as a vanguard that should lead the whole settlement project and the Jewish people toward redemption (Lustick 1988; Aran 1990, 1991; Friedman 1990; Feige 2009).

Rav Tzvi Yehuda Kook (the son) identified three overall stages of redemption. The first stage is expressed by the return of Diaspora Jews to the Land of Israel. But according to Rav Kook (the son) even while the Diaspora continues to exist, the next stage has already begun. The second stage is made possible by reuniting the Jewish people with the biblical heartland of Judea and Samaria. It entails

> *The complete resettlement in the Land and the revival of Israel in it... [and] the actual fulfilment of our inheriting the Land, of its being in our possession and not in that of any other of the nations nor in a state of desolation* (cited in Lustick 1988: 35).

It means that Eretz Yisrael should be in the exclusive possession of the Jewish people. In the third, and final, stage it is expected that by their contact with the whole Land of Israel, Jews will turn toward God and the observance of his commandments. In this stage, the final redemption will approach at a pace proportionate to the Jewish people's increasing level of religious observance. Hence, the relative tolerance toward secular Jews and especially toward secular Zionists is upheld to a certain stage, whereas in the last stage it is expected, as a necessary precondition for redemption, that secularism among Jews fades away.

In the previous case mentioned above, the territory of Haiti is just one among many territories around the globe where a religious battle between Christians and un-Christians takes place. Hence, its religious importance for the evangelicals is just like any other such contested and disputed territory. In contrast, the battle of Gush Emunim over the settlement and control of the Land of Israel has a unique, specific and paramount importance for this religious group; it is *the* territory. Only this specific territory has an important role in the redemptive process. Moreover, for Gush Emunim it is a battle over the territory of the ancient Hebrew forefathers; whereas in the case of the evangelicals, the participants do not necessarily fight over a territory where their ancient forefathers used to live. Furthermore, in the previous case the religious aspect of the conflict over territory is much more important than the national aspect; in the case of Gush Emunim, both aspects, the religious one as well as the national, are almost equally important. However, in both cases the religious battle over territory is a zero sum battle.

Another interesting point is that members of the Gush Emunim movement go to the periphery of contemporary Israel to establish new settlements. But this periphery can be also conceived as the heartland of the historic and ancient land of Israel. From a long-term historical view, this contemporary periphery was once central for the Jewish people and Gush Emunim expects it will become central again. It is in this perspective that Gush Emunim members see themselves as playing a central role in the history of the Jewish people.

(c) Inter-religious and intra-religious tensions and rivalries over territory, as well as a religious attachment to localities within national territories, are illustrated by the case of the Celestial Church of Christ, one of the African Independent churches. Even though globalization is sometimes connected with a loss of sense of place, African-style transnationalization goes hand in hand with territorializing the religious identity within an enlarged space. 'African-style transnationalization' describes the expansion, beyond its initial borders, of a religion that is rooted in a certain territory, notably through attachment to holy places. This process is revealed by Senegalese Mouridism, Ivory Coast

Harrism, Congolese Kimbanguism or the Celestial Church of Christ (Mary 2002).

At the birth of African Independent churches, their claim for identity became strongly linked to holy places, such as where original visions took place or the founding prophets are buried, and which have been transformed into pilgrimage sites. The project for the Celestial City of Imeko, near the border between Benin and Nigeria, was conceived by the Founder of the Celestial Church of Christ, Prophet Oschoffa and implemented from 1983 onwards. It related to a desire to territorialize the Church's message by giving territorial expression to the battle between the forces of Good and Evil. The choice of the site of Imeko is bound up with a vision reported to Papa Oschoffa in 1973 by a visionary. The message was that the Celestial City must be built at Imeko, on the precise site of a forest traditionally dedicated to the Yoruba deity Orunmila. The declared intention was to completely rooting out all pagan forces from the site and the area. The second message was that Mecca would be closed, that Jerusalem would cease to be in its accustomed place, and that God had chosen Imeko as the New Jerusalem (Mary 2002).

It can be argued that the new holy place has a dual peripherality. It is in the periphery of Nigeria, and Nigeria itself can be seen as peripheral in the global entity. But it is a periphery that has aspirations to become in the future much more central or even, the centre of the world. Furthermore, one can find here several inter-religious exclusionist motives: a similar motive as discussed in the first case, of completely rooting out all pagan forces from a particular place; an intention of replacing both Mecca and Jerusalem with the new holy site, Imeko.

After the founder's death, conflict over his succession led to an intra-religious tension that also had territorial aspects. The great majority of Benin Celestial Christians now celebrate Christmas at Seme, the beach area of Porto Novo, in their eyes the only authentic site of the Church. On the other hand, the Nigerian Church continues to gather at Imeko, which receives every year thousands of pilgrims from all-over Africa and Europe as well as from the USA. This case shows that immigrants can continue to maintain, especially through pilgrimage, their religious contacts and connections with holy places located in their countries of origin. In this case the most important holy places are located in the original territories of the founding fathers, and not in believers' current countries of residence (Mary 2002).

As Mary (2002: 115) observes:

> The unavoidable crossing of the paths of Benin partisans from Cotonou with pilgrims coming to Seme and those coming to Imeko takes place with affected mutual ignorance: they do not even greet one another, although they wear the same white robes. Equally astonishing is the fact that when the Imeko pilgrims have to cross Seme Beach or even Porto Novo, they are forbidden to stop, even though these are holy places for all Celestial Christians.

Hence, these intra-religious tensions have a territorial dimension and a certain religion can have two competing and alternative holy places that exclude each other.

Furthermore, in a certain respect the tradition of Christmas pilgrimage to the holy city of Imeko differs from some other pilgrimages. There is no expectation of a miracle or a drastic change in one's personal life: what we know about believers' expectations belongs rather to the social domain. Most pilgrims expect mainly the blessing of anointment, which is the condition of advancement through the ranks, within a Church that is very much hierarchical.

(d) Another example of a dispute over pilgrimage and holy places is characteristic of Islam, and it opposes Shiites and Sunnis (the two main fractions of Islam). Whereas the pilgrimage (*hajj*) to Mecca has the same significance for Sunnis and Shiites, the visitation (*ziyara*) to nearby Medina is of special importance to Shiites. The cemetery of al-Baqi, near the city of Medina, is the reputed resting-place of the Prophet Muhammad's daughter Fatima and four of the Twelve Imams. The Shiite practice at this cemetery is to pray for their intercession with God. However, the Wahhabists, the Sunni rulers of Saudi Arabia, who saw this prayer as a form of idolatry, have demolished al-Baqi entailing a longstanding controversy.

There were ups and downs in this pilgrimage controversy between Saudi Arabian Authorities and Shiite Iran. After the demolition of the shrines in the cemetery in 1926, al-Baqi ceased for many years to serve as a place of Shiite visitation. But after Iran's Islamic revolution, formal prayers were reinstated there against Saudi will—this time, however, outside a wall built by the Saudis to seal off the cemetery. Morevover, in 1986, in a concession to Iran, Saudi authorities allowed access to Shiite pilgrims to the cemetery itself. As a result, al-Baqi re-emerged as a major Shiite centre of pilgrimage with mass prayer conducted there by visiting Shiite clerics (Kramer 1990). At the same time, the

Saudis changed their exclusionist view with regard to al-Baqi cemetery illustrating how far a religious authority can change its view toward other religious fractions in accordance with political or other considerations.

(e) Since the early 1970s, new sacred sites of Jewish saints were established in Israel's urban periphery. These sites serve as pilgrimage centres and healing shrines. The initiators of these sites, as well as the visitors and pilgrims, are mainly Jews of Oriental origin (Mizrahim) and especially Moroccan Jews. These holy spaces are organized around tombs of rabbis who used to live in Israel or abroad (in Morocco or Tunisia, for example). In some cases, places are holy by the reinvention of a narrative of translocation of a saint from Morocco to Israel. Moreover, one also observes the emergence of new contemporary and still active saints and healers in Israel. These developments are strongly connected to the worship of saints in the Jewish and Muslim tradition in Morocco (Bilu 2005; Ben-Ari and Bilu 1997).

In brief, this case shows that immigrants can establish new holy places in their new country of residence that are anchored in their religious traditions in the country of origin. Moreover, in this case it appears that the more important holy places may well be the new ones established in the country of actual residence. In that respect, this contrasts with the case of the Celestial Church of Christ as priority is given to the new country of residence and not to the country or countries of origin.

At the organized level one witnesses in Israel the continuity of the competition, that originated in Morocco, between the descendants of two rabbinical families famous for the quantity of their members who became saints—the Abuhatzeira and Pinto families. The most famous is the tomb of Rabbi Yisrael Abuhatzeira (Baba Sali), in the town of Netivot which has become a major pilgrimage site (Bilu 2005; Ben-Ari and Bilu 1997). The competition between those families is mainly about pre-eminence and does not come up to exclusionist practices—worshippers may refer to the saints revered by both families and accede shrines of either camp.

Of special interest are the less well-organized shrines that are located in private homes and are dedicated to a saint buried in Morocco. The underlying belief is that the saint was thereby transplanted from Morocco to Israel and that he or she can now be honoured by the faithful. Such apartments that have a room spared for the cult of a holy person have thus become pilgrimage centres. For example, in 1973 Avraham Ben-Haim devoted a room in his small apartment to Rabbi David u-Moshe, a most popular saint among Jews in Morocco. This is but one case of a pilgrimage private center out of several ones that are still active today in Israel (Bilu 2005). In Morocco almost each Jewish community had its own saint while some saints were honoured by almost the whole Jewish population of the country. Furthermore, some of these saints were in Morocco holy for both Jews and Muslims.

In contrast to the pilgrimage to Imeko whose central purpose is advancement through the ranks, of the church, pilgrimage to the holy sites in Israel is motivated by the aspiration of solving various personal problems. In Israel, too, one has non-prestigious peripheral places moved by the will to become more central and prestigious, but unlike Imeko, the goal of the new sites in Israel is not to become the religious centre of the world, and the dead *tzaddikim* (saints) as well as those still alive, are not expected to constitute the vanguard that leads the entire Jewish people towards redemption, as in the case of Gush Emunim. Furthermore, by their illustrating typical features of some groups of origin, these new cults are deeply anchored in ethnicity.

(f) There are also cases where two distinct religions quarrel over a certain location regarded as holy by both. To this possibility responds the dispute between Hindus and Muslims with regard to the Babar Mosque in Ayodhya (India) which was erected on the ruins of a Hindu temple that, according to Hindu tradition, was built on the birthplace of Lord Ram, one of North India's most important gods. The Hindu temple was destroyed by the Moslem Mogul ruler Babar, and a mosque was built on the spot in the sixteenth century. Some of the old pillars of the original Hindu temple are still visible today and date to the eleventh century. The result of all this was that both Muslims and Hindus continued to worship the same compound (van der Veer 1987).

This background led to several clashes in the past between Hindus and Muslims. In the 20th century, one reports the events of 1912 and 1934 when Hindus launched attacks on the Babar mosque. In the 1934 crisis, hundreds of Muslims were apparently massacred and the army had to intervene. A fundamental change in the status quo concerning this mosque took place in the years following the Partition of 1947. Though, on December 1949, an idol of Ram suddenly appeared in the mosque, protected by an armed guard. This led to renewed riots that were halted with great difficulty by the police and the army. Following these riots, Muslims and Hindus were forbidden access to the mosque. Hence, Hindus organized a new devotional practice in front of the mosque (van der Veer 1987).

Still more trouble were to come. In 1984 a new Hindu organization voiced a demand to remove the mosques from Hindu sacred places including, besides Ram's birthplace, Krishna's in Mathura and the Viswanath temple of Shiva in Benares. However, according to van der Veer, at the local level of Ayodhya there were also certain Hindu groups and personalities whose economic and local political interests were in favour of retaining the status quo (van der Veer 1987).

Hence, the case of the Babar Mosque shows that relations between Hindus and Muslims may be influenced not only by religious considerations and motives but also by economic and political (national as well as local) interests. Moreover, not all the Hindus or all the Muslims necessarily share the same stance with respect to such issues, and they may be influenced by historical circumstances and concrete interests. Furthermore, the relations between Hindus and Muslims in India appear to imply ups and downs that were not solely, or even chiefly, characterized by tensions and conflict. In these ups and downs one finds a similarity with the case of the Sunni Saudi and Iranian Shiite relations discussed in the above.

(g) Sometimes contestation concerns two holy spaces located on the same ground and pertaining to a same church. This is the case of a Catholic church in Rincon (Cuba) consecrated to Saint Lazarus by members of Santeria, a religious group whose origins go back to Africa (the Orisha religion). In fact, two statues of Lazarus were set up in the church. The first, the 'official' statue, represents the Bishop Lazarus revived by Jesus. But, according to a witness of the 1995 pilgrimage, this is not the statue that was honoured by the pilgrims with flowers and candles and who address themselves to a second statue, representing a bearded beggar accompanied by two dogs licking wounds on his legs. Although the Catholic parish priest did his utmost to direct the pilgrims toward the statue of the bishop, his efforts were in vain.

The case shows that it is not unthinkable that a church comprises two alternative holy compounds which compete for believers' attention. Here too one witnesses, as in the case of Moroccan Jews in Israel, that people establish new holy places in their new country of residence, that are based on their religious traditions rooted in their countries of origin. Dianteill (2002: 129–130) comments on this phenomenon by pointing out that what is shown by Rincon is that:

> *Faced with this Afro-Cuban investment in the imagery and in Catholic places of worship, the Church has taken a tolerant line... of welcoming all the pilgrims into the sanctuaries and coming to terms with the heterodoxy of beliefs, while still reminding them, from time to time, of the 'official' point of view of the Catholic Church.*

This tolerant Catholic attitude also shown, as discussed earlier, in the readiness to get allied with Vodou in Haiti, contrasts, in this respect, with the intolerance of other religious allegiances.

Conclusion

The examination of the seven cases discussed in this chapter reveals differences with regard to perceptions of and attachments to territory. One such difference relates to the scope of the territorial unit involved in religious perceptions and attachments. The religious importance of the Haitian territory for evangelicals is just as any other such contested and disputed territory. In contrast, Eretz Yisrael is for Gush Emunim *the* territory, since only this specific territory has a role to play in the redemptive process. We already mentioned that for Gush Emunim its fight is justified by a perception that it is spoken of a battle over the territory of Hebrews' forefathers, unlike evangelicals' war over Haiti. Moreover, in the evangelicals' case the religious aspect of the conflict over territory is much more important than the national aspect; whereas in the case of Gush Emunim, both aspects, the religious one as well as the national are almost equally important.

Inter-religious and intra-religious tensions and rivalries concerning territory, as well as a religious attachment to local communities are manifested in the case of the Celestial Church of Christ. This case shows that immigrants may maintain, through pilgrimage, their religious contacts and connections with holy places located in their countries of origin.

In contrast to the pilgrimage to Imeko whose central purpose is advancement through the ranks, within the Church, pilgrimage to the new holy sites in Israel is intended to address personal problems. Here too we have a case developing in a non-prestigious periphery, however, unlike Imeko, one does not find here ambitions to become a religious centre of the world. Here, the *tzaddikim* (the saints) do not either see themselves a vanguard of the people like for Gush Emunim.

Furthermore, in several cases, ethnicity plays here a prominent role—which is strongly shown by Moroccan Jewish shrines. This case indeed exemplify how immigrants can establish a solid anchor to their religious particularism without depending on their countries of origin. The more important holy places for this population group consist of those places established in Israel. In this they are distinct from the Celestial Church of Christ, but quite similar to the Santeria members in Cuba.

These cases reminded here also reveal the importance of territorial aspects in human life in general, and in religious life in particular. This importance does not necessarily fade away in a world characterized by globalization. In fact, some of the cases enable us to pay attention to the existence of a certain dialectic between the global and the local. Thus, for example, in its concrete implementation, the evangelical battle against non-Christian territory that encompasses the whole globe also has a very significant local dimension—as can be seen in the battle over Bwa Kayiman in Haiti. Moreover, the Israeli Gush Emunim settlement movement whose territorial settlements' horizon can be seen as very local in scope nevertheless conveys a significant global impact that expresses itself in media coverage and international relations. Another example of a dialectic relation between the global and the local is manifest in the case of the Celestial Church of Christ. A relatively new transnational religious entity representing a manifestation of today globalization, it is also moved by global aspirations. At the same time, it illustrates a strong attachment to local realities and to the geography of its shrines.

In brief, the cases examined in the above show the continuous importance of the local and of re-territorialization. Both aspects are also sustained by the historic connection between religion and geography or territory. The examination of the cases may also be helpful in undertaking possible connections between religions and multiculturalism. Multiculturalism relates to the degree of intra-religious and inter-religious tolerance. Each religion, and especially so each world religion, conveys inherent aspects dictating exclusiveness and exclusion. Is religion an obstacle—or on the contrary, does it perhaps constitute an engine—on the way to achieving inter-group or intra-group tolerance, or in other words—achieving multiculturalism? As far as the cases examined here can say, the answer is positive regarding both possibilities. One can indeed find in several cases inter-religious intolerance (as in the cases of the evangelicals, Gush Emunim and the Celestial Church of Christ) and intra-religious intolerance (as in the case of the Saudi Sunnis and the Shiite pilgrims or the disputes within the Celestial Church of Christ) with strong exclusionist tendencies. But these are not the only possibilities and there are also cases that indicate the existence of inter-religious (Haitian Catholics toward Vodou or Moroccan Muslims and Jews vis-a-vis each other) or intra-religious (Rav Kook the elder toward secular Zionists) tolerance. Furthermore, it may be added, religious groups can show inter-religious tolerance toward some groups and inter-religious intolerance toward other groups.

The concretization, one may add, of the conflict potential that is endemic to inter-religious or intra-religious relations is influenced not only by religious themes and motives but also by economic and political (global, international, national and local) considerations and interests. This also has been shown by cases studied here. Hence, it can be argued that religions, in general and world religions in particular, are both programs, so to speak, enabling multiculturalism and bringing up its difficulties.

BIBLIOGRAPHY

Abduh, M. (1897). *Risalat al-Tawhid (The Theology of Unity)*. n.p.
Abrahamian, E. (1982). *Iran Between two Revolutions*. New Jersey: Princeton University Press.
Abu Lughod, J. (1989). *Before European Hegemony*. New York: Oxford University Press.
Adamir, F. (2005). *Osmanismus, Nationalismus und der Kaukasus. Muslime, Christen, Türken und Armenier im 19. und 20. Jahrhundert*. Wiesbaden: Reichert.
Agassi, J. (1990). *Between Religion and Nation*. Tel-Aviv: Papyrus.
Ahir, D.C. (ed.) (1982). *Dr. Ambedkar on Buddhism*. Bombay: People's Education Society.
—— (1991). *Buddhism in Modern India*. Delhi: Sri Satguru Publication.
—— (1994). "Dr. Ambedkar's Pilgrimage to Buddhism," pp. 1–16 in A.K. Narain and D.C. Ahir (eds.), *Dr. Ambedkar, Buddhism and Social Change*. Delhi: B.R. Publishing.
Akhtar, S. (1990). *A Faith for All Seasons: Islam and the Challenge of the Modern World*. London: Bellew.
Almog, O. (2000). *The Sabra: The Creation of the New Jew*. Berkeley and Los Angeles: University of California Press.
Almond, G. and Verba, S. (1971). *The Civic Culture*. Princeton: Princeton University Press.
Almond, P.C. (1988). *The British Discovery of Buddhism*. Cambridge: Cambridge University Press.
Ambedkar, B.R. (1987 [1956]). "Buddha or Karl Marx", pp. 439–462 in *Dr. Babasaheb Ambedkar Writings and Speeches*, edited by Vasant Moon, vol 3. Bombay: Education Department, Government of Maharashtra.
—— (1990 [1948]). "The Untouchables: Who Were They and Why They Became Untouchables?" pp. 229–382 in *Dr. Babasaheb Ambedkar Writings and Speeches*, edited by Vasant Moon, vol 7. Bombay: Education Department, Government of Maharashtra.
—— (1992 [1957]). *The Buddha and his Dhamma. Dr. Babasaheb Ambedkar Writings and Speeches*, edited by Vasant Moon, vol 11. Bombay: Education Department, Government of Maharashtra.
—— (2004). *Conversion as Emancipation*. New Delhi: Critical Quest.
Amineh, M.P. (1999). *Die Globale Kapitalistische Expansion und Iran—Eine Studie der Iranischen Politischen Ökonomie 1500–1980*. Münster, Hamburg, Berlin: Lit Verlag.
—— (2003). *Globalization, Geopolitics and Energy Security in Central Eurasia and the Caspian Region*. The Hague: Clingendael International Program.
—— (ed.) (2007). *The Greater Middle East in Global Politics: Social Science Perspectives on the Changing Geography of the World Politics*. Leiden and Boston: Brill Academic Publishers.
Amineh, M.P. and Eisenstadt, S.N. (2007). "The Iranian Revolution: The Mulitple Contexts of the Iranian Revolution", *Perspectives on Global Development and Technology* 6(1–3): 129–157.
Amineh, M.P. and Houweling, H. (eds.). (2004/2005). *Central Eurasia in Global Politics: Conflict, Security, and Development*. Second edition. Leiden and Boston: Brill Academic Publishers.
Amir, A. (1997). *I stick to my own: Thoughts and Reactions 1944–1996*. Tel-Aviv: Golan (Hebrew).

Ammerman, N. (1987). *Bible Believers: Fundamentalists in the Modern World*. New Brunswick, NJ: Rutgers University Press.
Amyot, R. and Sigelman, L. (1996). "Jews without Judaism? Assimilation and Jewish Identity in the United States", *Social Science Quarterly* 77(1): 177–189.
Anderson, A. (2004). *An Introduction to Pentecostalism*. Cambridge: Cambridge University Press.
Appadurai, A. (1996). *Modernity at Large. Cultural Dimensions of Globalization*. Minneapolis: University of Minnesota Press.
—— (2006). *Fear of Small Numbers: An Essay on the Geography of Anger*. Durham: Duke University Press.
Aran, G. (1990). "Redemption as a Catastrophe: The gospel of Gush Emunim", pp. 157–175 in E. Sivan and M. Friedman (eds.), *Religious Radicalism and Politics in the Middle East*. New York: State University of New York Press.
—— (1991). "Jewish Zionist Fundamentalism: The Bloc of the Faithful in Israel (Gush Emunim)", pp. 265–344 in M.E. Marty and R.S. Appleby (eds.), *Fundamentalisms Observed*. Chicago: The University of Chicago Press.
Arkoun, M. (1984). *Pour une critique de la raison Islamique*. Paris: Maisonneuve et Larose.
Armstrong, J. (1982). *Nations before Nationalism*. Chapel Hill, NC: North-Carolina University Press.
Armstrong, K. (2002). *The Battle for God*. New York: Alfred A. Knopf.
Asad, T. (2003). *Formations of the Secular: Christianity, Islam, Modernity*. Stanford, CA.: Stanford University Press.
Auffarth, C. (2007)."Religio migrans: Die 'Orientalischen Religionen' im Kontext antiker Religion. Ein theoretisches Modell", pp. 333–363 in C. Bonnet, S. Ribichini, D. Steuernagel (a cura di), *Religioni in contatto nel mediterraneo antico. Modalità di diffusione e processi di interferenza*. Pisa, Roma: Fabrizio serra editore.
Austin-Broos, D. (1997). *Jamaica Genesis: Religion and the Politics of Moral Orders*. Chicago: University of Chicago Press.
Avichail, D. (2004). *The Path of the Educational Campus in Mitzpe Ramon*. Jerusalem: Ministry of Education, Culture and Sport (Hebrew).
Ayubi, N.N. (1995). *Over-stating the Arab State-Politics and Society in the Middle East*. London and New York: I.B. Tauris Publishers.
Bamyeh, M. (2000). *The Ends of Globalization*. Minneapolis: Minnesota University Press.
Banac, I. (1981). *The National Question in Yugoslavia: Origins, History and Politics*. Ithaca, NY: Cornell University Press.
Barkey, K. (2008). *Empires of Difference: the Ottomans in comparative Perspective*. Cambridge: Cambridge University Press.
Barkey, K. and van Hagen, M. (eds.). (1997). *After Empire: Multi-ethnic societies and nation-building: the Soviet Union, the Russian, Ottoman and Habsburg Empires*. Boulder, CO: Westview Press.
Barth, B. and Osterhammel, J. (eds.). (2005). *Zivilisierungsmissionen. Weltverbesserungen seit dem 18. Jahrhundert*. Konstanz.
Basu, H. (2001). "Africans in India—past and present", *Internationales Asienforum* 32: 253–73.
Bates, S. (2008a) "Sarah Palin talks the God talk", http://www.guardian.co.uk/commentisfree /2008/sep/10/uselections2008.sarahpalin1, 10 September.
—— (2008b). *God's Own Country: Religion and Politics in the US*. London: Hodder and Stoughton.
Baumann, C. (2003). "Tamilische Hindus und Tempel in der Schweiz: Überblick und exemplarische Vertiefung anhand der Geschichte des Vinayakar-Tempels in Basel", pp. 275–294 in M. Baumann, B. Luchesi and A. Wilke (Hg.), *Tempel und Tamilen*

in zweiter Heimat. Hindus aus Sri Lanka im deutschsprachigen und skandinavischen Raum. Würzburg: Ergon.
Baumann, M. (2000a). "Diaspora: Genealogies of Semantics and Transcultural Comparison", *Numen* 47(3): 313–337.
—— (2000b). *Migration, Religion, Integration: Vietnamesische Buddhisten und tamilische Hindus in Deutschland.* Marburg: diagonal.
—— (2003a). "Von Sri Lanka in die Bundesrepublik: Flucht, Aufnahme und kulturelle Rekonstruktionen", pp. 41–73 in M. Baumann, B. Luchesi and A. Wilke (Hg.), *Tempel und Tamilen in zweiter Heimat. Hindus aus Sri Lanka im deutschsprachigen und skandinavischen Raum.* Würzburg: Ergon.
—— (2003b). *Alte Götter in neuer Heimat. Religionswissenschaftliche Analyse zu Diaspora am Beispiel von Hindus auf Trinidad.* Marburg: diagonal.
—— (2004a). "Global Hindu Diaspora. A Bibliography of Books and Main Articles", online www.unilu.ch/gf/3259_14461.htm.
—— (2004b). "Organising Hindu Temples in Europe, the Case of Tamil Migrants from Sri Lanka", pp. 379–391 in C. Kleine, M. Schrimpf and K. Triplett (eds.), *Unterwegs. Neue Pfade in der Religionswissenschaft. Festschrift in Honour of Michael Pye on his 65th Birthday.* München: Biblion.
—— (2006). "Performing Vows in Diasporic Contexts: Tamil Hindus, Temples, and Goddesses in Germany", pp. 129–144 in S.J. Raj and W.P. Harman (eds.), *Dealing with Deities. The Ritual Vow in South Asia.* Albany, NY: State University of New York Press.
—— (2007). "Götter, Gurus, Geist und Seele: Hindu-Traditionen in der Schweiz", pp. 223–237 in M. Baumann and J. Stolz (Hg.), *Eine Schweiz—viele Religionen. Risiken und Chancen des Zusammenlebens.* Bielefeld: transcript.
—— (2009). "Migration and Religion", pp. 338–352 in P. Clarke and P. Beyer (eds.), *The World's Religions: Continuities and Transformations.* London: Routledge.
Baumann, M. and Salentin, K. (2006). "Migrant Religiousness and Social Incorporation. Tamil Hindus in Germany", *Journal of Contemporary Religion* 21(3): 297–323.
Baumann, M., Luchesi, B. and Wilke, A. (2003a). "Einleitung: Kontinuität und Wandel von Religion in fremdkultureller Umwelt", pp. 3–40 in M. Baumann, B. Luchesi and A. Wilke (Hg.), *Tempel und Tamilen in zweiter Heimat. Hindus aus Sri Lanka im deutschsprachigen und skandinavischen Raum.* Würzburg: Ergon.
—— (Hg.) (2003b). *Tempel und Tamilen in zweiter Heimat. Hindus aus Sri Lanka im deutschsprachigen und skandinavischen Raum.* Würzburg: Ergon.
Baxi, U. (1995). "Emancipation as Justice: Babasaheb Ambedkar's legacy and Vision", in U. Baxi and B. Parekh (eds.), *Crisis and Change in Contemporary India.* New Delhi: Sage Publications.
Bazdogan, S. and Kasaba, R. (eds.). (1997). *Rethinking Modernity and National Identity in Turkey.* Seattle, WA: Seattle University Press.
Beckford, J.A. (1989). *Religion and Advanced Industrial Society.* London: Unwin Hyman.
—— (2003). *Social Theory and Religion.* Cambridge: Cambridge University Press.
Behdad, S. and Nomani, F. (2009). "What a Revolution! Thirty Years of Social Class Reshuffling in Iran," *Comparative Studies of South Asia, Africa and the Middle East* 29(1): 84–104.
Ben-Ari, E. and Bilu, Y. (1997). "Saints' Sanctuaries in Israeli Development Towns: On a Mechanism of Urban Transformation", pp. 61–83 in E. Ben-Ari and Y. Bilu (eds.), *Grasping Land: Space and Place in Contemporary Israeli Discourse and Experience.* New York: State University of New York Press.
Ben-Rafael E. (2002). "Ethnicity, Sociology of", *International Encyclopedia of the Social and Behavioral Sciences.* London: Elsevier, Vol. 7: 438–42.

Ben-Rafael, E. and Peres, Y. (2005). *Is Israel One? Nationalism, Religion, and Multiculturalism Confounded*. Leiden: Brill.
Ben-Rafael, E. and Sternberg, Y. (eds.). (2009). *Transnationalism: Diasporas and the advent of a new (dis)order*. Leiden: Brill.
Berg, I. (1979). *Industrial Sociology*. Englewood Cliffs, NJ: Prentice Hall.
Berger, P. (1990). "Foreword", in D. Martin, *Tongues of Fire: The Explosion of Protestantism in Latin America*. Oxford: Blackwell.
—— (1999), *The Desecularization of the World. Resurgent Religion and World Politics*. Grand Rapids, MI: Eerdmans Publishing Co.
Berger, P., Davie, G. and Fokas, E. (2008). *Religious America, Secular Europe: A Theme and Variations*. Aldershot: Ashgate.
Bergunder, M. (2008). *The South Indian Pentecostal Movement in the Twentieth Century*. Grand Rapids: Eerdmans.
Beyer, P. (2004). *Religion and Globalization*. London: Sage.
—— (2006). *Religions in Global Society*. London: Routledge.
Beyer, P. and Beaman, L. (eds.). (2007). *Religion, Globalization and Culture*. Leiden: Brill.
Bhardwaj, S.M. (1973). *Hindu Places of Pilgrimage in India. A Study of Cultural Geography*. Berkeley, CA: University of California Press.
Bilgrami, A. (1995). "What Is a Muslim? Fundamental Commitment and Cultural Identity", in K.A. Appiah and H.L. Gates (eds.), *Identities*. Chicago: University of Chicago Press.
Bilu, Y. (2005). *The Saints' Impresarios: Dreamers, Healers and Holy Men in Israel's Urban Periphery*. Haifa: University of Haifa Press (Hebrew).
Binder, L. (1988). *Islamic Liberalism: A Critique of Development Ideologies*. Chicago: University of Chicago Press.
Birnbaum, P. (2003). "Is the French Model in Decline", pp. 266–281 in E. Ben-Rafael, Y. Gorny and Y. Ro'I. (eds.). *Contemporary Jewries: Convergence and Divergence*. Leiden: Brill.
Birnbaum, P. and Katzenelson, I. (eds.). (1995). *Paths to Emancipation*. New York: Oxford University Press.
Blackburn A.M. (1993). "Religion, Kinship and Buddhism: Ambedkar's Vision of a Moral Community", *Journal of the International Association of Buddhist Studies* 16(1): 1–23.
Bloom, H. (1992). *The American Religion*. New York: Simon and Schuster.
Bönker, F., Müller, K. and Pickel, A. (eds.). (2002). *Postcommunist Transformation and the Social Sciences. Cross-Disciplinary Approaches*. London: Rowman & Littlefield.
Bourdieu P. and Passeron, J.-C. (1990). *Reproduction in Education, Society and Culture*. London: Sage.
Bovay, C. (2004). *Religionslandschaft in der Schweiz. Eidgenössische Volkszählung 2000*, in collaboration with Raphaël Broquet. Neuchâtel: Bundesamt für Statistik.
Brandt, J. (2002). "Konfessionelle und nationale Identität in Ungarn", pp. 31–72 in H.-C. Maner and M. Schulze Wessel (eds.), *Religion im Nationalstaat zwischen den Weltkriegen 1918–1939*. Stuttgart: Steiner.
Brass, P. (2003). *The Production of Hindu-Muslim Violence in Contemporary India*. Seatlle: University of Washington Press.
Breuilly, J. (1994). *Nationalism and the State*. Manchester: Manchester University Press.
Brockington, J.L. (1981). *The Sacred Thread: Hinduism in its Continuity and Diversity*. Dehli: Oxford University Press.
Browne, E. (1910). *The Persian Revolution (1905–1909)*. Cambridge: Cambridge University Press.

Brubaker, R. (1996). *Nationalism Reframed. Nationhood and the National Question in The New Europe.* New York: Cambridge University Press.
Brubaker, R. et al. (2006). *Nationalist Politics and Everyday Ethnicity in a Transylvanian Town.* Princeton, NJ: Princeton University Press.
Bruce, S. (1996). *Religion in the Modern World: From Cathedrals to Cults.* Oxford: Oxford University Press.
Bruckmüller, E. (1996). *Nation Österreich.* Wien: Böhlau.
Brumberg, D. (2005). "Liberalizations versus Democracy", in D. Carothers and M. Ottaway (eds.), *Uncharted Journey: Promoting Democracy in the Middle East.* Washington DC: Carnegie Endowment.
Brusco, E. (1986). *The Household Basis of Evangelical Religion and the Reform of Machismo in Colombia.* Ph.D. thesis, City University, New York.
—— (1995). *The Reformation of Machismo: Evangelical Conversion and Gender in Colombia.* Austin TX: University of Texas Press.
Buber, M. (1994). *Between People and its Land: The History of an Idea.* Jerusalem: Schocken (Hebrew).
Bundesamt für Flüchtlinge. (2006a). "Bestand im Asylprozess in der Schweiz nach Nationen am 31.12.2005". Bern: Bundesamt für Flüchtlinge.
Bundesamt für Statistik. (2006b). "Bilanz der ständigen ausländischen Wohnbevölkerung 2005, nach Staatsangehörigkeit". Neuchâtel: Bundesamt für Statistik.
—— (2006c). "Erwerb des Schweizer Bürgerrechts nach Staatsangehörigkeit, Art der Einbürgerung und Geschlecht, 1974–2005". Neuchâtel: Bundesamt für Statistik.
Bunting, M. (2009). "Religions have the power to bring a passion for social justice to politics", http://www.guardian.co.uk/commentisfree/2009/jan/12/madeleine-bunting-religion-social-justice?showallcomments=true.
Burdick, J. (1993). *Looking for God in Brazil: The Progressive Catholic Church in Urban Brazil's Religious Arena.* Berkeley, CA: University of California Press.
Bynum, C.W. (2007). *Wonderful Blood: Theology and Practice in Late Medieval Germany and Beyond.* Philadelphia: University of Pennsylvania Press.
Byrnes, T.A. (2001). *Transnational Catholicism in Postcommunist Europe.* Lanham: Rowman & Littlefield.
Byrnes, T.A. and Katzenstein, P.J (eds.). (2006). *Religion in an Expanding Europe.* Cambridge, MA: Cambridge University Press.
Carothers, T. and Ottaway, M. (eds.). (2005). *Uncharted Journey: Promoting Democracy in the Middle East.* Washington DC: Carnegie Endowment.
Casanova, J. (1994). *Public Religions in the Modern World.* Chicago: University of Chicago Press.
—— (1998). "Ethno-linguistic and Religious Pluralism and Democratic Construction in Ukraine", pp. 81–103 in B.R. Rubin and J. Snyder (eds.), *Post-Soviet Political Order.* London: Routledge.
—— (2006a). "Religion, European secular identities, and European Integration", pp. 65–92 in T. Byrnes and P. Katzenstein (eds), *Religion in an Expanding Europe.* New York: Cambridge University Press.
—— (2006b). "Rethinking Secularization: A Global Comparative Perspective", *The Hedgehog Review* 8(1–2): 7–22.
—— (2007). "Rethinking Secularization: A Global Comparative Perspective", pp. 101–120 in P. Beyer and L. Beaman (eds.), *Religion, Globalization, and Culture.* Leiden: Brill.
Castells, M. (2004). *The Information Age: Economy, Society and Culture, Volume II, The Power of Identity.* Second edition. Oxford: Blackwell Publishing.
Centre for Development and Enterprise (2008). *Dormant Capital: Pentecostalism in South Africa and its Potential Social and Economic Role.* Johannesburg: Centre for Development and Enterprise.

Cesari, J. (1997). *Islam in France: Social challenge or challenge of secularism?* Paper presented at the Middle East Studies Association Annual Conference, San Francisco, November.
Chang, H.J. (2002). *Kicking away the Ladder: Development Strategy in Historical Perspective.* London: Anthem Press.
Chang, M.H. (2004). *Falungong, secte Chinoise. Un defi au pouvoir.* Paris: Editions Autrement.
Chen, N. (2003). *Breathing Spaces. Qigong, Psychiatry and Healing in China.* New York: Columbia University Press.
Chesnut, R.A. (1997). *Born Again in Brazil: The Pentecostal Boom and the Pathogens of Povery.* New Brunswick: Rutgers University Press.
Cnaan, R. (2002). *The Invisible Caring Hand: American Congregations and the Provision of Welfare.* New York: New York University Press.
Cnaan, R., Boddie, S., McGrew, C. and Kang, K. (2006). *The Other Philadelphia Story: How Local Congregations Support Quality of Life in Urban America.* Philadelphia: University of Philadelphia Press.
Cohen, P. (1998). "Welcome to the Diasporama. A Cure for the Millennium Blues?", *New Ethnicities* 3: 3–10.
Cohen, R. (1997). *Global Diasporas: An Introduction.* London: UCL Press.
Cohen, S.J.D. and Frerichs, E.S. (eds.). (1993). *Diasporas in Antiquity.* Atlanta, Georgia: Scholars Press.
Cohen, S.M. and Blitzer, L. (2008). *Belonging without Believing: Jews and their Distinctive Patterns of Religiosity and Secularity.* http://www.jewishdatabank.org/Reports/
Cohen, S.M. and Eisen, A. (2000). *The Jew Within: Self, Community and Family in America.* Bloomington, Indiana: University of Indiana Press.
Cohn-Sherbok, D. (1996). *Modern Judaism.* London & NY: Macmillan & St Martin's Press.
Coleman, S. (2000). *The Globalization of Charismatic Christianity: Spreading the Gospel of Prosperity.* Cambridge: Cambridge University Press.
Collier, R.B. (1999). *Paths Toward Democracy: The Working Class and Elites in Western Europe and South America.* Cambridge: Cambridge University Press.
Cooper, J. (1998). "The Limits of the Sacred: The Epistemology of Abd al-Karim Soroush", pp. 38–56 in J. Cooper, R. Nettler, and M. Mahmoud (eds.), *Islam and Modernity: Muslim Intellectuals Respond.* London: I.B. Tauris.
Corten, A. (1999). *Pentecostalism in Brazil: Emotion of the Poor and Theological Romanticism.* Basingstoke: Macmillan.
Coward, H., Hinnells, J. and Williams, R.B. (eds.). (2000). *The South Asian Religious Diaspora in Britain, Canada, and the United States.* New York: SUNY.
Cox, R.W. (1987). *Production, power, and world order: Social forces in the making of history.* New York: Columbia University Press.
Crabtree, J. (2008). "Closing the God Gap", *Prospect Magazine*: 51, October. For an on-line version, see http://www.prospect-magazine.co.uk/article_details.php?id=10370.
Cucchiari, S. (1988). "Adapted for Heaven: Conversion and culture in Western Sicily", *American Ethnologist* 15: 417–41.
—— (1991). "Between Shame and Sanctification: Patriarchy and its Transformation in Sicilian Pentecostalism", *American Ethnologist* 18: 687–707.
Dann, O. (1990). *Nation und Nationalismus in Deutschland.* München: Beck.
Dassetto, F. (1993). *Islam and Europe.* Paper presented at the International Conference on Muslim Minorities in Post-Bipolar Europe, Skopje, Macedonia.
Davie, G. (1994). *Religion in Britain since 1945.* Oxford: Blackwell.
—— (2002). *Europe: The Exceptional Case. Parameters of Faith in the Modern World.* London: Darton, Longman and Todd.
—— (2006). "Vicarious Religion: A Methodological Challenge", pp. 21–36 in N. Ammerman (ed.), *Everyday Religion: Observing Modern Religious Lives.* New York: Oxford University Press.

Davies, N. (1981). *God's Playground: A History of Poland.* Oxford: Clarendon.
Dawisha, K. and Parrot, B. (eds.). (1999). *National Identity and Ethnicity in Russia and the New States of Eurasia.* Armonk, NY: Sharpe.
Delanty, G. and Kumar, K. (eds.). (2004). *The Sage Handbook of Nations and Nationalism.* London: Sage.
Deliége, R. (1999). *The Untouchables of India.* Oxford: Berg.
Delling, G. (1987). *Die Bewältigung der Diasporasituation durch das hellenistische Judentum.* Berlin: Evangelische Verlagsanstalt.
Dempster, M.W., Klaus, B.D., and Petersen, D. (eds.). (1999). *The Globalization of Pentecostalism: A Religion Made to Travel.* Oxford: Regnum.
Diamond, L. (2003). *Can the Whole World Become Democratic? Democracy, Development and International Policies.* Irvine: Center for the Study of Democracy, University of California.
Dianteill, E. (2002). "Deterritorialization and Reterritorialization of the Orisha Religion in Africa and the New World (Nigeria, Cuba and the United States)", *International Journal of Urban and Regional Research* 26(1): 121–137.
Diner, H.R. (2004). *The Jews of the United States.* Berkeley, Los Angeles: University of California Press.
Dorraj, M. (1992). "The Revival of Islam and the politics of Counter-Culture Mobilization in the Middle East", pp. 91–105 in C. Lehman and R. Moore (eds.), *Multinational Culture: Social Impacts of a Global Economy.* New York: Greenwood Press.
Dubois, T. (2005). *The Sacred Village; Social Change and Religious Life in Rural North China.* Honolulu: University of Hawaii Press.
Durkheim, E. (2008). *The Elementary Forms of Religious Life*, edited by M.S. Cladis. Oxford: Oxford University Press.
Eck, D.L. (1984). *Banaras: City of Light.* London: Routledge and Kegan Paul.
—— (1998). *Darśan: Seeing the Divine Image in India.* New York: Columbia University Press, 3rd updated edition.
Eder, K. (1991). *Geschichte als Lernprozess? Zur Pathogenese politischer Modernität in Deutschland.* Frankfurt: Suhrkamp.
Eickelman, D. and Piscatori, J. (1996). *Muslim Politics.* Princeton, NJ: Princeton University Press.
Eickelman, D.F. and Piscatori, J.P. (eds.) (1990). *Muslim travellers: pilgrimage, migration and the religious imagination.* Berkeley: University of California Press.
Eisenstadt, S.N. (1987). *The European Civilization in comparative perspective.* Oslo: Scandinavian University Press.
—— (1992) *Jewish Civilization: The Jewish Historical Experience in a Comparative Perspective.* Albany, NY: State University of New York Press.
—— (1994). "Center-periphery relations in the Soviet Empire", in A. Motyl (ed.), *Thinking Theoretically about Soviet Nationalities.* New York: Columbia University Press.
—— (1999). *Fundamentalism, Sectarianism and Revolution: The Jacobin Dimension of Modernity.* Cambridge: Cambridge University Press.
—— (2000). "Multiple modernities", *Daedalus* 129: 1–30.
—— (2002a). "Concluding Remarks: Public Sphere, Civil Society, and Political Dynamics in Islamic Societies", pp. 139–161 in M. Hoexter, S.N. Eisenstadt and N. Levtzion (eds.), *The Public Sphere in Muslim Societies.* Albany, NY: SUNY Press.
—— (2003). *Multiple Modernities and Comparative Civilizations.* Leiden: Brill.
—— (ed.) (2002b). *Multiple Modernities.* New Brunswick: Transaction.
Eisenstadt, S.N. and Giesen, B. (1995). "The Construction of Collective Identity", *European Journal of Sociology* 36: 72–102.
Elazar, D. (1999). "Jewish Religious, Ethnic and National Identities", pp. 35–52 in S.M. Cohen and G. Horenczyk (eds.), *National Variations in Jewish Identity.* Albany, NY: SUNY Press.
Eliade, M. (1954). *The Myth of the Eternal Return.* New York: Pantheon.

Elias, N. (1978). *The Civilizing Process*. Oxford: Basil Blackwell.
El-Or, T. and Neria, E. (2004). "The Haredi Walker: The Consumption of Time and Space among the Haredi Population of Jerusalem", in E. Sivan and K. Kaplan (eds.), *Israeli Haredim: Integration without Assimiliation?* Tel Aviv: Hakibbutz HaMeuchad and the Van Leer Jerusalem Institute (Hebrew).
Emerson, M.O. and Hartman, D. (2006). "The Rise of Religious Fundamentalism", *Annual Review of Sociology* 32: 127–144.
Engelke, M. (2007). *A Problem of Presence: Beyond Scripture in an African Church*. Berkeley: University of California Press.
Erlich, Y. (2008). "Hester Panim". *Makor Rishon* 13.04.08.
Esposito, J.L. (1983). "Muhammad Iqbal and the Islamic State", pp. 175–190 in J.L. Esposito (ed.), *Voices of Resurgent Islam*. New York and Oxford: Oxford University Press.
Evron, B. (1995). *Jewish State or Israeli Nation*. Bloomington: Indiana University Press.
Fackenheim, E. (1974)."The Holocaust and the State of Israel—Their Relation," *Encyclopaedia Judaica*. Jerusalem: Keter.
Fawaz, L. et al. (eds.). (2001). *Modernity and culture from Mediterranean to the Indian Ocean, 1890–1920*. New York: Columbia University Press.
Feige, M. (2009). *Settling in the Hearts: Jewish Fundamentalism in the Occupied Territories*. Detroit: Wayne State University Press.
Feldhaus, A. (2003). *Connected Places: Region, Pilgrimage, and Geographical Imagination in Maharashtra*. New York: Palgrave Macmillan.
Fernandez-Armesto F. and Wilson, D. (1996). *Reformations: A Radical Interpretation of Christianity and the World, 1500–2000*. New York: Scribner.
Ferrari, S. and Cristofori, R. (eds). (forthcoming). *Law and Religion in the 21st Century. Relations between States and Religious Communities*. Proceedings of the First ICLARS Conference (Milan, January 22–24, 2009). Leuven: Peeters.
Findley, C.V. (1980). *Bureaucratic Reform in the Ottoman Empire: The Sublime Porte 1789–1922*. Princeton: Princeton University Press.
Fischer, S. (2007a). *Self Expression and Democracy in Radical Religious Zionist Ideology*. Unpublished doctoral dissertation. Hebrew University of Jerusalem (Hebrew).
—— (2007b). "Nature, Authenticity and Violence in Radical Religious Zionist Thought", in H. Herzog, T. Kochavi and S. Zelniker (eds.), *Generations, Locations, Identities: Contemporary Perspectives on Society and Culture in Israel*. Essays in Honor of Shmuel Noah Eisenstadt. Tel Aviv: The Van Leer Jerusalem Institute and HaKibbutz HaMeuchad (Hebrew).
—— (forthcoming). "Fundamentalist or Romantic Nationalist?: Israeli Modern Orthodoxy", in S.M. Cohen, H. Goldberg and E. Kopelowitz (eds.), *Dynamic Jewish Belonging*. Berghan.
Fischer, Z. (2009a). "God-Forbid that a Man Should be Like This", http://www.shoresh.org.il/
—— (2009b). "When the Evil Inclination Rides on the Bus", *Ha'aretz* 11.8.09.
Fitzgerald, T. (2007). *Discourse on Civility and Barbarity*. Oxford: Oxford University Press.
Flood, G. (1996). *An Introduction to Hinduism*. Cambridge: Cambridge University Press.
Flora, P. (1999). *State formation, nation-building and mass-politics in Europe: The Theory of Stein Rokkan*. Oxford: Polity Press.
Fokas, E. (2006). "Greece, religion, nation and European identity", pp. 39–60 in H. Gulalp (ed.), *Citizenship and Ethnic Conflict: Challenging the Nation-State*. London: Routledge Press.
Fraser, N. (2007). "Transnationalizing the Public Sphere: On the Legitimacy and Efficacy of Public Opinion in a Post-Westphalian World", *Theory, Culture and Society* 24(2): 7–30.

Freitag, U. and Clarence-Smith, W.G. (eds.). (1997). *Hadhrami traders, scholars and statesmen in the Indian Ocean, 1750s to 1960s*. Leiden: Brill.
Friedman, M. (1974). *Society and Religion: The Non-Zionist Orthodoxy in Eretz-Yisrael 1918–1936*. Jerusalem: Yad Ben Tzvi (Hebrew).
—— (1986). "Haredim confront the modern city", *Studies in Contemporary Jewry* 2: 74–96.
—— (1990). "Jewish Zealots: Conservative versus Innovative", pp 127–141 in E. Sivan and M. Friedman (eds.), *Religious Radicalism and Politics in the Middle East*. New York: State University of New York Press.
—— (1998). "From Life Culture to Book Culture", in S. Deshen, C. Liebman and M. Shokeid (eds.), *Israeli Judaism*. New Brunswick and London: Transaction Publishers.
Froerer, P. (2007). "Disciplining the Saffron Way: Moral Education and the Hindu Rashtra", *Modern Asian Studies* 41(5): 1033–1071.
Fuchs, M. (2004). "A Religion for Civil Society? Ambedkar's Buddhism, the Dalit Issue and the Imagination of Emergent Possibilities", pp. 250–273 in V. Dalmia, A. Malinar and M. Christof (eds.), *Charisma and Canon: Essays on the Religious History of the Indian Subcontinent*. New Delhi, Oxford: Oxford University Press.
Fukuyama, F. (2006). *The end of history and the last man*. New York: Free Press.
Fuller, C.J. (1984). *Servants of the Goddess. The Priests of a South Indian Temple*. Cambridge: Cambridge University Press.
—— (1988). "The Hindu Temple and Indian Society", pp. 46–66 in M.V. Fox (ed.), *Temple in Society*. Winoma Lake: Eisenbrauns.
—— (1992). *The Camphor Flame. Popular Hinduism and Society in India*. Delhi: Penguin Books India.
Fuller, G. (2005). "Islamists and Democracy", in T. Carothers and M. Ottaway (eds.), *Uncharted Journey: Promoting Democracy in the Middle East*. Washington DC: Carnegie Endowment.
Garb, J. (forthcoming a). "Towards the Study of the Spiritual-Mystical Renaissance in the Contemporary Ashkenazi Haredi World in Israel", in B. Huss (ed.), *Kabbalah and Contemporary Spiritual Revival*. Beer Sheva: Ben Gurion University of the Negev Press (Hebrew).
—— (forthcoming b). "Mystical and Spiritual Discourse in the Contemporary Ashkenazi Haredi Worlds", *Journal of Modern Jewish Studies*.
Geertz, C. (1973) *The Interpretation of Cultures*. New York: Basic Books
Gellner, E. (1983). *Nations and Nationalism*. London: Verso.
—— (1992). *Postmodernism, Reason, and Religion*. London: Routledge.
Gerber, H. (2002). "The Public Sphere and Civil Society in the Ottoman Empire", pp. 65–82 in M. Hoexter, S.N. Eisenstadt and N. Levtzion (eds.), *The Public Sphere in Muslim Societies*. Albany, NY: SUNY Press.
Gerth, H. and Mills, C.W. (eds.). (1948). *From Max Weber*. London: Routledge.
Giesen, B. (1998). *Die Intellektuellen und die Nation. Eine deutsche Achsenzeit*. Frankfurt/M.: Campus.
Gill, S. (2000). *The Dynamics of Democratization*. London: Palgrave.
—— (2003). *Power and Resistance in the New World Order*. New York: Palgrave Macmillan.
Ginzburg, Y. (1994). *Kuntreiss Baruch HaGever: Five General Commandments which are five inner aspects of the act of the martyr R. Baruch Goldstein may God avenge his blood*. A lecture given by R.Y. Ginzburg, edited by Y.A. Leibovitz. Rehovot: Gal Einei (Hebrew).
Gitelman, Z. et al. (eds.). (2000). *Cultures and Nations of Central and Eastern Europe. Essays in Honour of Roman Szporluk*. Cambridge, MA: Cambridge University Press.
Glock, C. and Stark, R. (1965). *Religion and society in tension*. Chicago: Rand McNally and Company.

Goel, U. (2006). "Germany", pp. 358–361 in B.V. Lal, P. Reeves and R. Rai (eds.), *The Encyclopedia of the Indian Diaspora*. Singapore, Kuala Lumpur, Paris: Edition Didier Millet.
Göle, N. and Amman, L. (eds.). (2006). *Islam in Public. Turkey, Iran and Europe*. Istanbul: Bilgi University Press.
Good, A. (1987). "The Religious, Economic and Social Organisation of a South Indian Temple", *Quaterly Journal of Social Affairs* 3(1): 1–25.
—— (2001). "Multiple meanings in South Indian temple worship", *Culture and Religion* 2(2): 239–260.
Goossaert, V. (2006). "The Beginning of the End for Chinese Religion?", *Journal of Asian Studies* 65(2): 307–336.
Gorny, Y. (2006). *Converging Alternatives*. Albany, NY: SUNY.
Gräf, B. and Skovgaard-Petersen, J. (2009). *Global Mufti. The Phenomenon of Yusuf al-Qaradawi*. New York: Columbia University Press.
Graham, G.F.I. and Zaituna, Y.U. (1975). *The Life and Work of Sir Syed Ahmad Khan*. Oxford: Oxford Asian Historical Reprints.
Gramsci, A. (1971). *Selections from the Prison Notebooks of Antonio Gramsci*. Trans. by Q. Hoare and G. Nowell-Smith. New York: International Publishers.
Green, J. (2009). "What happened to the values voter? Believers and the 2008 election", *First Things*, March.
Greenberg, Y. (1997). *HaHephech (Au Contraire)*. Jerusalem.
Ha'aretz. (2003). "The Spirit of Yesha (Judea, Samaria and Gaza)", Special Rosh Hashana Supplement. 26.9.03.
Habermas, J. (1981). "New Social Movements", *Telos* 49.
—— (1984 [1981]). *The Theory of Communicative Action*, vol. I: Reason and the Rationalization of Society. Boston: Beacon Press.
—— (1987 [1981]). *The Theory of Communicative Action*, vol. II: Lifeworld and System: A Critique of Functionalist Reason. Boston: Beacon Press.
—— (1989/1992 [1962]). *The Structural Transformation of the Public Sphere*. Cambridge: Polity Press.
—— (1990). *Moral Consciousness and Communicative Action*. Cambridge: Polity Press.
—— (2008). *Between Naturalism and Religion*. Cambridge: Polity.
Haggard, S. and Kaufman, R.R. (1997). "The Political Economy of Democratic Transitions", *Comparative Politics, Transitions to Democracy: A special Issue in Memory of Dankwart A. Rustow*, 29(3): 263–283.
Hairi, A.-H. (1977). *Shi'ism and Constitutionalism in Iran: A Study of the Role Played by the Persian Residents of Iraq in Iranian Politics*. Leiden: Brill.
Halliday, F. (1999). "The Potentials of Enlightenment", *British International Studies Association*: 105–25.
Hanafi, H. (1987). *Min al-'aqida ila l-thawra* (5 Vols.). Cairo: Maktaba Mabduli.
Hann, C. et al. (2006). *The Postsocialist Religious Question: Faith and Power in Central Asia and East-Central Europe*. Berlin: LIT.
Hannerz, U. (1996). *Transnational Connections: Culture, People, Places*. London and New York: Routledge.
—— (1999). *Cultural Complexity: Studies in the Social Organization of Meaning*. New York: Columbia University Press.
Harris, J. (2009). "Statist Globalization in China, Russia and the Gulf States", *Perspectives on Global Development and Technology* 8(2–3): 139–163.
Hastings, A. (1997). *The Construction of Nationhood. Ethnicity, Religion and Nationalism*. Cambridge, MA: Cambridge University Press.
Haupt, H.-G. and Langewiesche, D. (eds.). (1999). *Nation und Religion in Deutschland*. Frankfurt/M.
—— (eds.) (2001). *Nation und Religion in Europa*. Frankfurt/M.: Campus.

Heard, J. (2007). *Re-Evangelising Britain? An Ethnographic Analysis and Theological Evaluation of the Alpha Course.* Ph.D. Thesis, London University.
Heelas, P. (1996). *The New Age Movement: The Celebration of the Self and the Sacralization of Modernity.* Oxford: Blackwell.
Held, D. and McGrew, A. (eds.) (2002). *The Global Transformation Reader.* Oxford: Polity Press.
—— (eds.) (2007). *Globalization Theory.* Oxford: Oxford University Press.
Helgesson, K. (2006). *'Walking in the Spirit'. The complexities of Belonging in Two Pentecostal Churches in Durban, South Africa.* Uppsala: Elanders.
Hengel, M. (1976). *Juden, Griechen und Barbaren. Aspekte des Judentums in vorchristlicher Zeit.* Stuttgart: Kath. Bibelwerk.
Hervieu-Léger, D. (1993). *La religion pour mémoire.* Paris, Éditions du Cerf.
—— (2001). *Le pèlerin et le converti. La religion en mouvement.* Paris: Flammarion.
—— (2002). "Space and Religion: New Approaches to Religious Spatiality in Modernity", *International Journal of Urban and Regional Research* 26(1): 99–105.
—— (2004). "Religion und Sozialer Zusammenhalt in Europa", *Transit: Europäische Revue* 26: 101–19.
—— (2009). "Roman Catholicism and the Challenge of Globalization", pp. 445–459 in E. Ben-Rafael and Y. Sternberg (eds.), *Transnationalism: Diasporas and the advent of a new (dis)order.* Leiden: Brill.
Herzig, E. (ed.) (1999). *The New Caucasus: Armenia, Azerbaijan and Georgia.* London: Royal Institute of International Affairs.
Hettlage, R. (1991). "Diaspora: Umrisse einer soziologischen Theorie", *Österreichische Zeitschrift für Soziologie* 16(3): 4–24.
Heydemann, S. (1999). *Authoritarianism in Syria: Institutions and Social Conflict.* Ithaca NY and London: Cornell University Press.
Himmelfarb, G. (2004). *The Roads to Modernity: The British, French and American Enlightenments.* New York: Knopf.
Hinnebusch, R. (2006). "Authoritarian Persistence, Democratization Theory and the Middle East: An Overview and Critique", *Democratization* 13(3): 373–395.
Hinnells, J. (1997). "Comparative Reflections on South Asian Religion in International Migration", pp. 819–847 in J. Hinnells (ed.), *A New Handbook of Living Religions.* Oxford, Cambridge, Mas.: Blackwell.
Hirschhausen, U. von and Leonhard, J. (eds.). (2001). *Nationalismen in Europa. West- und Osteuropa im Vergleich.* Göttingen: Vandenhoek & Ruprecht.
Hodgson M.G.S. (1993). *Rethinking World History: Essays on Europe, Islam and World History.* Cambridge: Cambridge University Press.
Hope, N. (1995). *German and Scandinavian Protestantism.* Oxford: Oxford University Press.
Horkheimer, M. (1972). *Critical Theory: Selected Essays.* New York: Herder and Herder.
Hosking, G. (ed.). (1991). *Church, State and Nation in Russia and Ukraine.* London: MacMillan.
Houweling, H. (2000). "Industrialization in East Asia. A Developmental Approach", pp. 1–50 in H. Kenks and I. Boxill (eds.), *The End of the 'Asian Model'?* Amsterdam and Philadelphia: John Benjamins Publishing Company.
Huber, E, Rueschemeyer, D. and Stephens, J.D. (1993). "The Impact of Economic Development on Democracy", *Journal of Economic Perspectives* 7(3): 71–85.
Hunt, S. (2004). *The Alpha Course: Evangelism in a Post-Christian Era.* Aldershot: Ashgate.
Huntington, S.P. (1968). *Political order in changing societies.* New Haven: Yale University Press.
—— (1991). *The Third Wave: Democratization in the Late Twentieth Century.* Norman and London: University of Oklahoma Press.

—— (1993). "The Clash of Civilizations?", *Foreign Affairs* 72(3): 22–49.
—— (1996). *The Clash of Civilizations and the Remaking of World Order*. New York: Touchstone.
—— (2006). *Political Order in Changing Societies* (new edition). New Haven: Yale University Press.
Husain, M.Z. (2002). *Global Islamic politics*. Second edition. New York: Longman.
Huss, B. (2008). "The Formation of Jewish Mysticism and its Impact upon the Reception of R. Abraham Abulafia in Contemporary Kabbalah", *Jewish Quarterly Review*.
—— (ed.) (forthcoming). *Kabbalah and Contemporary Spiritual Revival*. Beer Sheva: Ben Gurion University of the Negev Press.
Hutter, M. (2006). "Afghanische Hindus in Deutschland", supplement VIII—22 in U. Tworuschka and M. Klöcker (eds.), *Handbuch der Religionen*. München: Olzog.
Ichijo, A. and Spohn, W. (eds.) (2005). *Entangled Identities. Europe and the Nation*. Aldershot: Ashgate.
Illouz, E. (2007). *Cold Initmacies: The Making of Emotional Capitalism*. Cambridge, UK: Polity.
Inglehart, R. (1997). *The Silent Revolution: Changing Values and Political Styles in Advanced Industrial Society*. Princeton: Princeton University Press.
Inglehart, R. and Welzel, C. (2009). "How Development Leads to Democracy. What We Know About Modernization," *Foreign Affairs* 88(2): 33–48.
Iqbal, M. (1930/1934). *The Reconstruction of Religious Thought in Islam*. Oxford: Oxford University Press.
Ireland, R. (1991). *Kingdoms Come: Religion and Politics in Brazil*. Pittsburgh: University of Pittsburgh Press.
Islamoglu-Inan, H. (ed.). (1987). *The Ottoman Empire and the World Economy*. Cambridge: Cambridge University Press.
Issawi C. (1982). *An Economic History of the Middle East and North Africa*. London: Methuen and Co.
Iversen, H.R. and Oommen, G. (eds.). (2005). *It Began in Copenhagen: Junctions in 300 Years of Indian-Danish Relations in Christian Mission*. Delhi: ISPCK.
Jacobsen, K.A. (ed.). (2008). *South Asian Religions on Display: Religious Processions in South Asia and in the Diaspora*. London: Routledge.
Jacobsen, K.A. and Kumar, P. (eds.). (2004). *South Asians in the Diaspora. Histories and Religious Traditions*. Leiden: Brill.
Jacobson, D. (forthcoming). *Beyond Political Messianism: The Poetry of Second Generation Religious Zionist Settlers*.
Jaffrelot, C. (2003). *India's Silent Revolution: The Rise of the Lower Castes in North India*. London: Hurst and Company.
Jaoul, N. (2007). "Dalit Processions: Street Politics and Democratization in India", in J.C. Strauss and D.B.C. O'Brien (eds.), *Staging Politics: Power and Performance in Asia and Africa*. London: I. B. Taurus.
Jenkins, P. (2002). *The Next Christendom: The Coming of Global Christianity*. New York: Oxford University Press.
—— (2006). *The New Faces of Christianity: Believing the Bible in the Global South*. Oxford: Oxford University Press.
Joas, H. and Wiegandt, K. (eds.). (2007). *Säkularisierung und die Weltreligionen*. Frankfurt: Fischer.
Jowitt, K. (1993). *New World Disorder: The Leninist Extinction*. Berkeley: University of California Press.
Judt, T. (2005). *Postwar: A History of Europe since 1945*. London: Heinemann.
Juergensmeyer, M. (ed.). (2003). *Global Religions*. Oxford: Oxford University Press.
Kamenka, E. (1960). *Nationalism*. London: Hutchinson.

Kamrava, M. (2007). "The Middle East's Democracy Deficit in Comparative Perspective", pp. 177–202 in M.P. Amineh (ed.), *The Greater Middle East in Global Politics. Social Science Perspectives on the Changing Geography of World Politics*. Boston and Leiden: Brill Publishers.
Kann, R. (1974). *A History of the Habsburg Empire, 1526–1918*. Berkeley, CA: Berkeley University Press.
Kaplan, J. (2000). *Beyond the Mainstream. The Emergence of Religious Pluralism in Finland, Estonia and Russia*. Helsinki: Hakapaina Oy.
Kaploon, U. and Berekowitz, D. (2000). *An Outstanding Lad: On our "National Religious" Youth in Relation to the Spiritual-Psychological Condition of their Educators; Train the Child in the Way that is Appropriate for Him—A Suggestion for an Educational Agenda*. Jerusalem.
Karagiannis, E. (2005). *Flexibilität und Definitionsvielfalt pomakischer Marginalität*. Wiesbaden: Harrassowitz.
Karl, T.L. (1997). *The Paradox of Plenty, Oil Booms and Petro-States*. Berkeley/Los Angeles: University of California Press.
Karshenas, M. and Hakimian, H. (2005). "Oil, Economic Diversification and the Democratic Process in Iran", *Iranian Studies* 38(1): 67–90.
Katriel, T. (1986). *Talking straight in dugri speech in Israeli Sabra culture*. Cambridge: Cambrdige University Press.
Katz, D. and Popkin, R. (1999). *Messianic Revolution. Radical Religious Politics in the end of the Second Millennium*. London: Allen Lane.
Katz, J. (1973). *Out of the Ghetto: The Social Background of Jewish Emancipation, 1770–1870*. Cambridge, Mass.: Harvard University Press.
—— (1987). "Orthodoxy in a Historical Perspective", *Kivunim* 33: 89–98 (Hebrew).
—— (1998). *A House Divided: Orthodoxy and Schism in Nineteenth Century Central European Jewry*. Trans. Tzippora Brody. Hanover, N.H.: Brandeis University Press.
Kazancigil, A. and Ozbudun, E. (eds.). (1981). *Atatürk: Founder of a Modern State*. London: C. Hurst.
Keane, W. (2007). *Christian Moderns: Freedom and Fetish in the Mission Encounter*. Berkeley: University of California Press.
Keddie, N.K. (1968). *An Islamic Response to Imperialism: Political and Religious Writings of Sayyid Jamal ad-Din "al-Afghani"*. Berkeley and Los Angeles: University of California Press.
—— (1995). *Iran and the Muslim World: Resistance and Revolution*. Basingstoke and London: Macmillan Press.
Kedourie, E. (1992). *Democracy and Arab Political Culture*. Washington, DC: The Washington Institute for Near East Policy.
Kerr, M.H. (1966). *Islamic Reform: The Political and Legal Theories of Muhammad Abduh and Rashid Rida*. Berkeley: University of California Press.
Khazanov, A.M. (1995). *After the USSR: Ethnicity, Nationalism and Politics in the Commonwealth of Independent States*. Madison, WI: University of Wisconsin Press.
Khomeini, R. (1979). *Velayat-e Faqih: Hokumat-e Islami (The Jurist's Guardianship: Islamic Government)*. Tehran: Panzdah-e Khordad.
—— (1981). *Islam and Revolution, Writings and Declarations of Imam Khomeini*, trans. and annot. by H. Algar. Berkeley: Mizan Press.
Kiely, R. (1998). *Industrialization and Development: A Comparative Analysis*. London and Bristol: UCL Press.
Knott, K. (1986). *Hinduism in Leeds: A Study of Religious Practice in the Indian Hindu Community and in Hindu-Related Groups*. Leeds: Community Religions Project Monograph, University of Leeds.
—— (1987). "Hindu Temple Rituals in Britain: The Reinterpretation of Tradition", pp. 157–179 in R. Burghart (ed.), *Hinduism in Great Britain*. London, New York: Tavistock Publ.

—— (1991). "Bound to Change? The Religions of South Asians in Britain", pp. 86–111 in S. Vertovec (ed.), *Aspects of South Asian Diaspora*, Vol. 2, Delhi: Oxford University Press.
Kokosolakis, N. and Psimmenos, I. (2005). "Modern Greece: A Profile of a Strained Identity", pp. 105–118 in A. Ichijo and W. Spohn (eds.), *Entangled Identities. Europe and the Nation*. Aldershot: Ashgate.
Koselleck, R. (1988 [1959]). *Critique and Crisis, Enlightenment and the Pathogenesis of Modern Society*. Oxford: Berg.
Kramer, M. (1986). *Islam assembled: the advent of the Muslim Congresses*. New York: Columbia University Press.
—— (1990). "Khomeini's Messengers: The Disputed Pilgrimage of Islam", pp. 177–194 in E. Sivan and M. Friedman (eds.), *Religious Radicalism and Politics in the Middle East*. New York: State University of New York Press.
Krejci, J. (1990). *Czechoslovakia at the Crossroads of European history*. London: Tauris.
Krejci, J. and Velimsky, V. (1981). *Ethnic and Poltical Nations in Europe*. London: Tauris.
Kriedte, P. (1997). "Katholizismus, Nationbildung und verzögerte Säkularisierung", pp. 249–274 in H. Lehmann (ed.), *Säkularisierung, Dechristianisierung und Rechristianisierung im neuzeitlichen Europa*. Göttingen: Vandenhoek & Ruprecht.
Krings, M. (2003). "Diaspora: historische Erfahrung oder wissenschaftliches Konzept? Zur Konjunktur eines Begriffs in den Sozialwissenschaften", *Paideuma* 49: 157–177.
Kurzman, C. (1998). *Liberal Islam: A Source-Book*. Oxford University Press.
Lambert, Y. (1985). *Dieu change en Bretagne. La religion à Limerzel de 1900 à nos jours*. Paris: Cerf.
Lancaster, R. (1988). *Thanks to God and the Revolution: Popular Religion and class Consciousness in the new Nicaragua*. New York: Columbia University Press.
—— (1992). *Life is Hard: Machismo, Danger and the Intimacy of Power in Nicaragua*. Berkeley: University of California Press.
Landau, J.M. (1990). *The politics of Pan-Islam: ideology and organisation*. Oxford: Oxford University Press.
Lavie, A. (2003). "The Terror of the Hilltops", *Musaf Ha'aretz,* November 4, 2003.
Lebor, A. (1997). *A Heart Turned East*. London: Little, Brown and Company.
Lechner, F. and Boli, J. (2002). *The Globalization Reader*. Oxford: Blackwell.
Legg, K. and Roberts, J. (1997). *Modern Greece: A Civilization in the Periphery*. Basingstoke: MacMillan.
Lehmann, D. (1996). *Struggle for the Spirit: Religious Transformation and Popular Culture in Brazil and Latin America*. Cambridge: Polity.
Lehmann, D. and Siebzehner, B. (2006). *Remaking Israeli Judaism. The Challenge of Shas*. Oxford: Oxford University Press.
Lehmann, H. (ed.) (1997). *Säkularisierung, Dechristianisierung und Rechristianisierung im neuzeitlichen Europa*. Göttingen: Vandenhoek & Ruprecht.
Leon, N. (2005). *Mizrakhi ultra-Orthodoxy*. Tel-Aviv: Tel-Aviv University, Sociology Department (Hebrew).
Levi-Strauss, C. (1958). *Anthropologie Structurale*. Paris: Plon.
—— (1961). *Race et Histoire*. Paris: Gonthier.
Lewis, B. (1969). *The Emergence of Modern Turkey*. London: Oxford University Press.
—— (1990). "The Roots of Muslim Rage", *Atlantic Monthly* 266(3): 47–60.
—— (1996). *The Jews in the World of Islam*. Jerusalem: The Zalman Shazar Center (Hebrew).
—— (2002). *What Went Wrong? The Clash Between Islam and Modernity in the Middle East*. Oxford: Oxford University Press.

Lewis, P. (1994). *Islamic Britain: Religion, Politics and Identity Among British Muslims.* London: I.B. Tauris.
Liebman, C.S. and Cohen, S.M. (1990). *Two Worlds of Judaism.* New Haven and London: Yale University Press.
Lindsay, M. (2008). *Faith in the Halls of Power: How Evangelicals Joined the American Elite.* New York: Oxford University Press.
Linz, J. and Stepan, A. (1996). *Problems of Democratic Transition and Consolidation in Southern Europe, Latin America and Post-communist Europe.* Baltimore, MD: The Johns Hopkins University Press.
Lipset, S.M. (1959) "The Social Requisites of Democracy: Economic Development and Political Legitimacy", *American Political Science Review* 59: 1–22.
Lobo, L. (1996). "Dalit Religious Movements and Dalit identity", pp. 166–183 in W. Fernandez (ed.), *The Emerging Dalit Identity: The Re-Assertion of the Subalterns.* New Delhi: Indian Social Institute.
Logan, P. (1988). *Practising Hinduism: The Experience of Gujarati Adults and Children in Britain*, unpubl. report of the Thomas Coram Research Unit at the Institute of Education. London: University of London.
Lopez, D.S. (2002). *Modern Buddhism: Readings for the Unenlightened.* London: Penguin Books.
Luchesi, B. (2008a). "Mobile Tempel. Zur religiösen Festkultur hindu-tamilischer Gemeinschaften in Deutschland", pp. 353–374 in V. Gottowik, H. Jebsen and E. Platte (eds.), *Zwischen Aneignung und Verfremdung. Ethnologische Gratwanderungen.* Frankfurt/M., New York: Campus.
Luchesi, B. (2008b). "Parading Hindu Gods in Public: New Festival Traditions of Tamil Hindus in Germany", pp. 178–190 in K.A. Jacobsen (ed.), *South Asian Religions on Display.* London, New York: Routledge.
Luhrmann, T.M. (2004). "Metakinesis: How God Became Intimate in Contemporary U.S. Christianity", *American Anthropologist* 106(3): 518–528.
Luks, L. (1997). "Der 'Sonderweg' des polnischen Katholizismus, 1949–1989", pp. 234–248 in H. Lehmann (ed.), *Säkularisierung, Dechristianisierung und Rechristianisierung im neuzeitlichen Europa*, Göttingen: Vandenhoek & Ruprecht.
Lust-Okar, E. (2003). "Why the Failure of Democratization? Explaining 'Middle East Exceptionalism'", *Draft Paper Presented at the Spring 2003 Politics Department Seminars.* New York, Yale University.
Lustick, I.S. (1988). *For the Land and the Lord: Jewish Fundamentalism in Israel.* New York: Council on Foreign Relations.
Lynch, O.M. (2002). "Ambedkar Jayanti: Dalit Reritualization in Agra", *The Eastern Anthropologist* 55(2): 115–132.
Lyotard, J.-F. (1985). *The Postmodern Condition: A Report on Knowledge.* Minneapolis: University of Minnesota Press.
MacLennan, G. (2007). "Towards Post-secular Sociology?", *Sociology* 41(5): 857–70.
Madsen, R. (2007). *Democracy's Dharma: Religious Renaissance and Political Development in Taiwan.* Berkeley: University of California Press.
Makover, S. (2008). "The Women of the Ra'ala", *Ma'ariv*, 18.1. 2008.
Malloy, J.M. (ed.). (1977). *Authoritarianism and Corporatism in Latin America.* Pittsburgh: University of Pittsburgh Press.
Mandaville, P. (2000). "Information Technology and the Changing Boundaries of European Islam", in F. Dassetto (ed.), *Paroles d'Islam: Individus, Sociétés, et Discours dans l'Islam Européen Contemporain.* Paris: Maissonneuve et Larose.
Maner, H.-C. (2002). "Kirchen in Rumänien. Faktoren demokratischer Stabilität?", pp. 103–120 in H.-C. Maner and M. Schulze Wessel (eds), *Religion im Nationalstaat zwischen den Weltkriegen 1918–1939.* Stuttgart: Steiner.
Mann, M. (1993). "Nation-States in Europe and other Continents. Diversifying, Developing, Not Dying", *Daedalus* 122(3): 115–140.

—— (1997). "Has Globalization ended the rise of the nation state?", *Review of International Political Economy*, 4(3): 472–496.
—— (2004). *The Dark Side of Democracy*. Cambridge, MA: Cambridge University Press.
Maor, Z. (2005). *And Called their Name Adam: A New Jewish Look on Intimacy and the Family*. Efrat, Weat Bank (Hebrew).
March, G. and Olson, J.P. (1984). "The New Institutionalism: Organizational Factors in Political Life", *American Political Science Review* 78(3): 734–749.
Markus, V. (2005). *In der Heimat ihrer Kinder. Tamilen in der Schweiz*. Zurich: Offizin.
Marshall, R. (1993). "'Power in the Name of Jesus': Social Transformation and Pentecostalism in Western Nigeria 'Revisited'", pp. 213–246 in T. Ranger and O. Vaughan (eds.), *Legitimacy and the State in Twentieth-Century Africa*. London: Macmillan.
Martin, B. (1995). "New Mutations of the Protestant Ethic among Latin American Pentecostals", *Religion* 25: 101–117.
—— (1998). "From Pre- to Post-Modernity in Latin America: The Case of Pentecostalism", pp. 102–146 in P. Heelas et al. (eds.), *Religion, Modernity and Postmodernity*. Oxford: Blackwell.
—— (2001). "The Pentecostal Gender Paradox: A Cautionary Tale for the Sociology of Religion",pp. 52–66 in R.K. Fenn (ed.), *The Blackwell Companion to Sociology of Religion*. Oxford: Blackwell.
Martin, D. (1965). "Towards eliminating the concept of secularization", pp. 169–82 in J. Gould (ed.), *Penguin Survey of the Social Sciences*. Harmondsworth: Penguin.
—— (1969a). "Notes towards a general theory of secularisation", *European Journal of Sociology*, December: 192–201.
—— (1969b). *The Religious and the Secular*. London: Routledge.
—— (1978). *A General Theory of Secularization*. Oxford: Blackwell.
—— (1990). *Tongues of Fire: The Explosion of Protestantism in Latin America*. Oxford: Blackwell.
—— (1991). "The secularization issue: Prospect and retrospect", *British Journal of Sociology* 42: 466–74.
—— (2000). "Personal Reflections in the mirror of Halévy and Weber", pp. 23–38 in R.K. Fenn (ed.), *The Blackwell Companion to Sociology of Religion*. Oxford: Blackwell.
—— (2005). *On Secularizaton. Towards A Revised General Theory*. Aldershot: Ashgate.
—— (2006). *Pentecostalism, the World, their Parish*. Malden, MA: Blackwell.
Martinelli, A. (2005). *Global Modernization*. London: Sage.
Marty, M. and Appleby, R.S. (eds.). (1991). *Fundamentalisms observed*. Chicago: University of Chicago Press.
Mary, A. (2002). "Pilgrimage to Imeko (Nigeria): An African Church in the Time of the 'Global Village'", *International Journal of Urban and Regional Research* 26(1): 106–120.
Masud, M.K. (2000). *Travellers in faith: studies of the Tablighi Jama'at as a transnational Islamic movement for faith renewal*. Leiden: Brill.
Masuzawa, T. (2008). "The Burden of the Great Divide", *The Immanent Frame*, SSRC Blog, posted January 30th.
Maxwell, D. (1998). "Delivered from the Spirit of Poverty? Pentecostalism, Prosperity and Modernity in Zimbabwe", *Journal of Religion in Africa* 28(3): 350–73.
—— (1999). *Christians and Chiefs in Zimbabwe: A Social History of the Hwesa People c.1870s–1990s*. Edinburgh: International African Library.
—— (2002). "Christianity Without Frontiers: Shona Missionaries and Transnational Pentecostalism in Africa", pp. 295–332 in D. Maxwell (ed.), *Christianity and the African Imagination: Essays in Honour of Adrian Hastings*. Leiden: Brill.

—— (2006). *African Gifts of the Spirit: Pentecostalism and the Rise of a Zimbabwean Transnational Religious Movement*. Oxford: Currey.
Mayer, R. (2005). *Diaspora. Eine kritische Begriffsbestimmung*. Bielefeld: transcript.
Mazo, E.D. (2005). "What Causes Democracy," *Center on Democracy, Development, and the Rule of Law (CDDRL) Working Papers*. Stanford Institute for International Studies, Stanford University.
McAlister, E. (2005). "Globalization and the Religious Production of Space", *Journal for the Scientific Study of Religion* 44(3): 249–255.
McDermott, M.Y. and Manazir, A.M. (1993). *The Muslim Guide: For Teachers, Employers, Community and Social Administrators in Britain*. Leicester: The Islamic Foundation, 2nd Revised Edition.
McDowell, C.A. (1996). *Tamil Asylum Diaspora. Sri Lankan Migration, Settlement and Politics in Switzerland*. Oxford: Berghahn Books.
McGilvray, D.B. (1998). *Symbolic Heat. Gender, Health and Worship among Tamils of South India and Sri Lanka*. Middletown, NJ: Grantha Corporation.
McLoughlin, S. (2005). "Migration, Diaspora and Transnationalism", pp. 526–549 in J.R. Hinnells (ed.), *The Routledge Companion to the Study of Religion*. London: Routledge.
Meir , E. (2003). "The Last Kahanist", *Jerusalem*, 24.11. 2003.
Meissner, B. (1990). *Die Baltischen Staaten. Estland, Lettland und Litauen*. Cologne.
Mernissi, F. (1991). *Women and Islam: An Historical and Theological Enquiry*. Oxford: Blackwell.
Mesquita, B.B de and Downs, G.W. (2005). "Development and Democracy", *Foreign Affairs* 84(5): 77–86.
Metcalf, B.D. (1994). "'Remaking Ourselves': Islamic Self-Fashioning in a Global Movement of Spiritual Renewal", in M.E. Marty and R.S. Appleby (eds.), *Accounting for Fundamentalisms*. Chicago: University of Chicago Press.
—— (ed.). (1996). *Making Muslim Space in North America and Europe*. Berkeley: University of California Press.
Meyer, B. (1998). "'Make a Complete Break with the Past.' Memory and Post-Colonial Modernity in Ghanaian Pentecostal Discourse", *Journal of Religion in Africa* 27(3): 316–349.
—— (1999). *Translating the Devil. Religion and Modernity among the Ewe in Ghana*. Edinburgh: Edinburgh University Press.
—— (2004). "'Praise the Lord…'. Popular Cinema and Pentecostalite Style in Ghana's New Public Sphere", *American Ethnologist* 31(1): 92–110.
—— (2005). "Mediating Tradition: Pentecostal pastors, African Priests, and Chiefs in Ghanaian Popular Films", pp. 275–306 in T. Falola (ed.), *Christianity and Social Change in Africa*. Durham, NC : Carolina Academic Press.
—— (2009). "Pentecostalism and Neo-liberal Capitalism. Faith, Prosperity and Vision in African-Charismatic Churches", *Journal for the Study of Religion*.
Meyer, B. and Moors, A. (eds.) (2006). *Religion, Media and the Public Sphere*. Bloomington: Indiana University Press.
Meyer, M.A. (1999). "Being Jewish and…", pp. 21–34 in S.M. Cohen and G. Horenczyk (eds.), *National Variations in Jewish Identity*. Albany, NY: SUNY Press.
Meyers, A. and Hopkins, D.E. (eds.) (1988). *Manipulating the Saints: Religious Brotherhoods and Social Integration in Postconquest Latin America*. Hamburg: Wayasbah.
Micklethwait, J. and Wooldridge, A. (2009). *God is Back: How the Global Rise of Faith is Changing the World*. London: Allen Lane.
Ministry of Education, Culture and Sport. (2004). *Freedom and Choice in Education: Theory, Philosophy, Practice*. Jerusalem (Hebrew).
Minkenberg, M. (2005). "Germany: From Kulturnation to Europeanization", in A. Ichijo and W. Spohn (eds.), *Entangled Identities. Europe and the Nation*. Aldershot: Ashgate.

Mitchell, R.P. (1969). *The Society of the Muslim Brothers*. London: Oxford University Press.
Mittleman, A.L. (1996). *The Politics of Torah, The Jewish Political Tradition and the Founding of Agudat Israel*. Albany, NY: State University of New York Press.
Moore, B. (1966) *Social Origins of Dictatorship and Democracy: Lord and Peasant in the Making of the Modern World*, Boston: Beacon Press
Motyl, A. (1994). *Thinking Theoretically about Soviet Nationalities*. New York: Columbia University Press.
Münkler, H. (2003). *Über den Krieg: Stationen der Kriegsgeschichte in Spiegel ihrer theoretischen Reflexion*. Weilerwist: Velbrück.
Nadwi, S.A.H.A. (1983). *Muslims in the West: The Message and Mission*. Leicester: The Islamic Foundation.
Naficy, H. (1993). *The Making of Exile Cultures: Iranian Television in Los Angeles*. Minneapolis: University of Minnesota Press.
Na'ini, M.H. (1909). *Tanbih al-Umma wa-Tanzih al-Milla (The admonition and refinement of the people)*. Najaf: n.p.
Narain, A.K. (1994). "Dr. Ambedkar, Buddhism and Social Change—A Reappraisal", pp. 77–98 in A.K. Narain and D.C. Ahir (eds.), *Dr. Ambedkar, Buddhism and Social Change*. Delhi: B.R. Publishing.
Narain, A.K. and Ahir, D.C. (eds.). (1994). *Dr. Ambedkar, Buddhism and Social Change*. Delhi: B.R. Publishing.
Narayan, B. (2008). "Demarginalisation and History: Dalit Re-invention of the Past", *South Asia Research* 28(2): 169–184.
Narayanan, V. (2006a). "Creating Community Spaces in American Hinduism: Authority, Authenticity, and Identity", lecture at the Panel 'Comparative Studies in Hinduism and Judaism Group' (Congress of the American Academy of Religion, Washington D.C., 20.11.2006).
—— (2006b). "Creating South Indian Hindu Experience in the United States", pp. 147–176 in R.B. Williams (ed.), *A Sacred Thread. Modern Transmission of Hindu Traditions in India and Abroad*. Chambersburg: Anima Publications.
Nayyar, D. (1998). *Globalisation: The Past in our Present*. TWN Trade and Development Series. Penang: Third World Network.
Nekuda (2006). "On the Agenda: The Renewal of Jewish Emuni Creativity: The Start of a New Age?" (special section with various authors).
Neusner, J. (1995a). *Judaism in Modern Times*. Cambridge, Mass; Oxford, UK: Blackwell.
—— (1995b). *Muslims in Western Europe*. Edinburgh: University of Edinburgh Press, 2nd Edition.
Nielsen J.S. (1995). *Muslims in Western Europe*. Edinburgh: Edinburgh University Press.
Nye, M. (1995). *A Place for our Gods. The Construction of a Temple Community in Edinburgh*. Richmond: Curzon.
Obama, B. (2008a). *Dreams from my Father*. Edinburgh: Canongate.
—— (2008b). *The Audacity of Hope*. Edinburgh: Canongate
O'Donnell, G. and Schmitter, P.C. (1986). *Transitions from Authoritarian Rule: Tentative Conclusions About Uncertain Democracies*. Baltimore: John Hopkins University Press.
Oesterheld, J. and Günther, L. (1997). *Inder in Berlin*. Berlin: Verwaltungsdruckerei.
Omvedt, G. (2003). *Buddhism in India: Challenging Brahmanism and Caste*. New Delhi: Sage Publications.
—— (2004). *Ambedkar: Towards an Enlightened India*. New Delhi: Penguin.
Oosterbaan, M. (2009). "Virtual Re-evangelization: Brazilian Churches, Media and the European City", in J. Beaumont and A. Molendijk (eds.), *Religion, Politics and the Postsecular City*. Leiden: Brill.

Osterhammel, J. (2008). *Weltgeschichte des 19. Jahrhunderts.* München: Beck.
Outhwaite, W. and Ray, L. (2005). *Social theory and Postcommunism.* Oxford: Blackwell.
Overbeek, H. (1993). "Cycles of Hegemony and Leadership in the Core of the World System," *Working Papers Amsterdam International Studies. No. 31.* Amsterdam: University of Amsterdam, Department of International Relations.
Owen IV, J.M. (2006). "Democracy, Realistically", *The National Interest* (Spring): 35–42.
Owen, R. (1992). *State, Power and Politics in the Making of the Modern Middle East.* London and New York: Routledge.
Palmer, D. (2007). *Qigong Fever.* New York: Columbia University Press.
Pamuk, S. (1987). *The Ottoman Empire and the European Capitalism, 1820–1913.* Cambridge: Cambridge University Press.
Patai, R. (1983). *The Arab Mind.* New York: Charles Scribner's Sons.
Pearson, A.M. (1996). *"Because it gives me peace of mind": Ritual Fasts in the Religious Lives of Hindu Women.* Albany, NY: SUNY Press.
Peel, J. (2000). *Religious Encounter and the Making of the Yoruba.* Bloomington: Indiana University Press.
Permoser, J. and Rosenberg, S. (2009). "Religious Citizenship versus Immigrant Integration: The Case of Austria", pp. 259–289 in P. Bramadat and M. Koenig (eds.), *International Migration and the Governance of Religious Diversity.* Montreal and Kingston: McGill Queens University Press.
Perthes, V. (2008). "Is the Arab World Immune to Democracy?", *Survival* 50(6): 151–160.
Piekarz, M. (1998). *The Beginning of Hasidism: Ideological Trends in Derush and Musar Literature.* Jerusalem: Bialik (Hebrew).
Pollack, D., Borowik, I. and Jodzinski, W. (eds.). (1998). *Religiöser Wandel in den postkommunistischen Ländern Ost- und Mitteleuropas.* Würzburg: Ergon.
Przeworski, A. and Limongi, F. (1993). "Political regimes and economic growth", *The Journal of Economic Perspectives* 7(3): 51–69.
Qutb, S. (1980). *al-Adalah al-Ijtima'iyyah fi al-Islam (Social Justice in Islam).* Cairo: Dar al-Shuruq.
—— (1981). *Ma'alim fi al-Tariq (Milestone on the Road).* 14th edition. Cairo: al-Shuruq Publishing House.
Rachman, G. (2008). "Medvedev Will Not Declare Cold War", *Financial Times*, March 4, p. 11.
Ragussis, M. (1995). *Figures of Conversion: "The Jewish Question" and English National Identity.* Durham and London: Duke University Press.
Rahman, F. (1982). *Islam and Modernity: Transformation of an Intellectual Tradition.* Chicago: University of Chicago Press.
Rakel, E.P. (2006). "Conglomerates in Iran: the Political Economy of Islamic Foundations," part 5 in A.F. Jilberto and B. Hogenboom (eds.), *Conglomerates and Economic Groups in Developing Countries and Transition Economies.* London: Routledge.
Ramadan, T. (1999). *To Be A European Muslim: A Study of Islamic Sources in the European Context.* Leicester: The Islamic Foundation.
Ramteke, D.L. (1983). *Revival of Buddhism in Modern India.* New Delhi: Deep and Deep Publications.
Raphael, M.L. (ed.). (2008). *The Columbia History of Jews and Judaism in America.* New York: Columbia University Press.
Ravitzky, A. (1993). *The Revealed End and the Jewish State: Messianism, Zionism and Religious Radicalism in Israel.* Tel-Aviv: Am Oved (Hebrew).
Rawlins, W.K. (1988). "A Dialectical Analysis of the Tensions, Functions and Strategic Challenges of Communication in Young Adult Friendships", *Communication Yearbook* 12: 157–189, ed. J.A. Anderson. Newbury, CA: Sage.

—— (1992). *Friendship Matters: Communication, Dialectics, and the Life Course*. Hawthorne, NY: Aldine de Gruyter.
Resul, A. (2004). "Democracy and Democratization in the Middle East: Old Problem New Context", *Turkish Review of Middle East Studies* (14): 377–393.
Retlinger-Reiner, R. (2007). *Daring in Holiness: Religious Women's Theatre in Israel*. Jerusalem: Carmel (Hebrew).
Riesebrodt, M. (1998). *Pious Passion: The Emergence of Modern Fundamentalism in the United States and Iran*. Los Angeles: University of California Press.
Risso, P. (1995). *Merchants and faith: Muslim commerce and culture in the Indian Ocean*. Boulder: Westview Press.
Robertson, R. (1970). *The Sociological Interpretation of Religion*. Oxford: Oxford University Press.
—— (1992). *Globalization. Social Theory and Global Culture*. London: Routledge.
—— (1995). "Glocalization: Time-Space and Homogeneity-Heterogeneity, pp. 25–44 in M. Featherstone, S. Lash and R. Robertson (eds.), *Global Modernities*. London: Sage.
Robinson, J.A (2006). "Economic Development and Democracy", *Annual Review of Political Sciences* 9: 502–527.
Rose, A. (2007). "Are We Witnessing a Prague Spring? Haredim and the Internet", *Eretz Acheret* 41: 38–50 (Hebrew).
Rose, R. and Shin, D.C. (2001). "Democratization Backwards: The Problem of Third-Wave Democracies", *British Journal of Political Science Review* 31(2): 331–354.
Rosenak, A. (2000). "Who is Afraid of the Secreted Notebooks of Rav Kook", *Tarbitz* 69: 257–291 (Hebrew).
Ross, M.L. (2001). "Does Oil Hinder Democracy?", *World Politics* 53(3): 331–354.
Rotem, T. (2007a). "This is not Kabul—In Beit Shemesh also They Wear *Ra'alot*", *Haaretz*, 23.11.07 (Hebrew).
—— (2007b). Starting on 26.04.07 a series of six weekly articles in *Ha'aretz* detailing new professions acquired by Haredi women.
Roudometof, V. (2001). *Nationalism, Globalization and Orthodoxy. The Social Origins of Ethnic Conflict in the Balkans*. Westport, CT: Greenwood Press.
Roy, O. (1994). *The failure of political Islam*. London: I.B. Tauris.
—— (2006). "Islam in Europe: Clash of Religions or Conversions of Religiosities", in K. Michalski (ed.), *Conditions of European Soldiarity*, vol. II: Religion in the New Europe. Budapest: Central European University Press.
Ruach-Midbar, M. (2006). *The Culture of the New Age in Israel*. Unpublished Doctoral Thesis. Bar-Ilan University (Hebrew).
Rueschemeyer, D. et al. (1992). *Capitalist Deveopment & Democracy*. Chicago: University of Chicago Press.
Rukmani, T.S. (ed.) (1999). *Hindu Diaspora. Global Perspectives*. Montreal: Concordia University.
Russell, S. (1996). *Jewish Identity and Civilizing Processes*. Houndmills, GB: Macmillan Press; New York: St Martin's Press.
Rustow, D.A. (1970). "Transitions to Democracy: Toward a Dynamic Model", *Comparative Politics* 2(3): 337–363.
Sacks J. (1993). *One People? Tradition, Modernity, and Jewish Unity*. London, Washington: The Littman Library of Jewish Civilization.
Safrai, S. (1974). "Relations between the Diaspora and the Land of Israel", pp. 184–215 in S. Safrai and M. Stern (eds.), *The Jewish People in the First Century*. Compendia Rerum Iudaicarum ad Novum Testamentum, Vol. 1. Assen: Van Gorcum & Comp. B.V.
Said, E. (1978). *Orientalism*. New York: Pantheon Books.
Saint-Blancat, C. (1995). "Une Diaspora Musulmane en Europe?", *Archives de Sciences Sociales des Religions* 92: 9–24.

—— (2002). "Islam in Diaspora: Between Reterritorialization and Extraterritoriality". *International Journal of Urban and Regional Research* 26(1): 138–151.
Sakwa, R. (1996). *Russian Politics and Society*. London: Routledge.
Salentin, K. with Gröne, M. (2002). *Tamilische Flüchtlinge in der Bundesrepublik. Eine Bestandsaufnahme sozialer, ökonomischer und rechtlicher Aspekte der Integration*. Frankfurt/M., London: IKO.
Salentin, K. and Wilkening, K. (2004). *Technical Report of the 'Living together in Germany' survey* (in German). University of Bielefeld, Faculty of Sociology.
Salvatore, A. (2007). *The Public Sphere: Liberal Modernity, Catholicism, Islam*. New York: Palgrave Macmillan.
—— (2009). "Tradition and Modernity Within Islamic Civilisation and the West", pp. 3–35 in M.K. Masud, A. Salvatore and M. van Bruinessen (eds.), *Islam and Modernity: Key Issues and Debates*. Edinburgh: Edinburgh University Press.
—— (2011). "Eccentric Modernity? An Islamic Perspective on the Civilizing Process and the Public Sphere", *European Journal of Social Theory* 13(3).
Sarma, R.S. (2009). *Hinduistische Rituale*. Lucerne: own publication.
Sarna, J.D. (1995). "The Evolution of the American Synagogue", pp. 215–229 in R.M. Seltzer and N.J. Cohen (eds.), *The Americanization of the Jews*. New York, London: New York University Press.
Sassen, S. (2006). *Territory-Authority-Rights: from medieval to global assemblages*. Princeton: Princeton University Press.
—— (2007). *A Sociology of Globalization*. New York: Norton.
Sayyid, B.S. (1997). *A Fundamental Fear: Eurocentrism and the Emergence of Islamism*,.London: Zed Books.
Schalk, P. (2003). "Tamil Caivas in Stockhom, Sweden", pp. 379–389 in M. Baumann, B. Luchesi and A. Wilke (Hg.), *Tempel und Tamilen in zweiter Heimat*. Würzburg: Ergon.
Scharr, K. and Gräf, R. (2008). *Rumänien. Geschichte und Geographie*. Cologne: Böhlau.
Schatzki, T.R. (1996). *Social Practices: A Wittgensteinian Approach to Human Activity and the Social*. Cambridge: Cambridge University Press.
Schieder, T. (1992*). Nationalismus und Nationalstaat*. Göttingen: Vandenhoek & Ruprecht.
Schiffauer, W. (2005). "Migration und Religion", pp. 562–571 in E. Aytaç (Hg.), *Projekt Migration*. Köln: Dumont.
Schmidt, V. (ed.). (2007). *Modernity at the Beginning of the 21st Century*. Cambridge, UK: Cambridge Scholars Publisher.
Schmitter, G.P. and Whitehead, L. (eds.). (1986). *Transition from Authoritarian Rule: Prospect for Democracy*. Baltimore: Johns Hopkins University Press.
Schmueli, A. (1980). *Sheva tarbouiot Israel* (The Seven cultures of Israel). Tel-Aviv: Bialik Institute.
Scholte, J. (2005). *Globalization. A Critical Introduction*. Basingstoke: Palgrave McMillan.
Schomer, K. and McLeod, W.H. (1987). *The Sants: Studies in a Devotional Tradition of India*. Berkeley: Berkeley Religious Studies Series.
Schulze, R. (1990). *Islamischer internationalismus im 20 Jahrhundert: untersuchungen zur Geschicte der Islamischen Weltliga*. Leiden: Brill.
Schulze Wessel, M. (2002). "Konfessionelle Konflikte in der Ersten Tschechoslowakischen Republik", pp. 73–102 in H.-C. Maner and M. Schulze Wessel (eds.), *Religion im Nationalstaat zwischen den Weltkriegen 1918–1939*, Stuttgart: Steiner.
Schwinn, T. (ed.). (2006). *Die Vielfalt und Einheit der Moderne*. Wiesbaden: Verlag für Sozialwissenschaften.
Segady, T.W. (2006). "Traditional religion, fundamentalism, and institutional transition in the 20th century", *The Social Science Journal* 43(2): 197–209.

Seligman, A. (1999). *Modernity's Wager*. Princeton: Princeton University Press.
Seligman, A., Weller, R., Puett, M. and Bennett, S. (2008). *Ritual and Its Consequences*. Oxford: Oxford University Press
Sen, A. (1999). *Development as Freedom*. London: Oxford University Press.
Senghaas, D. (1988). "European Development and the Third World", *Review Journal of the Fernand Braudel Center for the study of Economies, Historical Systems and Civilizations* 14(3): 451–467.
—— (2002). *The Clash within Civilizations: Coming to Terms with Cultural Conflicts*. London and New York: Routledge.
Shafir, G. and Peled, Y. (2002). *Being Israeli: The Dynamics of Multiple Citizenship*. Cambridge: Cambridge University Press.
Shagar, S. (2004). *Broken Vessels: Torah and Religious Zionism in the Post-Modern Environment*. Ed. O. Tzurieli. Efrat, West Bank (Hebrew).
Shalev, M. (2000). "Liberalization and the Transformation of the Political Economy", in G. Shafir and Y. Peled (eds.), *The New Israel: Peacemaking and Liberalization*. Boulder: Westview.
Shari'ati, A. (1979). *On Sociology of Islam*. Trans. by H. Algar. Berkeley: Mirza Press.
—— (n. d.). *Mazhab Alayhe Mazhab (Religion against Religion)*. Tehran: Husayniyeh-e Irshad.
Sheleg, B. (2009). "The Outside is Unclean: Ramat Beit Shemesh as an Enclave", *Eretz Acheret* 51: 16–19 (Hebrew).
Sheleg, Y. (2000). *New Relgious Jews: A Contemporary Look at Religious Society in Israel*. Jerusalem: Keter (Hebrew).
Shokeid, M. (1995). "The Religiosity of Middle Eastern Jews", in S. Deshen, C. Liebman and M. Shokeid (eds.), *Israeli Judaism*. New Brunswick and London: Transaction Publishers.
Shulman, D. (2007). *Dark Hope: Working for Peace in Israel and Palestine*. Chicago: University of Chicago Press.
Siddiqui, A. (1998). "Muslims in the Contemporary World: Dialogue in Perspective", *World Faiths Encounter* 20, July.
Silberstein, L.J. (1996). *Postzionism Debates. Knowledge and Power in Israeli Culture*. New York and London: Routledge.
Skidmore, J. (2007). *Fire Burning in Snow: Baroque Music from Latin America*. London: Hyperion Records.
Skocpol, T. (1979). *States and Revolutions*. Cambridge: Cambridge University Press.
—— (1982). "Rentier State and Shi'a Islam in the Iranian Revolution", *Theory and Society* 11(3): 265–83.
Smidt, C., Kellstedt, L. and Guth, J. (2009). *Oxford Handbook of Religion in American Politics*. New York: Oxford.
Smilde, D. (2007). *Reason to Believe: Cultural Agency in Latin American Evangelicalism*. Berkeley: University of California Press.
Smith, A. (2001). *Nationalism*. Oxford: Polity Press.
—— (2005). *Chosen Peoples. Sacred Sources of National Identity*. Oxford: Oxford University Press.
Smith, B. (1994). *Classifying the Universe: The Ancient Indian Varna System and the Origins of Caste*. New York: Oxford University Press.
Smith, C. (1998). *American Evangelicalism: Embattled and Thriving*. Chicago: University of Chicago Press.
Smith, G. (2000). *Christian America? What Evangelicals Really Want*. Berkeley, CA: University of California Press.
Soloveitchik, C. (1994). "Rupture and Reconstruction: The Transformation of Contemporary Orthodoxy", *Tradition* 28: 64–130.
Soothill, J. (2007). *Gender, Social Change and Spiritual Power: Charismatic Christianity in Ghana*. Leiden: Brill.

Sorek, Y. (1997). "Ha-IM Ha Boreh Dati" (Hebrew), *Nekuda* 206: 55.
—— (1998). "Drusha Mahapecha", *Akdamot*, Ellul 5.
Sorotzkin, D. (2007). *The Eternal Community in an Era of Change: Conceptions of Time and Collective as a Basis for the Definition of Jewish Orthodoxy in Early Modern Europe*. Unpublished Doctoral Dissertation, the Hebrew University of Jerusalem.
Soroush, A. (1994). "Mudara wa Mudiriyat-e Mumenan: Sukhani dar Nisbat-e Din wa Democrasi" [*The Tolerance and Administration of the Faithful: A Remark on the Relation Between Religion and Democracy*], *Kiyan* 4.
Spannenberger, N. (2002). "Die katholische Kirche in Ungarn in ihren nationalen und gesellschaftlichen Bedeutungen", pp. 157–176 in H.-C. Maner and M. Schulze Wessel (eds.), *Religion im Nationalstaat zwischen den Weltkriegen 1918–1939*. Stuttgart: Steiner.
Spickard, P. and Cragg, K. (2001). *Global History of Christians; A: How Everyday Believers Experienced Their World*. Grand Rapids, MI: Baker Academic.
Spohn, W. (1998). "Religion und Nationalismus. Osteuropa im westeuropäischen Vergleich" pp. 87–120 in D. Pollack et al.(eds.), *Religiöser Wandel in den postkommunistischen Ländern Ost- und Mitteleuropas*. Würzburg: Ergon.
—— (2002a). "Nationalismus und Religion. Ein historisch-soziologischer Vergleich West- und Osteuropas", in M. Minkenberg and U. Willems (eds.), *Politik und Religion, Politische Vierteljahresschrift*, special issue 33: 323–345.
—— (2002b). "Transformation Process, Modernization Patterns and Collective Identities: Democratization, Nationalism and Religion in Postcommunist Germany, Poland and Russia", pp. 199–218 in F. Bönker et al. (eds.), *Postcommunist Transformation and the Social Sciences. Cross-Disciplinary Approaches*. London: Rowman & Littlefield.
—— (2005). "From Habsburg Empire to a Small Nation in Europe", pp. 55–71 in A. Ichijo and W. Spohn (eds.), *Entangled Identities. Europe and the Nation*. Aldershot: Ashgate.
—— (2008). *Politik und Religion in einer sich globalisierenden Welt*. Wiesbaden: Verlag für Sozialwissenschaften.
Srinivasan. (2007). *Hinduismus für alle. Eine Einleitung in die älteste Lebensart der Welt*, translated by Sharayu. Hamm: Sri Hindu Sankarar Kamadchi Ampal Tempel.
Stephens, R.J. (2008). *The Fire Spreads, Holiness and Pentecostalism in the American South*. Cambridge, Mass.: Harvard University Press.
Stölting, E. (1990). *Nationalitäten und Religionen in der UdSSR*. Frankfurt/M.
Strauss, S. (2005). *Positioning Yoga*. Oxford: Berg Publishers.
Stringer, M.D. (2008). *Contemporary Western Ethnography and the Definition of Religion*. London: Continuum.
Suny, G. (1983). *Nationalism and Social Change: Essays on the history of Armenia, Azerbaijan and Georgia*. Ann Arbor, MI: University of Michigan Press.
Szporluk, R. (2000). *Russia, Ukraine and the Break-up of the Soviet Union*. Stanford: Hoover.
Szücs, J. (1990). *Die drei historischen Regionen Europas*. Frankfurt/M.
Taylor, C. (1989). *Sources of the Self: The Making of the Modern Identity*. Cambridge: Cambridge University Press.
—— (1992). *Multiculturalism and "The Politics of Recognition"*. Princeton: Princeton University Press.
—— (2007). *A Secular Age*. Cambridge: Harvard University Press.
Tessler, M. (2002). "Islam and Democracy in the Middle East: the Impact of Religious Orientations on Attitudes toward Democratization in Four Arab Countries", *Comparative Politics* 34(3): 337–354.
Thomas, T. (1993). "Hindu Dharma in Dispersion", pp. 173–204 in G. Parsons (ed.), *The Growth of Religious Diversity. Britain from 1945*, Vol. 1: Traditions. London: Routledge.

Thomä-Venske, H. (1988). "The Religious Life of Muslims in Britain", in T. Gerholm and Y.G. Lithman (eds.), *The New Islamic Presence in Western Europe*. London: Mansell.
Tiesler, N.C. (2009). "Muslim Transnationalism and Diaspora in Europe: Migrant Experience and Theoretical Reflection", pp. 417–440 in E. Ben-Rafael and Y. Sternberg (eds.), *Transnationalism: Diasporas and the advent of a new (dis)order*. Leiden: Brill.
Tilly, C. (1975). *The Formation of National States in Western Europe*. Cambridge: Blackwell Publishing.
Todorova, M. (1997). *Imagining the Balkans*. Oxford: Oxford University Press.
Tölölyan, K. (1991). "The Nation-State and Its Others: In Lieu of a Preface", *Diaspora* 1(1): 3–7.
—— (1996). "Rethinking Diaspora(s): Stateless Power in the Transnational Moment", *Diaspora* 5(1): 3–36.
Trimberger, E.K. (1978). *Revolution from Above: Military Bureaucracy and Development in Japan, Turkey, Egypt and Peru*. New Brunswick, New Jersey: Transaction Books.
Troeltsch, E. (1960). *The Social Teaching of the Christian Churches* (2 vols.). New York: Harper Row.
Tromp, J. (1998). "The Ancient Jewish Diaspora: Some Linguistic and Sociological Observations", pp. 13–35 in G. ter Haar (ed.), *Strangers and Sojourners. Religious Communities in the Diaspora*. Leuven: Uitgeverij Peeters.
Turner, V. (1974). *The Ritual Process: Structure and Anti-Structure*. Harmondsworth, UK: Pelican Books.
Tzurieli, O. (2004). "Editor's Introduction", in S. Shagar, *Broken Vessels: Torah and Religious Zionism in the Post-Modern Environment*. Ed. O. Tzurieli. Efrat, West Bank (Hebrew).
Ukah, A. (2008). *A New Paradigm of Pentecostal Power*. Africa World Press.
Van der Burg, C.J.G. and van der Veer, P.T. (1986). "Pandits, Power and Profit; Religious Organization and the Construction of Identity among the Surinamese Hindus", *Ethnic and Racial Studies* 9(4): 514–529.
van der Veer, P. (1987). "'God must be Liberated!' A Hindu Liberation Movement in Ayodhya", *Modern Asian Studies* 21(2): 283–301.
—— (2001). *Imperial Encounters*. Princeton, NJ: Princeton University Press.
—— (ed.) (1996). *Conversion to Modernities. The Globalization of Christianity*. New York: Routledge.
van der Veer, P. and Lehmann, H. (eds.). (1996). *Nation and Religion. Perspectives on Europe and Asia*. Princeton, NJ: Princeton University Press.
Van Dijk, A. (1996). "Hinduismus in Suriname und den Niederlande", *Zeitschrift für Missionswissenschaft und Religionswissenschaft* 80(3): 179–197.
Van Dijk, R. (2002). "The Soul is the Stranger. Ghanaian Pentecostalism and the Diasporic Contestation of 'Flow' and 'Individuality'", in S. Coleman (ed.), *The Faith Movement: A Global Religious Culture?* Special issue, *Culture and Religion* 3(1): 49–67.
Van Unnik, W.C. (1993). *Das Selbstverständnis der jüdischen Diaspora der hellenistisch-römischen Zeit*, edited posthum by P.W. van der Horst. Leiden: Brill.
Veblen, T. (1947). *The Place of Science in Modern Civilization*. New York: Viking.
Vertovec, S. (1992). "Community and Congregation in London Hindu Temples: Divergent Trends", *New Community* 18(2): 251–264.
—— (1997). "Three Meanings of 'Diaspora', Exemplified among South Asian Religions", *Diaspora* 6(3): 277–299.
—— (2000). *The Hindu Diaspora. Comparative Patterns*. London, New York: Routledge.
Vicziany, M. (2007). "Understanding the 1993 Mumbai Bombings: Madrassas and the Hierarchy of Terror", *South Asia* 30(1): 43–73.

Virmani, A. (2008). *A National Flag for India: Rituals, Nationalism, and the Politics of Sentiment*. Ranikhet: Permanent Black.
Vital, D. (1990). *The Future of the Jews*. Cambridge, Mass.: Harvard University Press.
Vögeli, J. (2005). '*Ohne śakti ist śiva nichts*'. *Tamilische Geschlechterbeziehungen in der Schweiz*. Working paper Nr. 28. Bern: Institute of Ethnology.
Vulpius, R. (2005). *Nationalisierung der Religion. Russifizierungspolitik und ukrainische Nationsbildung, 1860-1920*. Wiesbaden: Harrassowitz Verlag.
Waardenburg, J. (1996). "Muslims as Dhimmis: The Emancipation of Muslim Immigrants in Europe: The Case of Switzerland", in W.A.R. Shadid and P.S. van Koningsveld (eds.), *Muslims in the Margin: Political Responses to the Presence of Islam in Western Europe*. Kampen: Kok Pharos.
Wächli, U. (2008). '*Ein Tempel ist wie eine Waschmaschine*'. *Die religiöse Organisation der indischen Hindus in der Schweiz*. MA thesis. Bern: University of Bern.
Wanner, C. (2007). *Communities of the Converted. Ukrainians and Global Evangelism*. Ithaca and London: Cornell University press.
Warner, R.S. (1998). "Introduction: Immigration and Religious Communities in the United States", pp. 3-34 in R.S. Warner and J.G. Wittner (eds.), *Gatherings in Diaspora: Religious Communities and the New Immigration*. Philadelphia: Temple University Press.
Warren, R. (2002). *The Purpose Driven Life*. Grand Rapids, MI: Zondervan House Publishing.
Weber, M. (1920). *The Protestant Ethic and the Spirit of Capitalism*. New York: Scribner.
—— (1946). *Essays in Sociology*. New York: Oxford University Press.
Weiffen, B. (2004). "The Cultural-Economic Syndrome: Impediments to Democracy in the Middle East", *Comparative Sociology* 3(3-4): 353-375.
Werbner, P. (1996). "The Making of Muslim Dissent: Hybridized Discourses, Lay Preachers and Radical Rhetoric Among British Pakistanis", *American Ethnologist* 23(1): 102-122.
—— (2003). *Pilgrims of love: The anthropology of a global sufi cult*. Bloomington: Indiana University Press.
Wertheimer, J. (1993). *A People Divided: Judaism in Contemporary America*. New York: Basic Books.
Wilke, A. (2003). "'Traditionsverdichtung' in der Diaspora: Hamm als Bühne der Neuaushandlung von Hindu-Traditionen", pp. 125-168 in M. Baumann, B. Luchesi and A. Wilke (Hg.), *Tempel und Tamilen in zweiter Heimat. Hindus aus Sri Lanka im deutschsprachigen und skandinavischen Raum*. Würzburg: Ergon.
Williams, R.B. (1988). *Religions of Immigrants from India and Pakistan. New Threads in the American Tapestry*. Cambridge: Cambridge University Press.
—— (1992). "Sacred Threads of Several Textures", pp. 228-257 in R.B. Williams (ed.), *A Sacred Thread. Modern Transmission of Hindu Traditions in India and Abroad*. Chambersburg: Anima Publ.
—— (2000). "Conclusion: Trajectories for Future Studies", pp. 277-287 in H. Coward, J. Hinnells and R.B. Williams (eds.), *The South Asian Religious Diaspora in Britain, Canada, and the United States*. New York: State University of New York Press.
Wittgenstein, L. (1961). *Tractatus logico-philosophicus, suivi de Investigations philosophiques*, traduit de l'allemand par P. Klossowski. Paris: Gallimard.
Wuthnow, R. (1998). *After Heaven*. Berkeley: University of California Press.
Xu, J. (1999). "Body, Discourse and the Cultural Politics of Contemporary Qigong", *Journal of Asian Studies* 58(4): 961-991.
Yadgar, Y. and Liebman, C. (2006). "Beyond the Religious-Secular Dichotomy: The Traditionists (Masortim) in Israel", in U. Cohen, E. Ben-Rafael, A.Bareli and E. Yaar (eds.), *Israel and Modernity*; In Honor of Moshe Lissak. Ben-Gurion University, Tel Aviv University, Hebrew University, Yad Ben-Tzvi (Hebrew).

Yavuz, H. (2003). *Islamic Political Identity in Turkey*. Oxford: Oxford University Press.
Young, M. et al. (eds.). (2007). *Nationalism in a Global Era: The persistence of nations*. London: Routledge.
Younger, P. (1980). "A Temple Festival of Māriyamma", *Journal of the American Academy of Religion* 48(4): 494–517.
Yuchtman-Yaar, E. and Peres, Y. (1998). *Between Consent and Dissent: Democracy and Peace in the Israeli Mind*. New York: Rowman and Littlefeld.
Zakaria, F. (2003) *The Future of Freedom: Illiberal Democracy at Home and Abroad*, NY: W.W. Norton
Zalcberg , S. (2008). "The Panic for Modesty: Terror for the Sake of Heaven", *Eretz Acheret* 51: 30–43 (Hebrew).
—— (2009). "The Redemption is on Their Shoulders", *Makor Rishon* 16.5.2008 (Hebrew).
Zernack, K. (1994). *Polen und Russland. Zwei Wege der europäischen Geschichte*. Berlin: Propyläen.
Zürcher, E.-J. (1993). *Turkey: A Modern History*. London, New York: I.B. Tauris.
—— (2004). *Turkey: A Modern History*. Amsterdam: Amsterdam University Press.
Zürcher, E.-J., Kazancigil, A. and Ozbudun, E. (eds.) (1981). *Atatürk: Founder of a Modern State*. London: C. Hurst.

INDEX

Abduh, Mohammad (1849–1905)   165, 169, 195
Abdul Hamid II, Sultan   194
Abu-Lughod, Janet   194
Abu Zeid, Nasr Hamid (1943–)   166, 174
Abuhatzeira, Yisrael (Baba Sali)   360
Abulafia, Abraham   331
ad-Darsh, Syed Mutawalli   206
Adeboye, Enoch   105, 106
Adorno, Theodor   202, 203
Advani, R.K.   267
Afghani, Sayyed Jamal al-Din (1838–97)   165, 169, 194
Agassi, Joseph   303
Ahmadinejad, M.   188
Akhtar, Shabbir   206, 207
al-Bana, Hassan (1906–1949)   165, 170
Al Hakim, Ayatollah Mohammad Baqir (1939–2003)   171
al-Ghazali   210
al-Mawdudi, Sayyed Abdullah (1903–79)   171, 195, 205, 206
al-Nasser, Gamal Abd   167
al-Qaradawi, Yusuf (1929–)   155, 174, 206, 207
al-Wahhab, Abd (1703–1791)   173fn
al-Zuwaihari, Ayman   197
Alkalai, Yehuda   307
Ambedkar, Bhimrao Ramji (1891–1956)   219–236, 261
Amineh, Mehdi P.   xi, 10, 11
An-Nai'm, Abdullahi Ahmed (1946–)   174
Anderson, Allan   130, 139
Appadurai, Arjun   34, 37, 282
Appleby, R.S.   4
Arkoun, Mohamed (1928–)   166, 174, 203
Armstrong, J.   3
Asad, Talal   131
Atatürk, Mustapha Kemal   164, 167, 195
Augustine   117
Austin-Broos, Diane   136
authority:
   all-commanding   109, 110
   bureaucratic   9, 109, 140

charismatic   9, 102, 109, 110
clientelist systems of   140
crises of   2
decentralized   6, 25
divine   149
fragmentation of   109
husband's   335
local patterns of   140
loci of   ix, 25
of halacha   294, 298
of scriptural tradition   259
pastoral   140
patriarchal   95
political   23
rabbinical   324, 333, 346
religious   ix, 8, 21–23, 25, 85, 92, 95, 102, 109, 110, 115, 138–140, 149, 205, 240, 254, 255, 259, 294, 298, 324, 333, 336, 346, 360
shift in   13, 240, 254, 255
spiritual   336
traditional types of   154
uses of   109
women holding positions of   115, 138, 139
authoritarianism/authoritarian   140, 159, 166, 167, 176, 263
and Islam   162, 171, 173, 175, 177
and Pentecostalism   140
industrialization   176fn
paradox of   182
path to modernization   167
persistence   159, 175, 177, 180–182, 185, 187, 189, 190
populist   181
post-populist   181
regimes   10, 151, 152, 159, 166, 167, 171, 173, 175, 177, 181, 182, 184–189
states   31, 72, 168, 184–188

Babar   361
Bach, J.S.   99
Bates, S.   49, 50
Baumann, Martin   xi, 12, 13
Baxi, Upendra   221
Bazargan, Mehdi (1907–95)   174
Beckford, J.A.   1

Behdad, S.   180
belonging without believing   15, 90, 315, 337–340, 342, 348
Ben-Gurion, David   302
Ben-Haim, Avraham   361
Ben-Rafael, E.   xi, 14, 15
Benedict XVI, Pope   260
Bengelius   114
Benjamin, Walter   202
Berger, Peter   1, 58, 133
Bergunder, Michael   102, 107, 108
Biden, Joe   46
Bilgrami, Akeel   214
Bin Laden, Osama   171, 197
Birnbaum, Nathan   301
Birnbaum, Pierre   280
Blitzer, Lauren   338
Bloom, Harold   112
Blum, Leon (1872–1950)   296
Bourdieu, Pierre   269
Brass, Paul   266
Bruce, S.   3
Brumberg, Daniel   182
Brusco, E.   125, 136
Buddha   230, 232–235
Buddhism:
    Ambedkarite   220–222, 224, 225, 230, 231, 233, 234, 235
    and Dalits   224–226, 228–236
    and de-marginalization   232–235
    and erecting statutes and monuments   222, 230–236
    and Hinduism   13, 220, 225–229
    modern/Navayana/new   12, 220–223, 235
buffered self   123
Bund   296, 297, 313, 314
Bunting, Madeleine   53, 54
Bush, George W.   46, 52, 53
Buxtehude, Dietrich   99
Bynum, Catherine   111

Calvin, John   98, 132
capitalism:
    American   133
    and democracy/democratization   161–164, 176, 177, 179, 185fn, 187, 189, 191
    and globalization   169, 172fn
    and modernity   163
    and Pentecostalism   133
    and pluralism   172
    and Protestantism   132
    competitive   181fn

expansion of   169, 172fn
finance   135
global   4, 32, 64, 103, 185, 273, 274
industrial   27, 163fn, 164
international   6, 32
market   7, 63
neo-liberal   135
postmodern   134
today   132
Western   171
Carothers, Thomas   182, 183
Carter, Jimmy   54
Casanova, Jose   59, 337
caste/castes   12, 107, 108, 168, 220, 221, 223–228, 230, 231, 235, 245, 246, 248, 250–252, 255, 261, 268, 283, 301, 309, 310
Catholicism/Catholic/Catholics:
    American   46
    and de-communalization   8
    and deterritorialization   92
    and reterritorialization   92
    and transnationalism   24
    anti-   116
    authorities   92, 100
    "Catholic Apostolics"   95
    China's attitude towards   264
    Church   140, 249, 259, 363
    clergy   73
    counter-reformation   70, 71
    cultural   46
    cultures   69
    East Central Europe   80
    Greek-   75
    Iberian   129
    identity   290
    in Africa   111
    in Cuba   362
    in Europe   87, 91, 92, 337
    in France   70
    in Germany   70, 71
    in Haiti   355, 363, 365
    in Hungary   74
    in Latin America   130, 136
    in Lithuania   75
    in Poland   73
    in Slovakia   74
    Latinos   43
    leaders   130
    "new communities"   88
    places of worship   363
    priest   362
    Roman   75, 92
    service   250

sociability 92
social 79
white 46
young 91
Cesari, Jocelyn 210
Chandrtamani, U. 228
Chavez, Hugo 102
church/churches:
  and the state 6, 47, 69, 73, 99, 101, 338fn
  attendance 8, 85
  Catholic 140, 249, 362, 363
  Christian 59, 85, 90, 93
  competition between 9
  Early 95
  established 110
  in Africa 120, 135, 357–360, 363–365
  in Brazil 130
  in Cuba 362, 363
  in England 97
  in Europe 51, 56, 85, 88, 104, 121, 337
  in Germany 97
  in Ghana 104, 135, 137, 138
  in India 107
  in Nigeria 105–107, 358–360
  in North America 104
  in South Africa 117
  in Sweden 140, 339
  in the Ukraine 114, 140
  in Venezuela 102, 103
  in West Africa 105, 111
  institutionalization of 16
  liturgies 140
  Lutheran 339
  mega- 47, 102, 104, 105, 109, 111, 125, 135, 140
  migrant 121
  mission-minded 100
  Orthodox 72
  Orthodox-Christian 71
  Pentecostal 9, 49, 91, 102–107, 110, 111, 117, 120, 121, 125–127, 130, 134, 135, 137, 138, 140
  Pietist 100
  positions of authority in 96
  Primitive 8, 93
  rival 109
  Romanian Orthodox 75
  Russian Orthodox 297
civilization/civilizations/civilizational:
  ancient 77
  and modernity 16
  and religion 258
  axial/axial-age 65, 66, 67
  Buddhist 12, 220
  challenge 145
  characteristics 122
  Chinese 14, 263
  clash of 4, 37, 159, 160, 199
  complexes 81
  concept of 40, 262
  constellation/constellations 6, 7, 21, 26, 40, 64, 81
  European 68
  formations 30
  framework/frameworks 32, 34, 39, 40
  identity 38, 65
  Indian 236
  Irano-Semitic 146
  Islamic 145–147, 150, 153, 169
  Jewish 280
  modern 1, 26, 32, 38, 119, 289
  monotheistic 23
  non-axial-age 65
  non-Western 3
  orientations 36–38
  others 259
  parish 8, 85, 90
  perspective 65
  premises 6, 38, 39
  relations 35, 37, 64, 78
  religions 66
  terms 40
  traditions 259
  transformation 21, 23, 37, 78
  transcivilizational ecumene 147
  transnational 67
  visions 6, 25, 26, 145
  Western 3, 171, 298
class/classes:
  and Islam 168
  and protestants 132
  business 134, 135, 187fn, 188fn
  capitalist 180, 181fn, 185fn
  conflict 230
  conservative 180
  crystallization 27
  distinctions 269
  interest expression 167
  life worlds of 27
  low/lower 171, 305
  middle 11, 96, 97, 106, 110, 111, 168, 170, 171, 178fn, 180, 181fn, 182fn, 183fn, 187, 188, 191, 269, 273–275, 287, 304–306, 317fn, 318, 335, 339

modern 164, 170, 176, 180, 188, 189, 191
new 132, 133, 162fn, 275
new bourgeois 181
new state-class 181, 185
Other Backward Classes (OBCs) 232
political 42
poor 172
relations 27
reshuffling in Iran 180
ruling 185fn, 187
scribal 148
struggle 296
transnational 274
Transnational Capitalist Classes (TCC) 185
transnational class consciousness 185
upper 305, 318
views on 96
voting 139
working 167
clientelism 102, 108, 140, 160, 161, 183, 187
Cohen, Stephen 280
Cohen, Steven 316, 317, 338
Coleman, Simon 112, 135, 140
communalism/communalization ix, 13, 23, 25, 35, 36, 38, 85, 86, 90, 91, 117, 261, 267–269, 275
de- 8, 86
community/communities:
  affinity 8, 92
  Ashkenazi 311, 346, 347
  black 136
  Buddhist 14, 23, 220, 235
  Catholic 88
  Chinese 272
  Christian 91
  confrontations between ix
  corporately defined 156
  cultural 8
  Dalit 221, 224, 227, 228, 231–235
  deprived 52
  diasporic 14, 24, 240, 272
  ethnic 6, 24, 67, 239
  Haredi 285, 286, 328, 329, 345, 346-348
  Hindu 14, 23, 244–246, 248, 249, 266-268
  human 90, 156
  imagined 94, 234
  Indian 12
  intimate (havura) 295

Islamic/Muslim 10, 11, 156, 193, 194, 196–199, 204, 209, 210, 214, 227, 266–268, 333, 345
Jewish 280, 282, 284–288, 290, 291, 293, 295–299, 301, 305, 306, 311, 312, 315, 318, 319, 321, 325, 326, 328–330, 340, 342, 345–348, 361
local 173, 363
Mizrahi 287, 288, 305, 340, 342, 361
moral 1
national 10, 29
natural 86
need for 90
new 3, 88, 125
New Age 337
religious ix, 2, 3, 8, 11, 16, 23, 67, 85, 88, 91, 172, 227, 239, 333
religious Zionist 318, 319, 321, 325, 330
Russian-speaking Jews (RSJs) 306
subaltern 234
Taizé 91
transnational ix, 2, 6
ultra-orthodox 326, 328, 329, 345–348
village 125
virtual transnational religious 24–26, 34, 37, 38, 90, 91, 353
worshipping 110
Confucianism/Confucian 13, 160, 257, 259, 261–264, 266, 274, 275
morality 13, 275
Cox, R.W. 186fn
Cragg, K. 5
Cucchiari, S. 138
Cunningham, Alexander (1814–1893) 261

Dahari, Sylvie 334–336
Dalits 219, 221, 222, 224–226, 228–236, 269
Dash, Ghazi 225
David u-Moshe, Rabbi 361
Davie, Grace xi, 6, 7, 337, 338
delocalization 15, 92, 353
  of religion 90–92
democracy/democratization/ democratic 7, 63
  and capitalism 161, 162, 163fn, 164, 176, 181fn, 185, 187, 189, 191
  and civil society 182, 183, 187, 188, 191
  and civilizational frameworks 65

INDEX

and fundamentalism   4, 173, 180fn, 190
and globalization   67, 78, 177, 183
and Islam   10, 160, 161, 173–175, 179, 180fn, 182, 190
and modernization   67, 161, 162, 167, 173, 176, 178fn
and modern nationalism   67
and Pentecostalism   140, 141
and state class   185
and the European Union   81
and the Muslim Middle East   10, 159–162, 175, 177–191
and the US   183, 184
conditions for   162–164, 176–191
debate   178
discussion   122
global   177
in China   271, 273
in India   273
in Iran   187–189
in Turkey   72, 76, 187
Jacobin   319
level of   179
modern   50, 53
participation   78
politics   151
prerequisites of   161
regimes   63
sequential   177
societies   16, 89
states   70, 71
values   2
variations in   64
waves of   178
Western   50
Deng Xiaopeng   271
Dharmapala, Anagarika   222, 262
Dianteill, E.   363
diaspora/diasporas/diasporic:
  and homeland   212
  Buddhist   14
  Chinese communities   272
  communities   24, 34
  enclaves   121
  Hindu   13, 14, 237, 240, 246, 255
  Hindu temple in   247, 249–253, 255
  identities   6, 30
  Indian   12
  Jewish   16, 239, 279, 280, 283, 285, 287, 289, 297, 299, 302, 311, 312, 356
  Mizrahi   287
  Muslim   197, 209, 212
  networks   24
  new   ix, 6, 24, 37
  newly founded places of worship in   248, 249, 251
  notion of   238–240
  religious   24, 34, 237
  studies   248, 251
  Tamil Hindus   244, 251, 255
  transnational   3
  ultra-orthodoxy   285, 287, 289, 299, 311
Dorraj, M.   4
Dubnow, Simon   297
Durkheim, Emile   1, 229fn
Dutty, Boukman   355

Eck, Diana   247
Eder, Klaus   151
Eisen, Arnold   316, 317
Eisenstadt, Shmuel N.   xi, 5, 6, 59, 60, 64, 78, 97, 98, 119, 121, 280
Elazar, Daniel   279
Elias, Norbert   262
elite/elites:
  bureaucratic   147
  business   135
  circles   282
  cultural   154
  economic   147
  in Africa   113
  in Israel   303, 304, 317, 330
  in the US   42
  intellectual   101, 102, 105
  Islamic   175, 209
  landed   100
  liberal   54
  military   189
  Mizrahi   288
  modernizing   260
  national   100
  noble   100
  political   122, 147, 154, 162, 164, 166, 168, 173fn, 181, 182, 184, 187, 188fn, 189
  religious   288
  ruling   166, 167, 187
  secular   42, 53, 165, 190
  socio-economic   105
  West European   6, 50
Emden, Jacob   292
Emerson, M.O.   3
Engelke, Matthew   108, 115
Enlightenment   28, 30, 37, 39, 41, 56, 71, 112, 118, 120, 122, 124, 128, 131, 136, 150, 151, 203, 222, 291, 292, 311
essentialism: cultural   159, 161, 189

Evangelical/Evangelicals/Evangelicalism:
  American   126, 136, 354, 355
  and Pentecostalism   103, 116, 117, 136, 275
  and transnationalism   355
  black   117
  Colombian   125, 136
  hymns   97
  in North America   117
  in Russia   99
  in West Africa   113
  missionary activities of   79, 94
  networks   257
  new wave of   354, 355, 357, 363–365
  revival   113
  vote in the US   45–48, 54, 55
exclusion   7, 27, 30, 36, 51, 81, 163, 166, 181fn, 204, 219, 227, 230, 233, 234, 340, 353, 354, 356, 358, 360, 365
Eybeschütz, Jonathan   292

Fackenheim, Emil (1916–2003)   294
family resemblance   15, 281, 309, 310, 313
Feinstein, Moshe   346
Feminism:
  and Pentecostalism   136, 138
  secular   136, 138
  ultra-orthodox   333
  Western   126
fiqh   200, 201, 208: minority   211
Fischer, Shlomo   xi, 15
Fox, George   100
Frankel, Zecharya   293
Fraser, Nancy   150, 152
Friedlander, David   292
Friedman, M.   328, 329, 347
Fuchs, Martin   235
Fukuyama, F.   3
Fuller, Graham   182
Fundamentalism   ix, 3, 4, 7, 15, 50, 60, 63, 64, 98, 170, 190, 268, 343, 344, 349
  Christian   4, 50, 98
  Islamic   4, 10, 15, 170–174, 182, 190, 195, 197, 198, 210, 268, 343, 344, 349, 359
  Jewish   15, 307, 308, 317, 318–325, 330, 326–336, 342, 343, 345, 346, 349, 355–357, 361, 363–365

Gandhi, Indira   267
Gandhi, Mahatma   221, 224, 226–228, 235, 274

Gangohi, Rashid Ahmad (d. 1908)   173fn
Geertz, Clifford   172fn
Geiger, Abraham (1810–1874)   292
Gellner, Ernest   68
Ghannouchi, Rachid (1941–)   174
Gifford, Paul   135
Ginzburg, Louis   294
Ginzburg, Yitzchak   323, 324
global/globalization   x, 5, 6, 8, 13, 21, 22, 24, 26, 33, 37, 39, 40, 55, 59, 64, 81
  actors   29
  and civilizations   3
  and conflicts   7, 79, 81, 365
  and delocalization   15, 353
  and democratization   78, 177, 178fn, 183–186
  and deterritorialization   15, 32, 353
  and fragmentation   7, 79, 81, 172fn
  and fundamentalism   60, 64, 172, 173, 316, 344
  and Hinduism   12, 237
  and identity/identities   ix, 37, 79, 80, 155, 259
  and Islam   146, 150, 153–156, 169, 172, 173, 174, 177, 193, 195–198, 209, 212, 213, 316, 344, 345
  and Judaism   315, 316, 337
  and local   27, 176fn, 353, 364
  and modernity/modernization   2, 3, 65–67, 120
  and nation-states   10, 66, 78, 79, 122, 153, 156, 172fn, 185, 186, 259, 262, 270, 275
  and Pentecostalism   94, 95, 97, 98, 102, 121, 122, 126, 128, 135, 137, 138, 275, 354
  and protest movements   34–36, 38, 39
  and religion/religions   2, 8, 15, 16, 55, 60, 63, 64, 66, 78–81, 85, 87, 94, 122, 160, 212, 257, 259, 275, 337, 348, 353, 357, 358, 364, 365
  and secular feminism   138
  and social boundaries   27
  and transnationalization   15, 29, 353, 357, 358, 364
anti-globalization movements   34–36, 38, 39
approaches   63, 66
capitalism   4, 32, 56, 64, 103, 155, 163, 164, 169, 172fn, 176fn, 185, 273, 274

centres of   33, 37
Christianity   7, 8, 58, 59, 139
communication   2, 94, 151, 155, 213, 259, 348
destructive forces of   81
economic crisis   43, 50, 135
era of   2, 8, 79
flows   15, 32, 282, 353
historical cases of   37
interconnectedness   2, 78, 146
movements   9, 197, 272–275
new patterns of   32
organizations   31
over-generalized theories of   7, 81
problems   32, 79, 159, 189
society   4, 259
glocalization   353
Glock, C.   3
Godwin, William   101
Goldstein, Baruch   323, 325
Golem   17
Gordon, David   301
Gordon, Judah Leib (Yalag)   292
Graetz, Heinrich   292
Gramsci, Antonio   166
Gross, Amnon   331
Guenzburg, Mordecai Aaron (1795–1846)   292
Gush Emunim (Bloc of the Faithful)   308, 324, 355–357, 361, 363–365
Guti, Ezekiel   106

Habermas, Jürgen   36, 150–153, 202, 211
habilitation thesis   151
hajj   194, 196, 213, 359
Halevy, Elie   98, 132, 133
Hanafi, Hasan   203
Hannerz, Ulf   27
Harris, Jerry   185
Hartman, D.   3
hassidim/hassidism   117, 285, 286, 288, 318, 320, 328–332, 335, 336, 345, 346
Hatam Sofer (Sofer, Moshe) [1762–1839]   285
Heidegger, Martin   39
Heine, Heinrich   295
Helgesson, Kristina   117
Hervieu-Léger, Danièle   xi, 2, 8
Herzl, Theodor   301
Hess, Moshe   301
Heydemann, S.   180
Himmelfarb, Gertrude   97, 118

Hinduism/Hindu/Hindus:
  and Buddhism   14, 225–229, 235, 261
  and Dalits   220, 225–228, 229fn, 231, 234, 235
  and globalization   37
  and Islam   260, 261, 266–269, 361, 362
  and transnationalism   270
  as a civilization   160
  Brahminical   12, 227
  communities   23, 268
  expansion of   260
  in diaspora   12–14, 16, 237, 251, 255
  in Europe   237, 240, 243, 252
  in Germany   240, 241, 248–250, 252, 254, 255
  in Great Britain   248, 255
  in India   13, 14, 140, 257, 259–262, 266–269, 273, 275, 361, 362
  in South Asia   248
  in Switzerland   240, 241, 243–245, 248, 252–255
  in the US   240
  nationalism   267, 268, 270, 273, 274
  priests   252–254
  ritual/rituals   245–248, 251, 254
  Tamil   238, 240–245, 248–255
  temple/temples   227, 240–243, 244fn, 245, 247–251, 253–255, 361, 362
  tradition/traditions   237, 240–242, 247, 254, 256, 261, 268, 269, 274, 361
Hinnebusch, Raymond   180, 183fn
Hirsch, Samson Raphael (1808–1888)   289
Hirschensohn, Haim (1857–1935)   290
Hobbes, Thomas   145
Hodgson, Marshall   145–148
Homberg, Naphtali Herz   292
Horkheimer, Max   202, 203
Huntington, S.   3, 159, 160, 177, 354
Hus, Jan   100
Huss, Boaz   331
Hussain, Dilwar   211

Ibn Adret, Shlomo (Rashba)   331
Ibn Taymiyya, Taqi al-Din (1263–1328)   173fn, 195
identity/identities:
  and flow   279, 280
  Buddhist   224–227, 229, 230, 235
  Bulgarian national   76
  civil components of   6

civilizational 38
collective 5, 6, 22–25, 27, 29, 30, 37, 65, 67, 68, 78–80, 280–283, 299, 315, 337
conceptions of 35, 280, 281
converted 131
cultural 27, 36, 90, 255, 345
Czech national 74
Dalit 224–227, 229, 235
democratic-pluralist 7, 63
diasporan 6
dilemma of 167
Estonian national 75
ethnic 122, 174, 338
ethno-national 7, 338
ethno-religious 300
European 337
French national 291
German national 71
Greek national 76
Hindu 226, 229, 245, 248, 251, 255, 257
Illyrian 75
Indian 146
individualization of 9
Islamic/Muslim 199–201, 208
Israeli 305, 340
Jewish 14, 15, 279, 281–313, 316, 338, 340
Latvian national 75
Lithuanian national 75
Masorati (traditionist) 340
Mizrahi 340
modern 119, 120, 122, 123, 131, 265
national 1, 13, 30, 64, 65, 67, 68, 71, 80, 121, 122, 257, 259, 260, 265, 275, 291, 300, 302, 303, 309
Pentecostal 97, 119, 125, 128
personal 88, 125, 245, 248, 321, 337
political 12, 221, 224
politics of 29, 36, 273, 275
portable 9, 97, 128
preservation of 164, 248, 251, 255, 284, 294, 298
primordial components of 6
religious ix, 6, 13, 22, 38, 78, 80, 85, 89, 121, 122, 127, 225, 226, 251, 255, 275, 322, 338, 357
Romanian national 75
Russian national 72
secondary 29
secular 65, 66, 72, 74, 75, 297
Slovakian national 74
small community 90

social 27, 225, 226
space of 14
subdued 29
sub-state 180
supra-state 180
Turkish national 72
universalistic 24, 25
ijtihad 208, 209, 212
inclusion 7, 27, 30, 51, 79, 81,148, 154, 181fn, 185, 230, 231, 234
individualization 79
  and modernization 65
  of beliefs 8, 85, 86, 89–91
  of religious life 17, 91
  relation between secularization and 279
Iqbal, Mohammad (1875–1938) 174
Islam/Islamic:
  and authoritarianism 162, 168, 175
  and Buddhism 260, 261
  and Christianity 75–77, 79, 260
  and democracy/democratization 10, 160–162, 175, 179, 182fn, 184, 190
  and globalization 37, 146, 147, 150, 153–156, 193, 195, 198, 212, 259, 344
  and Hinduism 260, 268
  and modernity/modernization 30, 147, 160, 163–165, 169–171, 174, 189, 190, 194
  and multiculturalism 11
  and Pentecostalism 94
  and territory 101
  and the state 72, 146–148, 155, 156, 169, 170, 172, 197, 344
  and the West 148, 149, 170, 199, 200, 214, 215, 344
  China's attitude toward 264
  civilization 145, 146, 150, 153, 159, 160
  clergy (ulama) 169
  contemporary 4, 7, 9, 58, 150
  conversion to 230
  cosmopolitanism 157, 193, 195
  critical 11, 201–203, 206, 207, 209, 213–215
  culture 160, 161, 199, 343, 344
  dimensions of 146
  egalitarianism 157
  empires 162–165, 167, 189
  fundamentalist/radical (Islamism) 4, 10, 15, 170–174, 180fn, 182, 183fn, 190, 193, 210, 214, 268, 316, 343–345, 349, 359

hegemonies 202
historical variant of 202
in Asia 260, 275
in Europe 11, 15, 16, 153, 198–201, 203–210, 212–215, 344, 348
in Germany 80
in India 268
in Iran 61, 175, 180, 188
in South Africa 117
intellectuals 166, 207, 209
interconnection of law and religion in 69
liberal 10, 174, 190
local or village 205, 207
movements 10, 156, 165, 169, 171, 172, 181, 197
normative variant of 202, 203
pilgrimage 359
political 10, 79, 153, 159, 162, 168–170, 172–175, 189, 190, 194, 195, 210
postmodern 203
pre-colonial 169
public 154, 155
reformists 170, 195
renaissance of 61
Shiite 359
sphere 147, 149, 153, 154
Sunni 70, 72, 80, 173fn, 359
traditions 154
transnational 10, 145, 149, 150, 153–156, 194, 196–198, 212, 213
understandings of the public 148
veiling in 333
view of the social bond 148
Islam, Yusuf (Stevens, Cat) 206
Islamophobia 204

Jacobsen, Knut A. xi, 12
Jefferson, Thomas 101
Jenkins, Philip 59
Jews:
　Ashkenazi 285–288, 309, 311, 326, 328, 332, 333, 339, 346, 347
　French 290, 291
　haredi/ultra-Orthodox 285–289, 299, 309, 311, 317, 326–334, 336, 342, 343, 345, 346
　Mizrahi/Sephardi 15, 287, 288, 305–307, 309, 311, 328, 332, 333, 339–342, 348, 360
　Russian-speaking 305, 306
　traditionist/masoratiim 15, 339–342, 348

Judaism:
　American 317, 325
　Ancient 302
　and Calvinism 115
　and Christianity 95, 117
　and emancipation 281, 282
　and modernity 279, 294
　and territory 101
　as culture 292, 311
　Biblical 283
　conservative 293–295, 311, 317
　contemporary 15, 337
　Eastern European 300
　ethnic aspects of 279
　ethno-secular 297
　Halacha 289
　historical 292
　in Asia 260
　in the US 293
　national aspects of 279, 286, 303
　Rabbinical 283
　reform 291–294, 311, 317
　secular 296–298, 313
　secular humanistic 297, 298, 313
　territorialization of 300
　traditional 14, 279, 281, 285, 292, 300, 301, 310, 321
　transformations of 280

Kalischer, Zvi Hirsch 307
Kamenka, Eugen 68
Kamrava, M. 182, 183fn
Kang Youwei 263
Kaplan, Mordecai 295
Katz, Jacob 279
Katznelson, Berl 302
Katznelson, Ira 280
Keane, Webb 111
Kedourie, Elie 160
Kemal, Namik (1840–1888) 169
Keren, Bruria 332, 333
Kerry, John 46, 53
Khalid, 'Amr 155
Khan, Aamir 269
Khan, Salman 269
Khan, Sayyed Ahmad (1817–1898) 169
Khan, Shahrukh 269
Khomeini, Ayatollah Ruhollah (1902–1989) 165, 171
Kierkegaard, S. 320
Knott, Kim 248, 255
Kook, Abraham Isaac (1865–1935) 307, 320, 355, 356

Kook, Tzvi Yehuda (1891–1982) 355, 356
Koselleck, Reinhart 151
Krochmal, Nachman 301
Kuhn, Bela 295
Kumari, Mayawati (1956–) 222, 231, 232, 235, 236fn

Laski, Harold (1893–1950) 296
Lassalle, Ferdinand (1825–1864) 295, 296
Lazarus 362
Lebor, Adam 213
Lehmann, David 101, 117, 137
Leiner, Mordechai Yosef 320
Levi-Strauss, Claude 86, 87, 284
Lévinas, Emmanuel 290
Lewis, Bernard 147, 159, 160
Lewis, Philip 209
Li Hongzhi 271, 272
Liebman, Charles 280
Lilienblum, Moshe Leib 292, 301
Limongi, F. 179
Loew, Judah (Maharal of Prague) [1520–1609] 346
Lust-Okar, Ellen 181
Luther, Martin 98, 99, 111, 117, 132
Luxemburg, Rosa 296
Lynch, Owen 231
Lyotard, J.-F. 203

Macpherson, Aimee Semple 98, 99
Madjid, Nurcholish (1939–) 174
Madsen, Richard 270
Mandaville, Peter xii, 11
Mann, Michael 78
Mao Zedong 265, 271
Mapu, Abraham 292
Marcuse, Herbert 202
marginality/marginalization/ marginalized 12, 56, 101, 103, 120, 164, 166, 174, 203, 223, 225, 231, 234, 255, 259, 262, 268, 273
  de- 232–236
Martin, Bernice xii, 9, 135
Martin, David xii, 8, 9, 57, 58, 69, 130, 132, 135
Marty, M. 4
Marx, Karl 223, 295, 296
Mary, A. 359
maslaha 210, 211
Maxwell, David 115, 128
Mazo, Eugene 177, 178
McAlister, E. 354

McCain, John 43, 45–49, 53
McDowell, Christopher 244
Medem, Vladimir (1879–1923) 296, 297
megairot (drawers) 334–336
Mendelssohn, Moses (1729–1786) 283, 291, 295
Mernissi, Fatima 203
Metcaff, Barbara 213
Methodism/Methodists 8, 70, 95–100, 108–110, 112–114, 117, 118, 131–134
Meyer, Birgit 133, 135
Meyer, Michael 279
Micklethwait, J. 55, 56, 60
mission/missionaries 270, 354
  civilizing 70
  of Jews 293, 302
modernity/modernities/modernization:
  and assimilation of Jews 302
  and conflict 163, 190
  and fundamentalism 316
  and globalization 66
  and Islam 10, 162, 164–168, 171, 189, 190, 316
  and nationalism 63, 64
  and pluralization 59
  and religions 10, 65, 66, 162, 164–168, 171, 189, 190, 302, 316
  and secularization 4, 21, 59, 63, 65, 66, 120, 121, 165, 195, 259, 260
  and traditional cultures 10, 164
  authoritarian path to 167
  cultural 161, 171, 189, 292
  economic 137, 161, 164, 166, 167, 171, 180fn, 189
  failed 165, 171, 190
  from above 166–168
  multiple 7, 59, 63–67, 81, 98, 119, 121, 122
  over-generalized theories of 7, 64, 81
  political 69, 161, 166, 167, 189
  secular 165
  technological 165
Mohilever, Shmuel 307
Moore, Barrington 180
Mossadeq, Mohammad 188fn
movement/movements:
  Agudat Israel 285
  Ambedkarite 221, 222, 224, 230, 231, 234, 235
  anti-globalization 34–36, 38, 39
  Bund 296
  charismatic 111, 121, 136

INDEX

Chinese spiritual   273–275
Christian   91, 101
Conservative   293–295, 311, 317
conservative   136
Dalit   224, 225, 233–235
egalitarian   107
fundamentalist   6, 10, 23, 25, 38, 59, 60, 172, 173, 190, 195, 197, 213, 355, 357, 364
global   9
Gush Emunim (Bloc of the Faithful)   308, 355, 357, 364
Haskala (enlightenment)   291, 292
Hassidic   286
Hindu   273–275
holiness   96, 97, 120
Islamic   10, 156, 165, 169, 171–175, 181, 190, 195–197, 206, 213
Keswick 94, 114
Megairot (drawers)   334, 335
millenarian   265
movement for secular humanistic Judaism   298
nationalist   68
new   3, 30, 31, 34, 35, 37, 274
peace   100
Pentecostal   97, 101, 104, 106fn, 107, 109–111, 113, 116, 118, 120, 121, 125, 130, 136, 138–140
protest   34–40
qigong/Falun Gong   271–274
Reform   292–294, 311, 317
reformist   38
religious   ix, 3, 9, 22–25, 38, 50, 57, 59, 106, 110, 113, 116, 120, 257, 260, 262, 270, 318
sectarian   24, 28
socialist/communist   295
transnationalism of   151, 196, 197, 213
veiled women   332–334
virtual   26
women's   104, 332
Zionist   291, 307
Muhammad, Prophet   193, 195, 208
multiculturalism/multiculturization   ix, 1, 5, 17, 28, 36
and Islam   11
and Pentecostalism   94
and religion/religions   1–3, 5, 7, 8, 14–17, 353, 354, 364, 365
and religious tolerance   353, 354, 365
and territory   16, 353, 364
in Europe   122
in India   12, 274
in Israel   306, 307, 309
in the US   94
Muslim   194, 209
mystic/mystical/mysticism:
  in Haredi community   320, 329–331, 336
  in Rav Kook's writings   320
  Jewish   334
  tradition in Islam (Sufi)   195
  type of Christian community (Spiritualismus)   91
Münkler, Herfried   40
Musharraf, Pervez   173fn
Muzaffar, Chandra (1947–)   174, 206

Na'ini, Ayatollah Muhammad Hussein (1860–1936)   165, 169
Nanautvi, Muhammad Qasim (d. 1880)   173fn
Narain, A.K.   225
Narasu, P. Lakshi   220
Narayanan, Vasudha   240
nationalism:
  and democratic-pluralist identities   7, 63
  and ethno-national identities   7, 63, 74, 76, 79
  and modernization theory   63, 64, 67, 69
  and multiple modernities approach   64
  and orientalism   262
  and religion   7, 64, 69, 70, 73, 76, 80, 168, 259, 262, 266, 318
  and the state   169
  and transnationalism   10, 156
  anti-colonial   266, 274
  Arab   347
  Bulgarian   76
  Central Asian   72
  Central European   68
  Confucian   264
  cultural   71, 72, 79
  Czechoslovakian   74
  East-Central European   68, 72
  East European   67, 68
  Empire-contracting   64, 67–72, 77
  formation of   68, 69
  German   71
  Greek   76
  Hindu   267, 274
  Hungarian   74
  in Central and Eastern Europe   7, 64

Jewish 292, 300, 302, 303, 307, 308, 312, 337
Mexican 116
modern 65, 67, 195, 261
peripheral 64, 67, 68, 70, 72–78, 81
Polish 73
revival of 63, 64, 68
Russian 71, 72
secular 63, 67, 69, 70, 72, 168, 195
Turkish 80
Ukrainian 77
West European 67, 68
Navroji, Sarah 107
Nazim, Shaykh 196
Nehru, Jawaharlal 221
Nietzsche, Friedrich 39
Nomani, F. 180

Obama, Barack 41, 43, 44, 46–56
Olcott, Colonel 262
Oschoffa, Papa 358
Osterhammel, Jürgen 70
Ottaway, Marina 182, 183

pagan/paganism/Vodou:
  and Catholicism in Haiti 355, 363, 365
  rooting out 358
  spiritual war against 354, 355
Palin, Sarah 48–50, 53
Parham, Charles 97
Patai, Raphael 160
Paul, St. 115
Pentecostalism 8, 9, 16, 49, 50, 56–58, 75, 91, 93–118, 119–141, 275, 355
  and fundamentalism 98
  and gender 136–139
  and modernity 122–126, 128, 139–141
  and transnationalism 115–118, 122, 125, 128
  characteristics of 101, 102, 111–115
  economic ethic of 131–135
  in Ghana 104, 105
  in Nigeria 105–107
  in South India 107, 108
  in Venezuela 102–104
  origins of 95–101
Perl, Joseph 292
Perthes, Volker 184
Piekarz, Mendel 334
pilgrimage/pilgrims 91, 99, 102, 112, 194, 234, 239, 243, 246, 247fn, 267, 330, 336, 358–363, 365

Pinsker, L. 301
priests/priesthood:
  Brahman/Tamil Hindu 246–248, 252–254
  shift of authority from family to 13, 240, 251, 254, 255
  diminishing number of 8, 85
  in Haiti 355
  of all believers 9, 108, 109
  of faith 99
  parish 85, 362
Protestant Ethic 98, 132; and Pentecostal economic ethic 131, 132
Przeworski, A. 179

Qutb, Sayyed (1906–66) 171–173
Qutub, Sayyid 39

Rabin, Yitzhak 308
Rabinovitch, Gamliel 330
Rahman, Fazlur 202, 203, 205, 208
Ram, Kanchi 231, 232–234
Ram, Mangoo 225
Ramadan, Tariq 4, 206, 210, 211
Ratosh, Yonatan 303
Ravidas (Raidas) 231
Rawlins, W.K. 1
redemption:
  and haredim 286, 301
  and Gush Emunim (Bloc of the Faithful) 357, 361, 363
  and Mizrahim 305
  and the veiled women 334
  and Zionism 300, 301
  messianic 286, 300
  national 320, 321
  Rav Avraham Isaac Kook on 355, 356
  Rav Zvi Yehuda Kook's stages of 356, 357
  universal 290
reformation:
  Magisterial 100
  of Islam 174
  Protestant 70, 103, 108, 111–113, 123, 129
  Radical 97, 100
Reines, Yaakov 307
religion/religions/religious:
  and authority 2, 6, 8, 22, 23, 25, 85, 92, 205, 336
  and civilizations 6, 23, 26, 29, 34, 38–40, 64–67, 81, 122, 160, 258
  and conflict 5, 17, 76–78, 80, 81, 355, 357–359, 363

and culture 15, 316, 344, 345, 348, 349
and democracy/democratization 161, 175, 190
and fundamentalism 3–5, 7, 15, 35, 38, 39, 63, 64, 66, 325, 355
and globalization ix, 2, 5, 7, 8, 12, 15, 33, 64, 66, 79, 81, 85, 98, 212, 259, 315, 337, 348, 364
and identity/identities ix, 5, 22, 23, 30, 36, 38, 65–68, 75, 76, 78–80, 85, 89, 121, 122, 127, 221, 224–226, 251, 255, 258, 259, 265, 275, 284, 291, 299, 300, 310, 322, 338, 340, 357
and modernity/modernization ix, 1, 2, 4, 6, 7, 21, 23, 30, 40, 55, 56, 58, 60, 61, 64–67, 88, 89, 91, 98, 110, 118, 119, 121, 126, 166, 258–261, 264, 270, 325
and nationalism 7, 63–70, 72–74, 76, 79, 80, 118, 168, 259, 261, 262, 266, 308, 325
and multiculturalism ix, 1, 5, 8, 14–17, 353, 354, 364, 365
and political arena ix
and politics 14, 24, 41–56, 72, 94, 106, 113, 161, 168, 172, 175, 221, 223, 230, 257–259, 267, 273–275, 318, 325
and public scenes/spheres 3, 23, 34, 37, 56, 58
and secularism/secularization ix, 1, 4, 7, 21, 59, 61, 63–70, 72–75, 79–81, 119, 122, 124, 168, 174, 259, 260, 262–264, 267, 269, 274, 280, 290, 307, 309, 311, 318, 327, 339, 343, 355
and state/states 10, 24, 33, 66, 70, 72, 73, 75, 78, 99, 121, 122, 148, 149, 160, 174, 257, 262, 264–267, 270, 274, 275, 298, 319
and territory/space 8, 13, 16, 17, 79, 85, 86, 90–92, 94, 116, 121, 149, 232, 240, 255, 296, 308, 324, 330, 353–355, 357–359, 363, 364
and tolerance 16, 207, 228, 353, 354, 365
and transnationalism 2, 6, 24, 25, 34, 67, 79, 81, 200, 212, 238, 239, 364
communities 2, 3, 6, 8, 11, 24–26, 34, 36, 67, 85, 91, 172, 227, 239, 291, 293, 318, 321, 325, 330, 333, 345, 347, 348, 353

definition of 1
dimensions of ix
diversification 2
in America 54–56, 58
in American politics 6, 7, 41–56
in Central and Eastern Europe 7
in China 13, 14
in Europe 51, 55, 56, 58, 59, 69, 86, 198, 200, 203–205, 207, 208, 212, 215, 259
in India 13, 14
in Latin America 110
indigenous 9, 127, 129
individualization/privatization of 6, 8, 15, 17, 22, 23, 65, 66, 72, 79, 86–92, 315, 316, 319, 320, 322, 325, 336, 337, 348
movements ix, 3, 23, 25, 26, 34, 36, 38, 59, 67, 110, 174, 257, 262, 270, 271, 274, 275, 318
New Age 318
orientations 6, 22–24, 34, 66, 240
resurgence of ix, 4, 22, 63, 64, 68, 75, 76, 79, 80, 110, 121, 257, 262, 263, 318, 327
sociology of 1
transformations of 2, 5, 14, 15, 17, 261, 300
vanguards 101
vicarious 338, 339
Resul, Ali 183
Reza Shah 165, 167
Reza Shah, Mohammad 165, 167
Rida, Rashid (1865–1935) 170
Riesebrodt, M. 2, 3
Robertson, R. 1
Rokkan, Stein 69
Rosenzweig, Frantz (1886–1929) 294
Roy, Olivier 197, 343, 344
Rustow, D.A. 180

Sacks, Jonathan 280
sacred spaces:
  and religion 16, 353
  Buddhist 219
Sadr, Mohammad Baqir (1935–1980) 171
Said, Edward 261
saints:
  Jewish 360, 361, 364
  martyr 129
  Muslim 268, 361
  tombs of 330
Salafism 169

Salvatore, Armando xii, 10
Sardar, Ziauddin 206
Sayyid, Bobby 214
Schieder, Theodor 68
Scholem, Gershom 331, 336
sectarian/sectarianism:
  and Islam 199, 206, 208, 214
  and Pentecostalism 97
  fissions 110
  groups/movements 24, 25, 28
  milieus ix
  roots of Jacobinism 97
secularization/secularism ix
  and civilizational constellations 64, 65, 81
  and democracy 174, 182
  and fundamentalism 4
  and individualization 279
  and Islam 4
  and Jewish identity/identities 287, 297, 301, 357
  and modernity/modernization 1, 4, 7, 21, 56, 57, 59, 63, 65, 66, 98, 119, 120, 121, 167, 169, 195, 259, 260, 281
  and nationalism 64, 68-70, 72-74, 76, 195, 262, 301
  and Pentecostalism 126
  cultural 69
  dimensions of 66, 67
  enforced 75
  in Central and Eastern Europe 7, 63
  in China 263-265
  in Europe 56, 59, 86, 92, 120, 121
  in India 13, 267, 275
  legacies 80
  levels 80
  liberal 53, 54
  process/processes 57, 65, 77, 86
  state 72
  strong 69, 74, 75
  theory/theories of 57, 58, 66, 69, 98, 121, 124, 260
  weak 69, 71, 75, 76
  western 121
  Western European 72
Segady, T.W. 4
Seligman, Adam 117
Sen, Amartya 269
Senghaas, Dieter 163, 164, 167
settlements:
  collective (kibbutzim) 307
  Gush Emunim (Bloc of the Faithful) 324, 357, 364

  Gush Katif 334
  new 308
  of monks 234
  West Bank 320, 321, 324, 325
Seymour, William 97
Shabestari, Mohammad Mojtahed 166
Shahrour, Muhammad (1938-) 174
Shankar, Guru Ravi 274
Sharett, Moshe 302
Shari'ati, Ali (1933-75) 171
Shazar, Zalman 302
Siddiqui, Ataullah 210
Siebzehner, Batia 117
Simons, Menno 100
Sivan, Emanuel 326
Sivanada 273
Smilde, David 102, 103, 115
Smith, Adam 131
Smolenskin, Peretz 301
Soloveitchik, Chaim 290, 347
Soothill, Jane 102, 104, 105, 115, 138
Sorotzkin, David 346
Soroush, Abdolkarim (1945-) 166, 174, 205, 207
sovereignty:
  modern 147
  national 7, 10, 63, 73, 156
  popular 173
  state 31, 68-70, 73, 78, 79, 145, 147-151, 185fn
spatial/spatiality:
  and Hindu ritual 245, 251
  exclusion 234
  imagery 354
  isolation 233
  organization 85
  new forms of religious 85, 86, 90
Spickard, P. 5
Spohn, Willfried xii, 7
Sri Paskarakurukkal 242
Stalin, J. 295
standardization: and subjectivization 87, 88; global 156
Stark, R. 3
state/states:
  and church/churches 6, 47, 69, 73, 99, 258, 338fn
  and civilizations 78, 145-149, 153, 169, 170, 172, 190, 198
  and collective identity 25, 67, 180, 265
  and globalization/global organizations 31, 32, 78, 79, 153, 155, 156, 169,

172fn, 184, 185, 196–198, 259, 260, 270, 275, 276
and Pentecostalism 9, 95
and religion/religions 10, 13, 24, 51, 52, 56, 63, 66, 69, 70, 72, 73, 79, 99, 109, 122, 145–149, 153–155, 160, 169, 170, 172, 174, 190, 198, 235, 257, 260, 262–272, 274, 275, 286–288, 290, 291, 298, 302, 303, 305, 308, 311, 319, 320, 324, 333, 339, 344
and social movements 31, 34–36, 156, 257, 270–272, 274, 276
and society/civil society 10, 25, 121, 166–168, 173, 176, 178–181, 182fn, 183–190, 257, 267, 269, 274, 324
agencies 31
authoritarian 168, 185fn
Baltic 74
big 69, 70, 78, 81
boundaries 31, 180
Central and Eastern European 7, 63, 76, 78, 79
centres of 35, 36, 72
democratic 53, 70, 71, 185fn
empire-contracting 78, 81
formation 7, 64, 65, 67–70, 73, 75–78, 81, 149, 155, 163, 165, 175, 176, 191, 258, 300
Imperial 70
in Europe 51, 56, 66, 68–70, 145, 169
Indian 221, 232, 235
Islamic/Muslim 4, 10, 11, 72, 145–149, 156, 160, 172, 175, 185, 189, 190, 197, 209, 344
modern 34–36, 53, 67, 70, 72, 121, 149, 152, 232
monarchial 75
nation 6, 10, 13, 21, 22, 25, 27, 29–31, 35, 36, 64–73, 76–79, 121, 122, 150, 153, 155, 156, 160, 163fn, 165, 169, 170, 172, 179fn, 180, 185, 188, 193, 257, 259, 260, 266, 270, 275, 300
new 78
old 78
peripheral 69, 73, 76, 78, 81
power relations between 30
revolutionary 21, 27, 29, 30, 35
secular 14, 72, 75, 168, 173, 258, 275, 339
service 152
small 71, 76, 78, 81, 164, 165, 190

South-Slavic 75
sovereignty 31, 70, 73, 78, 79, 145, 147–151, 185fn
strong 169
Turkish 72
swing 46
Ukrainian 77
weak 180
welfare 51, 52
Western 148
Westphalian 149, 150
stateness: strong 79; weak 79, 80
Stephens, Randall J. 95, 107
Sternberg, Yitzhak xii, 16
Sufi/Sufism 146, 154, 195
  brotherhoods (turuq) 146, 154
  connections 196
  orders 24, 154, 196
  practices 268
  resurgence of 196
  saint worship 268
  tradition 195

Talbi, Mohamed (1921–) 174
Tamil Hindus in Europe 238, 240–256
  rituals 245–254
  temples/templeisation of 240–243, 245, 247–255
Taylor, C. 39, 119, 121–126, 131, 319
theory, critical and traditional:
  of the Frankfurt School 201–203, 211
Tiesler, N.C. 4
transnationalism/transnational/transnationalization:
  African-style 357
  and Buddhism 261
  and Catholicism 92
  and civilizations 67, 81, 146, 199
  and globalization 15, 78, 94, 153, 196
  and Haredim 287
  and identity/identities 30, 67, 125
  and Islam 10, 145, 146, 148–150, 153–156, 168, 171fn, 193–198, 200, 209, 212, 213
  and Judaism 299
  and movements 10, 151, 156, 196, 197, 213, 270, 272
  and nationalism 156, 270, 273
  and Pentecostalism 9, 94, 107, 113, 117, 121, 122, 125, 128, 139
  and religions 5, 6, 9, 10, 14, 24, 30, 78, 92, 94, 107, 113, 117, 121, 122,

125, 128, 139, 145, 146, 148–150, 153–156, 168, 171fn, 193–198, 200, 209, 212, 213, 261, 270, 272, 273, 275, 287, 299, 353, 355, 357, 364
  and state/states   78, 79, 81, 156, 184, 275
  associations/organizations   30, 97, 184, 212, 213
  class/classes   274
  constellations   81
  diaspora/diasporas   3
  networks   ix, 6, 9, 121, 128, 139, 153–155, 171fn, 270
  religious communities   2, 24, 353
  Transnational Capitalist Classes (TCC)   185
Troeltsch, Ernst   90
Trotsky, L.   296
Turner, Victor   324

Ukah, Azonzeh   102, 105
Ullah, Shah Wali   194
umma/ummah   153, 193, 194, 200, 345
Unitarianism: rationalistic   99

van der Veer, Peter   xii, 13, 14
van Dijk, Alphons   254
vanguard/vanguards:
  and Christianity   100, 101
  Gush Emunim (Bloc of the Faithful) as   356, 361, 364
  Haredi spiritual   331
  Haredim as   286, 288, 289
  halutziut   318
  religious   101
veiled women: Jewish   332, 334–336
Vital, David   280

Vivekananda   274
Vögeli, Johanna   253

Waardenburg, Jacques   209
Waldman, Steve   46
Wanner, Catherine   140
waqf   147, 148
Warren, Rick   47
Weber, Max   98, 132
Weiffen, Brigitte   161, 179
Wesley, Charles   114
Wesley, John   113, 132
Wessely, Naphtali Herz   292
Wittgenstein, Ludwig   281, 310, 313
Wooldrige, A.   55, 56, 60
Wright, Jeremiah   48
Wuthnow, R.   3

yeshiva/yeshivot   285, 287, 320, 321, 326
yoga   271–275
Yosef, Ovadiah   341

Zafar, S.M. (1930–)   174
Zawahiri, Ayman   171fn
Zhitlowsky, Chaim (1865–1943)   297
Zilberberg, Tzvi Meir   330
Zindapir   196
Zionism/Zionists   285–287, 291, 300–305, 309, 311
  Pentecostal   115, 116
  post   303, 304, 308
  religious   307, 308, 317, 318–325, 330, 334–336, 343, 355–357, 361, 363–365
  secular   286, 300, 355, 356, 365
Zunz, Leopold (1794–1886)   292

INTERNATIONAL COMPARATIVE SOCIAL STUDIES

ISSN 1568-4474

In modern research, breaking boundaries between the different social sciences is becoming more and more popular. Discussions in which different disciplines are being invited to shed their light on such issues as migration, violence, urbanisation, trust and social capital are common in current academic discourse. Brill's *International Comparative Social Studies* focuses on presenting the results of comparative research by anthropologists, sociologists, political scientists and other social scientists.

1. WILSON, H.T. *Bureaucratic Representation.* Civil Servants and the Future of Capitalist Democracies. 2001. ISBN 90 04 12194 3
2. RATH, J. *Western Europe and its Islam.* 2001. ISBN 90 04 12192 7
3. INAYATULLAH, S. *Understanding Sarkar.* The Indian Episteme, Macrohistory and Transformative Knowledge. 2002. ISBN 90 04 12193 5 (hardcover) ISBN 90 04 12842 5 (paperback)
4. GELISSEN, J. *Worlds of Welfare, Worlds of Consent?* Public Opinion on the Welfare State. 2002. ISBN 9004 12457 8
5. WILSON, H.T. *Capitalism after Postmodernism.* Neo-Conservatism, Legitimacy, and the Theory of Public Capital. 2002. ISBN 9004 12458 6
6. ROULLEAU-BERGER, L. *Youth and Work in the Post-Industrial City of North America and Europe.* With an Epilogue by Saskia Sassen. 2003. ISBN 9004 12533 7
7. AALBERG, T. *Achieving Justice.* Comparative Public Opinion on Income Distribution. 2003. ISBN 9004 12990 1
8. ARNASON, J.P. *Civilizations in Dispute.* Historical Questions and Theoretical Traditions. 2003. ISBN 9004 13282 1
9. FALZON, M.-A. *Cosmopolitan Connections.* The Sindhi diaspora, 1860-2000. 2004. ISBN 9004 14008 5
10. BEN-RAFAEL, E. and Y. STERNBERG (eds.), *Comparing Modernities Pluralism Versus Homogenity.* Essays in Homage to Shmuel N. Eisenstadt. 2005. ISBN 90 04 14407 2
11. DOUW, L. and K-b. CHAN (eds.), *Conflict and Innovation. Joint Ventures in China.* 2006. ISBN 90 04 15188 5
12. SMITH, J. With an Introduction by S.N. Eisenstadt. *Europe and the Americas.* State Formation, Capitalism and Civilizations in Atlantic Modernity. 2006. ISBN 13: 978 90 04 15229 8. ISBN-10: 90 04 15229 6.

13. BEN-RAFAEL, E., M. LYUBANSKY, O. GLÖCKNER, P. HARRIS, Y. ISRAEL, W. JASPER and J. SCHOEPS. *Building a Diaspora*. Russian Jews in Israel, Germany and the USA. 2006. ISBN-13: 978 90 04 15332 5. ISBN-10: 90 04 15332 2.
14. ARJOMAND, S.A. (ed.),*Constitutionalism and Political Reconstruction*. 2007. ISBN-13: 978 90 04 15174 1. ISBN-10: 90 04 15174 5.
15. KWOK-BUN, C., J.W. WALLS and D. HAYWARD (eds.), *East-West Identities*. Globalization, Localization, and Hybridization. 2007. ISBN-13: 978 90 04 15169 7. ISBN-10: 90 04 15169 9.
16. MEULEMANN, H. (ed.), *Social Capital in Europe: Similarity of Countries and Diversity of People?* Multi-level Analyses of the European Social Survey 2002. 2008. ISBN 978 90 04 16362 1.
17. ROBERTS, C.W. *"The" Fifth Modality: On Languages that Shape our Motivations and Cultures*. 2008. ISBN 978 90 04 16235 8.
18. RAKEL, E.P. *Power, Islam, and Political Elite in Iran*. A Study on the Iranian Political Elite from Khomeini to Ahmadinejad. 2009. ISBN 978 90 04 17176 3.
19. BEN-RAFAEL, E. and Y. STERNBERG (eds.), with Judit Bokser Liwerant and Yosef Gorny. *Transnationalism*. Diasporas and the advent of a new (dis)order. 2009. ISBN 978 90 04 17470 2
20. STEFAN, A.M. *Democratization and Securitization*. The Case of Romania. 2009. ISBN 978 90 04 17739 0
21. AMINEH, M.P. and Y. GUANG (eds.), *The Globalization of Energy*. China and the European Union. 2010. ISBN 978 90 04 18112 0.
22. SMITH, K.E. *Meaning, Subjectivity, Society*. Making Sense of Modernity. 2010. ISBN 978 90 04 18172 4
23. BEN-RAFAEL, E. and Y. STERNBERG (eds.), *World Religions and Multiculturalism*. A Dialectic Relation. 2010. ISBN 978 90 04 18892 1